ANTARC
FIRST LADY

MEMOIRS OF THE FIRST AMERICAN WOMAN TO SET FOOT ON THE ANTARCTIC CONTINENT AND WINTER-OVER

Edith M. "Jackie" Ronne

Witness to the Pioneering Days of Polar Exploration

Clifton Steamboat Museum • Three Rivers Council #578, BSA
Beaumont, Texas
www.3riversbsa.org • www.AdventuresoftheElements.com

Library of Congress Control Number: 2004115176

ISBN-13: 978-1-57579-298-2
ISBN-10: 1-57579-298-2

Published by
Clifton Steamboat Museum & Three Rivers Council #578, BSA
Beaumont, TX

From, Three Rivers Council #578, BSA, the developers of the Adventures of the Elements Educational Trading Card Game and book series, comes the story of Antarctica's First Lady.

For more pictures of Jackie Ronne and the Ronne Expedition visit:

www.3riversbsa.org

www.AdventuresoftheElements.com

Printed in the United States of America
PINE HILL PRESS
4000 West 57th Street
Sioux Falls, SD 57106

Table of Contents

To my husband, Finn Ronne,
who knew I would continue the
family's historic interests in Antarctica.

Acknowledgements:

I wish to give my great appreciation and sincere thanks for the aid and very valuable suggestions given to me by Ann Hawthorne and Larry Conrad in the early editing process. My daughter, Karen Ronne Tupek, and son-in-law, Al Tupek, spent countless hours reviewing and typing new additions of the manuscript and scanning photos. To Polly Penhale for her suggestions and to Susan Sullivan and David Wilson, I am deeply indebted for their serious editing of my original diary inclusions so as to make the manuscript more concise, exciting and readable. All of those mentioned above are very knowledgeable in Antarctic affairs.

—Edith M. "Jackie" Ronne

Preface

With a lump in my throat and a tear in my eye, I sailed south across the Antarctic convergence toward the frozen continent. This, my fourth time, would be very different from previous visits, as my husband, Finn Ronne, was not with me. I had not thought it would be such a traumatic occasion. Finn had been gone for fifteen years, but in the Antarctic, I discovered he was still very much with me. Nostalgia engulfed me, remembering how he loved it so, how familiar he had been with every view and how surprised he would be to know I was there. I missed him deeply. As the pain of my loss intensified, I watched from the bow of the cruise ship "Explorer". We picked our way carefully through the pack ice. My tears obscured the intimidating icebergs floating majestically in open water just beyond. In the distance was the outline of the spectacular snow covered Antarctic continent. I had never expected to see it again.

We were attempting to make a landing at the Base where I had spent a year with my husband and which had now become the first American Historic Site in Antarctica. My daughter Karen, representing the family's third generation to visit the Continent, carried three large plaques she had made to place in the small museum depicting the Ronne Expedition's extensive exploration and scientific investigations of the area. It was good to see the buildings were still standing, including the twelve-foot square hut I shared for a year with my husband. But I viewed the once substantial base with very mixed emotions. Vandals from visiting ships of many nationalities during the intervening years had removed everything but the bare walls and floors. It was very sad and I fought for control of my sentiments and anger.

People have written many unkind things about my husband but I have always been proud to be his wife. I thought about the accomplishments, which made him one of our greatest polar explorers, as I walked around the scenes of one of his most important achievements. As one of the few people who truly knew him, I knew that he characteristically was a very disciplined Norwegian. Finn wanted things done his way, at times, considered to be rigid and intolerant. But more often than not, he was proven right.

I kept a very complete diary for that year but it took me forty-seven years before I had the desire or courage enough to read it again. The experience was too close to me. After many years had passed, as I peered into those huts again and realized that as the wife of the expedition's leader I was the only one who could tell the story of this place. When I finally mustered the courage to face the day to day occurrences which passed in those walls and were written in my diary and how I felt about them at the time, I found my observations and reactions to the things I lived through far more fascinating now than the day I recorded them.

This is my account of my observations, what I lived through and how I felt about it. But not only is this a historical account of the human triumphs and deficiencies of men and women in isolation on this particular expedition. It is an example of the breakdown of human relationships between people in isolation on expeditions past and present throughout history.

Expedition Members

Ronne Antarctic Research Expedition (1946-48)

Ronne, Finn.	Comdr. U.S.N.R,		Expedition Leader
Ronne, Edith M.	Mrs Finn,	"Jackie"	Recorder/Media relations
Adams, Charles J.	Lieut. U.S.A.F.,	"Chuck"	Pilot
Darlington, Harry,		"Harry"	Pilot
Darlington, Jennie	Mrs. Harry		
Dodson, Robert H. T		"Bob"	Asst.Geologist, Surveyor
Fiske, C. O.		"Larry"	Climatologist,
Gutenko, Sigmund,	Steward,U.S.N.,	"Sig"	Chief Commissary
Hassage, Charles		"Chuck"	Chief Engineer
Kelsey, Lawrence		"Kelsey"	Radio Operator
Lassiter, James W.	Capt.U.S.A.F.,	"Jim/Jimmy"	Pilot
Latady, William R.		"Bill"	Photographer
McClary, Nelson		"Mac"	Ship's Mate
McLean, Donald		"Don"	Medical Officer
Nichols, Robert L.	Dr.	"Bob/Nic"	Geologist/Senior Scientist
Owen, Arthur		"Art"	Boy Scout
Peterson, Harris-Clichy	"Harcly/Pete"	Physicist	
Robertson, James B.		"Jimmy"	Aviation Mechanic
Schlossbach, Isaac	Comdr.U.S.N.(Ret.)	"Ike"	Skipper/Second in Command
Smith,Walter		"Smitty"	Ship's Mate/Navigator
Thompson, Andrew A.	"Andy"	Geophysicist	
Valdes, Jorge de Giorgio, (Chilean)		"George"	Mess Cook
Wood, Ernest A.		"Woody"	Ship's Engineer

Falkland Islands Dependency Survey Base "E" Personnel (1947-48)

The British who shared Stonington Island with us:

Butler, Ken	Leader
Tomkin, John	Deputy Leader
Butson, Dick	Doctor
Freeman, Reg	Surveyor
Jones, Dave	Aviation Mechanic
Mason, Dougie	Surveyor
McLeod, Ken	(Falkland Islander)
Randall, Terry	Radio Man
Stonehouse, Bernard	Biologist
Thomson, Tommy	Pilot
Walton, Kevin	Chief Trailsman

Photograph of Jackie taken at the Base in Antarctica

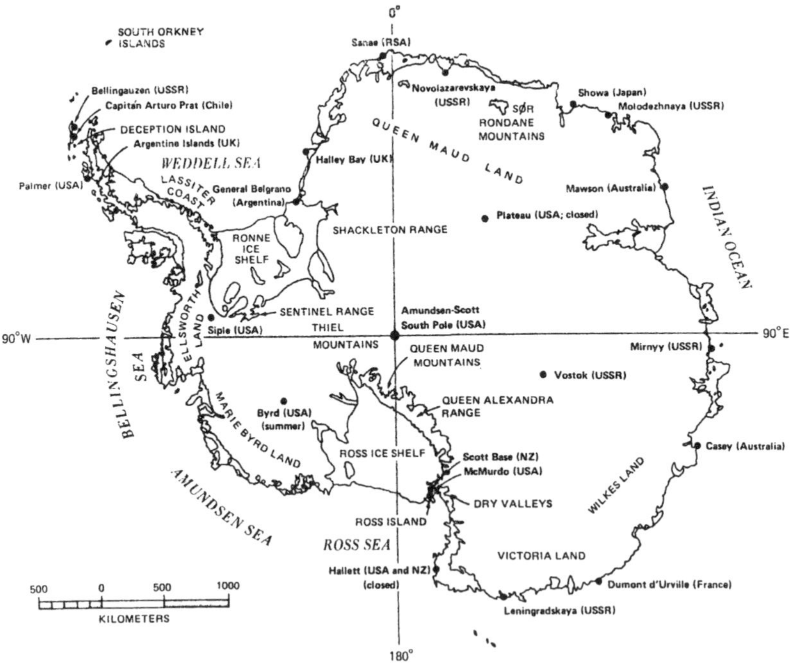

Map of Antarctica with main international bases

I

Antarctic Destiny

I started off for a year's stay on the Antarctic Continent with one small suitcase which contained mainly a good suit, a good dress, nylon stockings and high heel shoes – clothes about as suitable as Eskimo furs would be on a south sea island, but I didn't know I was going. How I got caught up in it all was a strange and unusual set of circumstances.

I met Finn Ronne on a blind date. Four of us spent a beautiful summer's evening picnicking by a meandering stream in Washington's Rock Creek Park. Other than the occasional roar of a distant lion in the nearby zoo, the setting was tranquil.

My friend, Bettie Earle, introduced us that evening in 1942, because she knew Finn and I were both interested in skiing. My own skiing ability consisted of gingerly attempting to navigate the Shoreham Hotel's slight incline in Rock Creek Park. Finn, was Norwegian and practically born on skis. He had already sledged in the Antarctic behind dog teams more miles than any other man living or dead. Fortunately, we found other things in common, as our skiing discussion did not last long that night.

Finn was twenty years older than I. He was quite nice looking but only about the same height, five feet, eight inches tall. I became enthralled by his conversation of Antarctic adventures and immediately liked him. But later, when he tried to kiss me good night, I pushed him away – after all this was just a first date and that is what good girls did in 1942 on occasion. The following morning when Bettie's boy friend, Charles, asked him how he liked me, he replied that I was very nice but somewhat of a "cold fish." That remark became a classic between us.

I came from a conservative, private family. My father, Charles Jackson Maslin, had several jobs, his last being with the B&O Railroad, before dying at the age of sixty-three of a massive heart attack. My mother, Elizabeth Parlett Maslin, should have taught school but like a proper married woman of her day, she stayed home instead. She went over my homework every night. I never went to school without knowing my lessons letter perfect.

I spent three marvelous summers away from home at a Girl Scout summer camp, Camp May Flather in Virginia, where incidentally, I learned to smoke. I quit when the Surgeon General's first report on the hazards of smoking came out in the early sixties. It was also at camp where I acquired my nickname. We decided to irritate the counselors and take nicknames just to be different. Most girls added an "ie" to their name, but Edith or Edie didn't lend itself to a peppy or spicy nickname. Some of us looked to our father's name for inspiration, but Charlie from my father's Charles, wasn't too feminine, either. So I used his middle name of Jackson and settled on becoming "Jackie". It was cute and it suited me. Back home, the name was forgotten after that summer, but it resurfaced later in college.

At the time, Baltimore did not believe in co-education in their public high schools. So I graduated from Eastern High School at sixteen without ever having had a date, except when I arranged for a classmate's brother to take me to the senior prom.

My first two years in college were spent at the College of Wooster in Wooster, Ohio. I had never been away from home before, except for summer camp. Naturally, the time there was spent majoring in boys. Since I had been a good student previously, my family quickly realized things could stand some improvement. With some sadness on my part, I transferred to George Washington University in Washington, D.C. In order to be near the college I moved to live with my aunt and uncle in Chevy Chase, Maryland, who were financing my education. The first person I recognized on campus was a girl from Girl Scout Camp. To her friends around campus, she introduced me as "Jackie", and everyone felt the name better fit my personality than Edith. That is the name I have been called ever since. I loved the college. I joined

Phi Mu Sorority, had a great social life, but also applied myself to my studies graduating with a major in history and a minor in English.

My aunt, Merriel Maslin Gardner, was a physicist with the National Bureau of Standards in Washington, and had married another physicist with the Bureau. My uncle, Dr. Irvine C. Gardner, designed the first telescopic camera able to take photographs of solar eclipses. He and my aunt traveled to numerous remote places in the world where total solar eclipses were to occur. I grew used to being around scientists and their discussions.

They were like second parents to me. I considered their house in the outskirts of Washington my home. They subscribed to educational and intellectual pursuits and often brought me along. One such event stands out in my mind. The National Geographic Society gave a very special "Welcome Home" to Admiral Richard E. Byrd and the members of his second Byrd Expedition of 1933-35. My uncle, who had done some favor for the Society, was given excellent seats in the third row from the front. I was very impressionable and my eyes were glued to the very handsome and charismatic Admiral Byrd, thinking and hoping some day I would meet a man like that. Little did I know that my future husband was sitting on the platform that night.

When I graduated from George Washington University in 1940, it was not an easy time to find a job with a mere undergraduate degree. I began a typing and shorthand course while looking for work. The National Geographic Society offered me a job typing lists of their new members. My lack of proficiency got me promoted to the New Member Desk where we checked for correct eligibility, hardly a position destined to change the course of history. After about nine months, I sought and got a government job at the Civil Service Commission at twice the salary paid by the Geographic. A few months later I moved on to the Department of State which more suited my interests and remained there in several different positions from file clerk to International Information Specialist in the Near and Far Eastern Division of Cultural Affairs.

About two weeks after we met, Finn invited me along with Bettie and Charles to his apartment to view his lecture film taken on the United States Antarctic Service (USAS) expedition 1939-41. I thought it was a spectacular film, which gave me opportunity to ask more intelligent questions about the Antarctic, his past and perhaps future work there.

Within a month I asked him to a dance given by the League of University Women and saw to it that he had a good time. After the dance, the four of us looked for a place to have a nightcap, but no place was open, so I suggested we go back to my house for some hot chocolate. Finn jumped at the chance and I learned that he was not a drinker and preferred hot chocolate to alcohol. We rolled back a throw rug and danced to phonograph records until Charles, half asleep, mentioned he couldn't believe Finn was enjoying the late hour, since he was an early-to-bed man and never stayed up that late. From that evening on, we began to see each other much more often. I enjoyed the fact that he was much older, and revelled on stories of his fantastic experiences. I liked his maturity and his nationality and charming accent. He was different than other men I had known.

As we spent more time together, I learned that Finn was born in Horten, Norway, in December 1899, the fifth of seven children of a family with an adventurous seafaring background. Like all inquisitive small children, Finn and his brothers had always been fascinated by their father's detailed stories of his numerous adventures at sea. Martin became, a veteran of high latitudes in both the Arctic and the Antarctic. For twenty years he remained the constant companion of Captain Roald Amundsen, the great Norwegian explorer who became the first to see both the North and South Poles. Finn was just 9 years old when his father, was selected by Amundsen to go on what everyone supposed would be a mission to attain the North Pole, but because of Robert E. Peary's announcement declaring his earlier conquest, it turned out to be an expedition to the South Pole instead. After Amundsen's untimely death in 1928, Martin decided to retire, but soon thereafter was persuaded by Commander Byrd to accompany him on the First Byrd Expedition, 1928-30. Finn, by now living in Pittsburgh, went to New York to see his father off and left feeling sorry he was not able to accompany him. While the expedition was at Little America in the Ross Sea, Antarctica, Finn received a radiogram which read: "If you are half as much a man as your daddy, I will be delighted to take you on my next expedition," signed RE Byrd.

Had he lived, Martin would have been persuaded to return to the Antarctic on the second Byrd Expedition in 1933-35. Already Byrd had asked him to begin the required preparations, and Martin had started to assist. However, he died suddenly in 1932 of a heart attack and Byrd offered Finn the vacancy his father left.

Finn had graduated as a mechanical engineer and took postgraduate studies in naval architecture before deciding to emigrate to the United States in 1923, becoming a citizen in 1929. He had soon joined the engineering staff at Westinghouse Electric Corp. in Pittsburgh, Pennsylvania, where he remained until July 1939. But the offer to be a part of a team seeking knowledge on an unknown continent easily convinced him to follow in the footsteps of his father.

On leave from Westinghouse, he served with Admiral Richard E. Byrd's 1933-35 expedition as ski expert and dog driver. Upon arrival in Little America, they dug their way down into Byrd's old Administration Building. Finn sought his father's former bunk. When Byrd showed it to him, they were both amazed to see Finn's name carved into the wood above the bunk. "I never saw it before," Byrd said. "It must have been the last thing he did before he left." "The old man must have known I would come," murmured Finn.

Martin's old bunk became Finn's. To his chagrin, Finn soon found out it was the coldest spot in the entire settlement. At night the door was kept open for ventilation. The cold raw air, at times in the lower sixties below zero, blew right into his bunk. While at Little America, Finn helped to build the base where Byrd spent the winter alone for meteorological recordings. Upon spring's return Finn sledged in Antarctica's interior doing geographical exploration and surveying as well as studying navigation and radio to further his interest in exploration. Martin had predicted well. Finn continued in his father's polar path.

Back with Westinghouse in 1935, Finn made plans for his own small expedition, which suddenly snowballed into the U. S. Antarctic Service Expedition when President Roosevelt intervened in favor of a government expedition. Finn's plans were taken over and conducted by the Department of Interior in 1939-41. He left Westinghouse in order to become second-in-command at East Base under Richard Black on the Antarctic Peninsula. He selected the site and oversaw its construction in 1940. Finn led the main southern sledge party that completed a 1,264-mile sledge trip in 84 days, exploring and delineating 450 miles of new coastline in the Pacific quadrant, and claimed that newly discovered land for the United States. (The United States has never made and formal claims to Antarctic territory, but their citizens were provided with claim sheets to be deposited in snow cairns in case any other country would make such future claims). By sledging around it, he proved conclusively that previously named Alexander I Land was actually an island and that Admiral Thadeus von Bellingshausen, Russian leader of a German expedition could not claim to have seen the Antarctic mainland at this point in 1820.

One night on the small field radio, Finn heard that Germany had invaded Norway. Aided by a hand-cranked generator, he sent a message back to the main base requesting that friends back home in the

United States find and send his necessary papers into the Navy Department applying for a Commission in the Navy. Upon returning to the States he was commissioned a Lieutenant in the U.S. Navy in May 1941, some months before Pearl Harbor. Finn served in World War II with the Navy's Bureau of Ships in charge of ship's tenders and repair ships for which he received the Navy's commendation medal.

We both worked within a few short blocks of his apartment in Washington and we saw each other almost every day. It was easy to meet after work and have dinner, go to the movies, take walks around Haines Point, play tennis, and ride bikes. He had friends who had been with him in the Antarctic and I learned much about various past episodes and the personalities of many of their mutual associates. I also became very knowledgeable about the Antarctic itself. It was obvious that all the men who had been there were captivated by the "out of this world" experience. He assured me, however, that having been on two expeditions, he would never go again. It was fortunate indeed that I did not take him too seriously. From the very start, it seems I understood this extremely motivated, ambitious, talented, and driven man.

For my birthday in October he gave me a beautiful gold watch but just couldn't wait until the actual day. It was obvious as to where we were headed. When he proposed before Christmas of 1943, he presented me with a lovely solitaire diamond ring with the excitement of a small boy. After more than a year's courtship, we were married on March 18, 1944, with Bettie Earle as my only attendant, and Carl Eklund, his former 84-day Antarctic sledging partner, as his best man. He was 44 and I was 24. On our honeymoon, we went skiing for a week at Stowe, Vermont. Finn was very solicitous in helping me up from my many spills on the easiest of the trails, but upon our return to Stowe the following year, he skied on one mountain, and I on the another. Over the years, my skiing ability did improve considerably, but I never matched his still at the sport.

After our wedding, I moved into Finn's small efficiency apartment. It was crowded but conveniently located. By now he was a Lieutenant Commander in the Navy and we lived just a ten minute walk away from the Bureau of Ships, while I worked just two blocks away in the State Department's Division of International Information and Cultural Affairs. We had not been married a year before the war began to wind down, and Finn started to make plans for his own expedition to the Antarctic once again. I was not surprised. For sometime I had felt this was being considered.

These were temporarily interrupted in the summer of 1946, when he was appointed to the Navy task force staff surveying the Canadian Arctic and northwest Greenland to set up weather stations and construct airstrips at the famous Thule Air Force Base, which he helped to site and plan.

Finn was a great organizer and planner. He always had a plan. He felt that anything was possible, if you planned for it. From his first introduction to the Antarctic Continent, he knew that at sometime he was going to lead his own expedition there. He had a most charming smile, an excellent sense of humor, and he knew how to be gracious to people. They responded to him. He captured their imaginations.

Finn's native language was not English, so I edited all of his correspondence and reports. Consequently, I too was closely involved in all of the planning for his new expedition. Evenings and weekends were consumed with countless plans, lists, and endless detail so necessary to the launching of such a venture. He needed money, sponsorship for scientific investigations, a ship, clothing, food, equipment, dogs, etc.

Since I became so knowledgeable of his many involvements and commitments, I was going to be in charge of the domestic side of the expedition while it was in the Antarctic. Regardless of what it took, I was committed to the success of the expedition. I had total confidence in him. If he couldn't get you out of a difficult situation, no one could. As a result people often sought his advice.

One evening, while we were discussing the plans, Finn received a phone call from the Naval attaché at the Norwegian Embassy, Christian Ostby, a friend since childhood from Horten, Norway. Christian said he had a young man there with some crazy idea of floating across the ocean in a raft, and he sorely needed help in raising some money for the project. Could Finn help? Although we were already operating at a fever pitch over our own problems, Finn agreed to see him and did indeed give him all of his own sources for raising funds and gathering equipment, such as the North American Newspaper Alliance for newspaper articles and the Army Quartermaster Corps for testing equipment under difficult environmental conditions.

The visitor was, of course, none other than anthropologist Thor Heyerdal, with plans to float a balsam raft, later to be named the Kon Tiki, across the Pacific Ocean to Easter Island. As he gratefully left our home that evening, Finn turned to me and said, "Can you imagine doing such a thing? Why that will never capture the public's imagination!"

Photograph of Jackie taken in cap and gown for college graduation

Finn had been a member of the Second Expedition of Admiral Richard Byrd in 1933-35, as well as the American Antarctic Service Expedition 1939-41, prior to meeting Jackie.

Jackie and Finn at their wedding in Chevy Chase, Maryland on March 18, 1944. Fellow Antarctic explorer Carl Eklund was best man and Bettie Earle, who introduced them, was maid of honor.

The newly-weds begin making plans for the expedition in their small Washington, D.C. apartment.

II

Against All Odds

Finn was the very spirit of adventure. He could always talk in an interesting manner. He could paint pictures with words, and he could make things come alive. He was an excellent lecturer. His Norwegian accent, which he never lost, was part of his charm. But it made him extra cautious of his pronunciation before the public. Even Dr. Gilbert Grosvenor, Sr., President of the National Geographic Society, once complimented him at the Explorers Club by saying Finn was the one person he could understand when he presided over the meetings.

Finn was very personable. His considerable knowledge, well thought out plans and dynamic personality made people who counted believe in him. The time was ripe for furthering American interests in Antarctic exploration. The Navy's Judge Advocate General's sponsorship of a Bill in Congress to lend a specific ship for Antarctic exploration amounted to a public announcement of intent in 1946. Since an individual cannot be given a naval vessel directly, the American Antarctic Association was incorporated by Finn to receive the vessel. He had created a great interest among government agencies and received strong encouragement and material support from the Office of Naval Research (ONR), the Army Quartermaster Corps, and General LeMay, who headed the Army's Research and Development Branch.

It should have been a piece of cake, relatively speaking. But, he also had almost overwhelming opposition from one extremely powerful man and that made all the difference in the world. Word travels fast in Washington. It wasn't long before Admiral Richard E. Byrd learned that Finn was planning an Antarctic expedition of his own. He could hardly have been surprised. After all, it was Finn's plans that had got the ball rolling for what became the United States Antarctic Service Expedition, 1939-41.

The Navy, particularly the Office of Naval Research, had been very interested in having Finn carry out his intended plans in the Antarctic on active duty under Navy auspices. But, it became painfully obvious that Byrd was not going to allow that. Byrd had no intention of having his powerful authority over American Antarctic exploration challenged. He knew Finn was capable, talented, ambitious, and probably presented somewhat of a threat to him – better to nip it in the bud as soon as possible. Although strongly endorsed by the ONR, all of Finn's attempts to remain on active duty were turned down. It became pretty well established that he would have to go on inactive duty in order to carry out his plans.

When the Office of Naval Research drew up a contract for the expedition to carry on scientific investigations and research as outlined by them, they could not receive approval for expedition funding from the Chief of Naval Operations Office for the amount of money they thought was reasonable. Even when they lowered the amount of money in the contract several times, the Office of Chief of Naval Operations refused to approve the contract. ONR was aware that Byrd was assigned to the Chief of Naval Operations office and eventually became so exasperated and determined to get the work done, they finally drew up a contract for the maximum amount they could by law without having the approval of the Chief Naval Officer. This sum amounted to less than one-third of the amount they considered reasonable. Finn's only choice was to accept it or not go. But it meant that members of the expedition could not be paid. Instead, they would all have to go as volunteers.

On the other side of the coin, General Curtis LeMay of the Office of Research and Development of the Army Air Corps, had been impressed by Finn and his plans. LeMay gave practically "carte blanche" orders to have much needed and necessary equipment issued to the expedition for important testing of that equipment under cold weather conditions. All equipment would be brought back for their evaluation upon return of the expedition from the field. General LeMay was his mentor. His reasoning was that this small privately financed expedition was a very cost-effective way of getting a variety of cold weather equipment tested under severe environmental conditions. A government undertaking would have been far more costly.

Meanwhile, Byrd's long arm stretched in many other directions as well. Suddenly, it was announced that Byrd would head a large task force called Operation Highjump to spend the Antarctic summer of 1946-47 doing trimetrogon photography over three different sectors of the Antarctic. Since our apartments were only one block apart and within a ten-minute walk of the Navy Department, Finn and Byrd often met enroute. I was with Finn on two of these occasions.

Byrd's conversation usually started off with, "Finn, you know I thought the world of your father. He was the salt of the earth. I was sorry he died before my second expedition, but I'm glad you were able to take his place. Now, I would very much like you to go along with me again. If you will give up your plans for your own expedition, I will see that you are made a Captain in the Navy." Essentially, this same conversation took place on three or four occasions, and Finn had no doubt that Byrd could have accomplished just that. But, Finn had been forestalled by Byrd once before, and he was determined to carry out his own plans this time

One time Byrd asked Finn to his office to show how much he intended to help. He had gotten the name of the contact man in LeMay's division who was arranging all the equipment to go with Finn. By telephone, he explained to this man that he was Admiral Byrd and that Finn was sitting in his office. He further explained that he was very interested in helping Finn and would appreciate any and all considerations that could be given to him. After the call was over, Byrd turned to Finn and said, "There, you see, Finn? I am helping you all I can." After Finn left his office, Byrd called the man back and asked him to ignore his first call and do just the opposite. In complete bewilderment, the man in question later reported both conversations to Finn.

One evening, Finn came home quite upset. Byrd had called him and said if Finn would show him a copy of his plans, he would help him in every way he could. What a quandary! Finn felt certain that if he gave Byrd his plans, Byrd would use them. And if he did not give them to Byrd, he would double his efforts to oppose Finn. Finally, but with great reluctance, Finn did give Byrd a copy of his entire expedition plan. The results had been predictable. Byrd barely changed the wording; Finn's main geographical objective of photographing the last unknown coastline in the world, a six hundred mile stretch of the Weddell Sea Coast from Mt. Tricorn to Coats Land, was made priority number one of the Bellingshausen Sea Task Group of Operation

Highjump. It is painful to record that the plane assigned to start that mission crashed into a mountain in bad weather, killing three of the seven aboard instantly. A rescue party found the other four in very bad shape and barely got them out with their lives. On Operation High Jump's way back north after concluding its summer operations, they passed our small ship headed south for a year, far apart at sea. Byrd radioed a message to Finn, wishing him the best of luck!

Years later, sometime in the sixties, way after the International Geophysical Year (IGY) of 1956-58, Captain Gambacorta of the Navy's supply ship *Wyndott,* part of the Task Force that built Ellsworth station where Finn was the Commanding Officer during IGY, asked us to his daughter's wedding in Annapolis. As we prepared to leave the reception, our host said there was someone anxious to meet Finn. We were still a bit mystified when he brought over a Navy captain and introduced him. After passing the time of day, the Navy Captain said that he had always wanted to shake the hand of the man who had had enough courage to stand up against the power of the U.S. Government. He continued to state that he had been Admiral Byrd's Military Aid in the Chief of Naval Operations Office during the time Finn was trying to get his expedition going. He told Finn he would never know the tremendous opposition Byrd had mounted against him night and day during that period. He proceeded to describe some of the unconscionable incidents against Finn that had taken place including Byrd's intercession with the Chief of Naval Operations Office to disapprove the amount of money the Office of Naval Research was willing to pay Finn for obtaining their desired scientific results, until it became so low ONR no longer needed their approval. Finn said that he did know, but, until now, had never before had the proof. The Captain quickly answered, "And you don't have it now, because if you ever repeated our conversation of today, I will deny it and swear that I have never met you."

To this day, I believe that the most miraculous thing about the whole Ronne Antarctic Research Expedition was that, with such opposition, it ever left the United States at all.

The Office of Naval Research had awarded Finn a contract for all of the expedition's scientific results and the North American Newspaper Alliance would carry stories of the progress. The act of Congress sponsored by the Navy, authorized them to provide a suitable vessel. In addition, there were some private contributions from friends and private scientific institutions. Many men, both in the Army and the Navy, had great confidence that Finn was capable of accomplishing his objectives, and they were willing to assist him to the limit of their ability. But, a great deal of professional jealousy and opposition existed as well. Try as he could, Finn was never able to raise more than $48,000 cash, a pittance in comparison to those who came after him.

Additional opposition came from a surprisingly unexpected source. As a result of some early publicity in *The Washington Post* concerning Finn's plans to return to the United States Antarctic Service Expedition East Base site in Marguerite Bay, the British Embassy informed the Department of State for the first time in September 1946, that British personnel were in occupation of that Stonington Island site. Under the secrecy of war, the British had launched Operation Tabarin in 1943, to counter Argentine and potential German activity on the Antarctic Peninsula (which they claimed as British Territory). Five British Bases had been established on the Antarctic Peninsula and were now run by the Falkland Islands Dependency Survey. The southernmost of their bases was on Stonington Island in Marguerite Bay. The British further stated that the American "hutments" on Stonington Island had been found in "considerable disorder" and that the Falkland Islands Dependency Survey had recovered the salvageable equipment and were preparing to return it to the United States during the next Antarctic summer.

The Department of State's reply sent to the British Embassy indicated that it was the intention of the United States Government to leave the buildings and supplies, such as coal, gasoline, and food, for the use of any United States scientific expedition basing in that area and that Finn Ronne was indeed planning an expedition to the area and for them to leave the things intact for further use. Additional information concerning the conditions of the buildings, equipment, and supplies was requested.

In December 1946, the Embassy sent the Department a report in which "the last Falkland Islands Dependencies Survey" found the "American huts and Property." It presented a very dismal picture of conditions at the Base. Referring to the Bunkhouse "practically all the canvas has disappeared and daylight shows through almost every joint. This has caused considerable damage.... The kitchen floor was solid ice, through seepage under the floor"; and referring to the science building... the whole place is in disorder with the floor littered with everything from clothing to chewing gum. There is very little equipment left in serviceable condition." Other information about doors being left open and ice accumulating as a result, plus wreckage and damage to equipment and general disorder was included, as well as the following paragraph:

> Inquiry is being made regarding the extent to which the huts in question are being used by the Falkland Islands Dependency Survey party already at Marguerite Bay. It is unfortunately the opinion of British Antarctic experts that, even if there were some space available in the huts, there would not be enough room for two parties or enough for their food and for their dogs at Marguerite Bay.

Obviously, a British group was in occupation of the American campsite and an American expedition to reoccupy it was not welcome. Finn had had no previous way of knowing that the British were there, all his plans had been made, and were dependent upon those buildings for a base. Finn had hoped to use the aviation gasoline left there to extend his flying operations, for it was possible to carry only so many drums of gasoline as cargo on the ship. The information about the lack of seals for dog food in the vicinity was ridiculous; but this was not all.

An international whaling conference was being held in Washington at the time. The British member of the conference had some intimate knowledge of the Antarctic was sent to call upon Finn by his government. Among other things, he asked Finn why he intended to go to British territory, which had been discovered originally by a Britisher (referring to Bransfield, who the British claim sighted the continent before U.S. sealer Nathaniel Brown Palmer, who the United States always recognized as the discoverer in 1821). Finn replied that there were various opinions about that and so far as he knew, the United States Government recognized no other government's claim to the Antarctic, nor had we made any formal claim ourselves, but reserved the right of any American citizen to go anywhere in Antarctica for exploration or scientific research purposes. Finn told him that, at this late date, it was impossible to make any other arrangements. When he saw that it was impossible to persuade Finn to give up the thought of going to the region, as he had been sent to do, he expressed the hope that Finn would cooperate fully with the British there. Finn assured him he would be very glad to cooperate with them providing they moved out of the U.S. buildings and found their own camp site.

But the British Foreign Office did not give up. As late as December 30th, Finn received another communication stating:

> We are further instructed to request you kindly to inform Commander Ronne that:
>
> (a) for practical reasons of which he is believed to be aware he could not support his proposed party at Mar-

guerite Bay without serious detriment to the operation of our party.

(b) nevertheless His Majesty's Government would welcome a visit by him to Marguerite Bay if he considers it essential to see the position for himself.

(c) if he is prepared to leave a very small party of say four or five men spend the Antarctic winter and work jointly with the British party of ten H.M.G. would be glad to consider whether this can be arranged on hearing what sort of specialists he would like to leave and what work he has in mind for them.

Beyond this, as Commander Ronne will himself best realize, it is difficult to go without serious physical risk to both parties involved.

As the Ronne expedition is understood shortly to be leaving for the Antarctic we should be grateful for urgent transmission of this message and of Commander Ronne's decision, in order that we may communicate the latter to London.

As a result of this message, the Department of State requested that Finn talk to officials of the British Embassy in person, which he did. At each rung of the diplomatic ladder, their staff expressed just "how beastly they considered it was of him to go to their territory." Finally, Finn had a very nice informal chat with Lord Inverchapel, the British Ambassador, who expressed his hope of future cooperation and wished the expedition the best of luck.

In the second week of January, just before the expedition was about to sail, Finn received another communication via the same source:

. . . the Foreign Office now wished to make known its fears lest, under Antarctic conditions, friction should arise between an American party so large as yours and the smaller British party at Marguerite Bay, parties at such close quarters disputes of one kind or another would be bound to arise and it was felt certain you would agree that would be undesirable. In these circumstances it was felt to be impossible that independent expeditions should be maintained in this small and restricted space; that the absence of previous joint planning, and essential differ-

> ences in methods, equipment, organizations, objectives, standards of living will all contribute to an impossible situation.

The message went on to state that:

> … no difficulties should, on the other hand, arise about a visit of short duration to the British station by your whole expedition but that for a wintering party accommodation of more than four or five men would be an impossibility; that these few men could be attached to the British party of ten and could work in close collaboration with them; that the British would of course be glad to make suitable wireless schedules available to them.

The message further stated that:

> …your request that such American property and scientific equipment as were found at the base be held there has been gladly acceded to; that unfortunately the American huts and property were found in derelict condition and the remains of one hut had been used by the British party to build a store-shed.

The foregoing exchange was particularly interesting in light of future happenings between the British and American groups.

Eventually the persuading, begging arm-twisting, interviewing, selection of personnel, collecting, and packing in Washington were finally over. Finn was elated that his months of planning and hard work were finally paying off and he could fly down to Beaumont, Texas, to oversee the ship and its loading. Soon I would take a two-week leave of absence from the Department of State to join him and assist with the hundreds of last minute details before the expedition could depart. Time was of the essence because Finn was aware of the tricky ice conditions at his designated base, the former East Base of the United States Antarctic Service Expedition, 1939-41, where Finn was second in command and oversaw the construction of the pre-fabricated buildings, in Marguerite Bay. This was the first time an Antarctic expedition had departed from a city as far south in the United States as Beaumont, Texas. Polar explorer Sir Hubert Wilkins came down from New York to see how things were going and lend a hand to the loading of the ship. At his own expense, he had already dispatched a couple of his own sledges, which had been stored at his Pennsylvania farm.

Sir Hubert, an Australian, was knighted by the King of England for his brilliant Trans-Arctic flight in 1928, from Point Barrow, Alaska, across the north-polar ocean to Spitzbergen, north of Norway. He also was the first to fly an airplane in the Antarctic. His most daring flight took off from Deception Island, across the Bransfield Strait, over the Antarctic Peninsula to the Larsen Ice Shelf on the east side of the 6,000 foot high Plateau, and continued south to within sight of Alexander Land, which was as far as the fuel would permit in his single engine plane. Since Finn's exploratory plans called for following-up where his plane flight had ended, Sir Hubert was vitally interested in what would be found on this expedition.

Sir Hubert was the consummate explorer. He had spent years in the Arctic with Steffanson; he had attempted to take a submarine under the Arctic ice cap, had flown around the world in the Graf Zeppelin, and had been the manager of Lincoln Ellsworth's Antarctic expeditions – all with little fanfare, great humility and considerate kindness to his fellow explorers, in itself a very unique quality in the polar fraternity. We were with him on numerous occasions and although he was always the focal point, he never repeated a story. He had great intelligence and proved to be a man whose ideas were far ahead of his time.

Sir Hubert and Finn had worked closely together at the Quartermaster Corps in Washington improving and developing new cold weather clothing. They were very good friends and were from the same mold, morally. When the American Polar Society held its meeting in Washington on the 40th anniversary of Admiral Robert E. Peary's supposed attainment of the North Pole, Sir Hubert was asked to be the Master of Ceremonies and Finn was asked to introduce him. Neither man believed that Peary actually had reached the Pole. Sir Hubert had the unenviable task of conveying this message diplomatically before an audience that included Peary's daughter, Marie Peary Stafford. As a well-known master of the English language, he rose to the occasion perfectly, starting to extoll Peary by saying, "We are not here this evening to honor a normal man. With toes amputated on both feet, Peary traveled unbelievable distances on snowshoes by dead reckoning, and without benefit of longitudinal calculations, over steep pressure ridges and extremely adverse conditions in record time, unequaled by any other normal human being." His daughter, Marie, who was sitting beside me, kept nudging me saying, "What an outstanding speaker he is," never once catching on that Sir Hubert's superlatives in describing

Peary were meant to alert the audience of the speaker's total disbelief in Peary's claim.

Some of the clothing and related equipment Sir Hubert and Finn had worked to redesign were already loaded aboard ship and stashed away in one of the holes for field testing. Much of the heavier equipment, such as three small planes, two over-the-snow tracked vehicles, called "weasels," and considerable photographic equipment came as a result of General LeMay's great interest.

Departure from Beaumont did not come easy. At the last minute, no one wanted to insure the vessel and without insurance, the ship would not be allowed to leave the United States. The Navy could not insure the ship because it was being privately operated. No company would touch it because it was a government vessel, except for Lloyds of London – dollar for dollar on what it was worth. One million dollars for insurance was not in Finn's skimpy budget. This unanticipated turn of events meant that Finn had to return to Washington for some congressional help. Judge Combs, congressman from the Beaumont District, went with Finn directly to the Maritime Commission and emphatically explained to them his great interest in the matter. Suddenly, within twenty-four hours, the ship became insured by the agency. Finn flew back to Texas that night. The expedition was ready to depart.

In early January I was asked by the North American Newspaper Alliance to write an article on why women had not ever gone to the Antarctic. I did the article and it was published in several newspapers around the United States including the Milwaukee Journal a copy of which I include here.

Because of the delay in getting the insurance straightened out, Finn asked me if I would go aboard and sail with them as far as Panama. There were many loose ends, a considerable amount of unfinished business, and last minute details he wanted to discuss with me before I returned to Washington. From then on, we would be completely out of touch except by ship's radio. With some reluctance, I agreed to go that far. I was torn between returning to the State Department from my two-week leave of absence and my desire to see how the somewhat disorganized expedition group would shake down. I didn't have time to think of what I was doing, as I barely had time to extend my leave, toss my clothes in my suitcase, and get on board in time for the farewell ceremony.

It was a hectic departure – "bedlam" describes it better. I was thrilled to christen the ship "*The Port Of Beaumont*." The Governor of Texas bade us farewell. The entire city was interested and involved. Articles appeared in the press daily. Schools were out and children were everywhere. School children, who collected money to help the rapidly depleted budget, lined the dock and they became intrigued by the type of sledge dogs being assembled dockside. Brass bands played. It was a festive celebration. The media were vying for attention and so were the sledge dogs that were being taken on board at the last minute by expedition members. Final good-byes were said, the ship was cleared of all guests, the anchor was raised, and soon we were slowly making our way down the Neches River. On the yard arm of the ship flew the Lone Star State flag of Texas, given to us by the Daughters of the Republic of Texas. Before long, the pilot boat left us and we were on our own. All hands continued making the ship ready for the open sea in the Gulf of Mexico. Tons of equipment had been loaded on board, sufficient to provide for every conceivable need for eighteen months: food for men and dogs, housing, medical supplies, scientific instruments, thirty tons of coal, one hundred and fifty-five gallon drums of high octane gasoline for the three small planes which were lashed down on deck. Dogs were everywhere, tied to the ship's stanchions and far enough apart so that they could not start a dog fight with each other, for separating dogs in a dog fight is really a chapter in itself.

The ship was being manned and operated by the twenty expedition personnel, only eight of whom had been to sea before. As we headed south in the Gulf of Mexico toward the Panama Canal, Finn had little time to be elated, but I was. His dream had become a reality at last. In spite of the almost insurmountable obstacles and hurdles put in his path, he had persevered. Under very adverse conditions, his diligence and determination had paid off. Many headaches had been overcome. But, we both knew only too well there would be many more to come. I had to pinch myself to believe that I was on board.

Finn loading the dogs on the ship in Beaumont

While being loaded aboard ship at Beaumont, Texas, the Trimetgon-camera-equipped plane dropped 40 feet to the dock when a lifting lug snapped. In Panama an identical plane was obtained as a replacement.

The damaged Norseman being lifted off the Port of Beaumont after it dropped to the deck while being loaded in Beaumont, Texas.

The citizens of Beaumont gave the expedition a grand farewell celebration, complete with live radio broadcast.

Port of Beaumont sails from Beaumont, Texas, down the Neches River

Jackie posed for a formal portrait, as did every expedition member.

Jennie Darlington and Jackie Ronne aboard ship on way south

Jennie and Harry Darlington

Some of the crew watches as the ship sails.

Group onboard Port of Beaumont near Panama (l to r): Sig Gutenko, Larry Fiske, Finn Ronne, Chuck Adams, Jackie Ronne, Chuck Hassage, and Andy Thompson

III

Heading South

Once in the open Gulf of Mexico, the expedition members quickly got their sea legs and settled down to the routine of running the ship in three watches of eight hours each. We had more time to start getting to know each other. Our skipper, Captain Ike Schlossbach, a veteran of several previous polar expeditions, as well as a retired Naval Officer, was understandably somewhat uncertain about the knowledge and efficiency of his untested crew. Although, all had served in the military during the war, they were volunteers without commercial shipping experience.

Ike, himself had cause to be jittery. He was an expedition "hobo". He could just smell when there was an expedition in the offing. He came down from his New Jersey home to find out if Finn could use him in any way; if not, he would just help load the ship, he said. He was retired from the U.S. Navy, was the only man who had commanded a surface ship, a submarine, and a squadron of planes. Ike had only one eye as a result of a plane crash. He had been navigating officer of Sir Hubert Wilkins' submarine expedition to the Arctic in 1931, had served on the Second Byrd Expedition in 1934, on the Greenland McGregor Expedition to northern Greenland in 1937, the United States Antarctic Service Expedition in 1940, as well as serving in the Arctic during the War.

Finn was in need of a skipper. Although Ike did not have a skipper' license, he immediately volunteered to enroll in a Merchant Marine school in New York. A well-known polar character, Iceberg Smith gave him his final exam, leaning over Ike's shoulder and shaking his head if Ike marked a wrong answer on the true or false portion. His license allowed him to take the ship to and from the Antarctic, but was invalid after his first port of call in the U.S. upon return. Ike never married, and he certainly enjoyed the vicissitudes of expedition life.

In the early pre-dawn hours of the day before we reached the Panama Canal, Walter H. Smith (Smitty), Second Mate and Navigator, informed Captain Ike that the lights ahead on our starboard side marked the entrance to the Panama Canal. Ike was skeptical and ordered the engines cut to idling speed until daybreak. But before sunrise a much larger ship, ablaze with light and coming full speed ahead from the opposite direction, expertly swung in front of us. "Follow that ship", Ike ordered. Smitty's navigation had been right on target. It was the Canal and the ship turned out to be the "Stellar Polaris", the well-known gleaming white Norwegian cruise ship. Ike never questioned Smitty's navigation ability again.

Finn, Ike, pilot Harry Darlington and Sig Gutenko, our cook who was a Chief Commissary Stewart in the Navy and had gone on inactive duty just to be with us, were the only four who had ever been to the Antarctic before. Finn had known Harry since he was the youngest member of the U.S. Antarctic Service Expedition 1939-41, when Harry was sort of jack-of-all trades. When someone told Harry to clean up after the dogs, Harry cleaned up after the dogs. He became a pilot during the war and when he found out Finn was organizing an expedition he came to see if he could help and sign on. He already had been very helpful in lining up some much-needed funds and advice, and so Finn had made him Third-in-Command and in charge of the aviation program. He and his wife Jennie had only been married a couple of months. When Finn insisted I go as far as Panama, I had asked Jennie to accompany me and we could both fly back from there. Jennie was delighted as she considered this her honeymoon. The four of us had become friends.

Dr. Robert L. Nichols was our senior scientist from Tufts College where he taught Geology. His assistant, Robert (Bob) Dodson, son of Finn's superior officer in the Navy, also helped with the dogs. Harries Clichy Peterson, called Harcly, not long out of Harvard, was to be our physicist and meteorologist, while Andrew Thompson was a geophysicist. Jack-of-all-trades, Larry Fiske, with a talking knowledge of many things, could and did pinch-hit as climatologist, lawyer, etc. Nelson McClary was First Mate and Smitty, Second Mate, while Charles (Chuck) Hassage was who had applied while we were loading the ship in Beaumont, Texas became the much needed Chief Engineer along with his assistant Walter Wood. Donald McLean, an intern in pediatrics just three months short of his final MD was our doctor. William Latady was the aerial photographer, while James Robertson was the aircraft mechanic. Lawrence Kelsey was our young radio operator. He was very tall, blonde only sixteen years old and had just returned to the States from working in the interior of Afghanistan. Most of these men were young and many of them over six feet tall.

Eagle Scout, Art Owen, had been the winner of a competition held in Beaumont to create interest in the expedition before we left. Major James Lassiter and Lieutenant Charles (Chuck) Adams (often known as the Air Force twins) were two excellent pilots who had delivered the three planes made available to us from General LeMay and had succeeded in convincing both Finn and the General to allow them to accompany us. They were a splendid addition to the roster.

After a fascinating day in transit through the Canal, we arrived at the Naval Base in Balboa while Naval personnel looked on in disbelief. We thought we had handled the docking with dispatch, but obviously the expert observers had some reservations.

I've always loved Panama – the weather, the afternoon downpours, the local color in Panama City that is as native as any found elsewhere in Central or South America, and, of course, the Zone. Balboa was so beautifully located and as American as an ice cream sundae. That Saturday night, Finn and I danced out-of-doors on a breathtakingly perfect evening beneath the sparkling stars at Fort Amador overlooking the Canal and Pacific Ocean. I was painfully aware that it would be a long time before we would dance together again or share such a carefree perfect night.

Several days after we left Beaumont, Finn had casually mentioned that there was really no one available to write the stories for the important contract we had with the North American Newspaper Alliance to cover the progress of the expedition. He could really use my help, he said. At first I thought he was joking and ignored him. We enjoyed being together, operated as a team, and often discussed how hard it would be to be separated for a year. But everything else was put on hold until the success of his longtime desire to lead his own expedition. However, now he wasn't joking. He persisted daily in trying to convince me that spending a year in the Antarctic was a piece of cake.

"It's nothing," he said, "it's the banana belt – hardly gets colder than ten or twenty degrees below zero," he continued. "You'd love it! It's gorgeous scenery, and you could ski on the glacier."

That did it! Obviously the man was getting serious! "Forget it," I said. "There is not a chance that I would agree to such a thing. I'm not even interested in going along; my thoughts are elsewhere. We have an apartment. I have a good job. I couldn't! I wouldn't! No woman has ever done it before and I'm not going to be the first! What would people think? No way!"

As the group was shaking down, he saw some other weak spots and doggedly insisted that I would be of more help by going the entire way. It was tempting. I was grateful to be needed. We had always worked well together and the success of the expedition had dominated my life as well as his. I loved this man and beyond anything else in this world, I wanted him to succeed. I wasn't even supposed to be aboard this ship. After tension filled weeks of tedious work of loading the ship in Beaumont, I had reluctantly agreed to accompany him as far as Panama only to wind up details. My wonderful boss in the Department of State had granted me another two-week extension to my leave of absence. We were a busy office – the department needed me.

Dogged persistence was certainly one of the qualities that had enabled Finn to launch his own Antarctic expedition. After all, how many Americans had succeeded in doing that? Only Richard Byrd and Lincoln Ellsworth had done so. Byrd was the consummate politician with wide influence through the government and a brother who was a U.S. senator, while Ellsworth was independently wealthy. Larry Gould had tried but in Byrd's shadow, didn't succeed. Finn had worked it and was on his way. As far as anything to do with the Antarctic was concerned, Finn never took "no" for an answer.

By the time we reached Panama, it was pretty well decided that I would continue on to Valparaiso, Chile, before having to make a final decision. That would be our last port of call, and I had the option of flying back from there. Jennie wanted to continue on to South America, and I was pleased to have her do so.

The expedition had been given permission to re-supply at the Navy Commissary in Panama. Because of limited refrigeration and freezer space going through the tropics before reaching cold climates, we had to take only boneless meat. An aircraft carrier had been in port provisioning just before we arrived, so there was very little choice left in meat selections. Among other things, we took onboard 6,500 pounds of frozen Argentine beef fillet – a fillet being something most had not seen since before the war.

We assumed that we had pulled away from the dock at Balboa rather smartly, so we were a bit chastened when the Navy's farewell message bellowed over a megaphone, "Good bye, good luck, and God help you."

Valparaiso, Chile, was to be our next and last port of call before heading south to the Antarctic Continent. If there was any chance that I would continue to accompany the expedition the entire way, there were plans to be made and several people to inform. I wrote a letter to my boss in the Department of State explaining this far-fetched possibility, and should it come to pass, I would offer my resignation from the U.S. Consulate in Valparaiso. The second letter I wrote went to my aunt and uncle explaining the circumstances and asking if they would be willing to dispose of our apartment, store the contents, and handle a few of the business matters in my absence. I realized it was a great responsibility and that I was asking a great deal of them. I also asked that they keep the news very confidential, as I was not interested in making headlines.

The ocean voyage south was delightful. We all enjoyed the calm seas and warm weather sailing through the tropics. When we crossed the equator, "King Neptune" came on board, following a long standing tradition, to initiate those of us who had not been in the Southern Hemisphere before. He was somewhat rough on the men, but we all took our duncking in stride.

On-board life had settled into a routine. The men stood regular watches – eight hours on and twelve hours off, thus rotating them daily to different positions. Aviation mechanic Jimmy Robertson and aerial photographer Bill Latady coated the planes with a plastic preservative to prevent damage from salt water spray in anticipation of rough seas ahead. Bill also painted the Ronne Antarctic Research Expedition emblem, which was a penguin, on the side of the Norseman plane. Chief cook Sigmund Gutenko, who had twenty years of Navy experience, was kept busy in the galley preparing our meals. The dogs were lazy and seemed happy, with only an occasional dogfight when one would manage to gnaw through one of his leather traces and torment one of his companions. However, within a few days we noticed that one or two became lethargic. Try as we could, they got worse. Although they had been given distemper shots before we received them, it was obviously that this disease that was affecting them. Unfortunately, we lost several dogs before the epidemic ran its course and we got to cooler temperatures. The scientists did some marine biology, made recordings of ocean temperatures with a bathothermograph, and took meteorological readings several times daily. These were radioed to the U.S. Weather Bureau. Physicist Harcly Peterson was able to set up his cosmic ray machine topside and get some important impulse data from space for the Bartol Foundation of the Franklin Institute in Philadelphia. It was a well-occupied, happy group.

In the Captain's cabin, Finn and I were always busy – Finn with plans and endless details, and I with writing daily articles for the North American Newspaper Alliance on the progress of the expedition (under Finn's name for, as yet, they did not know I was on board). I also had a lot of thinking to do. To go, or not to go?

By this time, the men began to suspect that I might be going the entire way and some of them were less than enthusiastic at the prospect. Of all the places on the surface of the earth, the Antarctic was considered a man's province. Undoubtedly, the thought of expedition life had appealed to some for this very reason. There was a lot of macho in them. We began to hear rumors about their feelings and what someone or other would do if I went – even to the point of quitting the expedition. Finn paid absolutely no attention to any of it. As yet the group really did not know him. He would have the first and last word about such a decision. So far as he was concerned, it was a matter solely between us and not a subject up for discussion. By the time we arrived in Valpariso, Chile, the final decision still had not been made.

The decision, however, could not be put off much longer. Finn and I hurried to the American Consulate to pick up the mail to see what reaction my news had wrought. My boss, John Steeves, had arranged to have my job held for one year and wished me nothing but good luck and God speed. I had, however, correctly anticipated the shock to my unsuspecting aunt, who would be the one to get rid of our apartment and store the furniture, as well as field many of the problems Stateside that I had knowledge of and would have dealt with. Indeed, there was a stack of mail from her, frantically listing all of the reasons why I should not go. Although, I had told her not to tell anyone, she had gotten several of my close friends to write, admonishing me as well. When she could think of no more warnings, in the last sentence of the last paragraph of the last page of the last letter, she dispiritedly cautioned, "And don't forget, you might ruin your complexion!" Something I certainly had not considered.

I felt guilty. I had a wonderful boss and a very challenging job. I felt certain the whole State Department's success rested on my shoulders.

(It has never ceased to amaze me that they have continued to fumble along without me all these years.) Then there was my disapproving aunt on whom I would place an appreciable burden. But above all other considerations, there was the publicity.

No woman had ever participated in an over-wintering Antarctic expedition and I did not want to create a sensation. The Office of Naval Research was counting on Finn to do a good scientific job. Certainly, I did not want them to think he had planned on my going as a way to capture the headlines, for such was definitely not the case. In the last analysis, this would become the main reason why, when Jennie Darlington wanted to accompany us the entire way as well, I persuaded Finn to allow her to come along. Her presence would soften the blow, I thought.

I need not have worried about the Navy. Upon our return, when I first met Admiral Paul Lee, Head of the Office of Naval Research, at a reception they held in our honor, he greeted me saying, "I'm very disappointed with you, young lady. I thought you would take this golden opportunity to produce the first citizen of the Antarctic." I suppose it would have helped in the very touchy politics of Antarctic claims, but I had my hands full as it was.

The final decision was made in our Valparaiso hotel room. We invited Head Scientist Bob Nichols to give us his very best advice. He definitely thought I should go, but he also felt it would be best if Jennie did not. For a while it seemed as though that would be the way it would work out. The decision for me had been made. I had always been committed to do anything to further the success of the expedition no matter what it cost, but I never dreamed I would be the first woman and third member of the Ronne family to go on a year-long Antarctic expedition. Harry Darlington was not in favor of either Jennie or my going. He stated emphatically that Jennie would not go. But when he realized it was definite that I was going, he backed down and gave his permission for his wife to go as well. Jennie was thrilled.

Once the final decision was made and announced to the men, they seemed to accept it and to my knowledge there was no more undercurrent or complaining. The die was cast. Last letters were hurriedly written informing my family, my boss, and a very few friends of the astonishing turn of events. And I submitted my resignation to the Department of State from the U.S.Consulate at Valparaiso. Even though my boss wanted to hold my job for a year, I hated to tie up that position. I didn't think it was fair.

Jennie and I picked up a few last minute items that we thought would be necessary for an extended stay in Antarctic isolation. Among other things, I remember buying a pair of Chilean-made ski boots, as none we had aboard seemed to fit me properly. Shopping helped, somewhat, to keep me from wondering whether I had made the right decision. I would be less than honest not to admit it was an uneasy time. Once past the point of no return, Jennie and I would be making Antarctic history. Along with all the other problems and considerations, how did one inconspicuously handle that?

Due to the prevailing rough weather, Finn decided to make one more port of call by sailing through the Inland Passage to Punta Arenas, Chile in southern Tierra del Fuego. After topping-off our ship's tanks with fresh water, fuel oil, and fresh produce, we departed from Valparaiso about noon and headed south to the open sea. There were twenty-three of us on board, two women and twenty-one men, including a young Chilean mess cook we signed on at the last minute to help our cook with routine galley duties.

For two days after leaving Valparaiso, we sailed in very rough open ocean. It was our worst storm thus far. I could barely keep my feet on the deck. Commander Torres, who would be our pilot through the Inland Passage, kept assuring me, "This good, weather – very good weather." I remained skeptical. We weren't far from the "Roaring Forties" historically known as "The Graveyard of the World." In the past, many ships had capsized in these waters and were never heard from again. We rolled so continuously that no one slept until five the next morning when we reached the first of the inland channels. We sighted our first albatross that morning, March 1st. Immediately, I thought of Samuel Tayor Coleridge's *The Rime of the Ancient Mariner.* The magnificent bird came sailing gracefully forward of the Bridge and followed us for a couple of hours before heading out to sea in a northwesterly direction.

Because of our extraordinary topside weight, Finn had decided we would take the more circuitous Inland Passage, both safe and scenic. Once inside, we had eight days of grandeur. On the afterdeck, some of the men used the opportunity afforded by the quiet waters to build a protective canvas covering for the dogs. As evening approached, our pilot informed us that the next channel was covered with fog and in order not to waste one or two days, it would be best to go around it by putting out to sea again.

From our port bow, we could see the high snow-capped Andes Mountain range, interspersed with snowfields, glaciers, and occasional volcanoes. But because of fog in the next channel, we reluctantly put out to sea again for a day and a half. It was miserably rough. Everything not secured was thrown to the deck. The ship bobbed like a cork. We experienced the greatest rolls of the downward voyage, 47 degrees on the inclinometer. Waves breaking against the deck caused spray to cover the decks. Wind and ocean swells from the southwest produced high, long, heavy rollers, but we continued to make about ten knots.

Navy Chief Commissary Steward, Sig Gutenko, who cooked for years on submarines and destroyers, said that either this trip through the roaring forties prevented him from keeping the contents of his pots and pans on the range for the first time, or else he was getting too old for his job. Soup and sandwiches were all he could manage. The scientists and others, who, until a month before had never been to sea, or even knew what it meant to box a compass, were acting as experienced sailors. Skipper Schlossbach had initiated them into the rudiments of seamanship. But Army pilot Jim Lassiter shook his head sadly, stating he would rather be a buck-private in the Army than an Admiral in the Navy any day.

About 9:30 the next morning, we came into another quiet channel, which gave everyone the opportunity to get some much-needed sleep. The scenery resembled Norwegian fjords. Mountains on both sides of us were covered with tall green trees up to the timberline and from then on many were snowcapped. Scenic waterfalls dotted the landscape. On both sides of the ship's bow porpoises played. Some men sighted what they thought were seals but later decided they were sea otters. Progressively, the weather began getting cooler and Dodson was very busy distributing woolens. The longhandle underwear were in big demand.

That evening about 6:30 we reached a bend in the channel, which resembled a large lake surrounded by hills and mountains. As was custom for ships using the channel, we anchored there for a short while and we soon saw why. Small primitive canoes headed for our vessel. The canoes had been very crudely made by hollowing out a tree trunk by hatchet. They were filled to capacity with Indians, both young and old, sitting on rough cut limbs and twigs to prevent the water in the leaky canoe from soaking them. These Indian natives were some of the most primitive in the world. Their features resembled the Seminole tribe. The canoes contained mostly barefooted women with babes in arms. Although clothed in rags with nothing to protect them from the cold damp weather, they displayed broad smiles revealing perfect sets of gleaming white teeth. Their language was an Indian dialect rather than pure Spanish. As soon as they saw me, they excitedly yelled, “Senora, tiene robes”? They wanted both clothes and cigarettes. As it became light, Photographer Latady took a flash bulb picture of them huddled below in their canoes. As the flash went off, they became very angry and covered their heads and faces. Obviously, they had hoped to pose for pictures in return for things we might give them. I scrounged around for a little something I could part with. About this time, some native Chileans pulled along side in a much better constructed boat. Sig traded one and a half pounds of sugar for some mussels and two-king crabs, the latter of which he steamed. It tasted better than any lobster I have ever eaten.

On one of the larger islands, we noticed a very nice house. Our Pilot informed us that it was the Headquarters for a branch of the Chilean Army Air Force. The large lake provided a fine emergency landing field for pontoon equipped planes. Even large Chilean Catalina flying boats had made occasional emergency landings there. A bit later, the Commander of this Chilean Air Force branch came on board. He was a tall, heavy set, good-looking Chilean of about thirty-five years who had been stationed at this outpost for five years. His growth of beard was the envy of our men who had been working toward such a goal for the past two weeks. While waiting for some difficulty with our steering engine to be fixed, we had a most interesting chat with him, using our Chilean pilot as interpreter.

On March 4th, we sailed on and the first glacier ice was sighted floating in the water. It had broken off from one of the glaciers in the nearby Andes. The scenery changed considerably. The Andean range tapered off until it reached nothing more than large boulders with breaks of water between them. With the cooler weather, as we traveled south, the vegetation decreased noticeably. As we sailed into the harbor of Punta Arenas about three o’clock on the afternoon of March 5th, we were blessed with one of those sunny days which are exceedingly rare in that part of the world. The perfect visibility afforded us a most unusual view of the then unclimbed Mt. Sarmiento, approximately sixty miles to the south of the town.

Punta Arenas, in the Straits of Magellan, was, remains the southernmost city in the world. With a population of 13,000 then, it was located at the northern extremity of Tierra del Fuego, and is the capital of Magellenes territory. It is a calling place and coal station for vessels passing through the Straits, deposits of coal occurring in the region and the anchorage being good. Lignite and wool are exported and cereals are cultivated. Its industries include meat preserving, refrigerating works, tanneries, and grease refineries. We learned that there were some Americans there drilling for oil, which fortunately they later found in quantity.

After talking with officials in the Inter-Oceanic Office, which controls the port of Punta Arenas, we discovered that a plane had left Valparaiso that would arrive in town the following day. As it was thought that this plane would be carrying our long needed steering engine spare parts and the badly needed dog vaccine, it was decided we would stay a day and wait for it. Shore leaves were given for the men to see this very quaint, clean, almost European looking town. After waiting for two days, we found out that the plane, which had been grounded at Porto Monte because of bad weather, might not be in for a week.

I found it very exciting to be in the southernmost town in the world. Also, it was my last opportunity to do some last minute shipping. Anticipating lots of time on my hands during the next year, I went in search of some knitting wool. I could purchase either American or Chilean produced wool. I chose Chilean, because it was different and it was cheaper. But the small store had no knitting needles or knitting directions for sweaters or socks. An elderly lady standing next to me overheard me say I was going to spend a year in the Antarctic. In excellent English, she said she was from Santiago and in Punta Arenas on holiday visiting her daughter. She had her knitting needles with her. If I would return to the store that afternoon, I could pick them up. I did come back and sure enough, her pile of needles was there. How wonderful they proved to be.

During the next year, I knitted mittens, socks, and after ski socks, along with ski headbands, and scarves, with only my memory to guide me in turning a heel and toe. A couple of these items are now on display in the Naval Memorial Museum in Washington, DC. My life long regret is that I was unable to send a message of appreciation to that gracious lady, as I had neither her name nor address.

Before leaving Punta Arenas, we were entertained at dinner in the beautiful home of Senor Francisco Campos and Senora Maria Menendez, parents of Chilean Congressman Alfonso Compos Menendez. Their guest book included a poem written by Sir Ernest Shackleton who had also visited their home before sailing for the Antarctic in 1916. I copied the poem and we used it later as a frontispiece in Finn's book, *Antarctic Conquest,* the story of the Ronne Antarctic Research Expedition.

While we were there the weather in Punta Arenas was bright and sunny with cool crisp winds blowing, but this was most unusual. The inhabitants said it was not uncommon to have eight or nine weeks go by without the sun appearing. Finn felt we had wasted too much time already, and if we intended to get into Marguerite Bay this year, we had to go without the material which we hoped the plane would bring us. Accordingly, we left the civilized world behind us at two a.m. on Saturday, March 8th. The scenery through the Straits of the Magdalena Canal was very rugged and barrenly beautiful. By four in the afternoon we had passed Cape Horn and were out of sight of land. It would be a year before any of us saw civilization again. I wondered what lay ahead as we sailed away south toward the icy continent – and into what, for me, was uncharted destiny. Ill prepared for a year's stay in Antarctica, my suitcase contained little more than the knitting needles, a good suit, a good dress, nylon stockings and high heeled shoes. Fortunately, I was able to pick out the appropriate size of men's clothing from the expedition stores.

The sudden shift to cooler temperatures created a great change in the behavior of the dogs. While in the tropics, they had laid around the decks, many suffering with distemper. Now they became full of pep and strained in the chains which separated them. Huskies are born fighters and the men had more than they could manage trying to stop dogfights. It almost seemed as the dogs knew that they were nearing their destination by their joyous howls and barking day and night. Frozen meat mixed with commercial dog food had been their daily diet since we departed from Panama. Dodson was in charge of feeding them. As soon as he appeared on deck, he was met with a chorus of deafening howls which nothing but chow temporarily quieted.

As we approached the great southern continent, those not on watch or sleeping hung over the railing as we encountered ice for the first time. Depending upon time of year and destination, various kinds of ice can be observed. Sea ice, bay ice, or pack ice found close to the shores or encasing the continent results from the freezing of salt water and is seldom more than fifteen feet thick. Large belts of ice, which have been broken up from the previous season and driven seaward by the winds and currents usually are seen first as a ship approaches. But once through the pack ice, the most spectacular ice formation in the ocean is the iceberg, composed of land-formed ice, broken from glaciers and shelf ice. In the North Atlantic huge sections of ice break off from the Greenland glaciers, float south, and even menace Trans-Atlantic shipping. Still larger icebergs are found in the Antarctic. Here they drift north and usually melt before reaching the shipping lanes. In the Pacific, Antarctic bergs are rarely found north of fifty degrees south latitude. Bergs that break off from glaciers are known as glacier bergs and those that come from the shelf ice are referred to as tabular bergs. In the Antarctic, the latter are usually the larger. Their enormous size can range anywhere from 10 to 250 plus miles in length and from a hundred to two hundred feet in height. Approximately six-sevenths of an iceberg is beneath the waterline, depending upon its density. We made up an ice pool and the one who guessed most closely the time of sighting the first iceberg would win the grand prize – a large can of sardines. The guesses ranged from 7 a.m. on March 10th to 7 a.m. on March 12th, with the most popular date as March 11th. We were surprised to find that there were a few theretofore-unnoticed personnel on board in the persons of Pedro McGuillicuty, Christopher Columbus, Chad, Joe Zilch, and Kilroy. These characters submitted guesses in line with their previously acquired reputations. But our cook and Chief Commissary Steward, Sig Gutenko, an Antarctic veteran who chose the early morning of March 12th, won the pool.

The overall general good fortune which had followed the expedition since its departure and would make itself evident time and again in the future, was with us on this last leg of our long journey. The five-day stretch of water from Punta Arenas to Marguerite Bay can, on occasion, be mighty rough and thoroughly unpleasant. Because of our topside weight, it was not something which I looked forward to with any pleasure, even though I do not get actively seasick. Actually, the elements favored us much beyond my hopes and expectations. The entire trip was made in perfectly quiet seas. We were able to obtain star fixes at night and had clear weather until March 10th, when fog set in. The radar worked well and with the waves and the wind from the northeast, we made an uninterrupted speed of ten knots toward our destination. When we reached the real heavy pack ice belt, I could hardly believe that this particular season's conditions allowed us to penetrate it with ease in just two hours. Beyond was clear blue open water with only the usual huge tabular bergs floating aimlessly about in the cold calm waters. Some were as large as ten story city office buildings and a block in width.

This tranquil scene was entirely different from the one which Finn had on his last view of Marguerite Bay eight years before on the U.S.Antarctic Service Expedition 1939-1941. That year, the bay ice surrounding the continent would not allow a ship to penetrate close enough for them to be picked up. They had been forced to evacuate this same base by two hazardous plane flights. Now, there was no bay ice, only clear blue open water ahead. From the bridge of our ship on

March 12, 1947, Finn sighted the first outline of the Antarctic continent in the distance. The expedition which he had planed for many years had arrived safely. Much worry and heartache had taken place. Many trials and tribulations certainly lay ahead. As those magnificent mountains loomed ahead and I stood with my husband I viewed the Antarctic continent for the very first time. We felt an overwhelming feeling of thankfulness that we had arrived.

Finn and Jackie on the fantail of the Port of Beaumont, with the Explorer's Club flag

Finn and Jackie working in their stateroom aboard ship, Port of Beaumont

IV

First American Woman

Finn pointed out familiar landmarks in the distance. There was Black Thumb Mountain, Red Rock Ridge, and the entrance to Neny Fjord. Even though I had seen this very scene in Finn's lecture film often, the magnificence of its reality defied description. Our navigator had performed his job well; we were exactly where we wanted to be.

Before sailing into Neny Fjord, Finn wanted to take a look at George VI Sound, near Alexander I Island, one hundred miles to the south. In our field work the following summer, Finn wanted to operate down this sound. If he could find a suitable place to establish a large cache of supplies somewhere in the vicinity now, it would save an enormous amount of work later. However, when we reached Latitude 67 degrees, 20 minutes, South, gigantic tabular icebergs stopped us. As soon as we saw the huge bergs slowly floating, side by side, all over the bay, Finn realized a further southern penetration by the ship at this particular time was impossible so we changed course and headed back directly for Neny Fjord. I was very excited as the rugged outlines took shape. Huge snow-covered mountains, stood out in greater detail as we approached. The startling grandeur of the panoramic scene certainly was one of the greatest thrills of my life. When I viewed it again nearly fifty years later, that original moment of sheer rapture remained etched in my mind as though it were yesterday.

Our little vessel, sailing at ten knots, passed numerous huge white and blue icebergs majestically floating like crystal palaces. As we passed Red Rock Ridge, Neny Mountain came into full view. The excitement and tension grew. Just two miles beyond Neny Island, which is entirely occupied by a mountain whose steep sides create a sheer drop off into the sea, lay Stonington Island, our Base site. As Skipper Schlossback had never been in these waters before and Finn knew the lay of the land, he piloted the ship to anchorage on the eastern side of Neny Island. It was 3:30 p.m. when we arrived. Before us, but still hidden by a small hill, lay our camp for the next year. Just in front of us, we could pick out the buildings of the recently built British base. Through the field glasses we could see several of the British feeding their dogs staked out on the snow. Finn was anxious to get ashore and see the condition of his former United States Antarctic Service Expedition's buildings.

A small boat was lowered over the side, and five of us, Finn, Harry, Latady, McClary and I, rowed through the heavy, slushy brash ice half a mile to the rocky beach of the island. Major K. S. Pierce Butler, Royal Signals, leader of recently built Base E of the Falkland Islands Dependencies Survey came walking down to the beach asking "Commander Finn Ronne?" It was reminiscent of "Dr. Livingstone, I presume?" Major Butler also welcomed me most heartily. I was very conscious of being the first American woman to set foot on the Antarctic Continent. It was a thrilling moment.

I later learned that other women had made fleeting visits into the high southern latitudes. All were Norwegian ladies whose husbands were associated with Norway's progressive whaling industry. In 1934, Mrs. Caroline Mikkelsen accompanied her husband, Captain Klarius Mikkelsen, on one of Lars Christensen's whaling ships. The event is described in a Norwegian publication.

> On 19 February, 1935, Klarius Mikkelsen of the "Thorshavn," discovered a new ice-covered land at 80 deg. 45 min. E. Long. and 67 deg. 50 min. S. Lat. and followed this to 68 deg.29 min. S. Lat and 78 deg. 36 min., E. Long., where the land was bare. On Feb. 20, he went ashore and hoisted the Norwegian flag and named the land Ingrid Christensen Land. His wife, Mrs. Caroline Mikkelsen, who also went ashore for six hours, is so far as is known, the first, and, up to now, the only woman to set foot on the Antarctic mainland.

Two years later in 1937, Lars Christensen, owner of one of Norway's great whaling fleets, was accompanied on an annual Antarctic voyage by his vivacious wife Ingrid, their daughter Fie, and two close friends, Mrs. Lill Rachlew and Mrs. Solveig Wideroe. On the *Thorshaven*, the same ship Mrs. Mikkelsen had traveled on two years earlier, they followed the outlines of the pack ice and circumnavigated the continent. From the ship they made several short flights over the coastal areas and on one occasion landed on Lars Christensen Coast where they deposited a cache of pemmican (concentrated food for emergency use or when traveling long distances). All the ladies agreed, it was a pleasant, exciting, stimulating, and truly different type of voyage.

In later years, I got to know Mrs. Christensen very well and, along with my husband and daughter, was a guest in her home in Sandefjord, Norway, several times.

The history of women in the south polar regions had thus been incredibly brief. Understandably, a decade later when I first landed it was next to impossible to believe the circumstances which had placed me there as the first American woman to set foot on the continent. In addition, I was to be the first woman to overwinter as a true working member of a pioneering Antarctic expedition, enduring all the hardships. Jennie had no regularly assigned job, but she fitted in as best she could.

After being introduced to five of the ten men who were staying there, the other four being on a field trip, Finn had a pleasant informal chat with the British leader. He informed us that the American Base site had been unusually popular that year, that two Argentine ships had visited the Island since the first of January and that the American buildings were in even worse shape as a result of the visit of two Chilean ships which had also paid visits that summer. One Chilean ship, the *Iquique,* had been there about one month before and the other, the *Angamos,* had been there just four days before our arrival. From this ship, 200 men had gone ashore and much looting had taken place. Major Butler then offered to accompany us to the American base just 100 yards over a small rocky hill. We could hardly believe what confronted us. The complete state of disarray of the base almost defied description.

As we viewed the three large and two small American buildings, there was shocking evidence of complete and utter vandalism. It's doubtful that any property could have been ransacked more thoroughly. Things were thrown in every direction. The entire place was littered with rubbish. Photographer Bill Latady took pictures of interiors of all the buildings. But there was also evidence that the buildings had been occupied and lived in over a period of time. Finn estimated that over 80 percent of valuable material had been taken or made unusable. The disastrous state of the buildings would delay our occupation of them for at least thirty days. The appearance of the base was a striking contrast to the way it had been left upon its evacuation in 1941. Then, everything had been thoroughly cleaned up and stored neatly. As was an Antarctic tradition friendly messages had been left, giving positions of a large food cache and other materials, in case anyone should visit the base and require emergency shelter.

Fortunately, much of the aviation gasoline, diesel oil, and coal supplies had been left more or less untouched. Even more important to us, however, was that the buildings themselves were in an excellent state of preservation, far better than Finn had been led to expect by the British correspondence. The structures had held up well under Antarctic winters and showed no exterior damage. These buildings had been built to stand for seventy-five years and unless outside forces offered more than mere weather, there was no reason to suspect they would not. Built in much the same manner as the ordinary cold storage vault, the walls were a half a foot thick, packed with heavy insulation. The doors were heavy with locks and releases comparable to the handles on an industrial refrigerator. The floors were double decked with bulkheads and insulation to keep the occupants above the cold air that circulates over the bottom of the room when the door is opened. There was a complete absence of windows with only wire-reinforced glass forming skylights to let in a maximum amount of light. The sleeping quarters in the main bunkhouse, which was twenty-four feet wide and sixty-four feet long, could accommodate twenty-six men. Finn had been the engineer in charge of erecting the buildings on the United States Antarctic Service Expedition and knew every inch of the compound.

Even the small shack, Finn's personal living quarters in 1941, had not been neglected in the general looting which had permeated the camp. Photographer Bill Latady could hardly portray its condition. One thing in particular did amuse us. The vandals must have received quite a shock when they broke open a varnished plywood box, nicely made, and with the well known name of radio commentator "Lowell Thomas, National Broadcasting Company, New York, New York, USA" neatly lettered on the outside. What they found inside was a rock, one foot square and four inches thick, wrapped in burlap bag. The box (which weighed about ninety pounds) was found where Finn had left it, while the lid, evidently in disgust, had been thrown one hundred feet from the camp site. This rock was intended to be included in a fireplace which Lowell Thomas built at his home in Pawling, New York. When they evacuated the base by plane in 1941, Finn had been unable to take it along and it was left with instructions to ship it to New York, C.O.D. by the first persons who happened to enter the base thereafter. Eventually Lowell Thomas was able to include this rock in his fireplace. For the time being, we had seen all we wanted of the camp's conditions, in fact more. Thoroughly disgusted and sick at heart, we returned to our ship.

It would be hard to place the blame for this looting upon any one group of individuals. Several ships with men of different nationalities had visited the base during the intervening years and undoubtedly many of them had a hand in it. While such wanton destruction is difficult to understand and explain, it was common during the war years and Americans were not without their share of the blame. The camp had been left unguarded in the Antarctic and what happened was a logical result, unexpected as it was.

Part of my Diary for March 12, 1947 reads:

> *We came back in about two and a half hours. Finn called a meeting and, told the fellows the situation. He told all of them to go ashore tomorrow and let what they saw govern their attitude with the British. An anti-pro British argument followed and was quite bitter. Most was anti-British. The question of raising our flag was involved. Harry and Bob Nichols wanted Finn to tell the British of our desire, others didn't.*

Finn renamed our headquarters, "The Port of Beaumont Base," and the following morning a large party from the ship rowed ashore to begin the clean up campaign immediately.

Thursday, March 13, 1947

> *I did not, as I felt a cold coming on. I tended to sick Jennie also with a cold and Chuck Hassage and then did the dishes. The men on shore began cleaning out the rubbish with evidence of British occupation of our buildings all over. They claimed to Finn they had been there only a week in February 1946, time they had occupied the island, but evidence was against them.*

The fellows on board got the dogs ashore and some 10 in 1 rations. Harry and Bill Latady stayed ashore to feed the dogs and keep the camp organized. Ike came in at night and he and Finn had a long talk about things in general, R.E.B. (Richard Evelyn Byrd) in particular. I continued to knit after getting the story off to the N.Y. Times. Visited Jennie who was suffering from itching among other things.

At the request of Major Butler, Finn and three others went to the British base for a conversation. Butler told them that he and most of the other men had been there already for one year. He informed Finn that the American buildings had been used by the British for a week in February, 1946, while they were building their own base and that the British had not been on the island before that time. They came under the strictest secrecy, being allowed to inform only their families of their destination. The British buildings, however, did not look to us as though they had seen an Antarctic winter and the American buildings, judging from the amount of British equipment and rubbish strewn around the place, looked as though they had been occupied by the British for much more than a week in February of 1946. They had used our generators for electric lighting; the water had not been drained, left to freeze; and the cold had cracked the cylinder block. Certainly the galley range had seen hard usage; the firebrick had been burned out. Such things could not have happened in a week.

The British ambassador in Washington had implied to Finn that they had been in occupation of the Base since 1944, and that they had found our buildings considerably demolished. This, of course, was not true and much later Butler was to inform Finn that their group knew he had not been told the truth, but it had not been their fault and that he had been embarrassed for he knew we could come and find out the truth. Butler said that he had relieved Commander Bingham, a former member of the Rymill Expedition, as leader of all five of the British bases in the Peninsula sector. He also informed Finn that they were still using our toilet and that if we requested they would build one of their own. Finn asked him to do that as we were now twenty-three people and, it would clearly be necessary. Our toilet was a small wooden structure a few yards away from our main buildings and perched on top of a cliff overlooking the back bay below.

Finn then told Major Butler that as we were reoccupying an American Base, on which there was American government property, we intended to raise the American flag, and that he hoped Butler would understand this action. The British leader protested and told Finn that were this done, he would be forced to inform his government and that he had strong objections to this action, as this was British territory. Finn replied that it was his understanding that the United States government did not recognize any other government's claim to territory in the Antarctic, nor did we make any formal claims. Later during an informal conversation with one of our men, Butler stated that he had no personal objection to our raising our flag, but that it was his duty to protest on behalf of his government.

At lunch, Finn informed the group that Butler had raised objections to the flag going up. Another big argument started. Finn called for a vote and about ninety percent of the men favored immediate raising.

That afternoon, Finn raised the American flag on the flagpole that he had put up in 1940. This was not a personal issue with either Butler or the British government and we certainly had no objection to their building their own flag pole, just as high or higher than ours. The British flag was then flying on their building. Admittedly, Finn was a flag waver; by tradition all Norwegians are. The precedent for his act lay in the fact that expeditions have always raised the flag at or near their campsite. As long as the United States maintained her present position, which she had announced officially, there was no reason why the American flag should not have been re-flown at a previously established American base. The next day, March 14th, Finn received the following note from Butler:

> I am directed by His Majesty's government to inquire the reason for the United States flag being flown on the North West point of Stonington Island. I assume that the United States government has made no claim to this territory and that the flying of this flag is merely an indication of the presence of a United States expedition. If that is so, I have no objection to raise. If, however, this flag is intended to represent a territorial claim, I am bound to protest on behalf of His Majesty's government, as this violates British Sovereignty and I shall have to report the matter to His Majesty's government for instructions.

It was signed as the "Magistrate, Marguerite Bay." On the same day, March 14th, Finn answered Major Butler as follows:

> I have received your note of March 14, 1947, inquiring as to why the United States flag is being flown on the American-built flag pole on Stonington Island. The Ronne Ant-

> arctic Research Expedition is reoccupying the base built by the United State government on the United States Antarctic Service Expedition, 1939-1941. The flagpole was built by this expedition as part of the United States Government's camp. As an American expedition reoccupying this base on Stonington Island, we have re-flown the American flag on the American-built flag pole at the American camp.

Thus ended the flag incident and our conscientious signalman, Larry Fiske, saw to it that the American flag flew day and night, through winds, storms, and blizzards, month in and month out, as long as our expedition was on Stonington Island. It was very incongruous that on a continent of six million square miles, four million of which were still completely unknown, such a ridiculous situation should arise.

In his next conversation, Butler told Finn that the Governor of the Falkland Island Dependencies Survey, Miles Clifford, would visit this British base on the *Trepassey* when she returned shortly and that he would undoubtedly wish to speak with him. Finn said he would be most happy to chat with him at any time. We felt that as individuals, the British party would meet us half way. Finn decided to endeavor, at all times and in every way possible, to cooperate and maintain cordial relations with them during our stay. He gave the others careful instructions on this matter.

We gathered the impression that their main interest in the area was to establish and maintain a small settlement for colonization and claim purposes; secondly, for scientific reasons, mainly meteorology; and thirdly, for local triangulation survey work. At the time, they had four men with three dog teams in the field surveying in a northerly direction where there were other British bases on the peninsula. A bit later, this group was unable to find an easy route down from the plateau. Finn turned over one of his maps from the previous expedition and Butler guided them down by radio using it.

The British had one small Auster plane, which had been brought down one month before, on the year's first visit of the *Trepassey*, but which had not been flown as yet. On their building was a large sign, which read "Graham Land Post Office, Marguerite Bay." There was no evidence of an established law court, however, except by Major Butler's signature.

The British gave every evidence of friendliness and repeatedly asked us over for tea, but we had much work to do to prepare the camp and so for the time being, we refused their nice invitations. Much later we learned that when the British first saw our group of men, they thought Finn had made height one of the prerequisites of selection. Twelve of our men were over six feet tall, five of whom were over six feet two inches in height. About seventy-five percent of them had been in one of the services during the war, and our average age was twenty-nine years.

One hundred yards away from the British camp, over a small hill, lay our American base. Our camp consisted of one large Bunkhouse, which I have described. The back end of the bunkhouse was devoted to the galley, and the mess table ran down the center between the bunking cubicles on either side of the large room. Each cubicle contained two bunks, and a small desk or washstand to one side.

The Science Building contained a radio room, photographic room, library, meteorological observatory and tower at one end, biological and geological space, as well as geographical plotting tables. The Machine Shop located next to the bunkhouse, behind the Science Building, was also a fair size and was complete with generators for electric lighting and to supply radio power, as well as containing space for machine and carpentry work. On the other side of the Bunkhouse, Finn had erected the small hut in 1940 for his living quarters and which we would now share. In addition to these buildings there was a Blubber House for cutting seals, and biological work, and one smaller storage hut.

The location of our base was exceedingly beautiful. The 2,500 foot long and about 1,000 foot wide Stonington Island was covered with boulders and large pebbles, which are partly exposed during the summer season, but covered by deep snows during the fall, winter, and spring. High snow covered mountains up to 4,500 feet in the immediate vicinity completely surround the island, making the scenery spectacular. Behind the camp buildings was the foot of the glacier, approximately 600 feet wide, which joined the island with the Mainland, and which lead up to the plateau, to an elevation of 6,500 feet. Right away Finn noticed that this glacier, which previously had been approximately 1,000 feet wide had broken back about 400 feet in six years, leaving Stonington that much closer to being a real island, (which it had become by the time I saw it again in 1995). Up this glacier and over the high plateau our trail parties would travel to the south. Be it a sunny day, cloudy, or an exquisite evening sunset, the colors on the mountains and snow were a rare treat which few in the world ever have had the privilege of witnessing. Within a few weeks when things were more settled, this glacier became my ski hill.

As a woman to see this forbidding awe-inspiring landscape for the first time, I realized I was very fortunate. But I was not the only one of the newcomers to be favorably impressed by the surroundings. The general feeling among all who were viewing the great southern continent for the first time was that of pleasant surprise. The erroneous impression that the vast landmass was nothing but a flat wasteland wilderness covered with ice and snow, gave way to the opinion that it was the most scenic and spectacular section of the world. The sapphire blue of certain towering, turreted icebergs which dot the bay and move like big grumbling animals through the smaller icebergs and growler fields; the massive thick, blue-white and green glaciers that push their green icy tongues to the sea and crack and crumble with sharp resounding shots, or deafening roars almost continuously; the steep sided, partially snow-covered mountains, which thrust their spiraling summits thousands of feet above sea level, with their rock slides reflecting a thousand colors and hues; an unsurpassed, long, lingering Antarctic sunset, tinting the snow fields pink; the wild beauty; the lack of vegetation; the whistling winds; – all make up the majestic, breathtaking setting, and at the same time give a warmth, and serenity, which only poets and artists can portray. Like countless men before me, I fell deeply in love with the Antarctic.

The men barely had time to accustom themselves to their new environment before they had to begin a rigid working schedule. From now on, it would be getting colder. Our first snow occurred the day after we arrived. To unload the ship and make ready the camp, we would have to work feverishly, so that all the outside work would be completed by the time winter asserted itself with heavy snows and strong winds. They were not far away; but few of us had any realization of how miserable the weather would become, and with so little warning.

On March 13th, the day after our arrival, we moved our ship from Neny Island, and steamed through the narrow strait between Penguin Island and Stonington, into the small cove, named Back Bay Cove. It was about three-quarters of a mile from camp and the same distance from the sixty foot barrier ice wall of the glacier. She was secured with one anchor and a stern line to the beach, a distance of one hundred feet. The personnel was divided into two groups, a shore party to clean up and repair the camp and a ship party to unload.

In the ship party, Lassiter and Adams began to get the gas drums clear of the deck. They lifted them over the railing to fall in the water below. In two small rowboats, Smith and Wood caught hold of the lines attached and towed six or seven drums at a time to the beach.

The four-ton motor boat that we brought was used along with one of the same size, which we had found in good condition and had re-launched. By lashing the two boats together and building a platform to cover them, the men provided a ramp to haul ashore the tons of equipment being unloaded. The winch and boom on the ship were used to hoist the heavy equipment onto the boat platform.

Friday, March 14, 1947

I got up did the dishes as Jorge was still in his bunk. Finn was on shore. After lunch I washed the dishes and Jennie and I went ashore. I helped Finn a little in our shack by fixing up the coal bin and throwing away rubbish.

Finn took out the single bunk and started tearing up the floor in order to put in a new one. The fire will dry the place out a bit and in about three days, Finn can lay the new floor. We had some tea, made by Bill Latady in the Bunkhouse, with the others, then Jennie and I tried to straighten up the galley by moving some of the junk out. The British brought back a little pile of things that included some canned nuts and candy.

Since one of the expedition's main objectives was to do exploratory flying and aerial photographic work, one of the first tasks was to get our small Stinson L-5 airplane ashore for reconnaissance flights. This airplane was equipped to fly from any surface, wheels for land, pontoons for sea, and skis for snow. As the terrain here was covered completely with snow and ice, the skis had been installed aboard ship to eliminate work in assembling the plane on the beach. On March 15th, three days after our arrival, five men removed the L-5 from the ship. After the airplane was secured to the raft, a lane through small icebergs and pack ice was picked to get to the beach. We also had the tide problem to contend with when unloading the plane onto the snow icefoot, one hundred feet from the base. After a 7000 mile trip exposed for more than two months to wind and high seas, there were small incidental damages to repair. Aviation mechanic Robertson began work on these immediately.

The next thing to get off the ship was the dynamite, and when all the heavy material had been brought on deck from the after hold, the boom was shifted to a forward position, so that all heavy material in the forward holds could be brought up on deck and lifted onto the loading platform on the two motor boats.

The dogs were taken ashore as soon as possible and tied to tethering lines. After a few days on a seal meat diet and some much needed exercise on the snow, they began to show distinct signs of improvement.

The camp was not ready to accommodate many persons, so each day the shore working party would come from the ship to continue cleaning the rubbish out of the buildings. Work was begun on putting heavy canvas tarpaulins over the buildings and nailing them down tightly, so that future winds would not be able to tear them off. The tarps covered the open seams in the roof to prevent snows as well as winds from penetrating the interiors. Those were hard days, with everyone working on some particular job from morning to night. During the middle of the afternoon, someone usually made tea in the Bunkhouse, giving the chance for a few minutes rest. It was a sorry looking group, using anything that could be found for a cup, drinking the tea and eating the cookies which had been found, then seven years old, until supplies could be moved from the ship. The first weeks of clean up on the beach were really camping out.

Relaxation was found, however, in the many little incidents that occurred. Things new and unusual to most of the expeditions went down in our memories to be recalled in group reminiscing. About 4:00 a.m. one morning, we were all awakened when a huge chunk of ice broke off the 60 foot barrier cliff about 1,500 feet away. The thunderous roar made the men come on deck to view the spectacle and an ensuing flood wave made the vessel rock. The berg floated slowly in the water, gently coming to rest alongside our ship. As it hugged the side for several days, everyone developed an affectionate feeling for it. Having a flat hard Irish head and being St. Patrick's Day, it was named Murphy. In spite of constant wind changes, Murphy remained devotedly attached to the starboard side. On the evening of the seventeenth, Murphy acquired a friend who came to rest on the opposite side of the ship. We named this new neighbor George. George also remained with us despite changing winds and, since both were about twenty feet high above the waterline, it was concluded that they were grounded. Our anchorage depth was seventy-five feet. Several nights later, the wind rose to storm proportions, and as George and Murphy were beginning to play rough by nudging the ship at least once every ten minutes, we hoisted anchor and parted company. Angered at the vessel's departure they accosted each other. When last seen, they were grinding together and George knocked off the head of Murphy, who then rose broadside floating out to the open waters in Marguerite Bay. George, feeling remorseful, gradually turned turtle and we saw no more of them.

At our new anchorage, the currents and winds brought other glacier bergs around us. Some were not worth worrying about and others were of such size and shape as to cause concern. The greater part of the berg that remains underwater provides the danger. Should one of them become lodged beneath our stern, any wave or wind action causing the berg to bob up and down, even turn over at times, might have meant serious damage to our propeller. When several of the larger bergs drifted too close for comfort, engineer Hassage insisted the penguin he observed on a small bergy bit nearby, wasn't calling for a mate but laughing at the skipper in his endeavors to pole-off the berg with a small two by four. Numerous ideas and suggestions to remedy the situation followed, but Sig's of throwing salt on it to melt it down caused the uproar. In their own good time, the bergs moved on, and peace was restored temporarily until the next one presented itself.

Even though we were at anchor and some of the extra weight had been removed, the concern of the skipper for the security of this heavily loaded ship on the way down still lingered in the memories of all. When it was discovered that our large search light was ready to topple from its perch, because all the screws holding it firm had been loosened, the only two explanations advanced were, either some hapless member had needed them for his scientific program, or else the skipper had been thinking of discarding this important item to decrease our topside weight.

A few straggler Adelie penguins, who as yet had not given up their summer playground for more northern and warmer climes, never ceased to hold everyone's interest. These funny fellows with their insatiable curiosity would often get themselves into difficulties. One day, Lassiter brought one on board to give him a better view of things, in the hope that he would stop cruising around the ship on a berg, complaining in such a manner as to distract everyone's attention. After taking a good look around the ship and bowing low Japanese style to each individual, he backed away, waddled through the hausepipe and jumped overboard.

We learned many things the hard way. On baking days, no one could slam the door because Sig's dough was on the rise. One could never leave so much as a thumbtack lying around, for that very item was always exactly what the next guy was looking for. When something disappeared, it was no longer a yell, "Who stole my knife?" but merely a casual remark that "Expedition Elmer" had borrowed it.

The two biggest problems of the week were, how to divide the fruit equally, and who stole Ike's Marlin Spike.

While work was going on at the base, I pitched in as mess cook by washing the dishes on board for Sig who cooked for 23 cold hungry people, wrote articles for NANA, or went ashore occasionally to help in our hut, chopped ice at caches here and there, made tea for the fellows at rest break and Jennie did about the same. There was always so much to do. I usually went to bed dead tired at night. My diary entries told it like it was.

Saturday, March 15, 1947

Finn went ashore early with Jorge. I awoke and helped with the dishes. The fellows had launched the old boat and came in cold for some coffee. Jennie and I talked for awhile, had lunch, and did the dishes. I stayed aboard to get some writing done. We have been getting off a huge amount of traffic to the N.Y. Times on conditions here.

Sunday, March 16, 1947

Sunday is like any other day – work and plenty of it. Slept late, washed dishes, had lunch and Jennie and I went ashore and started digging hard on the food cash. We wore ourselves out and got nowhere. We decided there must be an easier way. Jennie made some tea for the fellows, who managed to get the canvas over the science building. The British told Harry they had been authorized by their government to take anything they needed from this Base for their comfort.

Monday, March 17, 1947

Jennie and I got up late, washed the dishes, had lunch and went ashore. Fiddled around with the food cache for awhile, helped haul a great amount of stuff from the beach to the buildings. I chopped some ice outside the galley door and then started to make tea for the fellows who had been working pretty hard.

Finn received a note from the British saying the Governor would be glad to do anything he could. We were also invited to tea by the British, but Finn refused, because we had so much work to do around camp. Came back for dinner and had a chat about things in general later. About l0 o'clock the icebergs were up on us so they started the engines and moved the ship further away.

Gradually, the weather got noticeably colder. Before it became too late, Finn was anxious to make another trip with the ship down toward King George VI Sound, to lay an advanced trail cache in the area, if feasible. Only the lack of good weather held back a reconnaissance flight by the L-5 in that direction. The day after the plane had been unloaded, the wings were taken ashore and the assembly was started. Tail surfaces had not been removed so just the wings and struts had to be reassembled. Controls were hooked up, the electrical and radio system checked out, and the engine was given its periodic inspection and final check. A Steward Warner engine heater was used to warm the engine while the oil was being heated on the galley stove. As the temperature was much below freezing, the oil congealed very quickly. After two hours the engine temperature had risen to fifty degrees centigrade. The hot oil, also heated to fifty degrees centigrade, was poured in and the engine heater and cover were removed. After two or three tries, the engine kicked off and ran perfectly. When the engine had been given a test run of three hours, the L-5 was ready for its test flight. As we did not have a hanger and consequently lacked the ideal conditions for work as found in a repair shop, work in the open was a not very pleasant necessity.

Excessive winds and poor fall weather conditions delayed the test hop for a few days. However, the day dawned with perfect flying weather. The island did not offer a suitable take-off field because of its uneven surface with many rocks and boulders. In a few months the bay ice in Back Bay Cove would freeze to sufficient thickness for the perfect take-off field for all three planes, but until then the high, long, fairly level, glacier surface east of the camp provided the desired temporary flying field. From its previous island anchorage, aviation mechanic Robertson gave the plane all the power he could and managed to taxi up the initial four hundred foot glacier slope with the aid of several of the men pushing on the wings. When he reached the top of this slope, he continued to taxi the plane on the gradual uphill grade for about three-quarters of a mile to the aviation cache established by the former USAS expedition. This cache had been made from the large wing crate of the old Condor plane. It had been used extensively by the aviators at one time, but heavy snows in the six intervening years had covered the building so that only the long poles marking it could be seen above the surface.

After digging seven feet down, the entrance was reached. What had been a perfectly equipped shack was found in a considerable state of disarray. Several dog skeletons in the aviation cache revealed their escape from supposedly their humane destruction six years before, when the men on USAS were forced to evacuate the base in two very hazardous plane flights which did not allow them to take the dogs. Nearby on the surface, the L-5 would be tied down and well anchored, so as not to be carried away by the winds, as long as we continued to use the glacier for operations.

Harry, who was to test-fly the L-5, took-off quickly after a very short run. The orange and red colored plane silhouetted against the clear blue sky, made a great contrast to the glacier-filled mountains; the brightness of the sun contributed to the clear atmosphere. All three of our planes had been painted with brilliant colors as an added safety precaution when flying over this white continent. If ever a plane was forced to make an emergency landing in the field away from base, the bright colors would stand out against the background and it could be spotted easily from the air by a searching plane. After thirty minutes cruising in the vicinity of base, the L-5 was pronounced in perfect condition for future longer flights.

A sudden change in the weather, characteristic of this sector and with which we would cope for the next twelve months, prevented further flying for the day. The reconnaissance flight to George VI Sound was postponed until the following day, when the weather was suitable. During the interim, some additional preparations were made. Standard emergency equipment to be carried in the L-5 in case of a forced landing was assembled and packed in the plane. Such items as a large plumbers type blow torch for heating the engine, engine cover, battens for control surfaces, tie-down ropes and stakes, one man tent, skis and poles, alpine rope and ice ax, 30 days food ration per man, sleeping bags, primus stove for cooking, medical kit, and shovel, all were essential and no flight approaching major proportions could be made without them. My diary from the 18th of March read:

> *Finn and I spent our Third Wedding Anniversary together in the Antarctic. Some fun – guess I'm the first woman ever to do that. Got up late, had lunch and Jennie and I went ashore. We thought we had 100 lb. of salt with us to melt the ice over the food cash, but instead it was sand we had been lugging around – moral of that – don't steal the Doctor's salt.*

Bob Nichols, Jennie and I spent the afternoon on cleaning up the inside of the Bunkhouse. Finn worked some on our building, got the floor laid down and part of the insulation with canvas covering over it. The fellows were tacking down the canvas on the Science Building and practically finished it. Finn hitched up a dog team to carry supplies from the beach to the buildings. We all came back with a gorgeous sky and sunset, but dead tired. Had dinner with the first pie, wrote a story for NANA and went to bed.

The Expedition's Base including the machine shop, the main bunkhouse, and our hut.

Vandalism found at Base upon arrival

Unloading with visiting British ships Fitzroy and Trespassy in background

Ship anchored in Back Bay Cove with glacier and mountains in background

Adelie penguins near base

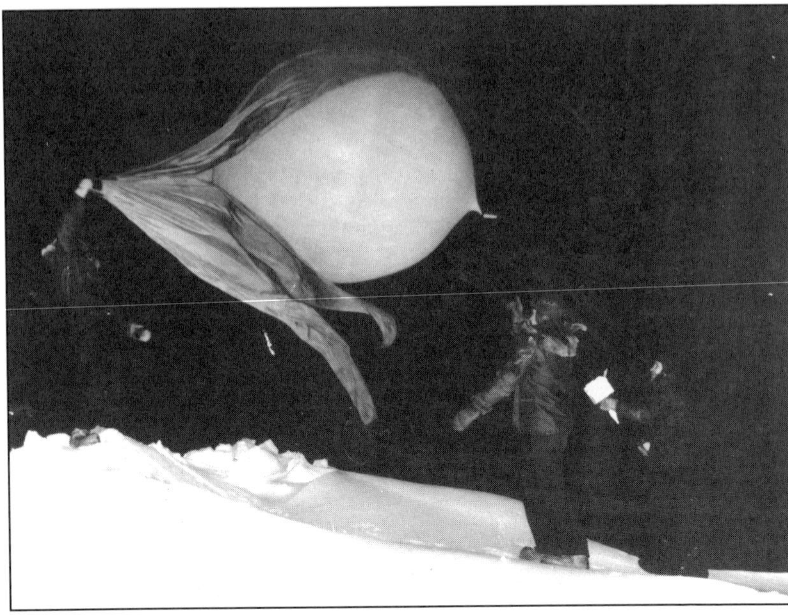

Meteologist Harcly Peterson releasing a balloon from the meteorological tower

Aerial view of Stonington Island showing Base and ship anchored in Back Bay cove

V

Foiled Again

Bickering between the men began almost immediately. It was about small things at first; who wasn't handling the equipment with care, orders criticized, etc. From two previous expeditions, Finn understood that these things happened and took it in his stride. But I hadn't been exposed to it before and it began to worry me. Finn had always managed to get away from living in the main bunk house (where there had been incessant bitching on both Byrd's second expedition and on the United States Antarctic Service Expedition), by building his own small shack nearby. Norwegians are considered loners anyway. They like their space no matter how small; it's one of the characteristics of their sparsely inhabited country. He intended to avoid it on this expedition by re-occupying his old shack, but the bickering concerned me, particularly when it was directed toward Finn and/or the success of the programs.

Wednesday, March 19, 1947

Today was a bad day! Started off by McClary's not waking Jimmy Robertson and not telling Bob Dodson to come ashore. Therefore, Harry could not take his flight until afternoon and he had to have gasoline up on the glacier, and there was no dog driver. Harry hooked up the team and, at the last minute, asked Finn if he wanted to go along to take a flight. Finn took me along up as far as to the glacier aviation cache. The view from there was beautiful. Bill was with us. Kelsey and Jimmy Robertson caught up with us. Finn took a flight with Harry, while I skied down a bit until Finn caught up. Then, Finn, Kelsey, and I went down, me using Finn's skis. Finn left the dog team with Harry to bring down the glacier. On a whim Harry and Bill took off on a flight to King George V1 Sound, leaving the dog team with Jimmy Robertson who doesn't know a thing about dogs. When the plane took off, the dogs began a fight. Jimmy couldn't separate them and came down the glacier for help. When Don, Bob Dodson, and Jimmy came back with the dogs, Big Stoop was nearly dead, probably from loss of blood suffered as a result of his wounds. He later died.

The flight was successful and the Sound was found to be open. Finn came on board to order the ship prepared for immediate departure. Bob Nichols, Dodson and Peterson remained on shore to feed the dogs and finish a little work. The ship group had been working all day and the fruit of this labor was on deck ready to be sent ashore. When they heard they had to stow everything in the ship's hole again and secure for sea, a bitching session, heretofore unequaled, began led by Ike. Everybody was mad at everyone else, but particularly everyone was mad at Harry for leaving the dogs with Robertson who could have been hurt. Harry had ignored Finn's request and as a result a dog's life was lost..

Coming out in the small rowboat, the wind blew up so that we almost capsized. The motorboat had to come after us. As it was getting dark fast, and the wind blowing, the boat could not go ashore again for the three fellows, so they were left there for the night. The fellows on board worked up to 10:30 stowing things away and making ready for sea. Then Sig made hot chocolate and we provided cookies as they turned in.

This was just the tip of an early iceberg, so to speak. They were all small things to be sure, but any expeditioner can tell you that in isolation, they will soon build-up to big things. If people think expedition life is like one big happy family, they are sadly deluded. It began to sadden and depress my unusually upbeat attitude and I kept thinking of some ways to correct and prevent it.

For the next two days, strong winds prevented us from leaving. The gusts went as high as sixty-five miles per hour. It was impossible even to launch our motor boat from the vessel's davits.

Thursday, March 20, 1947

> *Finn ordered the rowboat to go after the fellows on shore. When they were half way to shore, Harry ordered the rowboat back to the ship for him. Finn got sore at Harry for disobeying his orders again. The boat was tied to the ship but with a bad knot for it drifted away into the shore ice where it still is. The winds were very strong, up to sixty-five miles per hour. The cove was pretty rough. We were forced to wait for the wind to die down. The winds blew all day.*
>
> *Harry realized he had not done what he should have and offered to step aside as third in command. Finn straightened him out by calmly pointing out to him the thoughtless folly of his ways..*

Finn was not happy with the obvious carelessness. It was fortunate the winds were from the southeast, so that they carried the boat to the beach rather than out to sea, and we were able to retrieve it at a later date. But the men were left on shore overnight in severe weather unprepared all because of Harry.

I was very pleased with the incoming message from NANA that our British story had made the front page in the London Daily Telegraph and that NANA had given it good publicity as well. I kept very busy in our small stateroom pounding away on the typewriter. There certainly was a great deal to write about. Some went out under Finn's by-line, others under mine, or other members of the expedition. I must have averaged three articles a week covering all facets of expedition life. The North American Newspaper Alliance, or NANA as it was referred to was a syndicate of newspapers all over the U.S. including the New York Times, so our activities usually had good material coverage.

On the second day of the storm, Chief Engineer Hassage discovered a problem. One of the coils in the steering engine had burned out and there was no way of replacing it. The fellows on the bridge kept leaving the electric switch on and the only way of getting any place was to steer from the rear. The "twins" (pilots Lassiter and Adams) worked on it all day and had hopes of devising something to take the coil's place. We were anchored for awhile at Neny Fjord and then moved back into our cove. The wind continued to blow up to sixty miles an hour. We had no contact with the fellows on shore. I knitted quite a bit and straightened up the room. At night Jim Lassiter showed a Laurel and Hardy movie along with some other silly one.

The next day we sat at anchor all day again. The seas were calm so a shore party went to the camp and met the other three. All hands there worked on building the camp. They began work on the coal pile and finished some of the canvas work on the main bunkhouse. Pete came on board filthy dirty but happy. He had been working hard without anyone to call him down. The "twins" (Lassiter and Adams) slept all day, as they had been awake working on the steering engine for twenty-four hours. Around dinnertime, Pete joined them and the collective brains began again to repair the trouble.

Unless a way could be found for fixing it, the ship would have to be steered by hand from the stern and it would be impossible to make a dangerous trip down to the Sound such as we contemplated. All that day and all the following one, Engineer Hassage, Air Force pilot Chuck Adams, and physicist H. C. (Harcly) Peterson attempted to devise a gadget to take the place of the coil. Meanwhile, the storm had died out and the regular working party went ashore to continue covering the buildings with canvas, while others stacked coal bags alongside of the buildings for future use.

About 5a.m on the 23rd, the twins informed Finn that the engine had been fixed, so the order was given immediately to get underway.

After leaving the Neny Fjord area, we sailed south, about twenty-five miles off the coast of Marguerite Bay, within sight of the endless high, formidable, snow-covered mountains. We took bearings continuously as we passed by Terra Firma Island, Mushroom Island, and Cape Berteaux. In the southern part of the uncharted Marguerite Bay, at approximately latitude 69 degrees, 10 minutes south, and longitude 68 degrees, 55 minutes west, we discovered several groups of new islands and charted their position on existing maps. Three large islands appeared to be approximately one hundred feet above the water and the numerous small islands about fifteen to twenty feet above. We were approximately two miles away from the larger islands, which were ice capped with rocks exposed at the waters edge and upward, and we maneuvered among the smaller groups, which were free of ice and rock-exposed.

From the time we had passed Cape Berteaux, the icebergs became more numerous and from time to time we passed through light brash ice. There was no polar record of any ship having sailed further south in this particular sector, than to approximately latitude 68 degrees, 35 minutes. This was done by the *North Star* in 1940, when she made passage from Valparaiso to Neny Fjord. Then there had been heavy pack ice ahead, which prevented any attempt to penetrate further. At four o'clock in the afternoon, we had reached our southernmost point of safe penetration, at latitude 69 degrees, 20 minutes south, setting a new record for ship navigation in this region.

Under skipper Schlossback, our vessel picked its course, keeping to the east among the huge glacier and tabular icebergs, whose movement was coming from the southeast. They blocked the entrance to George VI Sound and made a landing anywhere in its vicinity impossible. The pack ice had gotten heavier the further south we went. Although Finn was unable to see the huge one hundred foot ice wall which denotes the head of the Sound, over which he had traversed in 1940, it was obvious that these gigantic tabular icebergs had broken off from there recently.

From the deck I was amazed to watch these ostentatious icebergs, many miles in length, sail by. We were viewing for the first time some of the real dangers as well as silent beauty provided by nature in that part of the world. The sun's shadows played over them revealing their various odd shapes and brilliant colors. In the distance, high mountains gave us a panoramic view and, with the sun dancing over their peaks, presented a color display impossible to duplicate, even in pictures.

The terrain was quite familiar to Finn, as he had traversed over this country previously by dog team. But he searched thoroughly for a glimpse of the Sound's barrier edge without result. As far as we could see toward Alexander I Island, icebergs blocked the passage. The Douglas Mountain range must be one of the most splendid seen in the Antarctic. Its steep, regular slopes descend from a height of 8,500 feet to the waterline, with rifts and valleys, partially covered with snow.

We were within two miles of Cape Jeremy, northernmost cape of the Sound, but the cape itself had broken off, as the mountains went straight down into the water. As far as we could see beyond, there was open water in the Sound, but blocked to us by the icebergs. This was a great surprise to Finn, for the Sound had not contained open water in 1940. Then its entrance was blocked by a one hundred and sixty-foot high ice barrier. Our plane flights many months later were to reveal this barrier edge had discharged icebergs, such as those we were sailing among, and its face actually had moved back thirty-five miles in six years, allowing open water in the sound for the first time in its recorded history.

Our passage was narrowing and closing in on us with less open water. As conditions ahead were not only such as to offer immediate danger to our only means of transportation back to the civilized world, but had we continued to search in the sound for a suitable landing place further to the south, the lateness of the season (the temperature was 30 degrees F.), bringing a sudden change of wind, might also have brought these huge icebergs down upon us, to block any possible exit for another year. The chance was too great a one to take, so as we were stopped and lay drifting momentarily, Finn decided we would return to open Marguerite Bay at once. An alternate plan of advancing supplies via an overland route would have to be effected at a later date.

The return trip was without incident. After drifting for the night in open water while our search light kept look-out for drifting icebergs, we arrived at Back Bay Cove by noon of the following day, just as the winds began to blow. The ship was anchored about one-third of a mile away from the base, where she remained permanently. Subsequent cold weather froze her in place for the winter.

It had gotten considerably colder on the trip. My diary for Monday, March 24, 1947, reads:

> *We arrived back in Marguerite Bay before noon and anchored. The wind came up rapidly and only one boat load of six made it ashore with difficulty. Finn gave Wood a partial talking to but he was as insolent as ever. I have been quite upset about the general gripes and buck passing and have become a little discouraged about it but I do hope it will work itself out when we get ashore. Finn wants the other two planes taken ashore now and the AAF fellows to get in some flying time in the L-5. This will mean another argument with Harry, as he thinks he should be doing all the flying.*
>
> *It is getting colder now, particularly aboard ship today with no heat. The camp work is lagging behind and things will have to start pepping up before the winter night comes.*

Fall was approaching and with it came the heavier snows. A warning was given to all several times not to leave tools lying around when it was snowing. The warning, naturally, did not sink in. One morning

Andy Thompson was spotted on his hands and knees grubbing around through mounds of snow in an effort to retrieve his hammer. It was just like the proverbial looking for a needle in a haystack. You could say good-bye to shovels, tools, and other miscellaneous equipment until the following summer's thawing would bring the rusty items to light once again.

Sig began to notice that as the weather got progressively cooler, the desire for cigarettes fell off, and a preference for sweets took its place. We had brought 7,000 pounds of candy, and there was more than enough to meet the demand. Men who, while in the States never ate over a pound or two of candy a year, consumed forty-two pounds of it in two days. Even a prankster's insertion of soap in some of the candy did not seem to deter the recently acquired sweet tooth. Ten amazed expeditioners watched Larry Fiske finish a box of the soap-filled candy without ever realizing the difference. But men on Antarctic expeditions sometimes acquire most peculiar tastes in the line of food. It was fast becoming apparent that our group much preferred the lowly hamburger to Grade A filet mignon of which they had become tired. Since our arrival in the Antarctic, the men had been actively plotting to encourage Sig to take a few days rest leave from his galley pots and pans. They were not so much concerned for the Chef's health and comfort as they were to realize their dreams of filet mignon made into delectable hamburgers drowned in oodles of catsup. I was not a totally impartial onlooker, for a hamburger about that time would certainly have appealed to my jaded appetite as well.

With hamburgers rather than soap-filled candy the uppermost thought in his mind, Larry Fiske received a surprise one evening after dark, when the supposedly gray rock he was about to step on, barked at him. It seemed as if the base was in the midst of a pup seal invasion, for Oscar, as he was named, had a friend close by. Antarctic seals know no enemy on land. They appear quite tame in their nosy way until danger is sensed and then they can become very vicious. They have been known to snap off a ski tip when it is poked in their direction. The Antarctic seals here were hair seals rather than fur seals and consequently had no commercial fur value. Their skins are badly marked from fighting. It was therefore no wonder that hamburger-conscious Larry's first thoughts, after recovering from his fright, were directed toward an easy catch. His disappointment was evident when someone's more experienced eye pointed out that his two barking companions were not more than four months old, weighed only about three hundred pounds, and were only five feet long, too young to bother with in the Antarctic. Oscar and his sister were made camp pets promptly, free to come and go at will.

As the galley at the base had not been cleaned up yet and our headquarters remained aboard ship for the time being, regular meals continued to be served there. Those few who stayed at the base lived off of army supplied E Rations and Ten-in-One. This situation and later similar occasions afforded us excellent opportunities to try out these rations under cold weather conditions. Made for tropical usage, it was necessary almost to double the individual portions in order to provide sufficient calories for working men in the temperatures we experienced.

Sig baked bread about three times a week, but the increased demand for sweets created a universal desire for more pastry desserts. We had the makings for a moderate amount of baked products, but men on a polar expedition consume unbelievable amounts of food. The same ship's limited storage facilities, which had led us to the filet mignon, made it impossible for him to get as many cases of frozen eggs or as much butter as he hoped. But Sig promised pastry in large quantities once we had moved to the base, providing a seven-year-old food cache containing these items was recaptured before the winter night set in.

The road to this cache was through twelve feet of solid ice with a pick and shovel. It had been made by the previous expedition in 1940, by chopping a vaulted room in the side of the glacier. An icebox is not hard to make in the Antarctic, but when it is seven years old, the covering ice has practically preserved it forever. Glacier ice, which is formed under pressure, is far harder to chop than regular commercial ice to which one is accustomed. The pastry lovers soon found that picking through this ice gives the same sensation as though it were iron. After several day's work and only two feet of achievement, the demolition squad was summoned to the rescue. Hassage placed a charge of dynamite approximately fifteen feet away from the assumed entrance to the cache. The resulting blast proved that the charge had been correctly placed, for all ice nearby was made so pliable that it could be shoveled away and the extra frozen butter was at the disposal of all. Thaws in the intervening years had spoiled the eggs, but our supply of dried eggs was plentiful and now we had more butter than we could use.

Wednesday, March 26, 1947

Got up early and went ashore with Finn. Harry informed us the fellows were bitching about mess cooking and he felt Jennie and I should do it. Finn informed him I was brought along for a specific job and that I would take my turn with the rest. I spent the morning washing a few dishes in our shack and the afternoon painting a bookcase. Had a long talk with Bob Nichols about things in general and for the most part it looks as though things are going pretty well now. The coal detail finished its job this afternoon and the canvas is just about on the two buildings.

For several days the dynamite gang were very much in demand. No sooner had the cache been brought to light than another infinitely more serious crisis required their touch. The sheer ice cliff of the glacier, which begins only five hundred feet from the campsite, is from sixty to two hundred feet high above the waterline and approximately a mile in length. The ship was anchored about a quarter of a mile away from it. For two weeks the unloading boats had been traveling back and forth to the ship in a parallel course to the cliff. Continuous cracking and groaning could be heard originating from the cliff and occasionally the glacier would calve off a few tons of ice at a time, and a new iceberg would be born.

There had been no evidence of any particular danger, until one morning the men in the first boat to go ashore noticed that one of the larger crevasses, on which a watchful eye had been kept, had opened to an alarming extent during the night. A one hundred foot by three hundred-foot iceberg was about to be born, but when, no one could say. The impending danger caused all unloading operations to be canceled temporarily.

On board the ship, discussions ensued as to what remedy could be taken, and a dynamite detail consisting of Lassiter, Hassage, and Adams volunteered for the assignment of removing the menacing mass of ice. Roped together the men climbed the glacier and carefully picked their way as close to the death trap as they considered safe. Eight charges of TNT were lowered slowly into the depths of the hard blue icy crevasse, and with wires connected to a blasting machine on the side of the glacier, the charges were detonated. The resulting concussion jarred the base buildings, and a multitude of echoes could be heard from the surrounding mountains. Several men from the British Base came rushing to the hill overlooking our camp, believing that some unforeseen accident had occurred. The ice cliff, however, merely gave a few groans and shook slightly, but otherwise, the large ice mass remained in its original precarious position.

Undaunted by his first failure, Hassage made another attempt the following day. Equipped with ice crampons on his boots, he carefully approached the edge of the tottering overhanging ice cliff from the top of the glacier. Then, tied by a rope which was belayed by Adams, he edged himself close enough to lower thirty-two sticks of dynamite far down into the ice cliff made crevasse. After a speedy retreat was effected, he detonated the cargo. The mighty blast was heard far and wide, but the seemingly indestructible ice cliff still remained. Hassage and Adams retired that evening discouraged that their day had been wasted. Early the next morning, to everyone's great surprise, the jutting cliff was not seen in its usual position but, instead it was discovered quietly drifting out to sea in the form of just another huge iceberg. The dynamiters had achieved their success, but in a manner which they had not expected.

Overview of base with planes

Finn and Jackie with white huskie puppy, Kasco

Huskies

Finn, Nelson McClary and Woodie lashing sleds in the Machine Shop

Exploration by dog sled

VI

Bitching Continues

Thursday, March 27, 1947

The day was a windy one, hence no one could go ashore. The fellows had their holiday and by the conversation at the end of the day, I think they would rather be busy. On this ship all you have to do is suggest a subject and immediately you have enough opposition for an all day argument. They spent all day discussing various things. There was a movie shown in the afternoon and again in the evening. Finn and I spent most of the day reading and writing. I wrote a story on Sig's hamburger and sent it in. Finn and I went to the movie in the evening, Sonja Henie, in "It's a Pleasure."

Saturday, March 29, 1947

I got up early and with Jennie and Finn went ashore taking my skis and poles along. While we were rowing to shore we saw the L-5 take off on its hop to King George VI Sound with Harry and Ike, once again without radio contact. Finn and I began working in our shack. I painted the bookshelves, Bill Latady came in for a long conversation about continuing repairs on camp.

Harry, Ike, and Jimmy came in to report about the flight. The weather was extremely bad and they saw practically nothing. If they make another reconnaissance flight, it will have to be in good weather. Finn made the frame for a window in our building. Bill Latady made some soup for lunch out of dehydrated lentils, celery, onions, and carrots left from the last expedition. It was much too salty. We came back to the ship and had dinner. Finn . . . sent Bob Nichols, Thompson, and Owen ashore to live. Bob Nichols came in for a long conversation on his program, who he would be able to take on the trail, and where he would go. Finn handled the conversation very well. Mac wanted a certain roommate, Latady, but was happy with Owen. Sig made us some cocoa and we talked late again.

Sunday, March 30, 1947

I spent the day on ship doing some writing. Finn went ashore and built a window in our shack. He said it has changed the whole appearance of it. Jennie and Latady are now making chow in the galley. They call it Jennie's kitchen.

Monday, March 31, 1947

We went over to the camp. I was working around the shack washing things and Finn was finishing the window. We saw that the weasel (a mechanized tractor) was coming ashore so Finn went down to help with it. Suddenly Jennie called and I looked out of the window to see two ships sailing into the sheltered cove. The larger one was the H.M.S. Fitzroy, the smaller, H.M.S. Trepassey. Excitement was high. We went down to the weasel and saw that it had dropped in the water while being unloaded to the beach. As the small plate in the bottom of the boat was out it sank and as much as the men pulled on the line, they couldn't get it up on the bank. A Britisher came over and gave a cordial letter from the governor to Finn inviting him on the Fitzroy. Bob Nichols and I went with Finn. The governor saw Finn alone with Commander Bingham. Bob and I were entertained by Captain White in his cabin with sherry. The governor and Finn joined up after 45 minutes and about 20 minutes later we left. The governor asked us for lunch the next day and Finn accepted. They were all very nice indeed. On board ship we found Harry was ranting around about his dog, Chinook, and acting the spoiled child. Found out from Pete, fellows had had a bitch session and held Finn responsible for the weasel, which was ridiculous as he had nothing to do with it. I cornered Peterson and Jimmy Robertson and had it out with them both and they agreed Finn was not responsible but Wood was. Jimmy came in and had a chat with us. Sig joined us and we all had coffee and a pleasant chat.

Little by little we learned that Harry had been undermining Finn for some time. As Third-in-command Harry was in charge of giving Finn's daily work orders to the men often adding "that's not the way I would do it but that's the way Finn wants it". At first the men had no way of judging who was right and so from the very start Finn was purposefully harmed in order to make Harry seem the better leader. Because of their long friendship, Finn excused Harry's obvious bad judgement, hoping that he would come to his senses.

The H.M.S. Trepassey, a wooden hull ship of approximately 360 net tons, was about half the size of our ship. Captain Burdon, a Newfoundlander and a veteran sailor in the Antarctic waters, was her skipper. The H.M.S. Fitzroy, a steel hull merchant ship, was approximately two hundred feet in length. Captain Freddie White of the Falkland Islands Merchant Marine was in command. This vessel carried the Governor of the Falkland Islands and their Dependencies, as well as Commander E. Bingham of the Royal Navy, formerly medical doctor on the British Graham Land Expedition, 1934-1937, and first leader of the five British bases which were then located on the Peninsula. Major Butler had replaced Commander Bingham just a few weeks before.

The two British ships were anchored close by The Port of Beaumont. To me the incident had its amusing side. In all of this vast frozen continent, this small cove had at anchor as much tonnage for its size as New York harbor. Stonington Island was Antarctica's leading and only seaport.

While discussing with the governor the mutually interesting matters arising from two different nationalities occupying Stonington Island, he expressed his deep regrets at the deplorable manner in which the Chileans had treated the American camp, and stressed his great desire for British-American cooperation in the Antarctic, particularly on Stonington Island, where both groups were interested in furthering scientific knowledge to the mutual advantage of all mankind. We fully agreed and pointed out that the Antarctic Continent was certainly large enough for the expeditions from various nations to cooperate in furthering scientific and geographical research. (A very prophetic view of the future International Geophysical Year and the subsequent Antarctic Treaty).

Major Butler and several of his men, and five of us were invited on board the Fitzroy for lunch. The Antarctic social season was at its height.

Tuesday, April 1, 1947

> *Finn and I stayed on board and got ready for the governor's luncheon. Finn, Ike, Harry, McClary, Peterson, and I went. The invitation for Jennie came after she had gone skiing with Latady and she did not go. I sat with the Governor. The luncheon was fine. Our group pictures were taken afterward on the sun deck.*

During luncheon, the governor proposed a toast to Finn and our party for continued cooperation and friendly relations east, south, north, and west between the United States of America and the British empire. Finn, in turn, replied that he hoped the cooperation between the two nations would continue to be as great as it had been during the war. From the portholes of the ship, we could see the American and British flags flying from their respective campsites.

Later in the afternoon, the rest of the members of our expedition and those from the British base "E" were invited to the Fitzroy for cocktails. Both occasions were very pleasant social affairs. As the two British ships were planning to sail north the following day, we said good-bye to the visitors until the following year, when they intended to come again. However, late that night, the Trepassey caught on fire as she was preparing to sail. We were unaware of the dramatic scene that was taking place only a short distance away until hours later, when it was well under control and other help was not needed. The two British ships were forced to remain a few days longer than they had anticipated in order to partially repair the fire damage to the Trepassey.

> *The fellows who went to the cocktail party in the afternoon came on board pretty tipsy. Jennie decided to stay on the beach. Finn called her back at 8 o'clock and George to come with her. Hassage and Adams went over to our base with an engineer from the Trepassey to fix*

the generators as the English gave us the spare parts for them. They came back without George and Jennie saying they had gone down the beach. Finn sent McClary and Adams back at 11 o'clock and we waited until after 4 before we heard a word from them. Finally Jorge came after a fire extinguisher and we knew for the first time a fire raged on board the Trepassey. We offered all help and assistance but it was declined with thanks. They thought the ship would blow up or sink but by about 8 o'clock a.m. it was out and situation under control. Finn found out Jennie and Jorge had taken the English boat and went on board "Trepassey" for a drink. Finn told her he didn't want her on shore yet, that he thought it was bad that she was working with Latady too much and that she should stay away from the boys. Finn told her to go to bed. All the night was gone.

Wednesday, April 2, 1947

As we did not get to bed until almost six o'clock in the morning, we didn't get up until mid-afternoon. There was definitely tension on board evidenced by the presence of Harry and Latady. It was discovered when Finn came back from the beach that Jennie had not gone to bed this morning as Finn had ordered, but instead went down below and talked about Finn's conversation with the fellows until 9:00 a.m. Jimmy Robertson went ashore and told Harry that Finn accused Jennie of an affair with Latady up on the glacier, which I know Finn did not do. Harry and Latady were ready to leave the expedition and return with the British. The rest of the fellows were furiously arguing about the running of the expedition and held their own meeting unbeknownst to Finn, but Harry then refused to do anything about it. Finn had a conversation with Bob Nichols and then had a talk with Jennie, Harry, and Latady and put them straight. He then called an open meeting which Jennie and I did not attend. Finn started by saying, "Let's have by gones be by gones and start afresh from the present."

After it was all over everyone said the feeling was better and a new regime was to begin.

Finn was disgusted and very upset with Jennie because she seemed to feel she could do just as she pleased on the expedition and her husband would take up for her with Finn. Finn thought since he had allowed her to come that she should have respect for him and decorum she didn't seem to possess. We really did not think there was anything serious between her and Latady. Certainly Harry did not seem to be jealous in any way.

We played host for tea to the British Governor, Captain White and Commander Bingham, all of whom greatly admired our ship.

The weather continued to deteriorate to the point that we all narrowly avoided a disaster. The winds had been blowing steady at forty miles per hour, with gusts up to sixty-five miles an hour, and the barometric pressure stood at 28.05. About one o'clock in the morning of April 4th when Mate McClary noticed that we were drifting toward the glacier ice cliff, the Skipper was awakened and gave the order to move forward. It seems that we let down more anchor and moved forward without the stearing gear attached. As we slowly moved, we swung suddenly to the starboard. The Fitzroy and Trepassey, lashed together since the fire, were drifting and also swung quickly. It was at this moment that the only three ships along the coast of this huge continent decided they all wanted to be in the same place at the same time. Our dory, hanging over the ship's side was crushed. Fortunately, no damage was done to any of the three ships, but it had been a tense moment.

Saturday, April 5, 1947

We woke up to a continuing gale. The Fitzroy Captain White came aboard expressing his hope the two British ships hadn't damaged our ship while drifting last night. Ike said, "Oh, no!" Just then Finn came down and not knowing the previous conversation told him the truth that it was our fault. They of course knew it was anyway but were too polite to say so. Both ships left around 11 o'clock. We gave them three blasts. They answered with same and we answered with one. Don McLean came in for a chat. In fun he had just practiced hypnotizing Kelsey. It was extremely cold aboard ship as we had no water and couldn't run the boiler. Finn and I read in our bunk for awhile. I wrote a story. Sig came in and we talked. McClary and Jennie came in and they wanted a holiday tomorrow with a good dinner and a movie.

The departure of these ships left the British and American camps on Stonington without further contact, other than radio, with the civilized world for the next year.

Despite numerous interruptions, little by little our work in establishing the base was progressing. The first dog team had been put into action for hauling the ship's unloaded supplies from the beach, up the snow-covered hill, to the camp. The dogs, which had been trained to pull in harness before departure from the States, were eager to get down to work. The other untrained dogs tugged at their tethering lines and put up an awful howl, because they were not among those chosen for harness. There was, as is usual in first attempts, the disconcerting fact that a dog team always wants to go in the direction least desired by its driver. A group of would-be drivers gathered around and began to take mental notes on the patient technique required for driving a team.

By the end of March, sufficient coal had been stored for the winter, and much equipment, including some food, the heavy radio transmitter, and the wings of the two larger planes had been moved ashore. The job of covering the buildings with canvas was near completion and, from time to time, more men were sent ashore to live, although the majority still remained on the ship. In bad weather, or after dark, the men on shore spent their time cleaning and making minor repairs inside the buildings.

With one group of men ashore and one on the ship, it was like one expedition operating two bases. Until the ship was frozen into the cove and systematically laid-up for the winter, it was necessary to maintain enough of a crew on board to move her in case of danger. This had to be done several times, because of the movement of large icebergs, and, in strong winds, when we dragged anchor somewhat. There had been many days, at least three a week, when the winds, or the presence of moving brash ice, made it impossible for a party to get ashore. During these periods, communication from ship to shore was kept by pre-arranged walkie-talkie schedules. We looked forward to the day when winter would assert itself by freezing our ship into position, so that we could all be together at the base.

During the second week of April, steady forty-mile-per-hour winds from the southwest, with gusts up to sixty M.P.H. an average of every thirty minutes lasted for five monotonous days. We were compelled to keep the main engines turning over slowly at all times to prevent dragging anchor. The wind rushed upon us through a mountain pass next to Roman Figure Four Mountain, three miles to the south. Figure

Four rises straight from the water's edge to a height of 3,400 feet. The mountain received its name from its rifts and valleys, which, when snow-covered, reveal a perfect Roman figure four. While riding out this gale, we dodged numerous large glacier icebergs, which the wind blew into our cove from the sea, and we watched the nearby glacier calving off smaller icebergs. We were relieved when the wind's direction changed to the northwest to bring calmer weather. Boat communication with the Base was established again, and the regular work routine continued.

Wednesday, April 9, 1947

Finn, Kelsey and Peterson succeeded in getting ashore. The weather was extremely calm, but there was much ice on the water to contend with. The evaporator finally produced water and the day on board ship was spent with that and melting the remaining ice on the decks. I read for awhile and then played cards with Jennie.

Finn, Peterson, and Kelsey came back bringing Latady, Harry and Jimmy Robertson with them. We had dinner and Finn called a short meeting to tell about the living plans for the women, and explaining about the naming of geographical places and the building up of the camp. Finn announced he intended to name the Beechcraft plane the "Ed Sweeney" and the Nordun "NANA."

The general feeling seems to be good now and the fellows are settling down to working better with each other. Finn had a good talk with Harry and told him he counted on his loyalty, which so far he hadn't gotten. Harry said he had stopped coming in for punch because the fellows were criticizing the fact that Sig was always in here. All of the fellows really seem to dislike Sig because he always throws cold water on their ideas. Don asked me to be his bridge partner and we took on Lassiter and Adams for a loss. Talked late with Sig and Chuck Hassage. Hassage talked about his woman trouble, wife and girls.

Wednesday, April 10, 1947

Everyone was able to go ashore today. After lunch, Finn, Ike, Harry, Chuck Adams, Jennie and I went in the newly rescued dory. We looked for a place to land the planes up on the glacier. Jennie and I inspected the changes in camp since we had last seen it. Jennie's room is just about finished. We all played with a stranded seal for awhile, and then Jennie and I took a walk around the island and up to the British camp. Major Butler came out and invited us for tea, which we enjoyed, then showed us their dogs, then their hanger and small plane. He was very nice and pleasant. He indicated that the British were seriously considering buying a ship like ours from the U.S. Their trail party is still not back, but probably will be soon. He had to request permission to write the article that I had asked him to do for NANA and has not received it from London as yet. We all went back to the ship in the Coast Guard boat and had a good dinner on board. Played cards with Jennie and Jorge for awhile and began to knit an ear covering ski cap.

Friday, April 11, 1947

Ike took off on a flight with Harry down the Sound. Finn and Kelsey followed their progress on the radio. The day was a beautiful one, sun shining and atmosphere clear as a bell. Ike said it was one of the most beautiful days in the Antarctic. Ice conditions were favorable, but a place to land was not found. Finn is thinking seriously of calling off another trip by ship because of general lateness in the year.

Jennie, Finn and I went over to Base. Latady came down from the glacier to sign a paper in case of an accident while flying. Finn allowed him to go up then with Harry to take a picture of camp. Finn cut one mattress off to extend the bed in our shack. They fit perfectly together now. The Darlington's room is nice as well. Jennie and I started up the glacier for a ski, but because of the ice, Jennie turned back and put on snowshoes. I continued to the top and had a nice ski half way up to the aviation cache. Scenery was beautiful and the day very cold. Came back to ship, had a good dinner, wrote an article on gale and had punch with Finn, Sig, Jennie and Jorge. Bob Nichols and Bob Dodson prepared for their geological trip for a several day's stay to Neny Island.

After the two additional flights in the L-5 to George VI Sound area failed to reveal any further information as to the possible establishment of a southern cache, and because of the lateness of the season, Finn decided to relinquish the idea of taking the ship to that vicinity again. There was, however, one thing more that could be done this fall to facilitate making plans for the following summer's field program. In the hope of being able to lay out a possible surface route which could be used by the weasels and dog teams, Finn made a flight over the Neny Trough area to see from the air if surface conditions had greatly changed since the last time.

April 12th dawned bright and sunny without a cloud in the sky. It was one of those rare, beautiful days with a temperature about twenty degrees below freezing F. In the brilliant sunshine, the plane circled the base in order to gain altitude sufficient to clear the mountains. They headed for Neny Glacier clearing the peaks by approximately one thousand feet, providing them with a good view. Glaciers wound through their wide and narrow passes, and where the permanent ice cap meets the rocky formations, bluish-green ice could be seen blending in with newly fallen snow. Finn describes the flight at two places more fully in his book "Antarctic Conquest."

Saturday, April 12, 1947

The small British plane was also in the air for the first time. Chuck Adams, Jim Lassiter and Arthur Owen rowed Nichols and Dodson over to Neny Island in the Coast Guard Cutter. The first three came back with five seals. Jennie and I stayed on board, did some knitting. I wrote an article on Ike's cup and made up some radio messages for Finn. Received a message from Bud Engle.

Jimmy Lassiter and Chuck Adams put soap in the candy as a joke so that no one could tell it. Ike was making such a fuss over somebody getting more candy than he, that Finn told him to ration it. Ike passed the thankless job on to Jorge and Jorge counted it and announced that each person could get two bars a day. This was the first day of the rationing and quite a shock when soap was found in it.

We started getting wise to McClary. The gun locker is constantly open and there are about ten guns around the ship. Jennie says Mac definitely wanted Harry to go home via the "Trepassey", so that he would have a bigger job on the expedition. Mac is trying to get everybody ashore, so that he can do as he pleases on the ship. Harry doesn't want them ashore yet and has told Mac that. Mac is constantly bitching, complaining and trying to get Finn discredited to anyone who will listen.

Sunday, April 13, 1947

We were not able to go ashore today because the ice was packed into the beach. Finn had a marvelous flight yesterday. It was one of the most perfect days he has ever seen here. We wrote up a good story about it. Finn planned a trip for tomorrow to follow up on the flight. Hopefully, he can get the weasel up Neny Fjord with Ike, Hassage, Adams, Owen, and Lassiter.

More of McClary's activities were revealed. He and Woody broke into some of the E rations and probably were the ones who broke into the issue room. Anywhere they can make trouble they do.

Apparently everybody on the beach is getting along well together. The two Bobs on Neny Island seem to be getting along fine. I finished working on my wool ear cap and it fits well. Fiske wrote something for us and we sent in one message to Fred Allen. Jennie has learned to make water with the evaporator. Jorge thinks he is in love with her and follows her around everywhere until now people are beginning to talk about it. Everyone is getting down on Sig. He butts into every conversation and the fellows are just getting so that they can't stand it. It is such a shame because Sig is so kindhearted, he would do anything for people who treat him decently. The fellows resent him being in with Finn every night. But he is so completely loyal to Finn that it is hard to say anything. I played bridge again this evening and went to bed fairly early.

Monday, April 14, 1947

I didn't feel well today, so I didn't get up until about three o'clock. I knitted for awhile. Finn didn't go ashore as the ice blocked the beach. The fellows worked around the ship. After dinner, Finn called Mac in and gave him the very devil. Mac had the nerve to tell Finn that the only two people he had confidence in on the expedition were Harry and Latady. Mac signed his death warrant and will be behind the eight ball from now on, 'cause Finn really let him know who was running this expedition. Finn felt betrayed and he didn't react well to betrayal. I played cards with Fiske, Jennie and Woody, who was supposed to be on watch. Finn played cards with Don, Lassiter, and Adams.

Earlier in the afternoon we discussed with Kelsey the possibility of setting up the mailbag every Saturday night with General Electric. Kelsey thought it better to wait until the radio stuff got ashore and he could estimate how long it would take him to set up the antennas.

Tuesday, April 15, 1947

The fellows finally got ashore again today. Finn went with about four of them. Smitty was sick, burning in the lungs, probably from all the painting of the small boats he has been doing. The camp seems to be doing well. The two Bob's returned from their geological trip to Neny Island. Nichols was most enthusiastic about the iron and copper veins, which he saw. I knitted with Jennie for awhile, then didn't feel well again, so rested. Didn't go to dinner, but felt better after dinner.

Finn talked to Ike about Mac and Ike said the dumb clucks don't know any better and that he certainly didn't have to use Mac as Executive officer on our way back. Harry got a radio message from his mother saying that Harry's stepfather, George Garrett, had been appointed Minister to Ireland and they would leave for Dublin in July. I received my first message from my Aunt since I arrived. It was a nice one and I was certainly happy to receive it at last. She evidently didn't receive all of the three, which I have sent.

Finn, Jennie, Sig and I talked for awhile. Finn played the mouth organ. Jennie left on the pretense of going to bed, but really went down and talked to Mac. Chuck Hassage came in and played the mouth organ for quite a while. Chuck is a nice fellow.

Thursday, April 17, 1947

I got up late today. Finn had already gone ashore. We had rice and meat to start off Sig's new luncheon menu program. Jennie spent most of the day wasting the good water she made by using it in the washing machine, which doesn't work properly and therefore doesn't get the clothes clean. I spent most of the day trying to work on Finn's book, but was interrupted by Sig's coming in to chat, mostly about nothing and consequently, I got very little done.

Hassage, Adams, McLean, Owen and Ike took more radio gear ashore. Finn, driving the weasel, worked on hauling the coal up to the camp, aided by Harry and Dodson. Lassiter is working on the tunnel or shelter, between the Science building and the Machine shop, for a weasel garage. Latady is working on the buildings and Nichols is helping Kelsey with the radio equipment. The weasel is working fine. More of the radio equipment went ashore. Finn is working on a second window for us and painting the walls white. He worked for a long time tonight on a future report recommending that this Base be kept up by the U.S. Government.

Friday, April 18, 1947

Finn went ashore early. I got up late. I spent the entire afternoon working on the report to be submitted to the government. Harry came on board and came in for a chat with us before dinner about the report, George Garrett, and the unloading of the airplanes. After dinner, Harry, Ike, and Finn had a conference. I spoke to Nichols at length concerning the report and he felt strongly that Finn should submit two plans for a group of bases on this continent. As a result of his conference, Finn decided to keep the planes on board until it freezes over, as that is really the only safe way of doing it.

We watched Don operate on a dog and evidently something happened concerning the ether, cause the dog was dead in a matter of minutes. It looked pretty much like Don's fault and Harry was madder than the devil when he found out.

April 19 was the first clear day in a week.

With a party of seven, Finn pushed off from the ship's side in our twenty-seven foot motor launch for the ten-mile trip into Neny Fjord to investigate a possible surface route south.

Although their main mission was to investigate a future trail party route, the trip also afforded the opportunity for some geology and sealing work. Nichols was amazed at how Finn crossed crevasses on skis, but he wouldn't follow. Nichols had a lot to learn about the trail. He made a brief close range study of the rock formations on the 6,000-foot high mountains that embrace Neny Glacier on both sides. He was at least able to get the general lay of the land. While they were thus occupied ashore, the rest of the group, Schlossbach, Hassage, Lassiter, Adams, and Owen spent their time sealing around the nearby islands in the Fjord.

One of their chores was to stock up on our seal supply early before winter, in order to provide enough food for the dogs until the spring returns and with it, the seals. Dogs thrive on seal meat. It not only appeals to their palate, but after a month on such a diet you could see an improvement in the thickness and glossiness of their coats. Since our arrival, a couple of members of the expedition had taken daily seal hunting trips around the nearby fjords to gather our supply while they were still very plentiful. It had become a very competitive sport among the men. On this particular day, Lassiter and Adams made a good catch by obtaining two large Weddell seals in an hour.

After the sealing mission, the launch returned to the cove to pick up the shore party only to find the wind direction had changed and had filled the cove with brash ice. The tide too was lower and a number of small reefs were visible near the beach. They approached slowly, cautiously picking their way through numerous patches of thick brash ice and ice growlers. But the swells speeded up their travel with such force that, in a matter of seconds, the launch became grounded on a small reef ten feet from the shore where Nichols and Finn were standing. Realizing the awkward situation and the need for quick action, the two waded up to their waists in the icy waters (approximately 29 degrees F.) and after a struggle, succeeded in helping to push the boat off the shoal with the aid of its own power. Unfavorable ice conditions and the oncoming twilight reduced the speed of the return trip, so that the party was very glad to get on board ship that night to replace their frozen garments, have a warm shower, and a hot meal.

A shower was a rare treat, reserved for those who absolutely needed it. Our camp snow melter had not been put into condition as yet and our ship's water supply provided little more than was necessary for cooking. We were relying solely upon the sluggish evaporator, which through a very complicated process turned salt water into fresh. With constant attention, Chuck Hassage was able to make up to six hundred gallons a day, but Chuck was a busy man, what with dynamiting ice cliffs and keeping all of the diesel equipment in good working order. Our weekly shower turned up every ten days or so. Before we left the ship, our water supply became so depleted that we collected ice in the small boats from nearby growler fields and lifted it on deck in nets, where it was melted by two Army emergency heaters. For several days, we had sufficient water for cooking, but not enough to keep the boilers going for heat on board and our living quarters were pretty cold.

> *Mac explained to Nichols tonight why he thought snowshoes would be better with a dog team than skis. He has a lot to learn too. Finn played cards with them for awhile.*

Sunday, April 20, 1947

> *The Night Watch (Mac) was undoubtedly asleep on the job for the Coast Guard boat was sunk this morning. The fellows spent the day trying to raise it. After lunch Finn, Nichols, Ike, McLean, and Hassage got into a discussion as to how far south in King George VI Sound the ship got. Harry had said they were not where we thought and that he could estimate by the flight. Finn proved to Nichols that Harry was all wet and Ike said there were no instruments in the plane to cause Harry to make such a statement. Chuck Hassage agreed that there was entirely too much bitching about things that were being done for the good of the expedition. Jennie was sick with a cold the whole day. Finn and I worked on stories for NANA and reports.*

Those of us who were still confined aboard ship enjoyed an occasional movie for an evening's relaxation. Jim Lassiter was the self-appointed projectionist. Upon request he never hesitated to tell you that the evening's showing would be "Duel in the Sun," the premier of which had not been shown up to the time we left the States. Sometimes our nightly feature would star Laurel and Hardy, and at times, Richard Dix, but its title never ceased to be "Duel in the Sun." The demand for movies grew to such proportions that he never had to take his turn at dish washing. Lots would be drawn to relieve him and conserve his strength for the nightly fight with the temperamental projector and sound track system, which were operating from different types of current.

During the month of April, the unloading and camp establishment program continued to go forward with full speed. The second weasel was hoisted by the boom over the side of the ship and floated ashore by Hassage. We now had both weasels in operation on the beach to haul the heavy equipment to camp. The two large and two small buildings were covered completely by canvas, making them ready for everything the winter ahead had to offer. Practically all of the heavy radio equipment had been brought ashore and Kelsey was busily working on the establishment of the base radio station.

Tuesday, April 22, 1947

The wind blew hard all day and no one was able to get ashore. Harry worked on aviation equipment and found it in pretty sad condition with need of future hard work and long hours. Finn and I worked on stories and reports the whole day. We got something done, but have hardly made an impression on what there is to do. Harry and Finn had a long chat here in the afternoon about future operations. One thing can be said about Harry, when he is interested in something, he really works hard on it. Things seem much better now. There is still a problem with Sig and Mac. No one paid any attention to Mac at dinner this evening and he felt pretty much out of it, I know.

Thursday, April 24, 1947

Finn left for shore this morning as the weather was good. He sent a note to Butler for him and his Second-in-Command, John Tonkin, to come aboard this afternoon. Finn finished both windows in our shack and had various conversations. Nichols wanted tea in the Science building. Finn finally squelched that by saying the thing would grow and it wasn't fair to all concerned. Peterson is grouchy these days. He has been sat on by everyone and thinks the expedition came for his programs alone. Jennie helped Smitty wash down the corridors, making comments about all. She was mad because Finn wouldn't let her go ashore this morning.

Butler and Tonkin came aboard and with Ike we had a nice chat after Finn showed them around the ship. The five of us had pie in our room. They know nothing about skiing, have very little fresh meat, except seal, have heavier tents, and worse pemmican. They stayed for dinner and Jennie was invited to sit at our table. They chatted until 8:30 and then left. The whole thing went off very well.

More and more of the personnel and our activities were being centered ashore. The buildings had been cleaned out and made more livable after minor repairs and alterations. Equipment brought to the beach had been unloaded, sorted, and stored in the proper buildings. A shelter was being built between the Science Building and the Machine Shop, which was large enough to house one of the weasels and protect it from the weather. This also offered an indoor passage way between the two buildings. A similar passageway was made between the Machine Shop and the galley end of the Bunkhouse. Later, when we finally did move ashore, Finn made a narrow tunnel from our small shack to the Bunkhouse. With this series of passages, we could go from one end of camp to the other without having to go outside, which was a great advantage during the winter's bad weather.

The galley in the Bunkhouse was about the only eye sore remaining in camp at the end of April. The range had been causing considerable trouble and no one had been able to remedy the trouble as yet. When least expected, minor explosions would occur, accompanied by great columns of black soot. Everyone there at the time would come out covered from head to toe. But as the men on the beach fortunately were living on Army rations, this necessitated the minimum amount of cooking. After a while the sameness of the food led them to investigate sources of change. Lassiter discovered some eight-year-old Jell-O powder and gaily made up a batch of lemon for dessert one evening. When the time arrived he went outside to collect it, only to find Chinook had gotten loose and lapped up approximately one-third of the treat. Dog or no, the men were in the mood for Jell-O and before long the other two-thirds had been consumed.

The dogs themselves were undergoing an organized period of exercise and training, and on April 27th, Harry started training Dodson, Owen, and Smith as the first dog team drivers. Daily trips were made up the glacier to haul aviation gasoline to the side of the L-5 by the aviation cache. After one or two such trips, the would-be trainers had about decided that a good dog driver was born and not made. No matter how many resolutions they made to the contrary, they found it impossible to keep a calm head and tongue when the dogs insisted upon playing such abominable tricks on them. On one such trip, one of the dogs in the team decided he was much too tired to continue and sat right down on his flanks, letting the rest of the team pull him down the hill sliding fashion.

Monday, April 28, 1947

> *Got up early and spent the whole day organizing Finn's book in its very, very, early stages. We have made a fairly complete outline to follow and I have been doing some elementary research in order to start organizing it somewhat. Finn was on shore painting most of the day. He and Harry came back and did much talking about future plans. Jennie and I took Harry and Lassiter over the coals in bridge. Hassage, Mac, Harry, and Finn discussed the work load for the next few days and because Lassiter was to take the rest of the food ashore tomorrow, instead of helping Harry do some work on the Nordun, Harry got mad, acted like a stubborn child, and walked out of the room. That broke up the conversation and Finn didn't care.*

It was against this background of continuing tension that we made our preparations to face the fury of the Antarctic winter.

VII

Freeze In

One of the main objectives of our program was to get scientific data and recordings in various fields over a period of at least twelve months. Therefore, work on setting up programs and instruments began within the first week of our arrival. Under the direction of our geophysicist, Andrew A. Thompson, a tidal shack, a non-magnetic shack, and a seismographic room were erected. At the bottom of the cove where the glacier joins the Island, only four hundred feet from the base, a suitable location was selected for setting up the tidal apparatus. His recordings began immediately along with his studies in terrestrial magnetism and seismology.

Physicist Harries-Clichy Peterson began his meteorological work aboard ship on our way down. As soon as we reached the base, his attentions were turned first to reconditioning the meteorological tower and establishing a first class weather station, without interrupting his observations. These readings continued to be forwarded daily to the Weather Bureau, where they formed a link in the complicated procedure of correctly making long range weather forecasts. Peterson's program included investigations in the field of cosmic ray measurements, solar radiation, and atmospheric refraction, but, for the time being, his hours were taken up with meteorological work and these additional branches had to be delayed for a few months, at which time they took a very important place in his daily schedule.

Senior Scientist and Geologist, Dr. Robert L. Nichols, had been spending many hours in helping to establish the base. Nichols never shirked responsibility. He was always there to carry his end of the load. But from time to time he was able to put in some time on the local geology work. His work would be greatest when he was able to get out on the trail later in the spring and summer, but before the winter overtook us, he was able to get out in the field for a few days of concentrated geological work.

Dodson studied the effectiveness of the sleeping bags, insulating mats, primus stove, tent, and the other equipment for the U.S. Army on short geological field trips with Nichols. Army "E Rations" supplying 3,800 calories daily were used. They are tasty, contain an interesting variety of appetizing food, and are conveniently packed for field use.

It was gratifying that results of our scientific program, which had begun already in a small way, began to accelerate even before we were able to move ashore to our base.

Tuesday, April 29, 1947

It was slightly blowy this morning. Finn did not go ashore, but worked instead on writing some of his family history and background for me to use. We also worked on a newspaper article. Adams, Lassiter, Kelsey, and Jorge went ashore in the coast guard boat taking some boxes of food with them. They took about 2 ½ hours to get ¾ of a mile, as the wind was so strong and brash ice blocked their way. They remained on the beach.

Received messages from Keller, Aunt, and Captain Dodson, saying stories are being well publicized in all the papers. Harry spent the afternoon in future planning with Finn. They worked out the routes and requirements for five major flights and wrote up a directive governing aviation personnel. Jimmy Robertson seems to be acting up these days, under the delusion that he is running things. Harry feels confident he can take care of that.

Thursday, May 1, 1947

Finn rowed ashore to get Kelsey on board for his contact. The diesel generator is finally started. Harry was up shooting the bull with the fellows until 4 a.m. Lassiter and Harry had it out about the condition of the Norseman plane. I worked on articles and messages to be sent out. Finn settled the complaints about who could use the hair clipper by telling them it was for the use of all concerned. General feeling seems to be fairly good. I read some of Stefansson's book on the early history of explorations of this continent.

Friday, May 2, 1947

Finn awoke this morning to find the cove definitely freezing out towards the ship. You could even watch it freezing around the ship in small particles. Finn was in the mess hall when Harry got up about noon. Finn asked him if he had so much work to do on the plane, why he was not up earlier and that if Jimmy Robertson was supposed to be the mechanic, why was the bad condition of the Norseman thrown in Lassiter's lap now. Harry was off saying he had done more work than Finn had and Harry was working while Finn had his picture taken in Beaumont, which was a perfect lie. Harry went into his room to stay. When Finn, Don, Lassiter and I were playing cards later, Harry came in shouting at Finn "I want to see you". Finn answered if you want to see me you can come to my room in ten or fifteen minutes.

I went to the "head" and found Jennie crying saying Harry was yelling and arguing with everybody, he had gone crazy and he had beaten her.

Harry barges in asking for his wife then went into the next head half-yelling and half-crying, " The whole thing is rotten, rotten I say". I told Finn about it, and he came up to our cabin. I had a long talk with Lassiter and found out Harry had told him in San Antonio that he was getting a regular commission and a next higher rank by going. Lassiter said he too would go under those conditions and wrote his name and qualifications on a card which Harry never delivered to Finn. Lassiter has twice as many flying hours as Harry and doesn't like the way he is running things. Lassiter also told me, he and Adams have told Harry about the condition of the Nordun and that Harry paid no attention. They had decided a week ago that they would not fly, but Harry's turning the Norseman over to them, fixed things up. Lassiter says he is the only one who could fix the Nordun up again and he pointed out the trouble to Harry, who was amazed. I think Harry is partly mad, because Finn told the boys he would take them on the trail and, of course, Harry wanted to do that because he wants to be the big cheese in everything. Harry never did come to speak to Finn and Lassiter told me Harry had been drinking.

The evaporator broke for good today and the water supply was so low that the heat was turned off and the ship was freezing cold all day. We went to bed cold and under tension because of Harry's actions.

The freezing ice could be seen approaching the ship rapidly. The speed with which the vessel was surrounded with a solid sheet of ice was quite a surprise to all. At noon, she was swinging as usual in the open water. In spite of the mild breezes blowing, small flakes of ice could be seen forming larger shiny patches which the southeast wind blew shoreward packing them in with the brash ice. Thus began the freeze, which advanced so quickly that by five p.m. the ship was surrounded completely and very little movement could be felt. The temperature stood at twenty-four degrees below freezing F. and during the cold clear night it fell to below zero. Days were getting shorter and the temperatures falling fast. A milestone in our history had been passed, for the "Port of Beaumont, Texas" had stopped swinging at its free water anchorage and was now frozen into her over wintering position, not to be released from the icy grip until February 1948.

On the following day, Finn tested the thin crust of ice, which had formed on top of the two feet deep ice flakes, and found that it was strong enough to support a man on skis.

Saturday, May 3, 1947

The ship was completely frozen in this morning and Lassiter and Finn skied ashore.

Lassiter was anxious to win his bet that he would be the first person to ski ashore from the ship, so he put on skis for the first time in his life, and started out. The swells from the ocean could be seen still moving the ice in long slow waves, so slightly that they scarcely were perceptible. At the shore, Lassiter met a tidal crack, extending around the Island. He negotiated this without difficulty and climbed to the beach. After his successful venture, his track marks led the way for others on what soon proved to be a very popular highway from ship to shore.

They were back for lunch and Harry came to lunch but said nothing and returned to his room. Hassage and Finn went ashore in the afternoon. I worked on some articles and knitted for a while. Harry did not come to dinner at all. McClary finished his dinner and went into talk to them for the evening. Finn has ordered that Robertson come on board tomorrow and as soon as the galley in at base is fixed up and the diesel running, we will make preparations to move ashore.

Harry is a spoiled child, who when he can't get his own way, goes into a perfect tantrum as though he hasn't good sense, which at times he certainly hasn't.

Sunday, May 4, 1947

Harry had a sudden change of face today and couldn't do enough for everybody. It was quite ridiculous. I went ashore on skis and had a long chat with Nichols and Andy Thompson about the articles I am writing on their programs. I was surprised to see how nice the shack looks. Finn has painted it white and we are ready to move in any time. Harry came to meals on the ship today, but invariably slammed the door on his way out. Lassiter gave Sig the word about 25 gallons of alcohol on board, which they really need for aviation, and which he felt sure it was about to be taken by the drinkers. We overheard Harry telling Lassiter he didn't realize Lassiter and Adams were interested in aviation – of all the ridiculous things!

Monday, May 5, 1947

Finn, Sig, and I spent about an hour between 2:30 and 3:30 am watching Mac go down the forward hold. We thought surely he was after the alcohol, but he coiled lines and we got so sleepy, we went to bed. Finn talked to Ike and we decided to move ashore tomorrow. We packed some things and began hauling them over. I skied over with Jennie and put away the things I brought. Finn and Latady had words about using more gasoline for the generator to do some work tonight. Harry worked on the planes and even volunteered to help me with a package, which I declined. I spoke to Jennie about his mood swings, but she wouldn't talk. Finn is actively thinking about putting Lassiter in charge of aviation, if Harry doesn't come to his senses. Ike agrees that this would be best. Finn intends to have the power cut off here tonight at 10:30 to have everybody get a good night's sleep after they were all down in the doctor's office last night. Harry did not speak one word at dinner.

On May 6th, the rest of the expedition personnel officially moved ashore.

Tuesday, May 6, 1947

Today we moved over to camp. Jennie wanted sheets. I referred her to Sig, who told her there were just enough to go back with. Finn and I took a load of stuff over early. I spent the morning fixing things up. Butler came over, at Finn's request, in the afternoon. They talked about cooperation between the two groups. Finn asked him to cooperate with keeping these fellows away from the British camp. Butler agreed with him.

Finn talked Butler out of the Weddell Coast job and to go east or north instead. Butler agreed there should be no duplication. He asked Finn many professional questions and took Finn's judgment. Shortly after Butler left, the power went off. Latady came over and asked to use more gas. There was a great misunderstanding about using the gas on the hill which Finn feels must be saved for aviation. Finn straightened it out, as it has caused much bitching. At dinner Finn explained it and appealed for unity and good feeling. Lassiter, Latady, Jennie, and I went skiing on the glacier at night. There was a beautiful moon and a gorgeous night and we all had a wonderful time. The feeling when I came in the mess hall was not good, but I ignored it.

A skeleton crew of four men including the skipper Schlossback and Chief Engineer Hassage remained aboard for a couple of weeks longer to decommission the ship's equipment for her long period of idleness, but they took their meals ashore with us. We were becoming one unit at last and looked toward settling down for the long winter night ahead. Considering it had taken nearly two months to make the base livable for all hands, we had much to be thankful for. We had arrived safely in the Antarctic, our ship was frozen-in and the four men still aboard were laying up her deck and engine room machinery for preservation against the elements; our scientific program had begun, and our camp had been established. As Finn and I settled down in our small twelve-foot square hut adjoining the Bunkhouse, we were approaching a new period of the expedition, the winternight. Unfortunately, it did not start off too well. My diary explains why:

Wednesday, May 7, 1947

> *We awoke for breakfast and I started to straighten up the room, when Finn and Lassiter came in and wanted me to take a flight today. Nichols was going to fly too. After fooling around for a while, we finally got off. We had much trouble getting the plane skis off the snow, but finally Jim got off. He landed twice and then took me up for five minutes. We secured the plane and all skied down and had lunch. Harry came screaming in asking if I had flown. I said, yes. He said, "you had a nerve, you know our Washington agreement about women not flying". I answered, "don't you talk to me that way, if you have anything to say go talk to my husband". (In Washington, there had never been any talk about my going on the expedition, and at no time, then or later, was there any talk about my flying. I hold myself totally responsible for Jennie being there. When I finally decided to go, I alone wanted her to come. At first neither Finn, Bob Nichols, nor Harry wanted her to go.) I finished my work. I went over to the Mess Hall where I found Kelsey, and Nichols, looking on while Harry was hitting the ceiling and laying into Finn in a crazy manner. He was absolutely wild, saying, "don't you do anything Finn Ronne without consulting me". I lit into him. Finn said little, he was fascinated with the scene. Harry told me "to get out". I told him I wouldn't. He said he wouldn't speak to Finn again as he hated him. At dinner tonight, I told Jennie we didn't take the sheets and didn't appreciate her saying we had. Nichols is trying to settle things between Harry and Finn. Finn thinks the*

situation unbelievable. Kelsey thinks that Harry is cracked completely.

I wondered once again how I had ever gotten myself into this situation. All I had ever wanted was for the expedition to be a success. I was worried. It had become obvious that Harry had been undermining Finn for some time, probably starting when he first moved to the base and was in charge of clean-up activities. As third in command, it was his job daily to tell the group what Finn wanted done that day. Instead of backing-up Finn, he would say something like, "That's not the way I would do it, but that's the way Finn wants it done." What he had in mind, other than trying to make himself popular, or where he thought this disloyalty was going to get him, is hard to say. But obviously, it had to come to a head sooner or later. We began to remember what Harry's mother, Mrs. George Garrett, had tried to tell us before we left Washington. Her words began to make sense in that she had tried to alert us to his peculiar ways.

Thursday, May 8, 1947

Had breakfast, and soon after, Bob Nichols came over to try to straighten things out between Finn and Harry. Finn was firm, he said he wouldn't retract anything, as he had nothing to retract – he was the same now as two months ago and he wasn't going to get on his knees to that spoiled kid. We worked on the camp organizational planning, mealtime, light time, educational programs and entertainment. When I went over to check these rough drafts with Bob in Science Building, Harry was sitting there. He left to see Finn. Finn shortly came after me. I went back to Harry in our shack and he apologized to me for his actions yesterday. I said, "Forget it, Harry." Finn came in. We told Finn about Bob's approval of the drafted memos and I typed them up. After dinner, everyone was there, Finn read the notices and told Bill Latady to put them on the Bulletin Board. Nichols gave a good pep talk. We had a few minutes leisure before the movie, "The Flame of the Barbary Coast". It was good and we all went to bed happy and in good humor.

Saturday, May 10, 1947

After breakfast and straightening up here, Finn and I went out to the ship. Hassage and Ike were arguing about the laying up of the ship. Finn settled things there by telling Hassage to lay up the engines as he thought best. We brought in a lot of stuff from the ship and spent the afternoon putting it away. Harry was all sweetness and light. We had a good movie at night and turned in after 12 o'clock.

Sunday, May 11, 1947

Although we still had several large projects to complete before the winternight curtailed many of our outside activities, today our first planned holiday, celebrating the setting up of our camp. We got up for a late breakfast. And later in the afternoon, we had a bacon sandwich. Boy, was it good. I read for a bit and we worked around here. Bob Nichols stopped over. Finn went out to the ship to get the champagne. We had a wonderful dinner around 7:00 p.m.: chicken soup, chicken fried, mashed potatoes, two vegetables, and Chilean champagne. It was wonderful. Finn worked hard on getting the radio in our shack set up and we managed to get some good programs. Kelsey was over helping. Larry worked on the lighting. Harry came in and talked to Finn about the power supply, which is getting bad. They still haven't gotten the diesel fixed and they are now working it on aviation gasoline. Bob Nichols came in and suggested Adams to go on the trail. He also wanted to fly many personnel to the trail. Sig came in for a few minutes. We all had a cup of coffee. Sig and Nic left, Harry stayed and discussed the British situation at length. Harry wants to be extremely friendly with them because of the dogs, he says. Finn wants to be aloof and maintain our independence. Wind blew hard all day. Chuck Hassage pierced his ear with his ski pole as he sailed in from the ship.

In total secrecy Finn established the Post Office today, dating it as March 12, 1947 the day we had arrived..

Before leaving Washington, Finn had been asked by the State Department to set up a secret post office in case the United States ever wanted to lay claim to this area, where our citizens had already done much pioneer exploration. The Base would be called Oleona, after Oleona, Pennsylvania, where the noted Norwegian violinist, Ole Bull, had set up a town designed to encourage Norwegian immigration. Finn was sworn in by the Post Office Department as a fourth class postmaster, the first ever to serve in Antarctica, and he carried the appropriate rubber stamps and caches for canceling several covers with opening and closing dates. The opening date was the day we arrived, March 12th, 1947, and the closing date was the date we departed, February 22nd, 1948. Later he returned a set to the State Department and to the Post Office Department.

Monday, May 12, 1947

As Harry stayed until 3:30 am last night or morning, we didn't get up until shortly before lunch. Finn fixed bacon sandwiches and coffee. I fixed up the room and we went into the bunkhouse for lunch. Spent the afternoon making canvas curtains for the shelves and finished the window curtains. Finn moved the radio antenna, sealed the wall cracks, etc. I went to the first navigation class. Smitty is a good teacher and it was interesting. Jennie didn't know a thing. After dinner, Lassiter and Adams came over for a game of cards. Lassiter said he would like Finn to send in their request for active duty in the Army. We read them an outline of our proposed government report. They said, they would seriously consider being here another year by themselves with recruits if the government would take it after that. Harry and Sig came in for a few minutes. We had coffee and fruitcake. They stayed until 2:30 playing cards by Coleman lamp, which was temperamental. Still having generator trouble and lights are going on gasoline generator. Often I wrote by flashlight. Wind blew hard all day. They tried to get the rhombic antennas up, but it was impossible.

Up until this time, Kelsey had maintained daily radio contact with the United States from our ship's station. Now our first major job was to set up the rhombic antennas for our Base radio station, which was the stumbling block, and with all of the other projects going on at the same time it took awhile to complete. Harcly Peterson worked out a formula for the antenna, which would beam our output on New York and catch a bit of New Orleans as well. The first of four poles would be sixty feet in height and raised close to the Radio Room in the Science Building. The pole furthest away would be twenty feet in height and placed on the glacier near the top of our hill. The other two steel poles would be raised on either side of the glacier at the appropriate height so that the tops of all four would be at the same height in a diamond shaped arrangement. The poles had been assembled and wired. They were ready to be raised in position as soon as the wind subsided. This was a miserable all hands job. Swirling snow of the oncoming winter made it doubley important to watch and know where you were going. Decreased visibility caused our first accident.

Thursday, May 15, 1947

It stopped blowing and was the first good day. Lassiter, Adams, and Finn went up to the L-5 plane on the glacier and dug it out ready, to fly it down to the Bay Ice. The plane needed a new battery, so they couldn't get it started. I cleaned the shack thoroughly as we had asked some of the Britishers for tea this afternoon. It really looked nice. The five Britishers came, Butler, Tonkins. the Doctor Butson, and two others, Harry, Jennie, Finn and I. Sig made French cinnamon toast and coffee. We had lots of fun talking and laughing and they seemed to enjoy themselves, but as soon as dogs were mentioned, they began to say how terrible their situation was. We had dinner shortly after they left and Finn announced there would be no movie because of the power situation. Kelsey's gasoline was for Kelsey only and his broadcasting. Bill Latady gave a lecture on skiing. Finn listened for a while, but said it was elementary and came back to our shack. We read and chatted by Coleman lamp, which is good, but definitely not electricity. Harry came over about the dog situation, etc., but said nothing about any dogs from the British. Twice today Finn had called in all the men who were trail candidates and laid the desperate dog situation before them to do something about. They became very enthusiastic and promised to get right on it and start training those dogs that we had.

I went to Navigation Class and it was very interesting. I understand it all.

Saturday, May 17, 1947

Harcly was talking to Finn after lunch. Ten minutes after he left, Smitty came tearing in yelling that Mac fell off the glacier. He was in the water about 50 feet down from the top of the glacier cliff.

While stretching out guy wires to one of the poles, McClary walked backwards toward the edge of the glacier cliff. With a parka hood covering an alpaca lined cap, he was oblivious of the warning shouts of his co-workers, Nichols and McLean, and continued past some orange colored danger flags which previously Finn had placed approximately twenty feet from the edge of the glacier in order to call attention to the danger. With amazing concentration on his job, McClary walked backwards off the fifty-five foot ice cliff, accelerating downward at thirty-three feet per second. On the bay ice below, he crashed through two inches of newly formed ice and plunged into the frigid waters. The sheerness of the ice cliff prevented him from being rescued immediately. While managing to keep his head above water, he made futile attempts to grasp the edge of the newly formed bay ice, which continued to break from his grip. He was further handicapped still by having his right arm in a cast up to his elbow, as a result of a broken hand suffered in an accident aboard ship on the way down. The broken bone in his hand had healed and the cast was to have been removed the following day. Robertson, who has a very level head in an emergency, crawled quickly to the edge of the cliff on his stomach and, leaning over practically by his toenails, threw McClary two heavy climbing lines with bowline knotted loops at their ends. With some difficulty Mac managed to sling them around his waist. From the time of the accident until he was hauled to the top of the cliff by means of man and weasel power, only eight minutes had elapsed.

Once back on the glacier cliff, he was rolled in blankets and McLean cut away the soaked plaster cast with a hunting knife. When brought into camp Doc. McLean warmed his toes with hot water bottles, but kept his limbs at room temperature. Someone also called Butson, the British doctor. An examination revealed, he had lost sensation in all fingers and toes and one man was assigned to massage each forearm and calf so as to increase the blood supply in the extremities. The Doctors were careful not to rub the frozen fingers, as they are particularly vulnerable to injury at such a time. His sensation returned gradually over a period of weeks during which time the skin of the finger tips became marble white, indurated, and eventually pealed, leaving the tender digits more susceptible to freezing than before. Had the bay ice been thicker, as it was a few weeks later, he most probably would have been either badly injured, perhaps even killed from a fall of that distance. It was a narrow escape and a true miracle that he survived the fall and his session in the icy water with no ill effects except moderate shock and exposure.

Nichols said tonight that he was spokesman for five of the guys who wanted to name that Nelson McClary glacier. Utter stupidity deserves merit is the idea.

Lassiter set off two powerful charges of TNT and it blew out the stuff in the Medicine Chest. Lassiter refused to run the projector, so Latady tried to run it, but pretty badly. Harry revealed this afternoon that Butler felt Finn would not cooperate with him in the Weddell Coast job, etc. This was all news to Finn and it is obvious that someone from here has been over there shooting his mouth off – now Finn has to iron that out. Just another day in the Antarctic!

Sunday, May 18, 1947

We awoke late to a perfectly beautiful day. Finn announced at breakfast that he would take anybody skiing his way. Bob Nichols and he went off right away. Bill Latady mooned around for a while jealously and finally went up to the aviation cache with him. Lassiter and Robertson followed. Owen took a dog team up. I went out on the hill skiing with Fiske and Don McLean. McLean is doing fair. It was a wonderful day and we could see Adelaide Island from the top of the glacier. The snow was ideal, the best I have ever seen. Harry took Jennie's skis, so she didn't go. Mac went into her room to chat and the British Doctor came over at 2:30. Nichols came back with Finn and came in for a long chat with him about future trail plans. We told him the latest about Harry and the British etc. It was an excellent chat. He wants Owen and Dodson, excluding Latady for his trail party. At dinner Finn gave a talk about the dangers here surrounding everyone at all times and how fortunate we were that Mac was still alive. Lassiter and Adams came in for a bridge game at night. Sig joined us and we had a good time. They didn't get the plane down from the glacier to the bay ice because the batteries were down.

Monday, May 19, 1947

The day was snowy and dull. Harry went out to the ship. Finn had the trail people in for a chat on how to handle and drive dogs. They got much out of it and went over to finish the dog shelter. At lunch, Finn again called attention to the dangers, even so two fellows had crawled to the glacier's edge this morning. He said he couldn't impress upon them enough how dangerous this was. I worked on the report for a little while and then Harry came in. I went to classes while Harry discussed flight and trail plans with Finn. We had a quiz in Navigation in which I got 87 and Jennie 52. The radio class began, but I am not too sharp in code I can see that. I came back and Finn and Harry had had a good talk on plans. Harry kept mentioning Latady as such a good man etc. We had dinner and a show afterward, "Incendiary Blonde". It was about Texas Guinan and very good. Went to bed late.

Tuesday, May 20, 1947

Work went on as usual, Harcly on rhombic antennas, and the trail party working on the doghouse. Jennie and I went skiing in the afternoon. The British Doctor and the silent fellow were there also. The Dr. can telemark right, but not left. Finn helped on the rhombics. In the evening Nichols came over and discussed trail plans at great length.

Wednesday, May 21, 1947

Finn found out this morning from Bob Nichols that after Bob left here last night, Harry was waiting up for him and asked him, "Well what did Finn have to say tonight?" It irritated Bob and he very pointedly told Harry, "nothing". The old argument about building the passageway between our shack and the bunkhouse began again and I told Jennie that they had better be careful how they tried to cross Finn's wishes, as he took just so much of it. Jennie said she had begged Bill and Harry not to consider her and that she was very content and happy about it.

Finn went on board ship to find out about Kelsey's wishes with regard to a possible Darlington move to the Library. He specifically stated that when the power was in good order at the Base, he wished to be on every night, seven or eight hours. So that settles Harry and Jennie moving over to the Library, which Finn told Harry. Hassage plans to shut down the electrical system on board ship before he comes over to fix the diesel, which will take about three more days. There were no classes today.

Harry talked to Finn at length about installing the framework in the Norseman to take care of the trimetrogon cameras, if they found it more feasible to use the Norseman on long hops. There is more in back of the story than meets the eye, I am sure, but it is, of course, the practical thing to do. I worked all day on the Government Report (that Finn was proposing for future government activities in the Antarctic). After chow, Andy Thompson gave a talk on boxing. Andy was terribly funny. He simply can't say what he means in front of anyone. He gave a demonstration with Smitty and he was really good. Bob Nichols and Fiske tried also. Bob Dodson and Latady came over on Finn's invitation for a chat. We had a good time and I read the Government Report to them. They were most, most interested.

Thursday, May, 22, 1947

Awoke this morning to find it blowing very hard from the N.W. Harcly recorded up to 30 mph. The temperature was 21 during the day, but dropped to 8 Deg. at night. The drift was so bad in front of the Bunkhouse that Finn and I had a hard time getting over. The fellows could finally see why Finn wanted a passageway and, after last night's conversation with Bill and Bob Dodson, Bill began working on the door with Finn's help and direction. He was very nice about it. In the morning, the fellows were out working on the doghouse and repairing the damage done by the unexpected wind. Finn had warned them that this would happen, but they paid no attention and did it their way. Harry did not come over all day. I was Assistant. Mess Cook and after dinner we cleaned up and had a movie, "Her Highness and the Bellboy". Bob Nichols worked on the Government Report rather than see the movie. Sig came over for a short while. We had classes and navigation is getting much harder. Radio class is more interesting. I find them both very enjoyable..

The bay ice over the cove, on the opposite side of the glacier cliff was thick enough now to drive the weasel back and forth to the ship to haul additional heavy supplies to our Base.

Friday, May 23, 1947

The wind died down today and Finn started them all off this morning with a memo that all the stuff had to be brought in off the ship before it was decommissioned. He got everybody in on it and they took a dog team out to do the hauling. In the whole day, they got about two tons of stuff ashore and lots of bitching done. Latady, Mac, and sometimes Harry worked on the door to the passageway. Harry was mess cook and a good one. Harry came over in the afternoon and said something about Finn having taken over the diesel so he stepped out. I informed him Finn did not, but had merely talked to Chuck Hassage, who said he preferred to stay on the ship until the electrical system was shut down and then he would come ashore.

Last night, Kelsey got contact for the first time in three weeks, and got some traffic off before he had to shift to another band. Jennie is beginning to take an interest in the Library now. We had radio class and I am beginning to show some improvement. Sig announced at dinner no loose dogs should run around camp because of the loose food. Bob Nichols came over to discuss the Government Report with me. Finn asked Harry and Jennie over for a hand of bridge. Finn gave the Britishers 6 bags of Kasco Dog Food. Nichols was most anxious today for a four man sledge party to include Don McLean as the fourth member.

Saturday, May 24, 1947

The fellows didn't get out to the ship with the dog teams until after eleven o'clock. Finn was out there early and became pretty disgusted with them. He came back for lunch bringing stuff on his back. Bob Nichols claimed he had a fall on the ice and Don diagnosed it as a fractured rib. Actually, he got it in the boxing with Fiske the other night. He felt pretty lousy and stayed in bed all afternoon. Don McLean ran one of the dog teams and Bob Dodson and Owen the other.

I worked on the report and my navigation in the afternoon. We did not have classes, as the fellows were too tired. After a good dinner, we had a murder movie, "Hangover Square". It was gruesome. Finn left and the fellows wanted another picture. I figured if they wanted them that way and they could stay up until twelve anyway O.K. Lassiter went over to ask Finn who said O.K. We all came over after the picture, Jim and Chuck to play bridge. Finn was in his pajamas and mad because of the second show. I took up for the fellows that they didn't see that they were doing anything wrong. Finn snapped out of it and we played a rubber of bridge in which Chuck and Finn licked Jim and me.

Sunday, May 25, 1947

Finn and I slept late but breakfast wasn't until 12:15 so we made that. The darkness of the winternight, certainly manages to throw off the normal schedule of the working day. Finn began working on the passageway and Jim Lassiter came out to help him. Together they worked for about two hours. Jim came in for a cup of coffee and brought some cookies with him. We learned from his long visit a number of things, mainly, all the fellows have loot boxes which contain all matter of things. Fiske has the largest one. The ship's ice box contained 33 fresh eggs, which are now divided among three people. The fellows have been stealing small caches of liquor from one another. The guns and ammunition has not been returned. Nobody but Latady, Mac, and Woody pay any attention to Harry. Mac is really vicious. Hassage is very temperamental at times. The Nordun should not have trimetrogon installed in it. The Nordun has enough of everything to fly to the Pole and back from advanced base. Jim would also like to fly to Punta Arenas on return. Jim continued to say that Harry has done more harm behind Finn's back than anyone else.

We had a ham dinner and I worked code with Bob Nichols, who is really feeling lousy. He had now thrown his sacro-iliac out of joint somehow and had been taking codeine. You can tell he really feels badly. I worked much of the forenoon on Finn's book and it will really be a tremendous job I know. Harry came over and shot the bull after dinner for a while. Sig was here. Harry didn't stay long and Finn and I went to bed about eleven o'clock. Early for a change.

Schlossbach, Hassage, and Adams finished their work on securing the ship for the winter. These men had taken extensive precautions to ensure the utmost safety and preservation of the ship during its period of inactivity in order to guarantee us our only means of transportation back to the United States. Her construction was sufficiently strong to withstand any ice pressure the bay ice in the cove could force upon her sides. She was anchored in thirty-two fathoms of water and frozen into the ideal position with her bow facing southeast. This was a great advantage, since the strongest prevailing winds occur from that direction and, to a certain extent, prevented large amounts of blizzard drift snow from collecting on her decks.

When everything possible had been done to preserve the vessel for the conditions ahead, the last small group of men moved ashore the latter part of May. It was a miserable day as they trudged over the bay ice man-hauling their personal belongings on small light sleds. The temperature had dropped suddenly from twenty degrees F., to eight degrees, and a thirty-mile per hour wind was blowing all the loose snow in the vicinity into hard packed drifts around our buildings and outside equipment.

Monday, May 26, 1947

Finn started working early this morning on the passageway and Jim Lassiter helped him. I made the bed and started melting snow for water, because the water jacket needs fixing and there is no water from the melter. It snowed heavily the last two days and is now almost as high as I am in places.

Harcly was busy working on the rhombic antennas for Kelsey, who hopes to get a radio contact tonight which would be about the first good one in four weeks. Owen and Dodson with a dog team were hauling coal, which is fresh out. Ike went to the ship, which is dangerous because of the warm weather. The ice is weak and the snow on it high and heavy. Bob Nichols is still feeling pretty lousy. Seven puppies were born to Goldie last night, but four froze to death before anyone could get to them. Three are alive and cute as they can be.

The other three, one male and two females, were taken with Goldie to the warm fire in the Blubber Shack. A few weeks later, when they were running around, the two female puppies unfortunately got too close to an adult female dog and never lived to grow any older. The almost completely white male puppy, which was Goldie's sole remaining offspring, was promptly named Kasco and soon became the favorite of everyone in camp. Over the weeks and months that followed, other puppies came along, but Kasco was destined for special attention. This attention he accepted in his stride and proceeded to grow larger and stronger than any dog on the expedition. Certainly his paws were by far the biggest of all the dogs at an early age. Characteristic of his breed, he was as friendly and gentle as a lamb in spite of his size and strength.

I worked a great deal on the book. We had ice cream for the first time, made by Lassiter, at dinner this evening. While we were eating it the British Doctor Butson came in asking for Don McLean. He had some ice cream and then Don took over. He said Butler would be over the following morning. Sig came in for a short while. The lights were out and we went to bed fairly early for a change.

The great Antarctic winternight was now upon us and, whether we liked it or not, we were now well and truly frozen in.

First secret U.S. Post Office set up in Antarctica.

Finn poses for secret photo taken by Jackie, to establish existence of post office, for potential future land claims.

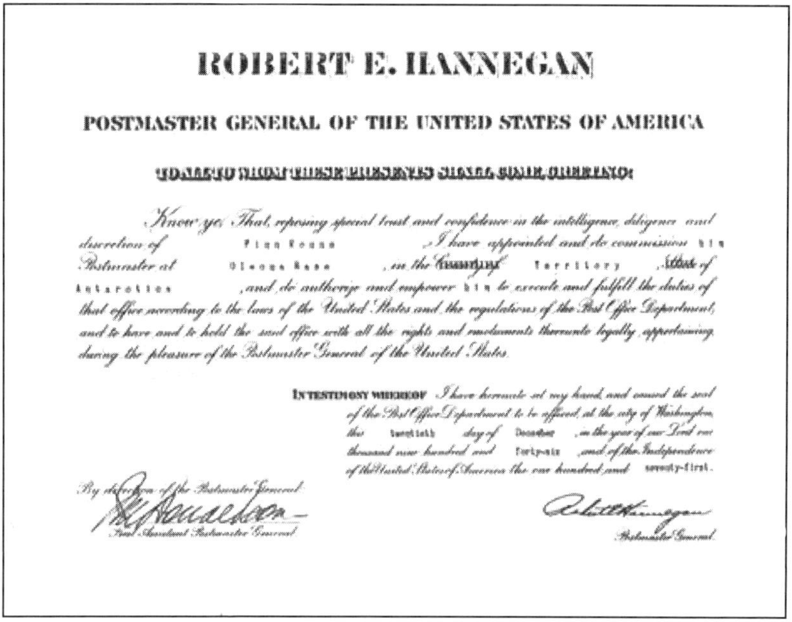

ROBERT E. HANNEGAN

POSTMASTER GENERAL OF THE UNITED STATES OF AMERICA

TO ALL TO WHOM THESE PRESENTS SHALL COME, GREETING:

Know ye, That, reposing special trust and confidence in the intelligence, diligence and discretion of Finn Ronne *, I have appointed and do commission* him *Postmaster at* Oleona Base *, in the* Territory *, of* Antarctica *, and do authorize and empower* him *to execute and fulfill the duties of that office according to the laws of the United States and the regulations of the Post Office Department, and to have and to hold the said office with all the rights and emoluments thereunto legally appertaining, during the pleasure of the Postmaster General of the United States.*

IN TESTIMONY WHEREOF *I have hereunto set my hand and caused the seal of the Post Office Department to be affixed, at the city of Washington, this* twentieth *day of* December *, in the year of our Lord one thousand nine hundred and* forty-six *, and of the Independence of the United States of America the one hundred and* seventy-first.

By direction of the Postmaster General

First Assistant Postmaster General

Postmaster General

A cover showing the "Oleona Base" cache. March 12, 1947, was the opening date of the post office and Finn's Postmaster Certificate

Port of Beaumont on Neches River in Beaumont Texas

This photo shows the front of a glacier close to the Ronne Expedition's wintering base.

VIII

Winternight

The winternight is that long stretch of cold and darkness, when the sun never rises above the northern horizon. During this period, the most miserable weather is usually experienced which confines activity mostly to indoor projects. Active men of varied backgrounds are forced to live in close proximity, with little exercise and no contacts, other than their everyday campmates. Each man must call upon his inner self to provide the stimulus to his interests, which he often may not receive from his associates. During this period, men's dispositions become tender and tempers flare over minor incidents which take on major proportions. It is the time, when the man himself is revealed perhaps for the first time in his life, and it is the most difficult period of an expedition.

Amundsen investigated his men thoroughly for six months prior to selection for his expeditions. The smaller the group, the more important it is to pick men who will get along well together. Every expedition leader has had problems arising from personnel difficulties and the reasons are not difficult to understand. Expedition life does not appeal to the average steady man, but rather to the individualistic, aggressive type who is attracted by the adventure and the unusualness which it offers. To live close together for twenty-four hours a day, day in and day out for weeks and months at a time, without any chance of getting away, would be difficult for any group even in civilization not to mention isolation.

Inside the camp, organization had been established by this time, and life was following a more or less daily routine. Aboard ship on our way down Finn studied the varied and different personalities of each man. He decided to select pairs of men with the least common interests to share each cubicle. On two previous polar expeditions, he had been subjected to lying awake night after night listening to great scientific discussions carried on by bunkmates, or just good friends chattering until the wee hours of the morning. To a great extent, he succeeded in eliminating this problem. One scientist shared a cubicle with one of the mates of the ship, another very talkative scientist shared space with one of the ship's engineers and so it went.

Around seven o'clock in the morning, the night watchman closed the huge icebox type door at one end of the building, and put an end to the cold air which had been rushing through the sleeping quarters since about eleven-thirty the night before. Fires were started in the small egg stove, the galley range, and Sig was called.

By eight o'clock, the men had partially emerged from their warm bunks and began performing a variety of acrobatics in their endeavor to get dressed as quickly as possible in the cold room. After Schlossbach moved ashore, he was in charge of running the camp, and had his own method of getting the late sleepers to their feet. Often you could hear him call "Hey, Hassage, get up, Robertson is up." Then immediately following came "Hey, Robertson! Hit the deck, Hassage is up." The scheme worked well for a few days but before long turned into mere routine. In any group of men, there are always a few who disturb the rest of others by talking in their sleep, which at times created most amusing situations. Many a time, Hassage was surprised to learn things about himself which were common knowledge to all, although he believed he had never told anyone.

The Air Force twins, Lassiter and Adams, were usually the first ones up each morning. During the winter night, dispositions were varied, nerves became frayed and tempers short, and breakfast table conversations can just as well be forgotten. As one man put it, "There should be a Continental Law that nobody be allowed to talk in the morning until after ten o'clock; by that time our grouches had been eased and we were fit company for each other." Hot cakes were the order of the day. They varied only by the amount of egg powder Sig put in them, increasing it daily until they nearly flew off the plate, then reversing it until they were just flour and water. After a pint of tomato juice and a full bowl of hot cereal had been consumed, I actually watched one of the men eat as many as sixteen hot cakes at one sitting. We had no shortage of butter or powdered eggs. As you would suppose, just about all hands began putting on weight, anywhere from five to forty-five pounds.

The daily maintenance of the camp itself afforded an endless number of routine jobs which had to be carried out through a rotation system, come what may. Mess duty was a task disliked by all. The married men, who had some experience in that line already, seemed to tackle the issue with greater surety but were equally lax in their zeal. Coal had to be supplied to all of the buildings. After each heavy blow the bags were well buried in eight-foot deep drifts, which called for a shoveling detail with the required amount of stamina in back of it.

Every second day, the ice brigade drove out to a large iceberg, which had been caught in our cove and frozen in place by the bay ice. They filled the weasel drawn sled with chunks of ice, which were towed back to the Base and dumped into the snow melter behind the galley range. The heat from the range warmed the surrounding water jacket, melting the ice, and in this way the camp obtained its water supply. There were numerous other menial tasks such as: sweeping the floors, and cleaning up the various buildings, carrying out ashes and garbage, etc., things which were tolerated by some and heartily disliked by others.

Our sense of values had begun to undergo a considerable change. We never thought of money for there was no use for it. We knew exactly where we would dine next and practically what the menu would be, i.e. steak six times a week. We were not bothered with traffic, crowds, shopping, income tax, or formalities of any kind. The men cut their own hair, grew beards, and if they missed a Saturday night bath, their conscience scarcely was troubled. But with twenty men living in one building, and especially when frequent blizzards and increasing darkness force all to remain indoors, monotony can easily prove to be an expedition's worst enemy. From two previous experiences, Finn knew that the winternight, which lay immediately before us, presented a formidable barrier, which has to be hurdled by all expeditions. The condition of the men in the spring, their viewpoint and interest in the expedition's common good is the determining factor for the success of any polar expedition where wintering is a necessity.

In isolation nothing can be concealed. Without the cover-up of civilization, weaknesses and peculiarities show up very quickly. The selfish motives of a few become glaring and temperaments clash. Hard work, set backs, and misunderstandings, produce situations continuously challenging to one's stamina. It is the old story of pioneering, only on a larger and more difficult scale. The challenge brings out the best in good strong characters and accentuates the worst in others, by reason of one's emotional and mental set-up, which is either an asset or a liability on such a venture. It is almost impossible to foretell those who will show the most stamina. During the war, the armed services often discovered that those whom they least expected to often performed the best.

It was essential to pick men with the ability and knowledge to accomplish certain objectives and Finn had been forced to make the selection without sufficient time or money to investigate thoroughly their suitability or temperament or emotional balance. Considering everything, we were very fortunate in our personnel as a whole.

It is true that we had many personality difficulties, but in spite of the hurried selection, these difficulties did not prevent the expedition from accomplishing its main objectives far beyond what had been expected. From my knowledge of some previous expeditions and conversations with many members of other expeditions, we probably had fewer problems than many groups under similar circumstances. Throughout history, they have all had major problems but never before had a woman been witness to the actions and reactions of men in the early history of the isolated Polar Regions.

Certainly it was the biggest challenge I had ever faced. I was angry that people could act this way, seemingly without good reason. It worried me constantly, and I was hurt, not for myself, but for how much it hurt Finn to be so utterly misunderstood on occasions. It became a very stressful time and I was always concerned as to what would happen next. In civilization you could get away from the constant bitching, but in isolation, you had to live with it night and day.

Fortunately the winternight is the period of time when the men must make the major preparations for the spring and summer fieldwork, and this factor is of considerable help. Keep men busy and you will keep them relatively happy. The program which our small group had confronting them was so extensive and wide in scope, that much real work had to be done if we were to produce good results. By the time the outside work had been completed, and the weather was no longer conducive to out-of-door activity, projects for the future field season had been begun in every part of the camp.

In the machine shop, Finn instructed Wood and McClary in the art of assembling and lashing trail sleds for the dog team parties. These sleds were made of hickory throughout and lashed together with rawhide, very similar to that used by Norwegian explorer Fritjof Nansen on his trip toward the North Pole in 1895, and they are well suited for hauling heavy loads with dog teams in Polar Regions. Dodson and Owen, assisted from time to time by Lassiter, Adams, and Smith, were in the harness business for quite a while during the winter. The dog harnesses were made from lampwicks. Dodson became an expert in the sailmaker's job of making the sledge tanks. When on the trail, all equipment, clothing, sleeping bags, radio trail set, and food are stored inside these tanks.

In the blubber shack, men worked in pairs making the dog pemmican for use on the trail. Nichols, Dodson, Smith, McLean, and Owen were the ones on this assignment. A total of three thousand pounds of dog pemmican was needed for use on the various journeys. Because the teams would be traveling mostly over terrain which contains no food such as seals for sustaining them, the sledges would have to carry the food for both the men and the dogs. Nichols was unable to do any heavy labor while recuperating from his broken rib, but was very anxious to see that the preparations for the field program were completed on time. He took over the tedious job of making trail flags, or trail markers as these small flags are sometimes called. These markers are of major importance to dog team parties wanting to retrace their tracks and of utmost importance when the party is traveling in a crevassed area. The rectangular flag markers are made of orange-colored light cotton material, and are sewed all around to prevent fraying.

The man food rations for use in the field also had to be made up during the winternight. All of the man food trail rations were made and assembled under the able direction of Sig Gutenko. Our cooking was done on a huge temperamental coal range. The most important item of the trail food was the pemmican. Sig is one of the few authorities on pemmican. He picked up his expertise during the United States Antarctic Service Expedition (1939-41). Upon his return from that expedition, they continued to improve the formula, making some changes, for use by the armed services during the Second World War.

It is grueling hard work for a sledge party to travel through pressure ice, crevassed areas, and to help the dogs with their heavy loads in climbing steep glaciers when the going is tough in temperatures at times as low as fifty degrees below zero. Eight hours or more of this hard work demands much physical exertion and the desire for a compact energy giving food is great. A highly concentrated food must be had which will furnish adequate heat and energy in addition to the essential vitamin and mineral factors, which also will not prove tiresome, and which at the same time will eliminate sluggishness in the digestion. Handy individual bricks of twelve ounces each make it extremely easy for the man in the field to prepare. I gave Sig a hand with the monotonous job of wrapping these bricks. It can be eaten raw if necessary, but preferably should be shaved into hot water to form, according to taste, a thick or thin highly nutritious soup, in appearance not at all unlike a heavy pea soup.

The second most important item in the trail diet is the biscuit, which consists mainly of oatmeal and whole-wheat flour. This provides a carbohydrate balance to the pemmican and offers something to chew on, as well as a substitute for bread. When the test batches were finished, the men tested them on short field trips in temperatures as low as forty degrees below zero, and the biscuit received a great many compliments – in fact for trail use or not, the supply disappeared completely.

Upon the completion of this work, the packing of the trail rations began and continued for several weeks. This was one job which Finn insisted the men who were to go on the trail perform themselves. With Nichols supervising, several of the men going on the trail packed the food bags. The complete ration in each large bag was food enough for one man for one month and is referred to in polar language as one man-ration. It weighed approximately 70 pounds and in 37 ounces of food per man per day it gives each man a total of 5,500 calories. This food which would be carried on the sleds is the only way for a party to exist when they are hundreds of miles away from their nearest food depot. Nothing must be left to chance, if the men are to have a fair opportunity of returning to their base. For this reason, infinite care to every detail must be given when making up the man food rations.

Dodson, with his many duties, was one of the busiest men in the whole group. He was the custodian of all clothing and miscellaneous equipment, caretaker of the dogs, and as ambitious as any in the general camp work. Finally, toward the middle of May, he was able to devote more time to his testing program to be carried out on the various types of equipment which the Air Force had sent along with us.

During the weeks that these tests were being carried on, the temperatures were generally about 25 to 30 degrees below zero F., and the wind often around 20 to 30 miles per hour, at times much stronger, and made for as good testing conditions as most climatic conditions will allow. When the men emerged from their outside living tents each morning and came into the bunkhouse for breakfast, their experiences and recommendations were noted by Dodson, and these experiments helped him to decide which items would be best suited for use on the trail. By this method, he was able to get a good and accurate check on many items such as sleeping bags, rubber mattresses, windproofs, underwear, fur socks, mushing boots, face masks, mittens, and other important items such as skis, ski boots, and ski bindings, which were also thoroughly tested. One can never be too certain – or cautious – about equipment carried when traveling in the Antarctic.

In spite of the hardships and dangers in the climatic and topographic conditions of Antarctica, the living conditions always have been considered one of the most healthful in the world. Certainly we were living testimonials to this fact. In spite of our fluctuating climate, which is hard on health in less-sterile environments, we were virtually an infection free group. We had no animal disease carriers, for there are no land animals; nor insect borne infections. Dogs do not even have fleas. The birds, our spring, summer, and fall inhabitants, come in contact only with fish, crustacean, and seals; and the temperature, which is usually below freezing, is unfavorable to the growth of bacteria. The danger of sickness lies in exposure to a new virile bacteria, which has never been contacted before and against which we have not had an opportunity to produce specific antibodies and antitoxins. Of course, we did have those bacteria that we brought along with us to which we had become immune. Many of the members brought along the common cold germs, and they were circulating around during the first month of the expedition's stay in the region. Also during that time, there were a few cases of sties, boils, and tonsillitis, and one case developed into pleurisy. This was the period when we were developing immunity for those infectious organisms carried by our companions. After a few months in the Antarctic, however, a person becomes well acclimatised, and it did not take long before we were each relatively immune to microbes found anywhere in camp. Vigorous exercise, invigorating air, much sleep, and freedom from vices and distractions of civilized society, built in us a more mentally straight and physically sound constitution on the whole. It was not until we returned to civilization that we became exposed to the ravages of virus and bacteria. Then they were more severe than exposure to infection under other circumstances, for the system of acclimatization had to be repeated on a larger and more gradual scale. Many of the men nursed bad colds upon our return to South America, while I did not sucumb until the middle of our reception ceremonies upon our arrival in New York city. However, there were certain medical conditions, which perpetuated themselves in spite of our isolation. A chronic sinus infection continued to be as debilitating for the duration as it was in the five years preceding the expedition, and one man continued to develop sties periodically as he had done in the past.

There was no decline in the progress of dental cavities. We recognized Arthur Owen one morning only because we were twenty-three persons who had been living in very close association with one another for some months. He turned a swollen cheek billowing like a cloud toward his twelve hot cakes and stated conventionally to McLean, "It hurts a little right here." Before long, Art found himself in an armchair with his head resting precariously on its under-stuffed back. When the tooth, extracted, lay in his hand, he claimed the ordeal was easier than in the States, and he is one of the few authorities.

Our food, while confined within the limits of the conventional polar diet, was plentiful, well balanced, and contained a sufficient amount of calories for maintaining a strong constitution. A great deal of fresh meat in the form of steak or beef five times a week eliminated any possible chance of scurvy, which rarely develops on the modern polar expedition. Bottles of vitamins were placed on the galley counter for the taking. Nearly everyone put on weight, as a result of the wholesome food and clean living. Kelsey gained 45 pounds in the first five or six months of the expedition. Interesting enough I lost weight as I tired of the steak and canned vegetables, but I don't recommend this experience to anyone contemplating a diet.

Although the three planes were secured for the winter, the five persons attached to aviation were kept very busy, both in their own field and in helping in other projects from time to time. A total of seven flights had been made during fall operations before the L-5 had been disassembled and stored for the winter. During the winter months, it was given an extensive inspection and all necessary repairs were made, The wings were completely recovered and unnecessary items such as landing and navigation lights were removed. The fuselage was also stripped in the same manner. The total weight removed amounted to approximately 68 pounds. The rear seat was removed and a platform 24 inches wide, and 68 inches long was installed for cargo carrying. A 10 gallon reserve gas tank was installed at the rear of the pilot's seat to give us a range of four hours, or four hundred miles. An automatic adjustable prop was installed in place of a fixed wood pitch to enable better take-off and cruising performance. Gloves could not be worn while handling tools as they limited the workers in many ways. When picking up tools with bare hands in temperatures of zero or below, you could lay a wrench down and walk away to find the wrench still sticking to your hand. Robertson survived the winter with a few blistered fingers.

Devices were built or revised during the dark months for use when flying over the mountainous terrain upon the sun's return. Latady and Robertson concentrated many long hours on the complicated trimetrogon camera installation for our Beechcraft plane. Their ceaseless efforts and untiring interest and determination were an inspiration and example to others for devising ways and means of doing things when some necessary material or additional personnel was not available. It should be remembered that at no time had an expedition ventured into the Frigid Zone with such a variety of projects on its agenda and with such a small staff to carry them out. There were only twenty-three persons charged with the responsibility of maintaining a camp, conducting scientific studies and investigations in geology, meteorology, seismology, terrestrial magnetism, solar radiation, atmospheric refraction, cosmic ray, tidal, and salinity observations. We were also carrying on a geographical exploration field program, which would include surface trail parties with dog teams and the operation of three airplanes for exploratory and aerial photographic work. This same group of men had been qualified to man and operate the vessel which traveled more than 7,000 miles to reach our destination.

Nevertheless, winternight is noted for its monotony. My Diary for a few days tells of the typical tedium that we experienced in our camp.

Tuesday, May 27, 1947

We got up early and cleaned up the shack as we were expecting Butler to call at his request. Jim Lassiter and Adams were working on the rhombics all day and completed them. Dodson and Owen had the dog teams out hauling, and they are beginning to work into shape. Chuck Hassage and Latady worked very late last night on the main diesel. They turned in, in a sleeping bag, in a tent for the rest of the night. The temperature went down to -18 degrees in the night, but in the morning, it came up to – 8 degrees. Andy Thompson recorded the first earthquake ever recorded on a seismigraph (a few others had been recorded earlier by other means) in the Antarctic during the night, and we sent the information to NANA. Kelsey got ten messages in, two from Kasco wanting dog stories to give publicity.

Butler came around 11 o'clock to thank Finn for the six bags of dog food. Finn took up the subject of cooperation. Butler denied what Harry had said about his first priority being the Weddell Coast. Finn said he would do the talking from now on for this group. Butler volunteered a dog team and driver for sharing results and the driver's experience with our equipment and methods and requested a member from here for their northern party. He said he could make two additional teams available for stand-by groundwork. They discussed this and agreed to think it over and meet at the British camp on Sunday to discuss it again.

I worked on Finn's book a while. We had classes and Harry went in to speak to Finn during this time. He said there was much work to do on the Beechcraft. Yesterday he had said there was not enough work to keep them busy. The movie was, "Murder My Sweet." Finn was unhappy because of three murder pictures in a row and walked out. I spent hours trying to convince him not to butt into this program. I felt strongly it was not worth the antagonism it would cause in trying to regulate their free time. Finn did take my advice as he usually did at such times. Bob Nichols came over and discussed the British proposal pro and con until three o'clock. They also discussed calling an aviation personnel meeting tomorrow and getting to the bottom of the confusion, plus eliminating using so much gasoline.

Wednesday, May 28, 1947

Awoke late because of being up so late last night. Worked on book. Finn worked on agenda for this afternoon's meeting with aviation personnel. After lunch Lassiter came in to talk while Finn went to the ship. I found out that Lassiter is fed-up completely with Harry but is hardly in a position to say much. Harry sent Jimmy Robertson over to the British two days ago to get some babbitt. Mac and Woody, with Adams and Lassiter listening, stayed up until 3 o'clock in the bunkhouse persuading Jorge he was not to wait on Finn. Lassiter overheard Harry say Finn does not do things the way he wants them done. Harry seems to think it is his expedition, and he is the one to be pleased (Some of the men would come in to talk to me alone from time to time in order to get their point across to Finn that way.

Finn held the aviation meeting, while I consulted Bob Nichols about the government report. Later Peterson came in and we read him the report. The aviation meeting was a success.

During the meeting, Ike said, "I know all about those mechanics. They open the hood of the engine and take a quick look inside, close it, and charge you $300." Robertson dryly said, "Well, a guy's gotta make a living!"

We invited Smitty, Owen, and Fiske in to discuss the government report. Latady came in to talk to Finn first. He felt he was very persecuted, etc. and they had a hard time at first. Latady claimed he didn't know whether or not he was photographer. He claimed Finn said he was a draft dodger (Harry was into this). He claimed he did all the odd jobs and Finn didn't like him. Finn explained to Latady that Finn knew Harry was undermining him with anyone who would listen. Latady agreed. Latady is a very capable, quiet man who is obviously in need of some recognition for all of the odd jobs he has done well. Finn promised him a memo outlining his work more specifically. Lassiter was very pleased with this afternoon's meeting. The other fellows came in and I read them the report. Sig came in later.

Thursday, May 29, 1947

We awoke late. Finn worked on the door. I cleaned up the shack and worked a bit. Bob Nichols came over for a while. After lunch, while I was at classes, Ike came in to talk to Finn about the plans. Ike felt more exploration and less flying around should be done. I came back from classes and he was still here. Bob Nichols came in to say Jorge and Sig were having a big argument, and Jorge had refused to work. Harry came rushing in with the same thing. Harry left to straighten it out and Ike left shortly thereafter. Bob and Finn started discussing new plans. Harry came in on the pretense of typing something on this typewriter, but you could see he wanted to get in on the discussion. Chuck Hassage came tearing in saying he didn't want to go south with the weasel. Finn did not try to talk him into it. Harry and Bob left. Finn and Chuck conversed leaving him to think it over and give Finn a decision at a later date. The story behind it was Jennie had teased him about walking to the South Pole with Nichols. While he was here, they tacked a notice on his bunk, "Have gone to the South Pole."

We had dinner and later a movie, "Twice Blessed." It was very good. Chuck Adams and Lassiter came over. Adams cut Finn's hair and Finn cut Adams'. We played cards for a while. Lassiter said the Chief Test Pilot at Kelly Field, after sizing him up, refused to fly with Harry in the Norseman. Peterson came in with the request to try his General Electric stuff, as weather conditions were perfect. Finn gave his O.K. Harcly came back later with very good results. He stayed and talked for a while.

Friday, May 30, 1947

Decoration Day – only nobody realizes it. Sig had trouble with the stove and with water so he didn't make breakfast until 2 o'clock. He called the fellows very late. Bob Nichols got up about eleven and came over to discuss plans with Finn. I straightened up, melted snow, and washed dishes. Finn worked on the door. We had lunch. The diesel was having trouble, there was no water, no radio contact, no work was being done, and the heating stove in the bunkhouse fell over on the floor. Things have been most discouraging!

Saturday, May 31, 1947

We got up late and had breakfast in the shack. Finn talked to Fiske about night watch and cutting down the stealing of food. We made up a memorandum on night-watch duties and also one to try and eliminate the stealing of food. There was no shortage of food, but some enjoyed hoarding for extra snacks now and then. Finn also did the report of conversation at the aviation meeting held on May 28th. Harry came in with a lot of drivel, as usual, about I told you in Washington and I told you in Beaumont, etc. Nichols was in discussing plans. Lassiter came in to approve a memo on aviation. Art Owen and Bob Dodson came in and discussed the dog situation for future plans. They now have fourteen dogs to be used, nine of which are excellent. Kelsey got a contact and we got some good messages. There is a great deal of publicity work to do and I must concentrate on it for the next few days..

Sunday, June 1, 1947

We awoke very late and had breakfast about 11:30 AM in bunkhouse. Found Art Owen, Latady and McLean had started off at 9 o'clock to climb Neny Mountain. Finn came back to work on his plan for the British meeting this afternoon. We went over at 2 o'clock. We had tea first; all the fellows were as polite and as interested in us as could be. Butler had gotten out of his northern commitment and wanted to work on the Weddell Coast. Finn outlined the plans as though we could do it all ourselves, without the help of their dogs. But if we took a Britisher, we would need an extra team. They were eager for us to have a Britisher and to take an American on their trip south. Finn invited them to a movie Thursday night. We came back and told Nichols the results. He was very pleased. After dinner, Finn announced the whole preliminary tentative plan to the fellows, along with tentative personnel selections for the sledge parties. Nichols, Dodson, Owen, and a Britisher for Weddell Coast. McLean to go with British party, Hassage, Fiske and Smith on weasels. McClary and possibly Wood to take Peterson to set up the Plateau weather station. All were terribly pleased and much interest was shown in plans. We invited Robertson, McLean, and Thompson over for a chat. I read the report Finn was preparing to send into the Government about the work we were doing and proposing that it be continued subsequently by others who could replace us. Finn gave Andy his liquor back and we all had a drink. It was a most successful party. They were all flattered and pleased, particularly Robertson. We laughed and talked about Panama and Chile. They left around 2 o'clock.

Monday, June 2, 1947

We woke up fairly early and had breakfast here in the shack. I began immediately to work on typing the final copy of the government report for Kelsey to get out on the radio tonight. We had lunch and I continued my work. Finn worked around here on his plans. I went to navigation class. It is getting harder definitely. I came back and finished the report. Kelsey came in and we had a chat as to what were the most important things to get out. I turned the report with all its copies to various government agencies over to him to send out on the radio. Lassiter certainly hates Harry. It was Harry's birthday today. Jennie made a cake and ice cream. Lassiter was pretty sour. He talked to Finn about the plans and what the Norseman could do. He also is interested in making a parachute jump with Adams, if he makes a jump. We had a big dinner and party celebration.

After dinner, something mighty interesting happened. McClary, of all people, came in to have a talk with Finn about his chances for the trail. It was really funny and a bit pathetic in view of all of his vicious underhanded nastiness discrediting Finn to date. He is really disappointed that he isn't going on the trail. He didn't want Finn to think he was shirking work – what a laugh. He stated his great interest in going and disappointment at not having been selected. Finn told him personalities did not count in this case, because it was to his advantage to get the best men out in the field.

Tuesday, June 3, 1947

Awoke late and had a stream of people tearing in and out all day. Bob came in about hearing the story on Mac. Harry interrupted the conversation. Sig came in later. Finn helped with training the dog teams and Lassiter and Adams chatted here with me for several hours about future plans and Harry etc. We had navigation class. When I got back Harry was here with Finn. Finn didn't want Ike to fly with Lassiter. Harry did. Finn said Ike's health was too bad. Harry said, "O.K. Keep him here with the ship which is a perfect excuse." We all agreed. Harry wanted Bill Latady to fly with Lassiter because Bill could do anything including aerial navigation. Now Bill knows no more about navigation than I do and, of course, Harry just wants to prevent Adams from flying with Lassiter.

We had dinner late as usual. Then an English movie followed, "Night Must Fall." It was terrible – just awful. We came back and talked with Sig until late. I worked a great deal on the dog story.

Wednesday, June 4, 1947

Up late with breakfast here. Bob Nichols came in after lunch. Harry followed shortly after. Bob previously admitted if Mac had acted the at Tuff's College the way he has, he would have kicked him out. Harry discussed Jorge, his lack of interest in mess cooking, his interest in radio, then a sudden unexplained leakage of messages from the radio room, probably by him, etc. Everybody felt Jorge had to have something to inspire him, in order to keep him out of trouble. Harry had Kelsey come over, and Finn talked to him about preventing leaks on the radio messages, as well as preventing people from racing through his shack to the Photo Lab. etc. Sig came in for a while.

Don McLean came over and upon request for information, told Finn that Ike was not fit to fly. Latady came in to show the pictures, which he had printed. About four were of Jennie and one lousy one of me. While all this stuff was going on, I was trying to work on the dog story, which I finished roughly. We had dinner. After dinner, Lassiter came in to say he had a big blow up with Harry up on the hill today. Jim says Harry punched three holes in the L-5 wing unnecessarily, and he told him a few things and offered to fight it out. Harry, of course, said the canvas was so rotten, he just touched it. Robertson gave him hell. I foresee another blow-up with Harry anytime and this will be final.

Thursday, June 5, 1947

Got up and straightened up shack pretty well, cause the British are coming tonight for a movie. I washed a few things. It blew some last night and made the snow drift in a different direction. The snow is packed pretty hard now and the skiing is good. Bob Nichols came in after lunch and talked about trail preparations. Harry came in and had an argument with Nichols about Dodson and Owen. Harry doesn't like them.

We got a message from Sir Hubert Wilkins last night. I worked on things around here and started to type the dog story. Sig came in and Mac and Wood. They all had a cup of coffee. I finished knitting my yellow socks to accomplish something while listening. Harry came in and discussed plane flights. I got dressed for tonight. Nichols came in reporting what he had accomplished with the fellows in field preparations. Bob Dodson came in and I read him the dog story. We had a hurried dinner and the British came over after dinner for a show. We had a glass of Rhine wine before the movies. Then Jim showed, "Incendiary Blonde." Jim made ice cream, and we all froze eating it. Nichols said the British doctor might go on the trail. Butler did not come because he had to take care of the radio schedules. Tonkin came over to our shack for a chat afterward. He suggested Butler come over to discuss things with Finn tomorrow. The British were not as nice a looking group as our fellows. All British seem to have bad teeth.

Friday, June 6, 1947

Awoke very late, had lunch, and came back for a talk with Major Butler. The British are very excited about cooperation. Butler and Tonkin stayed up all night figuring out a way to get their commitment to Hope Bay taken care of. They don't see how they can make Tricorn. Finn suggested the possibility of depositing a cache for them at Darlington Island. Butler was excited and grateful. They had a nice chat. Harry was sick today with upset stomach. Nichols came in and talked over with Finn the same old stuff. I got nothing done. Kelsey got the report out last night. I gave him the dog story tonight. We had dinner. Sig came over, we talked about a lot of nothing, and I was tired and disgusted because I am getting such a little bit done these days but when people are here I can't do much but be polite.

Saturday, June 7, 1947

Kelsey didn't get anything out last night. He got incoming messages for us from Carl Eklund, Larry Gould, Assistant Secretary of Navy, and Kay and Ed Sweeney, all with good news. Finn and I worked here all day long with very few interruptions. I got a story on summary of six weeks activity written for NANA and some more on the book. Finn worked on Latady memo for pictures and plans, somewhat. We had a nice dinner and a movie later, "Zombies on Broadway." It was really lousy.

Lassiter and Adams came in afterwards and we played cards and talked until 3 AM. Sig was here and made us good tuna fish sandwiches. Adams and Lassiter really have it in for Harry. Lassiter and Finn worked out weights for a Pole hop after the Weddell Sea coastline. They were both very enthusiastic about it. Finn just listened. Many of the fellows are sleeping nightly in the various tents, testing them for the trail and also for the Army. Jorge slept 18 hours in a sleeping bag and tent. He was too cold to get up, he said.

Sig and Jackie in galley wrapping pemmican that he made for trail parties

Jackie tended to normal activities,
like relaxing with a cigarette in her hut.

Bob Nichols, Finn and Captain Ike Schlossback planning a field party to King George VI Sound

Jackie working on articles about the expedition for the North American Newspaper Alliance while Finn plots aerial flights into the unknown

Jackie tended to normal activities, like making coffee on the primus stove in her hut.

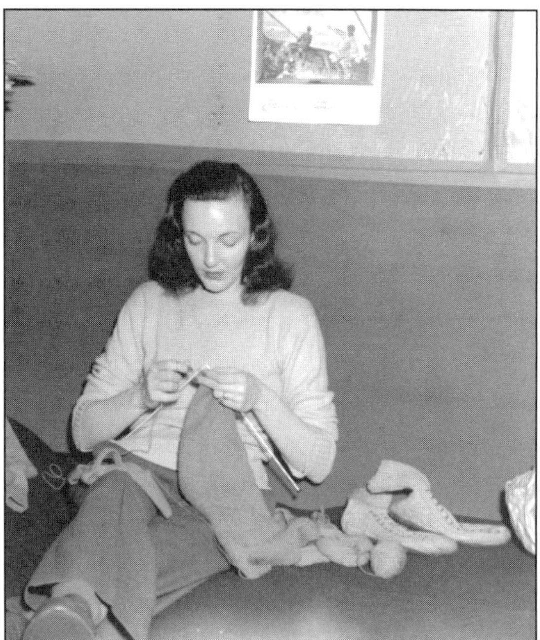

Jackie passed her free hours knitting with supplies she picked up in Chile.

IX

Problems Deepen

For, the most part, I purposely kept myself isolated in our quarters. First and foremost, I did not want the men to feel I was spying on them. As the wife of the leader, I was in a difficult position. I did not want to interfere with their work or butt into their bitching sessions. I never heard a curse word or a dirty joke on the entire expedition and I was always treated with respect. The men knew where I was and if they wanted to see me, they came to our shack to do so, and many did from time to time.

Most of the members of this research expedition had been chosen for their ability to do a particular job rather than for their previous polar experience, so nearly all were unfamiliar with the best methods of remaining comfortable and safe in extremely cold conditions. Those who had been in the polar regions before, tried, in an organized manner, to give the others the benefit of experiences which had been learned the hard way, so that in turn they would be capable of carrying out the jobs ahead safely and efficiently. In the beginning, very few of the men knew anything about the programs which were to be undertaken by the others. To alleviate this situation and to enable closer cooperation, talks were given on all the pertinent subjects. The plans of the aviation mapping program, geological, survey, exploration, the other scientific projects and how they fitted into the overall picture, as well as trail procedures and the mandatory safety precautions, were discussed so that the common goal of complete success could be reached through the cooperation of all concerned.

Each afternoon at four o'clock, all the men who were to participate in the field program stopped work on their various projects and attended two, one hour classes each day, in celestial navigation taught by Smith, and radio code taught by Kelsey and Fiske. These classes continued for eight weeks. There were about ten persons in the navigation class and about seven in the radio class. I attended the lectures regularly not because I intended to go out into the field, but because I greatly enjoyed them. McLean then gave lectures on First Aid, Peterson on meteorology, and Nichols described the geological aspects of glaciers and other terrain likely to be encountered in the field.

Our time was pretty well occupied with expedition work, yet the whole situation had its lighter side. Our necessary room perched on the the top of a cliff which dropped precipitously to the bay beneath offered such an example. While in the Bunkhouse taking to a group of the men one very windy afternoon, one fellow blew in the door and took over the conversation. He described having just come from the outhouse and demonstrated his attempt to get rid of his toilet paper by tossing it down the hole just as he was getting up. The paper blew up, so he grabbed it and tossed it down again, but the strong wind blew it back the second and third time. By now we all were hysterical because it was a familiar experience to everyone.

The skipper was definitely a character and was one of our best assets as a morale factor. His good nature and witty outlook on life created an atmosphere that all enjoyed. Ike's personal cup was ever a source of amusement. It was not especially fancy but rather a plain ordinary enamel job of pint size capacity. That particular cup got lost more than any other single item on the ship or at the base, which is saying a great deal. Each morning Ike began with "Who took my cup?" He put one of his sleuths on the case right away and the cup would be discovered either rolling about on the floor or miraculously hidden in his bunk amid various tools, towels, socks, and other items. This cup meant as much to the skipper as his sextant at sea for it had such varied usage. In it he heated water, soup, and coffee. When our water supply was low, it melted ice. It was never washed except by volunteers and then without Ike's consent. When such a deed was discovered, Ike went off mumbling "I was just getting that cup nicely coated so that all I would have to do is add hot water to make coffee and somebody's gone and washed it out again."

We all welcomed the relaxation provided by movies three times a week in the Bunkhouse. When our supply of fifty films was exhausted, some few movie films produced in 1935, 1936, and 1937, were found encased in six feet of ice left by the previous expedition and were used to supplement the ones brought by us. Those films had become brittle from the ice but other than that were well preserved. After all the films had been seen, the repeat performances were equally well attended. One scene in particular always amused us – a monotone professor describing a weekend sealing expedition to an island not far from the California coast drawled "And so we were off to great adventure." The remark hit home. Since Lassiter's nearest competitive theater was thousands of miles to the north, the audience showed great appreciation regardless of the quality of the film selected. The British members of Base E were invited over and either homemade ice cream or doughnuts with coffee was served after the movie was over.

Our well stocked library was in great demand, and many of the men took advantage of the encouragement given to write articles on their various fields of interest, which we sent out on the radio under their own name to the North American Newspaper Alliance for publication in a circuit of papers in the United States and abroad. Physical competition between the men was very popular as a subject for relaxation. Everything from pressing hand weight on a scale to Indian wrestling offered opportunities for diversion. The drop of a hat would bring on a spontaneous boxing match. Thompson, who had boxed while in college and later in a couple of professional matches, gave a hilarious lecture on the history of boxing as a sport and this increased the interest considerably.

Our weather was a big subject, full of the extraordinary and the unexpected. There was no complaint of sweltering days – Antarctic gales, low temperatures, and persistent snow were so far from the ordinary as to defy exaggeration. The polar sun cycle, the high polar plateau, and the warm South Pacific Ocean exposed our site to amazing weather changes. For two and a half months at our southern latitude in the winter, the sun never rose above the horizon. At noon there is faint twilight, but flashlights are needed for careful outdoor work. Moonlight was our best outdoor illumination and outside activities were planned more around the lunar cycle than the solar cycle. With clear weather and a full moon, visibility was phenomenally good. Every other two-week period the moon rises twice a day without going below the horizon. This phenomenon is extremely colorful. You can see the moon rise in the north in early afternoon and set in early evening, only to rise again in the southeast at night and then set to start the cycle all over again. Life is truly beneath the southern moon. Looking from one high mountain toward another, one can see clearly for more than two hundred miles. But when the moon is down and the skies are overcast, visibility is dangerously deceptive. The shadowless twilight blends sky, snow, drifts, crevasses, and precipices into a diffused nothingness. Safe ground travel is possible only at the end of a firmly held rope. One dull morning after a strong blow had re-situated the snowdrifts, Robertson ran outside to take a look at the planes. The low overcast made the visibility impossible. Three yards from the front door, he ran right off a five-foot snow bank and fell flat on his face. His censored remark to a few laughing onlookers was, "Disconcerting, isn't it?"

With clear skies during the sunless winter, the terrain radiates so much of its heat to the cold atmosphere above that objects actually cool below the air temperature and accumulate a deposit of hoarfrost several inches thick. This was a great strain on our antenna wires. After a while, the air would cool too and condense out a shallow blanket of ice crystal fog. Our coldest temperatures are reached during such radiation cooling. On cold still days when the temperature hovered around thirty degrees below zero F., and the sky overhead was clear as a bell, the stars were as brilliant and as numerous as I have ever seen. Directly above was the Southern Cross. The moon lit up the surrounding country and the spectacularly beautiful panoramic view revealed the high, snow-covered mountains encircling camp like somber ghosts and the shiny whiteness of the glacier leading up to the six thousand foot high Plateau. There is an indescribable coldness, and wild, forbidding beauty prevailing over the whole scene which can be found no where else in the world. On many such nights we enjoyed moonlight skiing on the glacier.

But there is another type of winter weather: the Antarctic blizzard coming down from the Plateau. During the months of June and July, these frequent blizzards also called katabatic winds raged over the area. The first warning we got was a fresh breeze from the southeast. Billows of snow were soon whipped up by the wind pouring off the Plateau crest twenty miles distant. The turbulent air beneath and the snow falling off the Plateau precipice hit the terrain underneath with a huge splash like a waterfall. Within an hour a gale would arrive at the camp with velocities upwards of forty miles per hour. Peak velocity clocked by Peterson in a minute was eighty-seven miles per hour. Only those who have spent a winter on the Antarctic Continent can fully realize the violence such storms can have. For many days and nights, endless winds howl and whistle through the ventilators and stovepipes giving you the feeling of living in a wind tunnel. The wind might stop for just a moment, only to start seconds later more intense than ever. On such days, it is hazardous to go outside for fear of getting lost. Any loose snow that may have fallen since the last blizzard is borne up into a blinding fury by the terrific force of the wind, beating so incessantly upon you as to forbid your facing the wind. Huge drifts pile up behind any obstacle and footsteps become obscured in seconds. Several such gales completely smoothed over a sixty-five foot glacial precipice, which we were able to use then as another ski hill. Only the feeding of the dogs and the most necessary outside tasks were performed on such days, for even with sealed windproofs and facemasks, it was a strenuous and miserable job. Fortunately we were spared extreme cold from these gales, for they must descend the 6,000-foot Plateau before reaching camp and are thus warmer like the Foehn winds off the Rockies. Ten to twenty degrees F., were the usual temperatures that blizzards arrived at the camp. The building entrances were covered with drifts up to ten feet high. As early as June, the buildings were well surrounded by snow, which acted as insulation to give more shelter and warmth.

Daily meteorological observations brought Peterson outside. This chore consisted of reading an elaborate instrument, a precipitation collector, and a snow stick three times each day, in addition to pilot balloon runs which were followed far into the stratosphere. To make his work possible, he improvised a pretty warm "Zoot suit" from a bright yellow life raft ensemble. Then to protect his head and yet have the needed visibility he made a Plexiglas dome with a special vent to alleviate frosting. No one had seen him make this "man-from-Mars" creation and he got quite a kick out of suddenly surprising his friends. Even the dogs were excited.

But there was an amazing contrast to the unfriendliness of the blizzards and occasionally, we had an unusual warm winter snowfall. When the cold southerly winds subsided a northwest wind picked up, bringing in warmth and moisture from the South Pacific Ocean. All were surprised, when in the middle of our winter month of July, temperatures shot up into the thirties and once we even had rain. A succession of warm fronts shot out temperature from minus thirty-six degrees below zero F., in an unprecedented jump to plus forty degrees, or a total of 76 degree change within a few hours.

Sunday was set aside as a day of comparative rest and relaxation, from the week's arduous work schedule. However, there were different opinions on how to relax. Latady, inspired by the view of Mount Aconcagua at Valparaiso and Mount Sarmiento near Cape Horn on our way down, and several other members of the expedition who were enthusiastic mountain climbers, bided their time until suitable opportunities arose. They certainly had no shortage of subject matter. Latady, who was thoroughly familiar with the techniques of winter mountaineering, was the leader of this group, and a number of peaks in the general area were climbed from time to time.

Sunday, June 8, 1947

We watched the mountain climbing group go up Roman Figure Four Mountain with two Britishers along with McLean, Fiske, and Owen. Finn worked on typing the plans and is beginning to think the weasel operation should be discarded. Sig was in for a short while. Harry, who was better from his stomach ailment for the first time today, came in for a while. He seemed to be in a pretty good humor. Bob Nichols came in to discuss plans. Finn is thinking more strongly of throwing the weasel plans out. Harry stormed in again worrying about Latady's climbing party and wanted to go over to the British to see if they were back there. Finn said no! We had dinner and Finn asked Robertson to come in and discuss weights. Nichols and I played rummy. Then Harry and Jennie, Nichols and I played Oklahoma for a while in the bunkhouse.

(Although I had been an active mountain climber before coming down here, I did not participate in any of these climbs, as it remained a man thing.)

Latady and the rest arrived with glowing tales of their trip, which was technically a very hard climb. They climbed the Pyramid instead of Figure Four. Jorge said he climbed Figure Four last night alone, but Bob and Jennie pressed him and caught him in a lie. When Robertson came out from talking to Finn, Harry asked, "Where did he come from?" (just as though no one should see Finn without Harry's permission.) I said, looking at him in a surprised manner, "Finn's." He got my look and said no more. We broke up the card game and I went back to the shack. Latady was telling Finn about their thrilling trip and was glad the fellows did not come out to search for them. Nichols came in later and continued to discuss plans and cooperation with the British.

Monday, June 9, 1947

Got up late and cleaned up the shack, for Butler was coming over today. Harry was sick again today and Finn found out for the first time that the rumor was circulating that Harry has been drinking for some time. That explains his inconsistent, stupid actions, somewhat. Finn found out that the harp on the issue room lock on the ship had been broken. At lunch, we saw McLean coming out of Harry's room. Jennie was definitely embarrassed when we asked her if Harry was sick again. Finn found out all the fellows in the tents overslept today and the beautiful day was wasted. The bearing of the diesel burned out again and it will take at least three days to fix.

Butler came over at 1:30 to discuss plans. Finn asked him to make calculations to take McLean with them the entire way to Tricorn. Butler, Tonkin, and Freeman are now making this trip. The British doctor will remain close to base. Finn has promised to deposit one cache, probably at Morency Island. Butler wants to cooperate with our meteorological station on the Plateau. Finn was willing. We talked about politics, etc. and the meeting was very friendly. Sig made a cherry pie for us.

We had dinner. Bob Nichols came in and chatted. He decided to go off night watch, because his rib was hurting him again. Don McLean came in and Finn told him the good news about him from the British. Don was very pleased. Finn asked him what was wrong with Harry. He said gastritis from excessive nervousness and probably from drinking before. He is on a diet and has stomach pains. Don thinks Harry is pretty scared about it. Fiske came in and chatted. Finn implied to him that he was doing too much, dog harnesses, sewing machine, weasel, radio, meteorology, electric wiring, Sig's food, studying law, and mountain climbing. He insisted he was not and would be able to get it all done. Sig and I had nice ham sandwiches and then he left about 12:00. Hassage, on night watch, told Finn the evaporator on the ship worked well. He just pretended it was broken to prevent Mac and Woody from taking showers every night. Temperature was -5 degrees.

Tuesday, June 10, 1947

We were up early this morning. Finn went in the bunkhouse for breakfast and brought me back hot cakes, to which I added bacon. Sig came in and the three of us chatted while I straightened up the shack. Harry and McLean were out digging up the tractor sled and Smitty, Owen, and Dodson had the dog team hauling coal, oil, etc. These dogs are terribly funny to watch. Finn usually has to go out and help the fellows who are working as hard as the dogs. It was still dark at 10 o'clock this morning. Bob Nichols came in for a few minutes. Finn was irritable. I worked all afternoon on the book and figure I have the first draft finished on about l/10 of it. Kelsey wrote Finn a very formal note about Peterson's taking copper wire for the amusement antenna. Peterson rushed in to explain his part and his stand in the matter. Finn told Kelsey and Peterson to come in together. He offered them both a piece of pie, but couldn't get them to make up. Kelsey said he had severed relations with Peterson, that he had taken all he intended to from him and he intended to have the materials he needed, when he needed them. Peterson said Kelsey was a disgusting, dumb, idiot and he'd like to poke him in the nose, etc. They would not speak directly to one another, but through Finn only. It was really funny and Finn had a hard decision to make.

Bob Nichols came in again and Finn was angry cause Dodson, Owen, and Mac had wasted the afternoon fooling around on the Bay Ice, instead of helping out around the base, so he called them in and told them so. We had dinner late. Harry came in took a look at Finn's aviation plans, said his figures were off and he wished Finn would consult him instead of other people in the aviation program, as he didn't intend to let the planes take off overloaded. We found out at dinner that it was Nichols' birthday. We asked Lassiter, and Adams to bring in some ice cream, and with Sig we gave Bob a toast with some of the Rhine wine. He appreciated it very much cause he was really low about his rib, which continues to hurt him.

Wednesday, June 11, 1947

Was tired this morning, got up late and straightened up around here. Worked most of the day on the book. Harry came in and in the course of thirty minutes made a number of statements, which didn't make sense. He said there wasn't enough work to keep the men busy and then discussed all the work there was to do and said the trail work wouldn't be finished. He wanted to use the scientists every third day to get ice. They are the ones who are very busy. He said there was much work to be done on the Beech, but he keeps pulling Robertson off for something else. He said he wished Finn would consult him on the plane figures as he had all the information and that Finn's figures were all wrong. Finn asked him to make up some and compare notes. We had a movie at night, "Return to Bataan." It was very good. Finn went over to the science building at 12:00. The lights were still on and he asked Hassage to turn them off. Robertson said "We can't even sit here and read a book" and then started bitching about Sig because he wouldn't give them tea. Sig has the tea here and lots of it, but won't give it until Fiske brings out his alleged cache of it.

Thursday, June 12, 1947

I was very very tired and didn't get up before noon. Finn was up early and with Harry straightened out the tents in the machine shop. They put one up outside our shack on the hill. After lunch, I did my navigation problems. Tomorrow is the last lecture on the theory. Monday, Dodson shows us how to use a transit. It has been most interesting and I have enjoyed it. Finn spent the whole afternoon typing up plans. Our radio was working well, so we had it on most of the time. Finn got a Norwegian news broadcast on U.N.R.R.A. from Oslo. We get Canada very well. Heard Truman make a speech in Ottawa. The weather was pretty warm today, but cloudy. The darkness is very pronounced now. Gets light about 10:30 and dark at 2:30.

Harry came in while I was at Navigation class. Finn told him he understood Harry had discussed the weasel with Chuck Hassage. Harry said sure, he would discuss anything with anybody. Finn said that was just the way he felt too, that he felt he could call anybody in and discuss anything with them and that included aviation matters. I came back from navigation and Harry left soon after.

We had dinner and Bob Nichols came in afterward, as did Sig. It was the same old conversation – would they be ready for the trail in time. Bill Latady gave a lecture on the techniques used in mountaineering. It was very good and he certainly hit at Jorge's supposedly going out alone. He said everyone should tell someone before they left camp, where they intended to go. The fire went out early in our little pot belly, coal burning heating stove, so we went to bed early.

Friday, June 13, 1947

Awoke late, Finn brought me breakfast in bed. I read Amundsen's book practically all day. It is most interesting, that must have been an almost perfect expedition – quite a contrast with some of the personalities we have along, although Amundsen also had problems with Johansen, who criticized Amundsen and later, after the expedition, committed suicide on a street corner in Oslo.

Finn worked on a memo to Harry, requesting him to give a detailed outline of the aviation program. There was a great discussion about the tea. Finn went on board the ship and got the lock fixed in the Issue Room. He found there 27 tea bags around loose. Lassiter and Finn got the eggs in the Paint Locker and Finn also found a case of raisins that probably Robertson had cached away. We found out it was Jorge's liquor which was stolen from the Issue Room. Harry and Jennie came in here for a chat this afternoon. Harry says his room on board Ship was ransacked and an Antarctic book was taken, as well as some personal things. He talked to Finn about a few things and Jennie and I talked mostly nonsense.

After dinner, Finn gave Harry the memo. He hasn't said a word since. Nichols came over and talked in detail about trail supplies and needs. Sig was here and offered his opinion now and then. Bob Dodson brought us some mukluks, etc. Mac and Owen came in to ask if they could go out over night on a trip. Finn said, no, not until he went out with them, when the sun came back. They brought up going to Debenham Island as did Harry this afternoon. Finn said not until the British gave their permission.

Monday, June 16, 1947

Awoke late straightened up the shack just in time for Butler's arrival. Sig also came in. Peterson came in too, and there was a lengthy discussion on the establishment of the Plateau Weather Station. The two groups will work in full cooperation in it, even to the extent of flying up supplies, etc. We had coffee and rice cakes. Much political discussion on world affairs, India, Britain, U.S. and Russia etc. followed. I tried to stress great things happening in world politics and cooperation, etc. Peterson and Sig left and Finn got on the other plans. Butler said their government had approved the plans for future cooperation. They outlined some more plans. Finn invited them to dinner next Sunday. Butler was most pleased. Finn told Butler how he had been held back by the British Embassy in Washington and said he had been disappointed and disgusted by that but had gotten over it now, intended to cooperate and suggested letting down the barrier of social intercourse, etc. Butler was very pleased, said fine, also said it was O.K. to go to Rymill's camp on a visit. Harry came in as Butler was leaving. Bill Latady a few minutes later. Both explained how slowly preparations for the trail were going and the seeming lack of enthusiasm. Finn agreed and said he would help and try to get the fellows going, etc. Finn announced all the news at dinner. The fellows were so pleased, they all gave him a big hand of applause. Finn went with Woody and Mac to lash sleds in the evening.

Tuesday, June 17, 1947

I had just gotten the room straightened when Butler came with a map of the upper part of this island. We had a short nice conversation and he left. Finn went back to his work with the boys, Mac and Woody, lashing sleds in the Machine shop. Jennie had made chocolate and served cookies for them all. They worked very hard and got one of the sleds finished. Finn got mad with Jennie running around taking pictures with the graflex camera. He told Bill not to let anybody use that camera and break it. Bill agreed. Kelsey has been doing well on the radio and got out all of our stuff. We got a message from Brundage (in the State Department) saying the report (for continuing future Antarctic research plans that Finn had sent) had been received a week ago and they were studying it. It was a most cordial message. Harry was in a good humor 'cause he had finished his aviation report for Finn. He came in at night and stayed until late, being just as friendly as he was in Washington and Beaumont. Many of the fellows went over to the British camp tonight. Peterson and Fiske on meteorology, and Kelsey and Jorge on the radio and Latady for some reason.

Wednesday, June 18, 1947

Harry gave Finn his memo on aviation plans today. He had not included the weight added or taken away from the plane, but he had put in a paragraph saying he expected Finn's 100% cooperation and to discuss anything only with him or other arrangements would have to be made. Finn was livid as was I, and Finn immediately sat down to write a memo back. The generator was acting up so the lights went out for several hours in the afternoon, which stopped all work until the fellows could fix it.

Later, I wrote an article on the British cooperation so the State Dept. might be swayed. Got a list of Britishers from Latady and saw some of the very good pictures he has taken. We had a nice chat in the photo lab. Finn got Mac and Wood back to work on the sleds until almost dinner-time. I was assistant mess cook and after dishes we had a movie, "Over 21." It was excellent and amusing. Nichols came over afterward and we discussed the British cooperation news article which Bob thought was excellent and the biggest news we might have. We also discussed Harry and how inconsistent the report was. By dividing the payload into the amount of gas required to haul, one would get 20 trips, while Harry, with no explanation, merely said 11 trips with good weather. We also discussed Finn's memo. Bob wanted to soften it up. The more we talked, the madder Finn got with Harry's casual attitude and inconsistencies regarding the payloads and amount of gas required on the long flights. Finn could not rely on his very loose figures. Lassiter had been in earlier in the day about a telegram from the Maharajah of Darbunga, who still wants him to be his personal pilot. He told us the interesting story of his many visits to his palace. Dodson and Owen worked on dog cakes all day. Owen also made a whip for the dogs.

Thursday, June 19, 1947

Awoke late was really tired. Sig went to the ship this morning to get some of the stuff for more pemmican, so we had ten-in-one for lunch. Bob Nichols had corrected the British cooperation news release and we went over it together. Finn was still working on the memo to Harry and his cooperation. Harry came storming in when Finn wasn't here and like a maniac raised hell with Nichols about the fire in the blubber house stove being left with the L-5 standing close by. Harry had Owen on coal and Dodson on ice, so neither could have been there. Peterson was also on ice detail after Finn had asked Harry to keep Thompson and Peterson off. Finn wrote another memo keeping Thompson and Peterson off along with Dodson and Owen while they were making dog food. Harry was crazy mad.

The day was a bit windy but clear. All lights went out cause all three generators are now broken. Woody and Mac stopped work on the sleds. Finn got angry with Fiske and Peterson cause they stopped hauling ice with the weasel while the lights were still out and no indoor work could be done. Peterson and Fiske started bitching at Finn right away. Fiske has so many jobs to do, he doesn't know how to get them all done and has thus become very irritable about them. Peterson came in this evening and tried to explain his point of view to Finn. After Finn gave his side of the picture explaining logically how important these thing were to the general running of the camp, Pete felt a little silly and tried to be more helpful. Each man saw only his side of a chore rather than the overall outcome to be considered.

The Antarctic Mid-winternight, June 21st or 22nd, is the most celebrated holiday on any expedition. It is the shortest day of the year, when the sun has reached its furthest northern declination. From this day on, the sun begins its slow return to the Continent, until December, when it is favored with the sun's light twenty-four hours a day. We decided to celebrate it on June 22nd.

A few days before, Finn had announced to expedition members that, after weeks of detailed discussion and planning, he and Butler had agreed that both groups would work in full cooperation with each other, both on the surface and in the air, in the coming spring and summer's geographical field operations. Whereas our expedition was extremely strong in aviation, their survey had great strength in dog power. The British had spent much time in breeding and training dogs for several years at their various bases and, at this particular Base, they had about seven well trained teams. They were anxious to make a long sledge trip, but felt it would not be possible to do so without considerable air support to maintain them in the field. Their small Auster plane, however, was not qualified for this job, whereas our two larger planes were. The most dog team power that we could muster, after our difficulties on the way down, was two nine dog teams. By supplying a two dog team sledge party by air, or even flying the dog teams to the edge of the unknown, we would have been able to make a long sledge trip far to the south, but it was felt at that time that by combining all strength available and traveling fast, we could carry out Finn's first plan with maximum results, as well as have two separate survey parties in the field. Their path of travel, of course, would not overlap.

This announcement was received enthusiastically by the personnel of both camps. It was the first time in the history of Antarctic exploration that expeditions of two different nationalities had been based in such close proximity. It certainly was the forerunner of the International Geophysical Year ten years later when many nationalities worked together both in the Antarctic and all over the world in a concerted effort to further scientific research. Many people had believed that we would not be able to get along together, but Butler and Finn felt that this presented an unusual opportunity to show that close cooperation between the two groups could be worked out for the common good of all. The historical Antarctic territorial disputes were not considered in any of our discussions. That difficult problem we left for our respective governments to decide. The idea of accomplishing the largest program with the maximum results for furthering Antarctic exploration was the major consideration.

Mid-winternight on June 22nd offered the opportunity to celebrate the newly announced cooperation with the British personnel of Base E.

Sunday, June 22, 1947

> *Awoke late and didn't have breakfast. The fellows were up earlier than usual for a Sunday and began cleaning up the Bunkhouse for the evening festivities. Finn went out to the ship for some more wine. Chuck Hassage came in while I was still straightening up the shack. He talked to Finn about his engineering end of it and submitted a plan including Robertson and Wood in the work to be done. Finn approved this. Chuck is unhappy still about his wife and talked about his family problems until late. I took the decorations in and Bill Latady started hanging them. Finally, I was able to get dressed and then helped a bit with the table. Jennie really looked glamorous.*

The occasion was a most festive one. The bunkhouse was decorated with streamers of red and green crepe paper which Jennie and I had made, with paper bells and alpine equipment entwined in green nylon climbing rope hanging from the rafters. Tin foil cut into tinsel added a touch of gaiety into the scene. The table, at which 32 people were seated, was decorated with Lassiter's newly painted red skis on which candles were placed. Place cards showing a picture of Stonington Island with the two camps, and the *Port of Beaumont* at anchor with the high glacier in the background, were made by Latady. Crossed white skis formed a backdrop at one end of the room. Dinner, expertly prepared by Chief Sigmund Gutenko, consisted of chicken noodle soup, previously frozen fried chicken southern style, peas, corn, rice with chicken gravy, and apple pie and coffee for dessert.

The British came, we had some wine first. Dinner was late an hour, but delicious when we finally got it. Latady took pictures, mostly of our end of the table. Harry had little to say. We had a movie later, Dorothy Lamour in "Rainbow Island" with Eddie Bracken. It was fair. Butler, Nichols, and Sig came into our place afterwards and we talked politics, etc. until about 2 o'clock over coffee, cake, and doughnuts. Harry came in about the work sheet tomorrow and made a fool of himself. He was obviously angry when he saw Butler, etc., enjoying themselves. Butler said the government had promised to send enough planes to do mapping work both last year and this year, but he hadn't seen them yet. It was a very pleasant evening and Butler greatly enjoyed it. He asked us over for next Sunday dinner and the following two, with eight persons coming from here each time.

Tuesday, June 24, 1947

Finn and I were both up early. Finn and Sig went to the ship for Sig to get soybeans for the pemmican making. Finn found all locks on the ship broken, etc. I cleaned up here and wrote for quite a while. Finn back at 11:30 said Harry was not up yet. He then decided to give Harry the long postponed memo today. Harry and Robertson were up until late last night digging out the plane from the windstorm which came up. They did not get up until lunchtime. Finn gave the memo to Harry. Harry did not say anything about it. Harry, Jennie, and Latady went over to the British for tea in the afternoon. Finn was angry when he found out they were going in working hours, but I persuaded him to say nothing for awhile. Lassiter told Finn Harry had been good for a week, but was starting something against Finn now. He didn't say what it was. Finn got the sleds finished today, all three of them. Mac, Woody, and Jennie oiled them tonight. Sig started working on pemmican today. He cut up the bacon, but did little else, although we were on 10-in-one rations all day. Nichols came in tonight. He was feeling much better, thought things were going well, but he was a bit depressed about personalities. Finn told him Mac had asked Finn if he really thought Bob would be well enough to go. Finn said he certainly hoped so. Bob said definitely yes. He had the most to lose with Finn if he did not go, but he definitely would be in condition to go. He played cards for a while with me and left about 12:00 midnight.

Wednesday, June 25, 1947

I received a fine message from my former boss, John Steeves, this morning. Things certainly do not look too good in the office these days and I am glad I am here with my worries instead of there. Jennie said something about not being able to get a message out of here and I really took her. Larry chimed in and I took him too. I went back later and took her again in her room and I hope gave her an idea of how little she counts, when the generators are bad and we have expedition business to transmit, which she seems to have forgotten. Incoming messages come in easily, but to get our daily scientific recordings out to various government agencies had to come first and radio reception often seemed to be a challenge with Kelsey.

I had not had a confrontation with Jennie before. It was not in my personality to put myself in competition with another woman on any level. We had been good friends, but the more Harry tried to work against Finn the harder it became not to feel some animosity. I knew that Jennie was very anxious for Harry to get along with Finn and tried to keep him from continuing his provocations. Jennie supported her husband and I supported mine. There was a lot at stake and obviously things were headed in the wrong direction. What exactly Harry hoped to accomplish eluded me.

Larry came in and had it out with Finn about the outgoing messages and he got straightened out too. Finn and Kelsey spent much time decoding a message from the Navy on doings of Task Force 68. They did little, but photograph Charcot, Alexander I Island, and Robert English Coast. Now they wanted Finn to establish good ground control points for them. Fine thing! Larry Fiske spent much time in here chatting. Lassiter told Finn that Harry was angry because Finn had revised his message to Ashley Snow. This is not true, Finn sent it out word for word. I read most of the day, but finally thought so much about things in general, that I stopped and wrote a long memo on visiting British during working hours, radio communication and use it is being put to, and the disgraceful condition aboard ship. Finn read it at dinner and the Peterson got up and said much of a constructive nature on the electric power situation. Fiske spent most of the evening in here polishing the good old apple to be sure he was on the right side of Finn. Went to bed about 2:30.

Thursday, June 26, 1947

I took a trip out to see Don in the Blubber House and saw "Kasco." He is a beautiful, large, white puppy and should grow into a beautiful dog. Finn had Nichols, Dodson, and Owen in for a chat after lunch. He jacked them up on their trail work and impressed upon them the fact that they would have to be alert at all times. Harry came in and out all day for various things. He seems in very good humor. He helped Finn code his answer to the Navy Department's message all afternoon. It was quite a job. Fiske was in, too. We received a message from Wheeler that our British cooperation story was published on the 22nd in N.Y. Times and London Daily Telegraph. Finn told the fellows at chow. Finn had Sig in and both he and Harry persuaded him to make the rest of the pemmican all at one time and get it over with. Lassiter and Adams moved the food boxes out of the Machine Shop entrance way into the clear, as they were a fire hazard. Mac, etc. worked on coal. Robertson was doping L-5 wings in Machine Shop. Bill got good pictures from Sunday's party. Harry was in again and wanted permission to go to Rymill's Base with Tonkin on Sunday. Finn said yes. Nichols said Lassiter had strongly defended Finn when some unidentified person suggested Finn's recent recommendation for their regular Army retention had not been strong enough, and was turned down for that reason.

Friday, June 27, 1947

Got up late as we read late last night. Jennie told me she wanted to give a cocktail party tomorrow afternoon. Finn was irritated with this, but finally agreed. Harry was in several times and was in quite a good humor. Finn started to put two skis together for a sled to take in the airplane. Lassiter got out the wire recorder and after dinner we had a community sing into it, to save later for a record. Then each man had a chance to say a few words. Finn gave snapshots of expedition life at random. It was good. I came next and then Jim called for Harry. He was not there and he called Jennie. Finn said, "Spread the women apart." Jennie was apparently insulted and went into her room. Jim and Chuck came over a little later to play us the recording. Harry came in and sat down to hear it too. Some of the things were terribly amusing and we all thought it quite good. Jim and Chuck left, Harry stayed until after 1 o'clock discussing things in general, war, Navy, and Bernt Balchen.

Saturday, June 28, 1947

Today was Harry and Jennie's First Wedding Anniversary. I got up for lunch. Then wrote some radio messages and read a bit. Sig came in with some canned peaches, which we opened. Finn worked all day on plans for a sled to be carried in the plane. Jennie came in and asked if we were coming to the party. I said I hadn't been invited. Finn would not go, for the same reason, but after Jennie insisted, I went in and had a drink with them. It was a very nice party. We had dinner and then a movie afterward. Got an article from Harcly to send out on weather forecasting. Lassiter and Adams were working on food bags for the trail. Before movies tonight, it was –19 F. and after, -21 degrees F., pretty cold. Lassiter and Adams came in to play cards. It was a dull game but Sig made us some good tuna fish and we had ice cream. It was about 2 o'clock when they left. They really feel dreadful about not getting regular Army, but we certainly hope that all is not lost and something will come of our good recommendations.

Sunday, June 29, 1947

Awoke to find most of the camp had gone up to Rymill's Camp in one form or another. (Britisher Rymill and his party had built this small camp in 1937 for surveying and meteorology studies as part of the British Graham Land Expedition, United States Antarctic Service personnel had visited it briefly in 1940.) Harry, Latady, and Jennie went with Tonkin and his dog team. McLean, Dodson, Owen, and Pete took our dog team. The rest went in various groups. Harry came back and said he saw cases of our food up there and cans of Phillips products (American supplies from 1940) on the shelves. All signs said, "Property of the Crown" – "Do Not Disturb." Finn wants to see this himself before saying anything. Finn and I worked around here. Finn worked on his sled. Bob Nichols came in for a few minutes and was quite angry about Sig's refusal to tell him where the tea was. Bob felt he was the one who usually took up for Sig, when other fellows bitched (about) him. Hassage and Lassiter said they couldn't go to the British dinner tonight. Hassage was not feeling well and Lassiter just didn't want to go. Don, Nichols, Smitty, Peterson, Adams, Latady, Finn and I went. We had a small drink before dinner. The table and decorations looked fine. There were place cards containing the dinner menu and an appropriate cartoon of everyone present. The dinner was delicious. We had a hot punch afterward. Some played the "Button Game" and then "Flesh, Fish, or Fowl," later "Liar Dice". During this time we had tea at two different times. The games were fun and the evening free of tension and delightful. It was just about the most pleasant since I left Beaumont, an interlude to an otherwise constantly on-edge existence.

Lately I had been living under considerable stress with the fear that some chaotic incident would bring an unforeseen disastrous situation to these inexperienced accident-prone men. This evening had been a relaxing interlude.

Independence Day came quietly to Palmer Land. After another unusual temperature change from minus twenty to plus thirty-eight degrees, a new snow commenced and quietly ushered in the Fourth of July. Neny Mountain, Figure Four and others loomed as dark shapes on the near horizon. The wailing's of the dogs foretold of the bright new moon. While most of the camp slept, the galley lights burned while Sig and Larry Fiske worked all night making some items of trail food. Their only audience was the night watchman and radio operator

Kelsey. Mid-winternight had passed and as this night wore on, a brilliant light, the first in two and one half months, showed on the horizon. This break in the clouds gave promise to the return of the sun before many weeks had passed. The partial light played on the flagstaff at the head of Stonington Island and the Stars and Stripes rippled gaily, saluting the new day perhaps a bit more proudly as it was a very special day in its history. In true American style, it was flying on a new frontier. With the coming of the twilight, the trail food makers and the night watchman turned to their breakfast and the arising personnel. The Base came to life and the men began their duties for the day in the southernmost place in the world flying the American flag.

Friday, July 4, 1947

Some were agitating for a holiday today, but Finn did not give it to them, as there was much work to be done. Bill and Chuck Adams were busy working on the diesel repair. Hassage was still sick. Nichols and Ike took a long walk. McLean and Smitty went with the dog team after the two seals killed yesterday. Lassiter, Mac, and Harry went out later this afternoon in back of Neny and shot five seals, which Nic and Ike had seen earlier. Butler came over this afternoon and told Finn that their pilot Tommy had an epileptic fit and so he had been grounded. We had a nice chat about setting up and manning the meteorological station, etc. and Nichols came in, and the question of rights to publish news was thoroughly discussed to everyone's satisfaction. Harry and Sig came in for a few minutes. After dinner Lassiter read the new ice detail. Apparently earlier Ike had objected to getting ice everyday for others taking a shower. Finn had Lassiter, Ike, and Harry in and discussed it. They decided everyone would get ice but Finn, this included Peterson, who was apparently the person they were all aiming at. Harry wanted movies tonight. Finn said no tomorrow night. Someone put diesel oil into 91 octane gas, thereby ruining it. Harry was concerned about the gas and wanted the radio program cut. Thompson came in about a new slant on a microseism program development. Finn gave him the O.K. to make daily weather maps etc. Larry Fiske came in about the dog driving tomorrow to get the seals. Everyone finally went home and we went to bed. Sig has six hundred and fifty pounds of pemmican made.

Saturday, July 5, 1947

Bob Dodson, Art Owen and the dog teams went out early this morning to bring back the seals. Finn and I skied out to meet them after lunch. It began to snow almost immediately and we could hardly see in front of us. It was about two and a half miles out to where they were. One of the British dog teams was out looking for seals. Bob and Art had gutted all of our seals and were packing them on the sled, when we got there. Just before we left, I spotted a crabeater seal on the huge iceberg. It had come up from the tidal crack. Art shot him. There was only one seal, but two bullets as he put it on automatic. They gutted him there and then while we watched. He had a good thickness of blubber. His heart continued to beat out on the ice for about fifteen minutes. We started slowly back with five seals on two sledges with fifteen dogs. The basket sled of Sir Hubert's turned over and partially broke, spilling some seal meat. We left some and went on until the rear sled got bogged down in slush twice. Finally, the dogs only pulled six feet at a time, so they left one sled and came in. It was pitch dark by this time. Actually, the dogs didn't do very well in pulling. With so much activity I was stiff in every muscle by the time we got back.

With difficulty, the men continued to train and exercise the dogs. The dogs were friendly enough and willing enough, but the drivers had not succeeded as yet in making them understand what was expected of them. They caught on right away that the command "Yake" meant to go but each dog had his own idea as to which way that meant. They were pulling to the right, to the left, some had their tails where their heads should have been, and a minority was pulling ahead. It took a number of weeks before they had a sledge team.

Monday, July 7, 1947

I was mess cook assistant today, so started in early, cleaned off the table and swept the floor. Jorge was quite amiable for a change. I worked on a draft for handling the meeting with Mac tonight. Nichols came in and was at first not in favor of having an open meeting with Mac, Harry, Dodson, Owen, McLean and Finn, but as he thought about it, he changed his mind. He worked over notes and points to bring up to Mac and he was very angry about it, as Mac had not spoken to him for two weeks. After dinner, at eight o'clock, the big show started. Nichols said Finn had first discussed his leading the Geological Field Party earlier in Boston and as this was a scientific party, everyone knew his choice of Dodson and Owen. It had come to his attention, he said, that Mac had said he was better qualified than any of these to go on the trail party. "Mac what do you have to say?" Nichols asked. Mac was flabbergasted and so was Harry. Mac brought up the dogs, preparations, canoeing experience, two geologists going along, etc. He had some nasty words with Bob about dirty campus politics of the selection. Bob was angry and gave reasons why he selected Art Owen and Bob Dodson. Mac refuted these reasons in front of the boys and said he thought, he, himself was pretty good, that he was a perfectionist. Bob then outlined why he didn't choose Mac. He gave him a chance to let the rest leave the room as Mac had accused Nic of putting him on the spot.

All stayed and Nichols told Mac he did not fit into an organization, that he had undermined Smitty, Harry, and Finn. With Harry, Mac wanted to know who told him. I said I did and was quoting Mrs. Harry Darlington on saying that she told me the following, so that I could use it in the best way to help the expedition: "I learn new things everyday about my husband; he has great loyalty on certain things. Mac tried to persuade him (Harry) to go home, (on board the British ship) because Mac felt he could get more out of the expedition in this manner and (later) when Mac started to get a certain group together to try to run certain things about the expedition, he asked Harry (to join them), (but Harry) said I will have nothing to do with that, because I am Third-in-Command". Harry and Mac almost went through the floor. (I spoke up, which was unusual for me, because I thought it was time that these two understood that we were on to their destructive antics of constantly making trouble against Finn).

Harry went out to get Jennie, came back to say she was in bed, went the second time and came back again to say he could not get her out of bed. Mac said if that was the case of what I had heard Jennie said about him, he didn't blame me for disliking him. I told him I had liked him at the beginning and felt him one of the nicest people on the expedition, but what I now felt about him was entirely of his own making. Nic got me out of the conversation and continued, that Mac had called for a show of hands on the women question (of our going) and, if on the trail, he might do the same thing. Don assured Finn that they would not have over run his decision on the women and, as it turned out, the majority were in favor of it anyway, that Mac was a poor sport in his inability to take the selection of someone else, and that Mac was his own worst enemy. Mac was furious and foaming at the mouth. He said Nic's integrity was nil with him and he wouldn't want to be with him, nor collect for him. Nic said the Commander had supported Mac and might have forced him to take him because of his good job in Beaumont, and wanted no feeling placed on Finn for this. Mac was pleased with this. Harry asked Nic how his program would fit into aviation. Nic reassured him, as it was his intention to cooperate in every way humanly possible. Nic assured Mac he had no feeling against him, he was only trying to help him. Harry once started to leave, Finn stopped him saying to remember he was here as Third in Command. Mac was a very poor sport and nasty and vicious. He has real hatred for Nic and was greatly embarrassed at his own position. They all left, finally; Bob too. Harry did stay and later said I shouldn't tell Finn things. I said don't be ridiculous, I would tell him anything and everything, just as Jennie did with him. (He and Jennie had done much bitching behind Finn's back and we knew it). Bob came back. Harry soon left. Bob chatted and thought things had gone well enough and, that his shoulders were broad enough to take Mac's hatred. Latady came in to tell Finn the diesel was fixed and running. That certainly was a step in the right direction.

Tuesday, July 8, 1947

It blew hard all day yesterday, but stopped by noon today. There was a succession of people through here all day, including Bob who had a new idea to get Mac out in the field. Lassiter brought in a pie, which he found in Fiske's weasel. Chuck Hassage came to discuss the diesel and Woody about problems on the ship coming (on the way) down. Sig came in, he had a fight with Jorge this morning over emptying the trash cans. Jorge hit him in the jaw and knocked two teeth loose. Sig was about ready to hit him back when Bob Nichols held his arm. The fellows bawled Jorge out, but Harry and Hassage thought Finn should relieve Jorge of mess duties, before something worse happens. Jennie wouldn't speak to me today, nor did she sit at our end of the table during lunch and dinner. I don't think this is going to affect my life to any great extent, but if she ever denies saying what I quoted her as saying, and I hear about it – boy is she going to hear about it and I don't mean maybe. I'll add a few more things to stimulate her poor memory about sitting down in the mess hall nights aboard ship to get information and trying to warn Harry and Bill about Mac, but saying Harry wouldn't listen to her. Too many people are trying to play one side against the other for their own self-interests now.

The diesel broke again tonight so Finn is faced with the same situation of using weasel gas for the radio. Harcly was in to discuss the Plateau trip with Finn. He had lost interest in it, because the fellows have been ribbing him about his work.

Thursday, July 10, 1947

Got up fairly early and spent most of the day writing on "The Battle of Washington" chapter, mostly about the ship. Finn wrote much of the material I needed for detail. Harry and Smitty took the pero team out with Chinook as Leader and Jennie sitting on the sled. They seemed to work fairly well according to Harry. Finn was most disturbed about the fellows' lack of interest and work in the program. He blew up about it to Nichols just after dinner.

They took a walk through the buildings and after Nichols saw all that was not going on, he too was disgusted.

Finn found Fiske working the trail set and he said he was working a ship at sea, then Finn heard him shout they were on a British frequency. This made Finn mad and he told Kelsey to take it away from them. Kelsey brought in a message from Wheeler asking information for Milton Reynolds if there was a suitable regular or emergency landing field here for a B-24. Reynolds was sponsoring a flight over both poles around August 10th. Lassiter was going to check, but he thought not, the bay ice is 30 inches and the glacier impossible because of crevasses. A B-24 would weight 65,000 lb. and be on wheels too.

Harry was in several times about the work progress tomorrow. Finn wants the dog food finished by Sunday, the rear end of the ship cleared off tomorrow. Bill came in and wanted to take a party skiing. Finn said no! too much work. Jennie came in and when all the rest left started talking about her name being mentioned the other night and she did have the conversation with me, but it was confidential and she thought I had misquoted her. I told her I had it written in my diary, that I was here to help Finn and had only one interest the success of the expedition. I didn't care what people thought of me, that this was not a popularity contest nor did I intend to try making myself popular. Her remarks to me were used for the good of the expedition, as she had requested, that the conference had been held to point out to Mac the reasons why he was not selected and if he didn't use it too good advantage, the way it was meant, it was just too bad for him. I further stated I felt very strongly about the way she disobeyed Finn, admitted it, and then went down and told a lie about him. I said I had been a witness and Finn had neither said nor implied that there was anything between Bill and her on the glacier. She said she felt Finn had implied it and I said she was dead wrong and her husband was considering going home on the Trepassey on a lie that she had told. She said everyone wanted to go home at that time anyway. I said poor sports on a situation they themselves had created. She said she had to live with those men and get along with them and that she was managing and the only thing she was interested in doing was to keep Harry on good terms with Finn and do the best job in aviation that he could both for the good of himself and the expedition. I asked her if lying about Finn this way was helping and if she thought Mac had improved any toward the overall good of the expedition since she had made the statement in question. She said, yes, and I said I didn't think so. Thus ended the conversation, both smiling. Finn returned and with a few light remarks, Jennie left soon afterward.

Friday, July 11, 1947

Awoke fairly early, cleaned up the shack and went skiing right after lunch with Latady, Adams, Jennie and Dick Butson, over on the big hill across from camp. We had a fine afternoon of about an hour and a half. Finn made a ski trip up the glacier this morning to see how it would be for a B-24 runway, but found it too crevassed. Jim Lassiter said the Bay Ice wouldn't do either. Finn sent Wheeler a negative reply to the query from Milton Reynolds about a suitable landing field here for a B-24. Sig was in with a definite black eye and swollen face after being hit by Jorge. He had very little to say and Finn read about Will Rogers most of the time. This morning Fiske was very upset about Finn accusing him of contacting a ship at sea, etc. and was most hurt. Finn calmed him down. Peterson wanted Finn to put in writing that he would pay for the Solar Radiation equipment to $200 if the Office of Naval Research or the Weather Bureau wouldn't. Finn said he would give him his word, but would not put it in writing and resented Harcly's asking for it. Finn gave Jorge a good talking to about hitting Sig. He told him it was assault and battery and he would get six months in jail for it in the United States, as he had disfigured Sig' face and should be ashamed of himself. If it ever happened again, Finn would deal with him in a stronger manner. Jorge said it would not happen again. Sig never should have insisted that this kid come along to help him with galley duties – he has done anything but!

During the winter night, while all of the activity was going on in camp preparing for third alternate plans to get at the problem. Being an expedition leader is never easy. the future trail work, and in between trying to sort out all the bitching and conflicts, Finn was scheming, planning, discussing, and working constantly on geographical plans for coordinating surface parties with airplane operations, taking into consideration weights to be transported in both cases. Gradually one main plan and three alternates evolved. The one, which would be put into effect, would depend upon certain physical factors and conditions which would present themselves at the time of execution. His plan, developed with Major Butler, was to operate into the unknown by using both dog teams and planes to establish an operational base in the southeastern most corner of George VI Sound. One of his alternate plans was also based on this desire. However, when the time actually arrived to carry out thisparticular plan, surface conditions and subsequent developments as a result of these ice conditions were such as to force him to adopt a combination of his second and third alternate plans to get at the problem. Being an expedition leader is never easy.

Jackie and Finn posed in front of Beechcraft while out skiing

Peterson and Fiske under plastic dome taking the wind velocity

Jackie washing clothes on stove with underwear drying on line above

British Leader K.S. Pierce-Butler having dinner with us

McClary and Art Owen relaxing in the bunkhouse

X

Ah, Spring!

Now that the worst part of the winter was behind us, we began thinking about putting some of our field plans into early operation. The glacier, which adjoins our Island, was our highway to the mile high Peninsula Plateau, which stretches for more than a thousand miles in a north south direction. It is necessary to cross this 6,000-foot obstacle either by dog team or plane before it is possible to get from our side to the eastern side of the Peninsula where Finn eventually wanted to establish an advanced base to explore further south.

The weather, which plays such an important part in either trail or flying programs, is at its worst on top of the Plateau where Finn also wanted to maintain a weather station for the duration of the training season. From the previous expedition, Finn knew that in a four-month period, the days that would be considered perfect for carrying out flying operations from the Plateau could be counted on the fingers of one hand. The temperatures and winds which we experienced down at the Base were mild compared to those experienced on the Plateau where winds could reach up to 110 miles per hour. Information from this strategic location would provide data for sending out surface parties and plane flights and would also be of value for meteorological research. Once established by a dog team party, additional supplies to keep it running could be flown up by the small plane, after a suitable landing field had been marked by the surface party.

By the middle of July, trail preparations were sufficiently completed to enable the first surface party to depart. Finn was anxious to give our equipment a test and the trip would provide an excellent opportunity to train personnel. After a man has been able to stand up against the rugged conditions experienced in a few days trip to the Plateau, he can consider himself initiated into life on the trail. He decided to take Latady, Owen, Adams, Peterson, and Dodson with him. They would establish the station and leave Peterson and Dodson there for several weeks until two other men were flown up to man the station for another few months. Another reason for starting so early was to give Peterson his opportunity to obtain some refraction measurements before the winter was over, and the sun was still very low on the horizon. Dodson also wanted to make a series of test experiments in severe cold weather conditions on the trail for his report to the Army. They were ready to leave on the first suitable day.

Monday, July 14, 1947

Nichols and Sig got up at three to finish the man trail ration. Finn was busy all day with preparations for taking a trail party up tomorrow. Harry was in and out. Finn caught Don doing his business in the Blubber shack. Sig came in and chatted. Finn and I made up orders for Peterson while on the Plateau and Ike (who would be in charge of base while Finn was away). After dinner Butler brought over a map made by Dougie of the glacier. Gave us regards from Captain White of the Fitzroy. We talked about various and sundry things and had a pleasant evening. Ken asked us over for tea next Sunday. I got out an article on the radio on the weather and on trail food. Finn left me in charge of radio communications while he would be away, since I was the one most familiar with his wishes and policy. Dodson and Owen worked late loading the sled.

Tuesday, July 15, 1947

Got up at eight o'clock, first time since I've been here. All were up for breakfast. At nine o'clock Finn and I went out – Finn ready to leave. The sleds were all packed over by the blubber shack, but no one was there except Mac. Finn got sore and went in to find McLean performing a medical examination on Art Owen at the last minute which should have been done days ago. Finn was so disgusted, he wanted to cancel the trip. Dodson was running around. They finally hitched up the dogs and got going by 9:30. It was still dark. Peterson came out all dressed up in the Alpaca suit donated by a company for each member of the expedition. He will be awfully warm (we thought at the time, but it may well have saved his life). All the rest were wearing windproofs. The take-off was gruesome. The dogs did not behave too well and the fellows were all screaming and yelling and didn't handle them properly. Harry, Mac, Smitty, Lassiter, and Andy went up part way with them. Smitty and Harry came back less than an hour later saying the dogs were not pulling well and some of the junk would have to be left at the aviation cache to be taken up later by plane. Art Owen forgot his crampons and Harry took his back to him. When Harry got back late this afternoon, he said he caught them about 6 ½ miles up the glacier.

A week of strong winds made a hard icy surface good for dog team traveling. In spite of the bad start, they had made good time climbing the gradual Northeast glacier slope during the twilight hours, and utilized to the fullest the few hours of daylight during the middle of the day. Finn pointed out crevasses, explained how they could be recognized and how necessary it was to be on the alert constantly for existing dangers. He reviewed previous instructions in the method of traveling on skis through crevassed filled terrain, as well as the mandatory safety precautions to be observed at all times. The rock faces of the mountains on either side revealed the movements of greater glaciers that had existed not so long ago. Hanging glaciers flowing like lava over the rock cliffs from the ice cap of the Plateau and numerous avalanches made dramatic sights. They made thirteen miles the first day and camped after dark a couple of miles from the steep slope leading up to the Plateau. However, they didn't meet their eight o'clock radio schedule that night. The temperature went down to twenty degrees below zero, and for those who had never slept in a sleeping bag on the trail before, it was a great surprise.

Wednesday, July 16, 1947

Got up very late, as I was not feeling well. Had lunch and then came back to lie down. Harry came in and in a very round about way I found out that Don, Andy, and Smith had gone over Neny way sealing and wouldn't be back until tomorrow. Apparently, Ike either suggested that they go or gave permission to the idea. I slept all afternoon, getting up for dinner. After dinner a few of us played Liar Dice until the British came over for the movie. Butler and Tonkin were both here. We had a cat cartoon, then Jinx Falkenburg in, "The Gay Senorita," which was lousy and Shirley Temple in, "Kiss and Tell," which was very good and funny. Kelsey did not get contact with Finn and party. Butler wanted the map of Neny trough. I came over to get it after the movie, while they started to serve ice cream. When I came back Ken and John Tonkin were both in Jennie and Harry's room. I had some ice cream and then stuck my head in telling Ken I had found the map. Harry and Jennie said come in – I said I had to attend the fire in my small stove. Ken said he would come over with me for the map. I invited him to sit down and chat, which he did. Then offered him some coffee, which he accepted. I went over to invite the other three in but Harry had just opened a bottle of slaunch (wine), so Ken and I went over there. The conversation was very boring and not very friendly. I suffered with it for 30 minutes and then left, the British soon after me.

Thursday, July 17, 1947

Read until 2 o'clock last night, so I slept until noon. Started to work in the afternoon, but Sig came in, so we played solitaire all afternoon. Bob came in just before dinner and we began talking about Don McLean and his not getting the medical reports done and his dirty habits. Nichols revealed that Don had told him Harry had said that Finn was angry with Don about doing his business on the ship and that Finn was thinking about not sending him on the trail. I know Finn never said this about Don and that Harry was misquoting. Bob Nichols was going to speak to Don about his medical reports.

Lassiter came in about this time and asked me what Finn would say if he went sealing tomorrow. I read him part of Finn's message to Ike saying no one should leave camp. Lassiter said that was all he wanted to know. He left and

Harry came in, all in the air. Bob Nichols asked him to put Don on work list for medical exams. Harry said he had, but that Don had gotten Finn's permission to go seal blubbering instead. Harry said he was through with the work sheets, that Ike ran the camp the way he wanted to and that he, Harry, knew Finn did not want the fellows away from camp at night. They were camped near an iceberg, which only had to turn over once, Harry continued, and complained that he had never had to kill seals at night before.

Learned that Ike had given his OK to Thompson, Smith and McLean for a man hauling trip over the frozen surface of Neny Fjord and the party was camped in the lee of a berg, which was the size of two city blocks in length and as high as a five story building. It was not likely to turn over, as Harry had suggested. During their two-day stay, they secured six seals that had climbed on the bay ice from the tidal crack around the berg in order to sun themselves.

Seal hunting in the Antarctic is a very poor sport from a sportsman's viewpoint. Arctic seals have become very wary and they are relatively difficult to get, but the Antarctic seal knows no enemy on land. For countless millennium, they have been able to assume that they are safe once they come out of the water. When a man approaches a seal, often it will lift its head lazily in a disinterested fashion and peer blankly at you with two huge eyes. It will make no attempt to get away, or even to move. Few men would have the desire to kill a seal merely for the sport of it. As five of their catch were Weddells, which weight approximately seven hundred pounds each, and one was a crabeater weighing around five hundred pounds, it was impossible for the three men to man haul this load back to the base. It would afford an excellent opportunity to find out what our Army weasel would do on the comparatively smooth bay ice.

Previously in the day, Harry asked me what we were going to do with the puppy (Kasco). I said take him home to the States, and Harry said then one person should feed him. Woody and Mac said they would feed him until Dodson got back. After dinner, Lassiter, McLean, and Andy came in for a game of bridge. We had a good time. Larry Fiske dropped in and later Nichols. Larry said Kelsey had gotten radio contact with the Plateau. They were safely there and asked for the plane to come up tomorrow. Jennie spent the day with the British. I read Sam Houston until 2:30 a.m.

Saw the Aurora Australis over our hut at dinnertime. Beautiful red glow.

It was a lively display of Antarctic beauty – one of the things which makes men go back to this desolated Continent for the second and third time. Looking southward, we could see the most splendid display of the Aurora Australis. These beautiful Southern Lights were intense in their color strength. There were rapidly occurring changes from streamers to curtains and, at times, the horizon of the high mountain chain could be seen bathed with a red glow like the sun, giving the appearance of a distant fire in the made to order display. As we were not based in the aurora belt of the Antarctic, such a display was the unusual, rather than the usual.

Friday, July 18, 1947

Got up for lunch at noon. Found it blowing so hard, Harry couldn't fly up to the Plateau. Ike made a deal with the British for us to clear a runway for their plane, if they would give us enough gas to go out and get the seals with the weasel. So after lunch, off everybody went to watch the fun. Hassage went too. They brought back all of the seals on the tractor sled and apparently did very fine.

For dinner the camp had their first taste of seal liver and kidneys from the more tender crabeater seal. Comments were varied, but most felt that the taste was interesting, in spite of the slightly blubbery odor. Even I tried it –ugh!

I started to work on the book, but Jennie came in with a can of jellied consommé, which we had. Sig came in and then Harry. After a short conversation on children, they all left and I worked on the book for the rest of the afternoon. I can't seem to get this expedition out of Washington. We also had a good steak dinner, as Sig is back on day work now.

That day, July 18th, the first egg was laid in the Antarctic by Chick Petunia. The credit, of course, goes to the chicken, but Chief Sig Gutenko felt more than a little proud and, when considering all the thought and care chickens living on a polar continent must be given, decided he had been repaid by the actual result of his scientific program. When Petunia presented concrete evidence of her worth and, when sufficient eggs had been collected so that everyone had been presented with two, styled to preferences in place of their usual morning's hot cakes, the chickens became more popular. So popular in fact that they were allowed finally to occupy a suite on one of the floors of Peterson's meteorological tower. This pleased Gutenko, the Scientists, and mainly the chickens, which continued to produce larger eggs more frequently.

Saturday, July 19, 1947

Woke up late had lunch, started to do some writing, but was interrupted by Don McLean. He obviously was sent over by Bob Nichols to be nice to me. He showed me some pictures, tried to be utterly charming and stayed about two hours. The wind blew very hard all day, so the planes could not take off. Britisher Terry worked Finn on the radio better than Kelsey and said they would start down today, they needed kerosene, food, and dog food. I wrote an article on, "The Egg and I," the first egg in Antarctica to be laid. After a good dinner, the British came over to see, "National Velvet." Ken brought back the map and I invited him and Reg in with Nichols and Sig. We talked until 2 a.m. and had a very pleasant time. I read for an hour.

Sunday, July 20, 1947

Got up around one o'clock, fixed breakfast here, had a thorough wash and went out to find that Terry had been over to say Finn would start down today. The wind was blowing furiously. I came back and at 2:45, John Tonkin came to conduct me to the British camp for tea as it was blowing so hard. I had a wonderful time with all sorts of goodies, nice conversation, etc. Larry came in and made himself at home. Ike came tearing in worried about Nichols out for a walk and afraid Finn had started down. Ken insisted I stay for dinner which I did, and Larry too, although I didn't notice that he was included in the invitation. They had a radio schedule with Pete and could not hear him well, but he heard them perfectly. He went on

CW, we on voice. I said hello to Finn. Wind was blowing 75 mph so he had not been able to start back.

Came back to find dinner was just over. I made my fire and came back to help Jim Lassiter with the dishes. He told me Harry had blown-up when he found out I was censoring radio messages yesterday and again today. Said he would have it out with Finn as soon as he got back. Jim also said Ike had gotten in an argument with Harry and had relieved him of Third in Command. Lassiter said the other fellows had said forget about it, except those certain few. Lassiter had thought Harry was on his way to bawl me out and he started over to throw him out. Robertson got the 35 mm projector working and showed, "Love, Live and Learn," and 3 reels of "Captain Fury" until 1 o'clock. I read for a while and then turned in about 3 o'clock.

Monday, July 21, 1947

I awoke around one o'clock. It was so cold and windy I could hardly get up. Everything was frozen. The barometer was down and the wind blowing harder than ever. I had a hard time making the fire start. Went into the Bunkhouse to find Jennie helping Sig to make Ravioli and the fellows had just finished putting grooves in a bunch of trail flags. Had lunch. Don, Bob Nichols, and Ike went for a walk, while the rest of us saw "Tom Sawyer." Afterwards I came in to write. Don came in to chat, more of his same program of being friendly. I started telling him about the book, Finn's life and his troubles with the admiral. Larry came in for part of it. We talked until six and went to have some doughnuts and coffee. Had another movie, the last two reels of, "Captain Fury," three cartoons, and then, "Algiers." Terry came over with a message from the plateau party giving the position 0f their camp as half way between the British cache and the American Met Station. Wind had covered antenna, radio key broken, and tent under great strain with 75 mph wind. I was a bit depressed and concerned.

Living under continuous tension, among men who had rivalries and jealousies between themselves, and who were always looking for some reason to blame Finn for their problems, was a never ending strain. It was not a cohesive happy family of all working for the same goal. Each had his own priorities and when those priorities weren't satisfied they became hard to deal with. Even Finn, who was familiar with the various tensions on expeditions in isolation, was perplexed. The men were young, almost all in their twenties, inexperienced, they were not paid and therefore felt little reason for loyalty if they didn't get what they wanted when they wanted it. The steady nine to five individual did not seek out the opportunity to spend a year in Antarctica. Finn worked hard to eliminate the disagreements by discussing their concerns with the individuals or groups, calmly explaining the logical reasoning governing decisions. It took all of the diplomacy he possessed. Even the most level headed among us would lose his cool when he didn't get what he wanted – anyone that is except for Chuck Adams. Adams always did what he was asked to do, did it well and never complained about anything in any way. Beyond any doubt he was the most perfect expeditioner anyone could ask for. But, there was no doubt there were a few trouble makers who took pleasure in keeping things stirred up with little chance of retribution.

Tuesday, July 22, 1947

Woke up very late around 1 o'clock. Went in to find them working on trail flags, sewing them on the sticks, Jennie, Bob Nichols, Don and Smitty. I fooled around with them for a while and then did some work in here. The barometer was steadily rising and we thought Finn might start back. Lassiter, Harry, and Robertson began digging the plane out. Lassiter urged Harry to fly saying the wind was not more than 20 mph. Just then the British plane flew over head. Harry checked and found an 18-mph wind. Harry flew for a few minutes and then landed, loaded the supplies and took off for the Plateau. In an hour he came back saying he could not get higher than 6,500 feet. Lassiter said he only needed 6,300. We had dinner about 5 o'clock and soon after the movies started, while Lassiter and I were having a chat about the planes. He said he was disgusted with the organization of things and was only flying to collect his pay and he wanted the maintenance of the Nordun.

We saw "The Hurricane," with Lamour and Don Hall. At 8:30 Harry came back from The British radio contact with the plateau, announcing Finn and 3 others had left the top at 8 a.m. He then came over and told me and I thanked him. He started in bitching on why they were coming down then, etc. There was no reason for this – Finn was in charge up there and the judge of when they were coming down. After the movie, Bob Nichols came in and we had a long talk about conditions. I was pretty much disgusted and Bob said there were many more undercurrents than even I knew about, that Harry was under great tension and very unhappy, as all the fellows ribbed him. Bob said the situation was just a result of many people of different backgrounds, coming down here for different reasons and the crosscurrents were unbelievable. The only thing to do was make the best of the situation and the personnel. He left about 12:45 a.m. and just as he walked out Finn came in. We sat up until 5 o'clock talking about his trip and what had happened here in his absence.

Finn said they had a good, but hard trip. Adams was excellent helping out in every way possible. They had faced low below zero temperatures with the penetrating wind made life miserable. These men, some of whom were immature were quickly initiated into trail life, by experiencing some of just about the worst Antarctic has to offer to the man sleeping in a tent on the snow.

After eight days, Finn decided that the four in the support team must return to base in order not to consume the food and fuel designated for the use of Peterson and Dodson, who were to remain. Momentarily the sun peaked over the mountains and went out of sight again, but they thought they had better utilize this break in the weather to advantage. On the way up the final ascent, they had placed orange colored trail flags about one-quarter of a mile apart, so they could follow the same route on their return. Around noon on July 23rd, Adams and Finn left to stake out the trail flags every fifty feet to give them the direction of the descent by the time the dog teams were ready to start. Through the whirlwind snowdrifts they managed to find the exact spot where they had climbed six days before and with the trail flags which they had just set up, they had no difficulty tracing their steps back to the tents. Finn considered that they would have no difficulty in negotiating the glacier back to camp, once they reached the lower limits of the land. The men took off with their loaded sleds with a man in the lead for the dog teams to follow the flagged trail. Peterson and Dodson watched the others disappear in the snowdrifts.

The descent of the returning party was easily accomplished. After traveling for eleven hours they arrived at Base, at one a.m. in the morning to find only the night watch up. However, it did not take long before the remaining members were up to greet the return of the first trail party. They were ravenously hungry and rapidly devoured the food that Sig generously prepared for them, and their story was related until the wee hours of the morning.

We had not heard the end of the Winter plateau trip, however. From the time they had left camp on July 15th, it had been the understanding that the first good flying day after they had reached the top, the L-5 would fly up additional supplies. Because of the ruggedness of the terrain, it required from two to three days to make the 17 mile climb by dog team, whereas the plane could cover the distance in 30 minutes. Up until the time the four of them had left Peterson and Dodson to man the station, there had not been one suitable flying day. For the next three or four days after their return the wind continued to blow, not as hard as it had for the previous week, but enough so that the weather remained unsuitable for flying.

During this time, a second trail party was making ready to leave camp for the plateau. This party was destined primarily as a second training trip to give other personnel a chance to experience trail conditions. At the same time, they would carry a few additional supplies to the two men on top in case continued bad weather delayed the plane's departure. This was merely a precautionary measure, as Peterson and Dodson had been left with an 18 day food supply, which if necessary, could have been stretched. The evening the four returned to camp, we had radio contact with the two men on the Plateau, at which time they said the wind was blowing hard there, that it was impossible to work outdoors, but they did not state anything unusual in the conditions they were experiencing. The next two nights, Kelsey was unable to contact them. Finn was not particularly concerned, as he knew Peterson had been having difficulty with the radio and was doing a bit of experimenting with the antenna. He reasoned there was nothing that could have happened to them, confined as they were to their tents, except the possibility of inexperienced men being overcome by fumes from the kerosene primus stove. Finn did not give credence to this, however, because both men knew enough to use the primus only for cooking and not for heating without taking the utmost precautions. Dodson had experience in the out-of-doors. He had been vice-president of the Harvard Mountaineering Club and was a good skier and climber. Were the bad weather to continue for a week or two, thus preventing the plane or a trail party from leaving, both men knew the location of a British cache less than one-half mile from their position, which contained kerosene and two tons of supplies.

Thursday, July 24, 1947

Awoke around 11 o'clock. Finn went in to find no one up and nothing was getting done. He was most unhappy and he told them so. Found out there was no night watchman to call them. Around 2 o'clock, I took a ride on John Tonkin's dogteam for about twenty minutes. We had a fine time and it was good to get out in the air. Came back to find Harry and Ike in discussing affairs with Finn. Ike and Harry had an argument about who controlled the camp while Finn was away. Ike claimed Finn hadn't left him enough directions and that Harry didn't give him a correct list of what had to be done and that Harry was a liar. Harry said he wouldn't control it while Ike ran things, was going to be too busy with aviation to run things any way. Blew up when he heard about my control of outgoing radio messages. I told him he had no right to talk behind my back. Finn said that was the way he wanted it and explained why to Ike, who understood. Ike said Harry should have control of the Beech and he the other two planes, that Harry couldn't run the camp and wouldn't be able to run aviation. Harry said Ike would be remaining here anyway and that started things. Ike said he came down on false pretenses and that Finn said he would be a pilot. Finn denied this and explained Ike's physical conditions, dependence on him as Skipper, etc. Harry said he wanted Ike as copilot with Lassiter, but that Lassiter wouldn't fly with Ike. Lassiter was called in, who said he would. Lassiter said he was fed up with Harry constant lying and offered to go out and fight it out with him. Robertson was called in and it was decided that he should be responsible for all maintenance with Lassiter's help, but didn't understand why all three planes had to fly at one time. It was all very hectic and after it was over, Lassiter came and said he didn't want to go up the glacier with Harry on Saturday, but wanted to go manhauling with Chuck. Finn said O.K. and is sending Don instead. Latady came in with a story.

Thompson recorded a whopper of an earthquake on his seismograph today. Very nerve wracking times.

Saturday, July 26, 1947

Finn let me sleep until noon. He was up working. Jennie was up for the first time in three days. She wanted a record from my diary of Harry's previous flights. I began washing my hair.

Any washing in our hut was a major undertaking. I would first go into the Bunkhouse and tap off of a bucket of water from the central source of supply (a spigot) near the galley range where the snow melter had melted the water from hard blue ice or snow. Then I carried it into our hut to heat it on our small coal burning stove for a couple of hours. If I hadn't changed my mind by the time it was finally hot, I'd proceed with washing clothes, hair, or myself, as the case may be. Sometimes by that time, I decided not to wash my hair. It really didn't matter, as I was not going anywhere and no one was coming to visit. A month or two didn't make much difference. The men had a slogan that they were sure to take a shower every night, but you must remember that the night lasted three months during the dark part of winter. The men had rigged a make-shift shower in the machine shop which I had tried once or twice, but actually I found it easier and more convenient to do my meager bathing by taking a sponge bath in our own quarters. A clothesline was permanently strung across our room for drying my unmentionables, etc. The men had gotten quite used to ducking beneath the line, filled or empty, and coming up on the other side whenever they came in to talk to Finn.

Around noon on the fourth day after Finn's return to camp, the weather cleared sufficiently to permit the L-5 to take off. As the bay ice over the cove was sufficiently thick to use for a flying field, our future flight operations were conducted from there.

Harry flew today, but did not see the tent. Adams then flew, found the tent easily, flew over it four times, but saw no one.

Previously, the men on the Plateau had been told to signal the plane by panels to indicate the direction of the wind and the condition of the surface for landing. Adams was not able to land because he estimated that a 30 mile-an-hour surface wind was blowing and without someone on the ground to give him information, it would not be safe. If he had landed under such conditions and something happen to prevent him from being able to take off again, he would have been stuck there alone without assistance. It is not safe for any one man to be in the field at any time; two is the minimum number. We thought it possible that the men were inside their tent and that the wind had caused so much noise that they could not hear the motor of the L-5. Finn asked Harry and Adams to fly up again in the Beechcraft, try to raise them, and then to cover his previous route of sledge travel, in case they had left camp for some reason. They did this, buzzing their tent at least six times without response. The missing men were not seen on the surface at any time. When the fliers returned and gave Finn this information, he became alarmed for the first time. Still he was not able to reason logically what the trouble was, or what possibly could have happened even though they had not come in on the radio schedule for the last 36 hours.

> *Harry's dog team party was supposed to go up today, but last two days of blow canceled it until tomorrow. The barometer was slowly going up and the wind had stopped, but the atmosphere was still a bit misty.*

The days were still short and now twilight was approaching. It was too late to unload the small L-5 plane of sufficient weight for allowing another man to accompany Adams so that together they might land. Finn had little information to work on, and with the whereabouts of two men unknown, certainly he did not want two additional men taking rash chances with darkness coming on. The only alternative was to be sure the trail party left early the next morning and at the same time hope for good flying weather. In times of stress, the worst things which could happen always come to mind first.

Finn had requested Peterson and Dodson not to go beyond calling distance of their tent alone and, if they went together, to be sure to wear skis at all times. However, there had been a great deal of discussion about the Weddell Sea and the possibility of seeing it from the Plateau on days of perfect visibility had been mentioned. He knew both men were anxious to see as much as they could of the Antarctic and were eager for the program to start. What if they had gone off in search of new scenery and danger had befallen them? Perhaps they became separated and couldn't find their way back before a storm had overtaken them? Maybe they hadn't worn skis and one or both had fallen down a crevasse? Had both of them gone down a crevasse, we wouldn't have a chance in a million of ever knowing what had happened. Before we could reach the spot, blowing snow would cover their tracks and we would not know where to begin searching for them. If we stayed in the Antarctic until eternity, we would never be able to search every crevasse in the vicinity.

Inwardly, Finn was very concerned, but actually he didn't know how close to the truth his thoughts were traveling. At that very moment in the twilight, their trouble was overtaking them, while he was pondering and powerless to aid. It would be foolhardy to start on a wild goose chase unprepared. He would have to wait until morning and hope that it was a good day. Finn was worried that evening, but couldn't believe there wasn't some reasonable explanation. My Diary read -

> *Ken Butler came in as I was in the middle of washing my hair. He sat and chatted all afternoon. Finn was particularly concerned that the 30-mph surface drift, which prevented the plane from landing, also prevented the sacked in Dodson and Peterson from hearing the plane. Ken had taken a long flight over Neny Trough today. We discussed world politics for hours. Finn gave him a large heater, of which we have six, to heat up their plane before starting. Harry showed definite concern about Dodson and Peterson's welfare and wanted to start first thing tomorrow morning. Finn said, yes, by all means, and wondered if anything could have happened to them in their tent, but reasoned that it was impossible as they wouldn't have used the kerosene for heating instead of eating. We had dinner and the British came over for a movie while Finn was listening to the 8 o'clock schedule from the trail party, which did not come on. We saw the "Buccaneers," without Finn, who was in our shack, because he had seen it so many times.*
>
> *After about five reels, Bob Dodson stormed in the galley white as a ghost, bumped into me and said, "Where is Finn? Pete went down a crevasse. I did everything I could to help him, but had to come back for help, leaving him there."*
>
> *The lights snapped on. I went tearing after Bob Dodson into our shack. Butler asked if he could come – I said, "yes", and yelled for Ike.*

Dodson's words made Finn numb with shock and surprise. Eventually the reality of the situation dawned and Finn's mind raced to obtain certain information. Finn was always very calm in an emergency.

> *Bob Dodson said Pete was up on the glacier about eight miles. He had called to Bob to throw him a knife. Bob lowered it on 120-foot line, but couldn't reach him. Heard no more from him and so yelled to him that he was going after help. Butler said he would get a dog team ready. Bob said he was ready to go again after eating. I got Sig to get Bob's chow ready and helped him. By that time, most of the fellows were running around preparing for the outgoing party. Finn was afraid he could not go, because of the very bad blisters on his feet from his recent trip, but I assured him I could fix them up, so he announced twice that he was going. Finn told Ike not to go, but while I was fixing Finn's feet, Lassiter came to tell Finn that Harry, Ike, Bill and Bob had started. It was about 10:30. Finn was disturbed Ike had gone. McLean came in and wanted to go. Finn said O.K. go with the British. He and Finn went over to the British camp where they were loading the sleds and two dog teams with all rescue apparatus, tent, rope, block, lights, medical equipment, etc. They got off about 11:15 or 11:30. Jennie and I went out back to see them start off. Finn left sitting on the sled, but we later heard he soon got off and ran along side.*
>
> *Hassage and Nic came in for some coffee. We talked of how horrible the accident was and of what his chances of survival were. The same thought was in everybody's mind, but we dared not mention it. They left and Jennie and Sig came in. We talked and watched out of the window looking for lights. Woody, Mac, Owen, Smith and Andy took a light up to the aviation cache to guide the party back in the dark. Lassiter and Robertson were getting the plane ready to take off at dawn. Larry Fiske had half an hour walkie-talkie schedules with the group at the aviation cache.*
>
> *Three of the four remaining Britishers slept while one took night watch. Everybody was active and worrying. I could think of nothing but Pete's family and wondered what Finn could say to them and what an awful tragedy*

it was. Jennie brought in some wine, which we drank. Sig went into his bunk to sleep for a couple of hours. Jennie and I had some tomato soup and a steak sandwich. We went outside several times and finally, it began to get light. Each hour we thought we would learn some news. We all sat chatting by the fire in the bunkhouse. People urged me to go to bed, but I insisted upon waiting – I couldn't sleep then.

Finally, the British plane and our plane took off and returned with word that they spotted the searchers preparing the dog teams in the middle of a badly crevassed area and that they had flashed a signal, but could not read what it was.

The time was 15 hours after 6:30 the previous evening when Bob Dodson had left Pete. We gave up hope, thinking it impossible that he could have survived 15 hours of it. Bob Nichols and I took a walk out to the ship and Bob told me I had to prepare myself for the worst. We watched the two planes take off again, and land without encouraging word. Everyone was discouraged and we knew that Harry was on top of the glacier coming toward camp with the news. Everyone went out to meet him and found that Pete was alive and well except for bruises and a little exposure. The story is as follows:

On Thursday morning they began having trouble with their tent. It had blown continuously since Finn left. Their sleeping bags were wet, frosted over, and frozen. They forced themselves to eat, but they were getting cold, particularly Pete. When the trouble came with the tent, they decided on Saturday to leave, as they did not consider the weather good enough for the plane to fly that day. This was their first mistake. They left, without making a sign that they had left, around noon. They were down the steep glacier when they heard the plane overhead and set off smoke bombs. They figured it would take them a couple of hours to get back up to the plateau and by then the plane would have given up. They decided the only thing to do was to get back here as soon as possible. (What they both purposedly neglected to tell Finn then was that they had been lost in a highly crevassed area for three hours and were just beginning to find their way out of it). Pete was the weaker of the two. They were having trouble traveling against the sastrugi (wind blown snow ridges). They decided to take off their skis to make more time – a disastrous decision. Bob led for a while dragging his skis. He fell once and Pete thought he had gone in a crevasse, he was petrified, but fortunately it was only a ridge. Pete started to lead and fell several times. They were not roped together, as they certainly should have been. Bob stopped to adjust his backpack and suddenly, with a gasp Pete was gone. Bob approached the crevasse and heard Pete yell for a knife. Bob lowered a knife on a 120-foot rope, but to no avail. He heard nothing else and yelled to Pete that he was going on for help. Wisely, he put his skis on and came back to camp at about 9:45.

The rescue party got to the area and searched for the crevasse for 3 ½ hours. Finally, they picked up Dodson's ski tracks and with the searchlight found the flags Dodson had left to mark the crevasse. Dick Butson, the British doctor, who was a small man, volunteered to lower himself down on a rope, asking Finn what to do with the body, if Pete were dead. Finn had puzzled about this very problem on the way up and asked Ken for advice. Ken said leave it there pending word from the family. Butson got down to Pete and found him alive and talking to him. Within 30 min., they had him out and soon in a tent, with the doctors working over him. Latady and Harry were also in the tent. Finn asked Harry to get out and let Dodson in, which he finally did. Pete thought he would never be rescued, after two hours, and thought of other things beside the base. He said it was a horrible way to die. He couldn't move a thing and the more he moved the tighter he became wedged in. He had fallen head first, 110 feet below the surface, wedged in, with his arms pinned behind his back and his backpack over his head, so sound couldn't get to the surface. He hollered, but all sound went below. He heard them looking for him for about three hours. He was a lucky fellow. His face was bruised and cut. He was stiff and cold, but apparently no bones were broken. And apparently, the alpaca suit we had been amused to see him wear when he left for the trail, was partly responsible for saving his life by protecting him from the numbing cold.

The two doctors cut off his clothing, treated him for shock, examined for any fracture and placed an arm and leg in splints as a precaution, until a more thorough examination could be made at camp. Then he was stowed in a large sleeping bag for the choppy ride down to Base. Although no bones were broken, movement of any sort was painful because of the pressure that had been exerted on his body while in that distorted position, crammed and prone on his side between the converging ice faces. The plexus of nerves to the right arm was injured with the resulting partial paralysis of that arm. This and the numerous scratches on his face and arms healed perfectly in a matter of a few weeks. On our way back to camp, Lassiter flew overhead in the L-5, awaiting instructions if he should land and perhaps take Pete back by plane. They waived him off, as it would have been risky to land on the surfaces over which they were traveling. Lassiter had taken the signals to mean that either they had not found Peterson, or were not bringing him back. It was not before they reached camp finally that we knew the safe outcome of their mission.

On that same eventful night, Schlossbach froze his big toe so badly that the entire tip underwent a dry gangrene. During the successive three months period a large area sloughed and was replaced by new tissue. Up until the time we left the Antarctic, his toe bore a star shaped dimple at the very tip as his only memento.

Dick Butson did a magnificent job. The British came in for breakfast of tomato bullion soup, cake, tea and coffee. Everybody went to bed. We slept until dinner, which Sig brought in to us, ham, sweet potatoes etc. Sig chatted for four or five hours. Harry came in and talked about how dumb Bob Dodson had been, saying also, they hadn't eaten recently because they would have to go outside the tent to relieve themselves. Harry said he didn't know Finn was going on the rescue party. Finn had told Harry he was going and Harry had answered, you are – good! We went to bed around 2 o'clock in the morning.

Peterson's narrow escape was an all too vivid reminder that the Antarctic is perilous country, with danger lurking everywhere. One false move is all that is necessary to forcibly bring home this very serious fact. The greatest enemy of any expedition that has ever come to the Antarctic, is the inexperience of its personnel. Experience can be obtained only through individual realization of the great dangers the terrain can afford and having the foresight to take all the necessary precautions to compensate for any unforeseen emergencies. The two narrow escapes that this group had been fortunate enough to see safely concluded, were glaring examples to all concerned, which they were not likely to forget. The lessons were obvious – the Antarctic cannot be treated lightly. The knowledge of its unknown mysteries can be revealed only through patience, over a long period of time, and by observing the cardinal rules of safety at all times. Finn was not happy with either of the two men involved in this nearly fatal episode and did not hesitate to point out their poor decisions and many mistakes which he had covered with them in the past, such as not leaving camp without. at least, leaving an indication in the snow that they had done so, since they knew Adams would be flying up to them on the first good day. They were not roped together in a highly crevassed area and they had removed their skis, a devastating decision, as skis will usually cross over a snowbridge of a crevasse safely by distributing the weight of a man over the ski's surface. The men were aware of these points, but had just been thoughtless and careless in their hurry to get back to base.

Monday, July 28, 1947

Sig's birthday today. We got up for a twelve o'clock breakfast. The crowd had already started making some tent flags. Finn called in Dodson and found out all the particulars of last two days. Finn called Harry in to get Pete's eating story straight which Dodson denied. Finn was angry with both men for not obeying safety rules and taking orders. I talked to Pete for some time. He was very thankful he was alive and safe. Nichols came in and talked about the accident. It was the second beautiful day in a row, with the sun out and perfectly clear – could see for miles. Some took a walk and stopped into the British for tea, I guess. We had a good dinner of roast pork, etc. The British came over for a movie, "Letter of Introduction." They were all tired out after yesterday's jaunt. We discussed how very lucky Pete was and how little hope anyone had for his being alive and how appreciative we were of their aid and readiness. After the movie, Butler,

Tonkin, Walton, Freeman, Ike, McLean, Hassage, and Sig came in and we drank a toast of thanks to the British then had ice cream, tuna fish sandwiches and coffee. We had a nice conversation and a good time. They left about 12 o'clock.

Fortune allowed us a few days to catch our collective breath before we had to cope with other problems. One thing about an expedition, each day brings forth the unexpected and life is rarely dull.

Two days later the second Plateau sledge party departed from camp. McClary, Robertson, Owen, and Dodson went up to move the fateful Plateau campsite from its position, two miles further along the Plateau. They too were given instructions to pick out a landing field and wait for the L-5 to arrive with additional supplies. A week later, after several tries only to be forced back each time by bad weather, Adams finally was able to make a landing on the Plateau. The dog team party was busily establishing the new camp. It was one of those rare cloudless, cold Antarctic days.

In a small way thc spring field season had begun. The sun was with us again. It had appeared for the first time over the glacier rim about 10:30 EST on Sunday July 27th. In time, its return had a far-reaching effect and as it grew noticeably brighter it brought with it slightly longer days. As we looked toward the mountains southward, we measured its daily advance by the way it played more and more over the peaks. What a grand sight it was and what satisfaction it offered to all.

Finn discussing flight plans with Ken Butler, leader of nearby British "E" base, posing by Beechcraft plane "Ed Sweeney."

Jackie and Finn peer out of the window in the passageway between their hut and the main bunkhouse.

Discussing trail and flight plans in our hut – top row: Fiske, Finn, Peterson; front row: Latady, McLean, Ike, Thompson, Nichols and Dodson

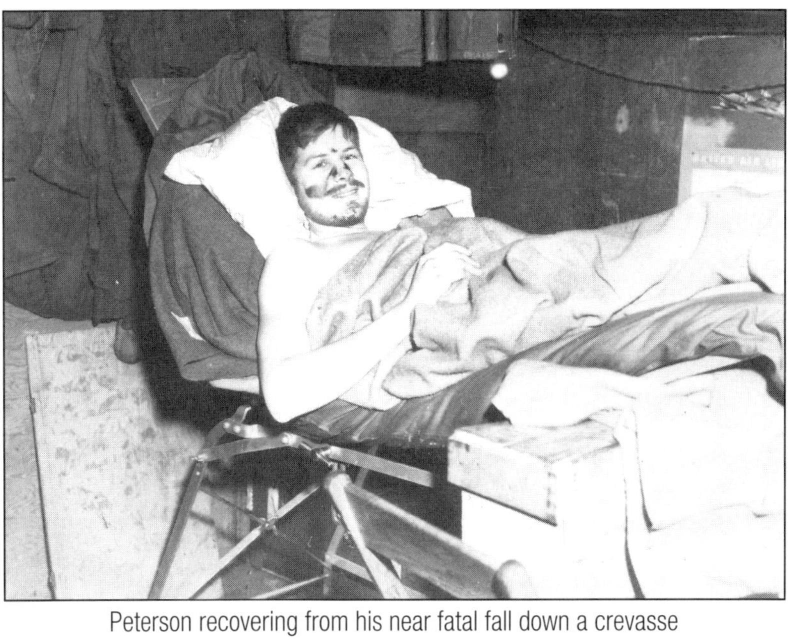

Peterson recovering from his near fatal fall down a crevasse

Our little "Necessary House" on the hill with Science Building on right

Our cook, Sig Gutenko, serves up fresh pies

XI

Warming Up

Thursday, July 31, 1947

Awoke fairly early, spent part of the morning chatting in the science building. Harry's trail party left about 9:40. Took an afternoon ski half way to Figure IV with Jennie and Nichols. Nic had man-hauled coal with Don all morning. Came back and Jennie brought in some chocolate. Ken Butler came over. He and Finn chatted about Peterson with regard to his fall. Finn discussed with Ken possibility of supplying their party for the whole Weddell Coast trip as Finn was afraid to let our personnel out. Ken was pleased to death naturally. I was shocked to death. Obviously, Finn had been shaken to the core.

Before dinner Kelsey informed Finn that he had intercepted a communication between Harry and the British base saying a sled had broken and they were returning to Base tomorrow. Finn was so mad with Harry for making a schedule with the British without his knowledge that he told it to the whole dinner table. Not everyone understood what he was talking about, but those who did, certainly did not side with Harry. For some time, Harry had chosen to continue pushing Finn too hard. Nichols and Ike came in afterward to discuss the whole situation, which looks pretty bad. Discussion was interrupted by the movie, "Andy Hardy at College." It was Reg Freeman's birthday and everyone sang him a song.

Ike, Finn, Sig, and I came back and chatted. All agreed that Harry's attitude is, and has been hopeless, and that Kelsey should do better on the radio. Bob Nichols came in for a few minutes and then all left except Sig. We talked to Finn until 3 o'clock in the morning, about what he could do to get more out of the fellows and the expedition. We offered suggestions back and forth and I hope accomplished something.

Friday, August 1, 1947

After staying up until 3 o'clock, I was dead tired this morning. Finn made me some tomato juice and a bacon sandwich. Bob Nichols came in after lunch and discussed Kelsey's complete lack of interest in radio during the last several weeks, and what the possible cause could be. A couple more Britishers came over to try on the alpaca suits (the type that Peterson had been wearing) that Finn is giving them and. which they were delighted to get. Nichols came in again and discussed the trail operations. Finn told him he had discussed with Butler the possibility of us supporting the British trail party along the Weddell Coast. Nichols said Finn was retreating and I agreed. Bob pointed out that the personnel would not be endangered in taking chances, because no chances would be taken without the utmost safety precautions being observed.

Harry got back and came in. He had heard that Finn was angry and they let each other have it. Finn told him definitely, he wanted to know about anything and everything going on with the British. Harry said O.K. and calmed down telling Finn all the things which went wrong on their trip: the tent was no good, the sled broke, the pemmican was no good, the radio was wrong, the gang lines and tethering lines and harnesses were wrong, and the dog pemmican fell apart. After that we had dinner and Finn, and I spent the evening working. Andy received another earthquake on the seismograph. Pete felt well enough to lie in Jennie's room listening to records.

Admittedly, Finn had a short fuse, but he had been uncharacteristically patient with all of Harry's very trying antics, hoping that Harry would come to his senses and recognize what was happening between the two of them and straighten himself out before Finn lost all patience. In spite of all of the very trying inexplicable things that Harry had done, Finn felt sorry for him. They had known each other for a long time. He had been so very helpful when Finn was organizing in Washington and Finn had rewarded him by taking him into his confidence, making him Third-in-Command and taking his wife along with us. What more did he want? Were the trouble makers urging him on? Did he want to take over the expedition himself? What was it? Finn really tried to get to the answer but it hurt him that Harry was not and for a long time had not been loyal.

Saturday, August 2, 1947

Another beautiful day. The sun is certainly on its way back now. It is already shining on the British camp. Finn did lots of work around the hut and outside while I spent my time busily answering for radio transmission a list of messages, which we owe. Jennie took my picture standing outside. She has been running around with Bill's camera. Bill presented us with an album of pictures taken thus far. He did the book binding himself. He told Finn he had given the fellows several copies of the expedition pictures. He also suggested they be allowed to obtain any copies they wanted at a future date. Finn said he hoped to be able to present them all with a selected picture album upon return. He told Bill after a year that it would be O.K. if Bill wanted to use any of the mountain pictures in a publication of his own. Bill also said he had enough materials to develop the fellows' private films. Bill volunteered to help sell Finn's film upon return, which was a nice offer. Finn made up a memorandum of picture policy to be followed and gave it to Bill, as a result of this conversation. We had dinner and the British came over to see, "Oklahoma Kid". Finn invited Butler, Walton, Butson, Jennie, Harry, McClary, and Sig in for a chat. The obvious 3 had little to contribute, which was interesting. We think Butler sees through them.

Sunday, August 3, 1947

We awoke late and Finn fixed breakfast here. We had some of the recovered eggs, which were tasteless, probably because they had thawed and refrozen. Finn called Harry in, to find out why he didn't want to lead the Plateau trip again. They talked very calmly but Harry refused to give a good reason why he wouldn't go, just saying he was in too many things, that he would train elsewhere but not there, that Finn didn't have confidence in him, etc. Finn let him go, saying that's all I have to say to you now. He then brought Nichols and Ike in and it was decided to let Mac lead the party and send Dodson in Harry's place. The fellows were brought in and told and were very pleased. Nichols has been asked by Butler to go on their short trip to Neny Trough.

Finn and I were invited over to the British for tea and found Larry just leaving. We chatted as usual, but just before we left, Finn had a chat with Butler, explaining Harry had not informed him regarding the radio matters and did just as he pleased. Butler said Jennie had started bitching about Finn to John Tonkin Thursday evening and John was very surprised and could say nothing. Ken said Harry was impossible and he did not see how anyone could live with him. He had also told his men not to take sides in any controversy over here and when our fellows came over and started bitching, he always changed the subject. Ken said the Falkland Islands were going to broadcast to us this coming Friday and wanted Finn to say something over the air. We came back for dinner and saw "The Castles" after dinner. Nichols told Finn of his conversation with Ken regarding a future joint trail party, which Finn has now changed his opinion on, for the better, I believe. They discussed Harry, Nichols saying Harry had told him in confidence, the real reason why he wouldn't go up to the Plateau again. An albatross flew calmly over camp today circling about, leaving little doubt as to open water nearby.

Monday, August 4, 1947

I worked on an article of "Women in the Antarctic" and later prepared for transmission an excellent article by Andy Thompson on earthquakes and microseisms. Bob didn't leave on the British party today, as the prediction was for a storm, but he and Butler instead took a trip to the Debenhams. They had a long talk about to what extent the two expeditions would cooperate and naturally he wants to do the long 400 mile sledge trip from Darlington Island. The issue begins to get dreadfully confused and I am against Finn arranging for the British to do it.

Most of the fellows were out working on gas drums. Bob reports that McLean is disappointed at not going, either on the British trip, or the Plateau trip. Finn says he can go on the depot-laying trip to Cape Berteaux. Bob says Smith has done a good steady job of things and deserves to be complimented. Harry appeared amiable today and tonight they had a big party in their room. Bob says Butler understands a great many things and is a good friend of the expedition. Bob got angry with one of Sig's illogical conversations and walked out early. I had a pointed discussion with Sig, as to why he constantly has to criticize everything Nichols does.

Tuesday, August 5, 1947

Bob Nichols was in and out discussing all possible plans to follow for the trail work. While practicing on the glacier Don McLean broke his ankle skiing just before lunch.

He was endeavoring to become more proficient in skiing on the glacier in back of camp. This was a very sorrowful accident to him, particularly because he was one of the trail candidates and the occurrence about eliminated him for a long while.

I worked on the preserving of the ship article and finished some washing from yesterday. Had a movie after dinner, "Topper Takes a Trip" – lousy. Before movie, Bill attempted to take some group pictures. Jennie immediately sat herself in the middle of the second row, which made Finn upset and so he went over to the side. The fellows were most discourteous and filled up the first row, not allowing the expedition officers to be in the center of the picture. They took two this way, then found out Lassiter was not even in the picture. Finally Sig, Bob, and Finn rearranged them with the Expedition officers in the front row, the scientists in the second row and one of the women on either side of second row and one picture was taken of this. I felt embarrassed about the whole thing. Tonkin came in here after the movie and spent several hours telling us about his most amazing experience during the War. He is a very nice fellow and exceedingly interesting.

Wednesday, August 6, 1947

Ken Butler invited me to go on a sledge trip to Rymill's Base at the Debenhams. We left about quarter of eleven and had a seventy-minute run in the sunshine with the dog teams. It was a perfectly beautiful day. Once there, we had some hot orange juice and some tea, took a quick look around the shack and a view from the former meteorological hill. Millerand Island was close by. On the way up, Ken asked me all about Harry and told me he had shown his uncontrollable temper several times at his place, his lack of defining a problem, his unstableness and his discussing Finn's ideas to his own advantage, example, the British Weddell Coast Trip, when Finn had asked him not to say anything. On the way back, I told Ken how terribly the British Embassy had acted toward Finn before he left and why Finn had such a turned-off attitude upon our arrival. Ken understood perfectly and said Bingham had been angry because of the lies the Foreign Office was telling about the condition of this Base and when the Britishers arrived, which was not three years ago. He felt it could be traced to the mismanagement of one or two people and he regretted it.

We got back and had a cup of tea. Their plane had just made 11,700 feet. Lassiter had ours at 10,050 feet and had to come down because of the cold. I asked Ken over for dinner, and he came. After dinner, he and Finn had a long talk about trail plans and the plateau weather station. Finn said our party would leave tomorrow and it was a good training trip for them. Sig came in mad at

Harry and the conversation turned to him. After much was said and explained to Ken, he said he thought Harry to be hopeless. He didn't see how anyone could live around him and he couldn't see how Finn could operate through him, under the conditions which now existed, and thought it would be better to replace him under the circumstances.

Thursday, August 7, 1947

Got up late and found that the second Plateau trail party had finally left about 8 o'clock this morning, with McClary, Robertson, Owen and Dodson. They really got an early start (on their mission to move the original Plateau Station two miles further along the Plateau). At lunch Finn announced the two planes would fly the stuff to the glacier soon and Woody and Britisher McLeod would follow in about two weeks to man the station. Also, he said Adams would fly the L-5. Harry butted in to say the British plane had been grounded for the year. He mumbled something about his not flying again and he would get things straightened out etc., and asked to speak to Finn.

Harry and Finn went into our shack. I took my time and then went in. They were arguing loudly. Harry disagreed with Finn's flight plans over the Weddell Sea Coast. He thought they were too dangerous, although when discussing them thoroughly in Washington, he had thought they were great. This was the first time Harry had indicated his fear of flying the flights Finn had planned as the major geographical objective of the expedition. Harry asked me to leave. I said I couldn't see why I should. Finn calmly said she stays. Harry said O.K., he would get out. Finn said that was O.K. with him, but they continued to yell by the door. Harry said, yes, he was disloyal and couldn't see any reason why he shouldn't be, that Finn couldn't have any confidence in him. He said that he was over 21 and would do as he pleased about orders and obeying them. Finn let him have it and said O.K .that was the way it would be. Harry then backed down and said he thought things were running well. He left with tears in his eyes. We were really mad.

For a very long time Harry had had some misguided idea that he knew more than Finn and was running things. For months Finn had been unbelievably patient with him, hoping he would straighten out. Outwardly Finn took this blow-up very calmly, but it was obviously the beginning of a major break with Harry and I knew that Finn was very unhappy about it.

After dinner and movies, "Wilson," which was excellent, Finn brought Ike in and they talked until 3 o'clock. Finn decided to replace Harry in aviation by Ike and Ike agreed that Harry was irresponsible and hopeless. It was decided Ike could be responsible to Finn and not allow Harry any authority. Lassiter had been in, in the afternoon, making more plans with Finn regarding a proposed polar trip. Already, Harry had indicated to Lassiter, that he thought Finn would turn the aviation program over to him, but Lassiter said he was crazy and he didn't want it. Lassiter is working on a new antenna for Kelsey. Nichols is getting in condition by long ski trips to Figure IV Mt. twice a day. I sent in "Women in Antarctic" story to NANA .

Friday, August 8, 1947

Awoke in time for lunch. Typed Dodson's report. Nichols began work on two geological abstracts. I typed up a justification for relieving Harry as head of aviation. Sig came in for a talk in the afternoon. Jennie was very sick with an upset stomach. Harcly Peterson wanted to go up to the aviation cache. Finn said, no! He didn't want Harcly near a crevassed glacier again. Harry appeared very friendly. Finn asked Kelsey to go over to Butler and ask that they stand-by the radio for the trail party. After dinner, we listened to a broadcast from the Falkland Islands and London. Freddie White gave regards to Ronne, etc. Lassiter spent the day on the antenna and got an 80-foot pole up straight. Chuck Adams came in and talked with Finn about flying stuff to the Plateau tomorrow. Nichols went over the trail gear and estimated weights with Finn. They discussed 3 or 4 man party. Bob suggested asking Butler for more dogs, that he thought it for the good of the expedition, to have a 4-man party. We got to bed fairly early around midnight.

Saturday, August 9, 1947

Awoke fairly early and straightened up the room. Lassiter worked on getting up the antenna. Bob Nichols spent most of the afternoon trying to persuade Finn not to abandon Harry. Harry had talked to him much about how sorry he was of some things he had said and that it would be better if we all were friends again. Bob told Harry he had done many things wrong and Harry agreed, perhaps he had, etc. Bob said Finn knew Harry had bitched about him at the British camp. Finn told Bob it was impossible to go on like this and he couldn't stand it any longer. Finn had a long talk with Ike about the organization of it and worked things out pretty well. Finn discussed with him about not piloting and he was very understanding. He said he disagreed with the Doctor and with Finn's reasoning about his piloting with only one eye and lack of depth perception, but as long as Finn had his mind made up that way, it was O.K. by him to act only as co-pilot.

Adams was going to fly (to the Plateau), but Harry didn't tell him the weather was O.K., so he felt he was between Harry and Ike and didn't fly.

Latady was bothered with sinuses again and was in bed most of the day. We didn't get the trail party on the radio. After dinner, we had a movie, "Drums", then Tonkin, Tommy, David Jones, Lassiter, Adams, Smitty, Doug Mason, Sig, and later Andy came in for a chat and sandwiches, coffee, and ice cream. They didn't leave until around 2 o'clock. Harry was very sweet all day, but began getting morose at night. Harry approached Ike as to what they had decided and Ike said they were waiting for Harry's resignation. Harry said he would make it up today, but never did. He had also told Ike, if Ike took over aviation, he guessed he would be continued with the management of the Beechcraft.

Sunday, August 10, 1947

I took Hassage's place as Mess cook so he could go to Red Rock Ridge with the British. Smitty became a father during the night, as Pansy had seven puppies, five males and two females. Later in the afternoon, she had one more, a female. Little Pansy, it was amazing.

Chuck Adams decided to make a flight to the Plateau, but just as he left it clouded over, so he was forced to come back again. Finn and Bob skied out to Neny. The plane in landing got stuck in the slush ice, so the weasel went out and hauled her out. Lassiter fixed a new radio antenna for us and it is considerably better than the other one we had.

Lassiter and Adams came in for a cup of coffee and we played some bridge, after which Finn talked to them about the new plan for aviation. They felt it was the only thing that could be done and they would do anything they could to help the program within the limits of safety.

After dinner, at which Harry was very friendly, Finn called him and Ike in. Finn asked Harry if he had any suggestions for making it a more peaceful group. Harry said he thought he and Finn should start over again from the beginning. Very calmly Finn said, he had already done that many times before but each week brought a new crisis with Harry and he could stand it no longer. Finn told him what he proposed to do and read him why he was relieving Harry as Head of Aviation. Harry still admitted he was disloyal, but said Finn was removing him from aviation when all the things Finn didn't like had happened in other fields. This, of course, is by no means completely true, but Finn let it go. Harry said he had come in to make other suggestions, but as Finn had made up his mind, he refused to argue any further and so far as he was concerned, he came down here as head of aviation and was not interested in any other camp work or Third-in-Command, so it was all or nothing for him. Finn said O.K. and Harry left. Ike said it was too bad, but that's the way he was, and only a few days ago, he had said just handling the Beechcraft would be O.K. with him.

Monday, August 11, 1947

After Harry and Ike left last night, Lassiter came in and Finn told him the news. Lassiter stated again, that he had told Harry, that he would come down on this expedition under the same conditions, which Harry had said he was coming i.e. a regular Navy Commission and a promotion in rank. Of course, this had been a misrepresentation by Harry, who was already out of the Navy. Lassiter also said, Washington told him directly that he should go any place or do anything for the expedition and he was the judge of the two (himself and Adams) over safety.

When we awoke fairly early this morning, Harry, of course, had made no work list. At lunch, Jennie and Harry sat close by us and Harry particularly was very friendly. It was amusing in one way, but sad really to see what he had done to himself.

Don came in and spent quite a while discussing Harry with Finn. He had spent much time with Harry, had discussed with Ike and was glad to get Finn's side. He felt it was a case of personalities not getting along and felt if Finn could take over the aviation program, with the pilots as consultants, without Harry having to go through Ike, it would be more agreeable to Harry. There are, of course, many obvious things against this. Larry Fiske spent a long time chatting after dinner, then made up the weather report for NANA. Lassiter came in later saying Harry had taken Chinook for a walk past Hawkins and the two of them got into a fight. Everybody yelled for a gun and before the fellows could throw water on the fighting dogs Lassiter shot Hawkins in the leg. They put it in a splint and he is O.K. now. Harry asked to be night watchman and Finn agreed to it. The eight puppies are getting along fine and are husky little devils.

Tuesday, August 12, 1947

Butler came over for the afternoon telling Finn of the bad luck with the Auster's flying and how messages were mixed and confused in transmission and how angry the Governor was. He asked Finn to broadcast for 15 min. on Thursday to all the other British Bases. Finn called an aviation conference with Ike, Lassiter, Adams, and Latady, telling them of his change in Harry's job. They discussed the possibility of Harry's coming back to fly the

Beechcraft and Finn told Bill if he could talk Harry into it well and good. Bill quite agreed with Finn, that Harry was disloyal and temperamentally unfit for the job.

Butler came in for a few minutes while I was working up Sig's pemmican story. We then saw, "Are Husbands Necessary", and a repeat of "Its a Pleasure". Butler came in again for a few minutes afterward and it ended in a discussion on Harry. Butler thinks him quite impossible and making a dreadful ass of himself. He hasn't shown up all day today. Jennie took his meal at dinner into him. Finn bumped into him tonight in the Science Bldg. and he spoke friendly, as though nothing had happened. In the aviation discussion Lassiter tried to pin Ike down as to who would be flying the planes. Ike refused to be pinned down. Lassiter said he had no objection to flying with Ike and Ike said, "Well I can't see why you should, you're lucky to get such a good man to fly with".

Wednesday, August 13, 1947

Today proved to be one of those rare beautiful days. Chuck Adams got the plane ready and took off for the Plateau. He found the fellows at the new met station, landed, and unloaded his cargo.

When Adams returned to camp, he came nonchalantly into the Bunkhouse and drew his chair up to a cup of warm tea without taking off his hat. One of the men made some remark about it and he sheepishly removed it to reveal a large blood stained emergency bandage. On their way to the dispensary, the men found out that after Adams had unloaded the supplies at the Plateau Met Station, he bent down to kick the sticky skis of the plane loose from the snow, preparatory to taking off. Suddenly he slipped and fell right into the revolving propeller.

Robertson and Dodson, who were close by, said they heard the prop hit Chuck several times before he fell to the ground. With a level head, Robertson stopped the plane's engine quickly and examined Chuck's three-inch long gash in his scalp. Dodson raced for a medical kit. Adam's heavy fur cap and tough windproof parka had saved his life. He assured the amazed men that he had thrown himself to the ground merely to get away from the prop's motion and was perfectly capable of flying the plane back to Base. After Robertson made him an emergency bandage from the first aid kit in the plane, Chuck made a long run in the deep soft snow and came back to camp.

McLean was forced to cut away a large area of hair before taking four stitches in Chuck's scalp. Another quarter of an inch and he would have been done for. Chuck waited anxiously for this to grow in around the ugly scar, afraid that it would remain a permanent bald spot, but he had nothing to fear. Few men in this world have ever made contact with a rapidly revolving airplane propeller and lived to tell the tale. Chuck Adams was fortunately one of these few.

> *Lassiter took his place and flew an additional three loads up to the Plateau, making a total of four for today with four hundred pounds of supplies and equipment each trip.*

Upon Lassiter's return, Adams made another trip to the Plateau Met Station with supplies. One ton of supplies had been landed there in the five flights within the past two days. Planes can do much work once they get a break in the weather. Lassiter and Adams were in agreement that the low atmospheric pressure on the 6,000 foot Plateau causes a loss of engine power which made their take-offs from there somewhat of a problem on each flight.

> *Jimmy Robertson returned on the third trip plenty glad to get back. Finn, Smitty, Woody, and Nichols spent the morning shoveling snow on board ship. The puppies, all eight of them, are definitely growing and doing fine. The little devils. Harry had the nerve to ask Lassiter last night, to ask Finn if he, Harry, could go on the man-hauling trip with them. That's a good joke. Jennie is having little to say to us these days, but doing plenty of yelling with the fellows . . . . . I wrote up Andy's article on tides and helped Finn decode one of the few messages from the State Dept. Bob Nichols was preparing to leave on a sledge trip with Butler tomorrow. They will go up Neny Glacier, Fjord, and Trough and be gone about ten days. Finn spoke to Ken about one of the Britishers accompanying Lassiter on a flight to find a good way across Neny Trough to the Weddell Sea. Ken said take Dougie Mason. After dinner, Jimmy Robertson came in and talked about Harry with Finn. When Finn read him a partial list of things Harry had done wrong in aviation, Jimmy agreed Harry was a funny guy and hard to do business with.*

Nichols' trail party finally left camp over two weeks later.

Saturday, August 30, 1947

The trail party departed in full glory this morning at 9:00 am. Bob Dodson was the driver of the first team of thirteen dogs which pulled two sledges. Finn and I went to the British Base to see off the supporting team and Kevin's team of eleven Labrador huskies and say good-bye to Bob. He gave the "Yake" signal and with a forward jerk, they almost disappeared in the flurries of ten inches of newly fallen snow. We had a cup of tea with Ken and got back about 10:30. Harry came in while we were there and was very surprised to see us.

I worked all day on writing articles of getting the planes off and naming them, and the departure of the trail party. Kelsey had a good contact with them at 8 o'clock and they reported to be nicely settled 12 miles away at Refuge Island, in back of Red Rock Ridge.

Less than a week later, we would be astonished by what they had to say about their problems.

Friday, September 5, 1947

We had dinner late and while at dinner, Kelsey got contact with the trail party bringing the message to Finn that Nichols was turning back and returning to Base, that the dogs would never cross the southern part of the plateau. Ike and Finn were most disturbed about this change in plans. The two Jimmies came in to suggest that they fly them out, or do everything by plane. The best suggestion to Finn was to fly two men and nine dogs over to Cape Keeler and let them go down the Weddell Coast. Robertson said the Norseman would be ready to fly on Sunday, if not tomorrow. We were up late, conferring and talking. Lassiter said Owen was the best man of the lot. Hassage was concerned about the weasel. Finn said get it ready to try and meet the trail party coming back on Sunday and see conditions for yourself.

Saturday, September 6, 1947

Hassage prepared to leave in the weasel tomorrow. Butler and Tonkin expressed regret that Nichols was returning. There was no radio contact with Nichols tonight. Finn caught Fiske opening the box of a new vibrator, which he stopped immediately because it was not needed.

Monday, September 8, 1947

Spent day working. In the afternoon about 4 o'clock, Hassage came in saying the Nichols party was on its way back. Larry Fiske was sick in the stomach and lungs, so Hassage who wanted to go on, decided to come back after talking to Nichols, who said it was impossible to get down there.

The two groups had rendezvoused at Red Rock Ridge, nine miles from Base. Struggling along with a surface drift and a nasty southern wind at their backs, the dogteam party was happy to see the weasel. When most of the load had been placed on the tractor sled, the dog-teams made an easy two hour run back to Base. They had traveled fifteen miles that day, during which time the temperature dropped to the fifties below freezing. Their faces were frostbitten and their beards were matted, and they were delighted to be back, satisfying themselves with dry clothing, hot tea and coffee. Nichols told Finn the story.

He said they could have made advanced base, but Kevin wanted to come back and reorganize the party and train our dogs better. Kevin and his sled went through the ice and fell in the water. Bob also fell in the second time. They were in water in their tent while camping. Bob didn't want to come back. After more difficulty, Kevin insisted the dogs would not make the complete trip. Bob consulted the rest and made the decision to come back and sent Finn the message, not wanting to have a long discussion with Finn over the radio. On the way back, they made good mileage, but decided they couldn't even make the Weddell Coast and decided what they would do, was a geological trip down the Sound. They also made an agreement that the four of them would stick together and no three would go out without the others. Finn presented his new ideas of flying the three to Cape Rymill. Bob said sell it to the boys and it is O.K. by me.

After dinner, Finn tried to work out some agreeable new plans to settle a difficult situation called the four men in plus Ike and outlined the plans. They were all interested, but insisted that Art had to go along. Finn said it was impossible for 21 dogs to carry the supplies and equipment for four men and that only three could go. Finn asked the two Bobs and Kevin each if he wanted to go on a three man party. Each man said, no! Finn said, then this is an ultimatum. They said, no, not exactly. Kevin apologized. We had some hot chocolate and they left, except Bob Nichols, who argued with Finn a bit about having a four man party.

Tuesday, September 9, 1947

Nichols came in before I was up and stayed until lunch going round and round about three and four man party. Bob said, safety, assistant, Finn said, 21 dogs, which were all we had available, and cited Knowles 3 man geological party on USAS Expedition, etc. Bob said the others would not go if Finn asked them, but suggested Finn talk to Dodson. Finn called Dodson in after lunch, to ask him if he would go on a three man party. He said I'll stick to Nichols because I can't see Art Owen sitting around here. Finn was very upset and told him to leave. Bob Nichols came in again and argued. Finn kept pointing out to him that 21 dogs would not be able to take four men. Bob suggested a compromise to avoid an impasse. Finn said it was ridiculous and Bob was making the impasse himself.

At dinner I got furious with Jorge for mimicking Finn when Finn asked for a harp, and I told Jorge he was not funny. Everyone was most surprised including me, as I did not usually enter into controversies.

After dinner, Nichols, Ike, and Finn started talking again. Bob told Finn he hadn't given him an opportunity to do geology. Finn was furious, having presented him with every possible opportunity and pointed out in the early days, he had come on the beach many a morning at 10 o'clock to find Bob sleeping. Bob said you mean I'm inefficient, got furious and walked out saying, "I will never lead your three man party". He banged doors and knocked over chairs in the Bunkhouse, he was so mad. Sig came in and the four of us bemoaned the state of affairs. Ike did not agree with Nichols, saying you had to have a roof over your head first. We all felt pretty sorry for ourselves.

I was discouraged and disheartened. It was a particularly hard time with seemingly no possible solution.

The leader is certainly pressured by everyone from every angle. Each person thinks his own self interest outweighs any other project and if he is not successful in getting his own way, he will turn sour. His current attitude was out of character for Nichols, who was usually a steadying influence on the group. We went to bed late, tired and disgusted.

With ample justification, Finn was becoming very jittery about the alarming run of very serious accidents and the continuing failure of trail parties. Here we had our entire geographical program before us and the most dangerous time of the expedition was yet to come. If we continued to have such a proportionately high number of close calls, he was afraid our luck would soon run out.

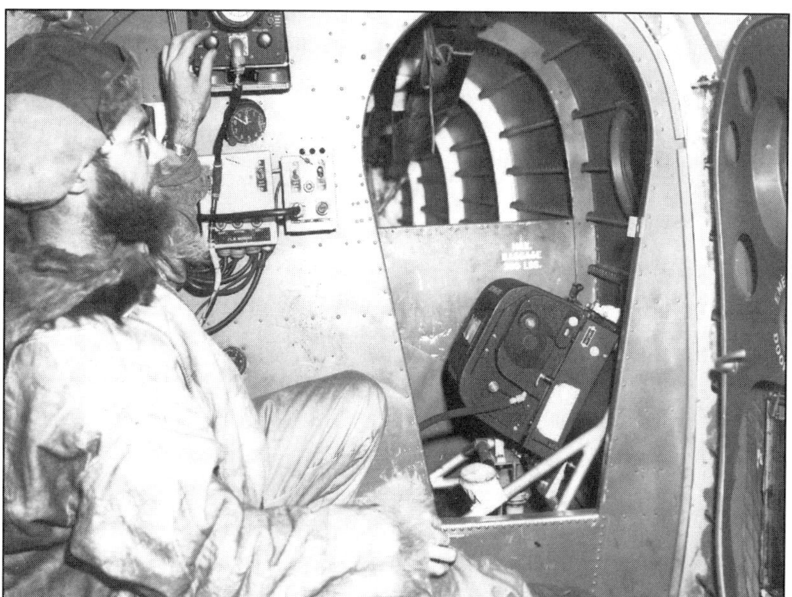

Bill Latady operating the trimetrogon cameras in flight in Beechcraft

Harry Darlington

Finn saying goodbye and good luck to Bob Nichols at the start of his sledge trip down the coast

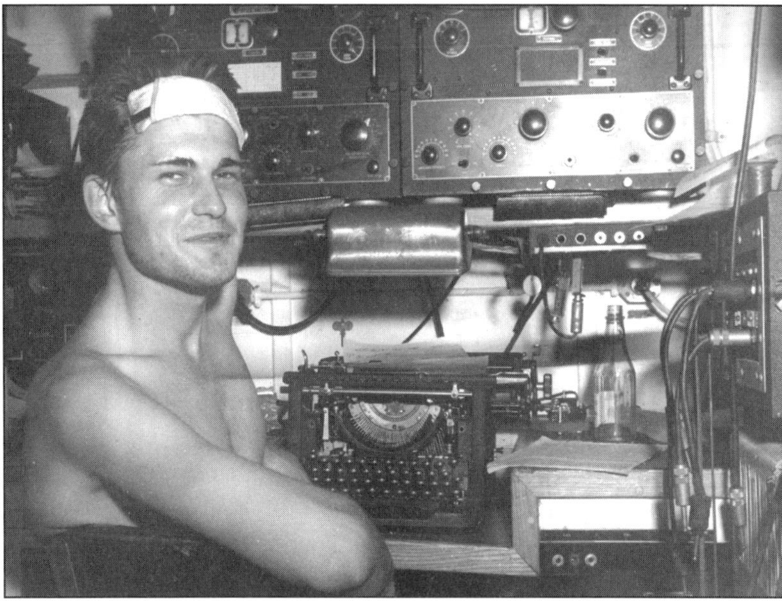

Radio Operator, Lawrence Kelsey in our radio shack

The three British airmen rescued after their plane crash stand between Finn and Ken Butler – Reg Freeman, Navigator; Bernard Stonehouse, Co-pilot; and W.H. Thomson, Pilot

Our two Air Force Pilots, Lassiter and Adams in front of Norseman plane

Weasel (with Beaumont sign) takes gasoline drums to planes for fueling

XII

Disaster Averted

Wednesday, September 10, 1947

Butler came over early this morning to talk to Finn about future plans. He felt, if Finn went down the coast they shouldn't, and suggested a four man combined party – British-American with the three best British dog teams to Tricorn. From there an American Party south. One of their teams was ours, and our responsibility. They would wait at Tricorn for the American party and travel back together.

In late afternoon the Norseman with Lassiter and Ike took off on its test hop. They had trouble getting the skis loose, but once they were, her performance was perfect. Adams, Robertson, and Harry came in for coffee as Ken left. Before dinner Finn called in Mac, outlined the plans for him and he was delighted. He asked for Owen. Finn said find out how much he had to do with the famous agreement and let him know later.

Bob Nichols caught me at dinner, asking if Finn would agree to send Art, when Bob needed him for geology. I said it is too late Bob, Finn has made other plans, which

I think are better for the expedition. He said that was fine, he was sorry he had gotten mad. I said Finn would never stand for their agreement, that Finn knew the trail, and he didn't, and that Finn was the leader. Bob came in to our shack after dinner and Finn said it was too late, he had given Bob the opportunity, but he didn't take it and that he had made better plans which he couldn't break and Bob would have his opportunity, also, to do what he could. Bob begged Finn not to leave Art out as he had a moral responsibility for him. Finn asked how much Art had to do with the agreement. Nichols said zero with the ring removed. Finn said nothing about his plans for Art, but told Bob about the Weddell Coast plans. Bob asked Finn to sleep on his compromise, that he was interested in the Coast, he could leave in two days and lead it with three men, but that the Sound plans for him and Dodson were also wonderful and to have a dog team instead of man-hauling would be wonderful. Hassage and the weasel would be a help, but Hassage wasn't interested in geology. Bob pleaded again for Art Owen and Britisher Kevin Walton on moral responsibility before he left. Mac came in saying, he had talked to Art, who was more or less forced into the agreement. Finn called Art in and told him the story. Art was thrilled to death about it, and both men told Finn how much they appreciated the opportunity and promised to do a good job for him and Mac promised to write a good report. As soon as they left, Bob came rushing in saying how wonderful it was, Finn had the best two men in camp, and he was pleased with his trip too, and once again, pleaded for Kevin Walton and asked me to speak to Finn about it.

Robertson, Sig, and Ike had coffee with us and we discussed the day's events, everyone happy at what had transpired. Ike could see no reason why Kevin should go down the Sound with Nichols' party.

In the morning today's temperature was -18 Deg. F, at noon it was -10 Deg., and in the evening -24 Deg.

Thursday, September 11, 1947

Bob went over and had a talk with Kevin and found out that he was perfectly satisfied to stay around here and do survey work, which is what he was sent down to do, so Bob didn't feel he had too much of an obligation to him anymore.

The fellows, including Butler, worked on the Beech. Butler came to lunch and also dinner. Finn talked to Ike about the flights and about Harry. Latady asked Finn about Harry. Finn told him what he wanted from Harry and Bill said that was very fair. I sent the Potomac Appalachian Trail Club story in. Finn told about the new plans at the table tonight. They are definitely better plans and everybody seems very happy about it.

Friday, September 12, 1947

After lunch, Finn had an aviation conference here. It was finally decided to use the L-5 and Norseman the first good day to set up the Tricorn Operational Base, at Cape Keeler leaving Fiske and Smitty there to man it. Smitty decided not to go with Nichols, but is thrilled to death to go to Advanced Base. When the weather people are there, trips will be made back and forth building a cache there. The L-5 and the British Oster will fly the Cape Keeler cache. As soon as the Beech is finished, she will fly the trimet over the Weddell Coast.

I went with Dodson and Nichols on a dog team seal trip this afternoon to Neny and the Figure Four, where we found a seal which Bob killed. We were out for a couple of hours and saw first hand that Bob Nichols was far from being a dog man. The dogs need training badly. Harry told Finn this morning, whatever he decided on Harry's note was O.K. by Harry. Nichols is very pleased with the plans and at dinner tonight Finn told Don he could go, which greatly pleased Bob and Don, so everyone in camp is now doing what they want to do and it is a very happy camp. It looks as though, if everything works out well, it will be a bang up program.

The aviation group, consisting of, Ike, Lassiter, Adams, Tommy, and Ken, which was supposed to meet at the British camp met a deadlock and adjourned to our shack. The British wanted the Norseman to take the load of 19,000 pounds over to Cape Keeler. Finn wants to save a landing of the Norseman and conserve 87-octane gas. Butler understood this, but was rather obstinate. It was finally decided that on the first really perfect day, the L-5 with Adams and Smith, would fly with the loaded Norseman with Lassiter, Ike, and Fiske, to Pullen Island to establish the Advanced Base. If the day was only partially good, the Auster would fly to Cape Keeler with the Norseman, which would parachute the load to the landed Auster. It was left this way, hoping tomorrow would be a good day.

Sunday, September 14, 1947

We were up fairly early and had breakfast in the shack with a later breakfast around 10 o'clock in the Bunkhouse. Finn put Kasco in harness and had him pull Finn on skis. He is a strong little devil and works hard and seems to love it. He could actually pull Finn along on the level. I worked on an article of Nichols return and the test hopping of the Norseman plane. Lassiter and Adams worked all day in the snow, loading the Norseman for the trip to Cape Keeler cache. They came in later and talked to Finn about the loads of the first and second flight to Pullen Island. They think with an Advanced Base as far south as Pullen is from here, they will be able to go to the Pole and back to this Base easily. Finn did not comment, as getting to the Pole was not a priority with him.

Sig had an argument with Don McLean about staying out of the galley and Don took two swings at him. Sig is half Don's size with a bad back and legs from severe war injuries.

Harry began talking to me this morning, when I was out watching Finn play with Kasco. He asked me if I would like to see the Beech and took me down and showed me through the plane. Most of the conversation was the same old stuff, of how he viewed the trimetrogon and flying the Beech situation, etc.

We took it easy in the evening and listened to the radio from the States, Town Meeting of the Air, and all about news of the United Nations. Jorge came in with a long radio message typewritten in Spanish. Finn told him to limit it to 50 words and put it in English. He left without a word. Ken offered Kevin Walton and team to help Bob down the coast for three days. We went to bed fairly early.

Monday, September 15, 1947

Finn worked on loads for the first and second Norseman flight to Cape Poindexter. I worked on a draft of the agreement to be made with Ken for the Joint British-American Sledge Party. The aviation gang began working on the planes.

Finn went over to see Ken after lunch and it was decided that the Auster would go up and take a look at the weather on the other side and if good, cruise around and wait for the Norseman by the weather station on the plateau. The Oster reported weather clearing, so after much ado about putting last minute stuff in, and Latady loaded down to the gills, the engine was turned over. Lassiter was pilot, Ike co-pilot all dressed up in polar kit. Robertson and Latady, with the baggage, hopped in the open side door. Lassiter rounded the end of the island before he managed to get off the ground. We listened to Terry on the radio, while Finn discussed the weights of the first flight to Cape Poindexter with Smitty, Adams, and Fiske. He told them to be ready to leave tomorrow, that if the Keeler cache was laid today, and there was good weather tomorrow, the first flight would take place to Poindexter. We heard Terry, the radio operator at the British base, say the Auster was flying over Fleming Glacier. Then he kept asking Jim who was piloting the Noresman if he saw the Auster.

On the radio Thomson, the British pilot, reported that he had decided to go on, as the Norseman was the faster plane by some thirty miles per hour and could easily catch up. At the moment, 4:00 p.m. he was flying over Fleming Glacier at 9,000 feet on the other side of the Plateau. Lassiter was informed, and he started to catch up with the Auster. This was the last message received from the Auster plane.

Finn went over to the British camp. Harry and Jennie were having tea. Finn talked to Ken, listened to Jim on the radio, and got a promise from Ken that the Oster would take Nichols' stuff down the Sound, because the L-5 would remain at Pullen Island.

About 6:15 the Norseman taxied in. I went out to see them and Pete said they looked heavily loaded and wondered if they were able to dump the stuff out. I said, "oh, certainly"! When the fellows got out of the plane, we found out they never once saw the Auster plane, they didn't meet at the rendezvous, and they kept flying past Cape Keeler all the way to Cape Rymill, circled both places twice and came back to land in dense fog with 1400 lb. over load. Everyone said it was a perfect flight and were extremely enthusiastic about the Norseman's performance. Terry kept calling and calling, but nothing has been heard from the Auster since going over Fleming glacier.

Finn told Ike to get Butler. As Butler was on his way over, he bumped into Lassiter and Harry coming to see him. They all came in together. Finn called for Ike and asked Harry and Lassiter to wait until the three had finished discussing it. Ken said Harry told Thomson at the last minute there was a good landing place around Cape Rymill. Ken was obviously disgusted with this way of Harry's doing things. Finn told Butler everything was at his disposal, but suggested the L-5 be used to search. Butler agreed with Adams and Dougie, but suggested getting a trailing antenna put on. Finn called Adams and Robertson. Both men said the L-5 didn't have the searching range and couldn't drop any gear because it couldn't carry any. Ike agreed that the Norseman was the plane to use, so Finn said get it ready. Robertson said he would patch it, unload it and get the antenna on. Adams would help him and Lassiter would sleep, so as to be the pilot tomorrow. Dougie, the British Doctor Butson, and David Jones the mechanic, would go along. Ken was his usual polite gracious self, but terribly worried and intended to stay up all night, keeping the radio schedule. The men got to work immediately.

The British radio continued to call their plane all night and the hours dragged on, with no report. Because the storm made it impossible for the planes to begin a search, Finn suggested that he take a surface dog team party to look for the missing men. After some discussion, it was felt that the area to be covered was so extensive – a one hundred and fifty mile radius – that it would be impossible to find the group via dog team before it had been narrowed down by a plane survey. All hopes were placed in our three planes, one of which still was being assembled and as yet had not been test hopped.

Although the blizzard raged outside, we hoped the following morning would bring clear weather. Members of both camps worked on the planes all night in thirty mile an hour winds and swirling blinding snow. Hassage, Ike, Robertson and Adams reloaded the Norseman with additional food and emergency equipment in preparation for the following day's search. Robertson and British Mechanic Jones checked and rechecked the engines of both NANA and the L-5. Jones was very upset about the possibility of a mechanical failure in the Auster, but had difficulty believing that such a thing could have happened for he had given it a complete one hundred hour check two days before.

Tuesday, September 16, 1947

It was a miserable day, after having snowed hard and blown all night. Hassage, Ike, Robertson, and Adams were up working on the plane all night, until 5 a.m. this morning. Ken Butler got the radio fixed and rigged up a trailing antenna. The day was extremely bad, still snowing and ceiling zero, so no search for the missing plane could take place. Jorge and Don McLean were up all night too. Jorge did not get up until noon, when Don got him up and helped him with the dishes. After lunch the fellows started to work on the Beechcraft. Lassiter cleared the Norseman of snow in case the weather cleared up.

We did practically nothing around here. I typed some geological collecting notes for Nichols and wrote a story for Kasco, Dog Food Company but little else. Ike came in for a cup of coffee and toast and he talked about how hopeless these young fellows were in taking orders and how Tommy had given the impression that he knew it all and wherever he was now, was paying for it.

We had a movie, "The Lost Canyon", which was a cowboy picture. Later Finn caught Jorge, McLean, McClary, Robertson, and Hassage, in the galley making cocoa. He gave them hell! Later Don came in and Finn let him have it about breaking into cargo, whether or not they got extra coffee, tea, and cocoa. Finn said, if we had to remain longer than expected, we would run out of food and the fellows would really bitch then. He said he could show invoices of all the needed food. The British didn't dare touch their supplies. Don admitted he had some of the apricot nectar and Finn said yes he knew that to be true and now it would not be available for Thanksgiving or Christmas.

Wednesday, September 17, 1947

Awoke early and had breakfast in here. The day was again a bad one with very poor visibility and winds. The planes could not take off. The fellows were out working on them, particularly the Beechcraft. At times, the overcast showed signs of breaking and everyone prayed for clear skies, but in a matter of minutes, it clouded over again. Our thoughts were with the lost men and what has happened to them. They have 7½ lb. of food, or six rations, a two man tent and one sleeping bag. Pete came in and wanted to have a telephone line put in between here and the British camp. Finn said no, he could not see it. If they wanted to go over, go and take the exercise.

Finn made up a memorandum to Bob Nichols, tying him down in what to do on his trail trip, so that Finn is covered as to his safety and in case he goes astray in not taking the proper precautions. Finn brought Ike and Bob in. They had the same kind of a discussion, if this happens, then we can't do so and so, and is it worth a week's geology, etc., etc. It all depends on the surfaces. He still wanted Don and another plane flight of supplies. Jorge continues to be hopeless. Jennie said a cheerie good morning to Finn today. Surprise, things are picking up.

The storm continued making flight operations impossible. We knew that the lost men were not prepared to meet the emergency. The flight had been considered a local one and two of them were not dressed warmly. Their plane had not been able to carry sufficient emergency supplies for all three. The all important thing was to find those men in a hurry.

Thursday, September 18, 1947

> *The Norseman plane took off early this morning at 7:15 with Lassiter pilot, Adams co-pilot, Dr.Dick Butson, Mechanic David Jones, and Dougie Mason in the back. Finn was up to see them off. I got up shortly thereafter. It was a beautiful day, but the wind was blowing strong on the surface. After flying for two hours, they came back and landed over in front of the British camp. They said the ground was completely covered with clouds, mist, and fog over on the Weddell Sea side. They had a bumpy ride and had a hard time getting back because of the clouds.*
>
> *After lunch the L-5 plane went up to look at the weather and after an hour and a half, came back because of impossible visibility. Ike came in for a chat in the afternoon and said he had heard the Governor heard about the lost plane and had reported it to the papers. In the late afternoon, it looked as though it were clearing, so Finn went over to the British Camp and ordered the Norseman to fly again. Within 30 minutes, she came down after climbing 5,000 feet because of engine trouble and after seeing the visibility was still hopeless.*

The Plateau Weather Station being operated jointly by Woody and Britisher K. E. McLeod proved most valuable in giving us their observations and standing-by for the flights during the entire time. At the main Bases, Kelsey and Britisher Terry Randall alternated in covering a twenty-four hour a day radio watch. All search information was being broadcast to the Auster before each flight, in the hope that her receiver might pick it up and that the men could give the searchers some signal from their position. The planes, the Plateau, and later the ground party were all on the same frequency to correlate available information.

> *Ken came in and Finn spoke to him about releasing the news. Ken said he understood and would tell the Governor to say nothing until the plight of the flyers was discovered and would then give us priority on releasing the*

news. Ken was very worried, but still was not in favor of sending out a sledge team.

John Tonkin wanted to start tomorrow morning with a dog team. Butler came over and was terrified, excited, nervous, and depressed. He suggested sending the L-5 up tomorrow and if it was a good day, have the Norseman ready to take off. If it was bad on the other side, have the Norseman take Tonkin, Walton, and Owen to the top of plateau so they could man-haul to Bill's Gulch and Fleming Glacier, to report how high the ceiling was beneath the layer. Finn called in Art and he was eager to go. Finn also called in Kelsey and he promised to fix up two trail sets, one for the Norseman and one for the man-hauling party.

Friday, September 19, 1947

The L-5 took off early this morning and Adams found a hole for the Norseman to go down under the cloud layer so he came back to report. Ike decided he wanted to go as co-pilot and Lassiter objected because he wanted Adams. Butler came over and asked Ike to stay because of his visibility; Adams would be more good, so Ike did. Jones didn't go either, because he stayed to help Jimmy Robertson get the Beech ready. The fellows were up for three hours and 45 minute, and landed back in a 60 mph surface wind.. They had headed thirty miles out to sea and found a hole in the clouds and went down under. They saw perfectly, from Cape Joerg South to Cape Rymill, and covered every square inch finding no trace

With one area eliminated, Butler decided that the only hope of making a sustained search of the Weddell Sea area, from Bill's Gulch south to Cape Rymill, was to have either one or both planes proceed to Mobileoil Bay and operate from a ground base there. To utilize the fairly decent weather, the Norseman took off at 2:30 p.m that same afternoon.

Harry was watching over by the plane, as sour as heck. Jorge was pretending to help, but actually doing nothing. Apparently Hassage washed the lunch dishes.

With a 2,000-pound overload, Lassiter flew with only half-mile visibility into the Mobileoil Bay area. There he deposited Tonkin, and Dougie Mason of the British group and Owen, from our Base, at Cape Joerg with food and supplies to last thirty days.

> *John Tonkin was going to establish a base there and man-haul out from it, in every direction and when the area had been covered, move upward to another area. Lassiter landed safely back here and preparations were made to take the other party up to the plateau. The plateau weather station was standing by constantly, the plane and John were all working the same frequency and Terry was also working another Base, who was delivering Ken a message from the Governor. Ken sent an answer, telling the Governor of the constant operations of the American planes over the area and of the negative results to date. Also, told him he was in control of the ground and air search parties and that all search information was being broadcast to the Auster each time an operation started.*
>
> *The weather began to close in and it was already getting dark at 6:15, so the Norseman boys decided not to take off for the Plateau. On their way back from the last flight, they had a look at Fleming Glacier but saw nothing. Dinner was quiet except for Sig announcing that there would no longer be a permanent Mess Cook and explaining how he intended to do the dishes. Finn, in that connection, announced that Jorge had been relieved of all duties and no longer had any privileges on the expedition. Jorge asked, "Why?" Finn said, "You know why." He said, "Well, the fellows don't know why." Don said, "I don't know anything about it," and looked at me, as if asking for an explanation for Finn's actions. I stared him down. Mac looked at me and I stared him down. Of course they were the two who were putting him up to his pranks. Finn told Jorge to slow down. After we came into the shack, Jorge came in and wanted to know why Finn treated him so. Finn let him have it full blast. He admitted to cutting the wiring to our shack, but said other people had also been implicated. He said he had more friends than Finn thought he had. I let him have it then. He said he had never been out with men before and he likes to do*

childish tricks, etc. etc. Finn told him to go with the bitchers and stay there, he was through with him and he had failed to take advantage of the opportunity offered him on the expedition.

Saturday, September 20, 1947

The weather was bad again this morning with partial sun, clouds, and a strong surface and upper wind. John radioed for the L-5 to land with some necessary articles for them and prepare to take local hops in that area. Lassiter thought he should fly the plane, but Chuck was obviously so disappointed, Lassiter didn't press the point and Chuck took off. After one and a half-hours, he was forced to come back because of downdrafts and wind. Everywhere he flew he lost ground in the area and couldn't get to Cape Joerg. Harry certainly feels out of things these days and shows it. He runs around and tries to butt in and looks as though he is running things or busy working, but nobody pays any attention to him, whatsoever. Finn went over to talk to Butler about sending a team up Neny Trough, with the weasel for support. Within a few minutes the weasel was off for the trough with Hassage, Latady, and Butson.

They went to take a look down Neny Trough with the field glasses in case the men were on their way back through the channel and had not been seen from the air because of the overcast. Several hours later the party returned, saying that winds up to eighty miles an hour made it impossible and that they couldn't even hold the field glasses up in their hands to see through them.

Finn asked Butler to ask the Governor for permission for Finn to release the story to Wheeler to hold, until the Governor sent him a message to release. It takes Wheeler four days to receive our material.

When Ken talked to the Governor last night, he asked that we not publish the information until something was definitely known, and then he promised that it would be released in our papers first.

Finn asked Ken and others to dinner and movies. Ken was in middle of his dinner but decided on a movie. However, just then a message in code came in from the Governor. In the middle of the movie, "Delightfully Dangerous", Ken came in and he and Finn went into our shack. Ken said the Governor wanted to know if Finn could send news in code. Finn said, no, but it is going to a Government station. He also wanted to know if Wheeler could be counted on to hold stuff. Finn said he thought so. Then Ken muttered something about the Governor informing the Colonial Office. Finn suddenly thought that he would have the Governor recommend Lassiter and Adams highly for the regular Army and went in and told Lassiter who was very pleased.

Sunday, September 21, 1947

Things started off with a bitching bang this morning with Harry and Bill Latady coming in to see Finn about not knowing what was going on. Harry claimed he didn't want to get in this, in fact he wanted to stay clear of it, but he had been standing by for five days (which wasn't the truth) and didn't know what was going on. He wanted to get the Beech ready for flying, if he was going to fly it, and who would go, if the other planes were down. Finn said probably Bill and probably myself. Sig came rushing in saying, "Finn call in Ike", there has been much bitching out here and its been exaggerated, "call in Ike". Finn told them he had put everything at Butler's disposal and Harry and Bill claimed they didn't even know that. Finn said he would talk to Ken and have a general meeting. Finn went over to Ken and he said he would be over, but he became so busy, it was impossible.

Sig said later that Robertson began it by coming in with frozen hands, after trying to gas the L-5 without help, as everyone was over with the Norseman. He thought everyone should listen to Ike only. Ike came in with another story, saying that Lassiter wanted Adams to fly with him in the Norseman. Ike said the L-5 should go too and Adams should fly that and the two planes fly together. Lassiter went into Butler and Ken asked Ike to let the Norseman go alone without the L-5, as the weather wasn't good.

After the Norseman got off, we heard John report the visibility 20 mi., with 5,000 foot ceiling approach through the Traffic Circle. Mac on plateau said wait 5 min. The Norseman was climbing then, 5 min. later they reported clouds moving in from the North. We heard that they were over the Traffic Circle. Then Ike had the generator turned off which had been running all night. Hassage didn't get up this morning either.

Just before lunch, Lassiter and Adams came back. They had deposited their load plus Kevin Walton at Mobileoil Bay. They flew back over Bill's Gulch, Neny Trough, and told Finn that they had given up hope of finding them, as they had covered everything. They thought it best to fly both planes over with gasoline and operate from there. At the lunch table, Harry put out a lot of stuff and unfortunately, Lassiter said to Harry he had given up hope. Harry, of course, will go straight over to Ken with it. Harry is starting a lot of this bravado stuff. Jennie spoke to me in the Machine Shop today for the first time in ages, when I was looking at the puppies. The weather closed in and Lassiter and Adams couldn't fly NANA and the L-5 to Mobile Oil Bay. Ike came in and said it was Ken's fault, as Ike wanted it to go in the morning, then it would have been there. Sig told us in the evening that Lassiter was trying to persuade Latady to talk to Finn, about taking a surface party up on the Glacier. Latady said he thought men should be saved for the Beech, but he felt the search was disorganized. Ike in his room heard Bill and came out making a long loud speech in defense of Finn, saying the fellows had done nothing but bitch since arriving on the expedition. Finn knew this territory in and out better than any of them ever would, but that the fellows persecuted him, so they didn't give him a chance to tell them anything. Ike told them once again that Finn had turned all facilities over to Butler to run the search and if anyone was to blame it was him (Butler), who he (Ike) believed to date had made three major mistakes, which he would tell him to his face anytime:

1)letting Tommy go so late with not more emergency food.

2)not sending out a surface party as Finn suggested the first night.

3)not sending the L-5 with the Norseman this morning.

Jennie, Latady, Lassiter, Jorge, McLean, Smith, Hassage, Nichols, and Dodson all heard him. Butler was over for dinner. Finn told him, we had to send in the news, if the Colonial Office knew. Just then, Terry brought a message from the Governor saying the Colonial Office was informing the families and would release news to London papers 12:00 GMT tomorrow, which was 8:00 am NY time and our time. Finn was frantic, as it did not give us enough time to get our story in. Ken said, send it through the Falklands, which we decided to do, at our own expense. I quickly wrote 400 words, which Terry got out. It was supposed to be in N.Y. by 5 a.m. Butler also sent a message to the Governor asking him to request the Colonial Office to hold it for another twenty-four hours until we could get the story up to NANA. The Governor replied, he would endeavor to do so. As soon as Ken left, I wrote a two thousand word article giving more details and Finn requested Kelsey to stick with the article until he got it out by radio some way, some how. But Kelsey didn't get it out.

Monday, September 22, 1947

Dawned with high winds that had been blowing at night and complete overcast. No flying could be done today. Finn and I didn't get up until lunchtime, because of the weather. It seemed like Sunday to everyone. In the afternoon, we read Lassiter and Adams the story, which is to go out and then, Finn brought Kelsey in to try to get the story out. He said nothing could be done until tonight. Ike and Robertson came in for a cup of coffee with us and Adams and Lassiter. We also read them the story. Lassiter went over to the British side to take a look at the Norseman plane and stopped by to see if Ken had heard anything from John. Ken rushed out and said come here, I have something very important to tell you. Ken told Jim, that Harry had just come over to him and said, he thought Ken ought to know, Ike had said Ken had made mistakes in the search party and was completely incompetent to handle it, and was a poor leader, and it was also rumored in our camp, that Ike was responsible for the loss of the plane. Jim was so mad, he said he would go out and punch Harry in the nose. But, instead, he came over and told

Finn. Jim said, he knew he wasn't liked, but didn't realize Harry was actually as dangerous a person, as he had now proved himself to be. When Ken came in here after dinner, he told Finn about it and at first thought it would be well to have it out with Harry, with Ike in here, right away, but he didn't want to do anything which would hinder the search. He asked Finn then, if he could say a few words to the camp at the movie. After the newsreel, before the main picture which was, "Texas Guinan".

Finn called everybody together and asked Robertson to get those persons in Harry's room. Robertson reported they were playing bridge. Finn said, I still want them to come out here for a few minutes. Out came Jennie, Don, and Andy. Finn said where is Harry, so finally Harry came out. Ken said, he had two things to say: 1)Thanks to Finn and particularly Adams and Lassiter for all they had done. 2) He had heard rumors of persons beginning a post mortum of who was to blame, which he hoped would stop right away, until after the search was over. He said, no one at all on this side of the Hill was to blame and if anyone was to blame, it was himself, or possibly an error on the part of the pilot, but the first thing to do was to find out what had happened to the lost men. After the movies, Ken said, Harry was the most dangerous man anyone could ever hope to have around. He felt definitely, he was the cause of most of Finn's trouble with the other fellows and knew that he had tried to work up a group of Ken's men against him. He said, he was the kind of man who stirred up one side against the other side and then sat back to watch the fun, hoping in the meantime, all parties would think what a wonderful guy he was. David Jones said, when working over here, he wasted more time trying to find jobs for Harry to do and that he had seen a lot of RAF pilots during the war and felt Harry was probably a flashy pilot and not too good a one at that.

That evening we heard the BBC announce the disappearance of the plane and state that "two flyers from an American expedition had searched the area for thirty minutes". We were more than a little shocked by their underplaying our efforts.

Up until the afternoon of September the 23rd, NANA had made three trips to Mobile Oil Bay, taking with each load, a ton of supplies over the Army's prescribed maximum allowed cargo load. During this time, a thorough aerial search had been made between the Base and Cape Rymill. The day dawned bright and sunny for the first time during the search and both planes were operating in different sectors, Adams in the L-5 around Mobile Oil Bay and Lassiter in NANA further to the north. After the morning search, there was no doubt about the complete coverage of the area. My diary describes the day.

Tuesday, September 23, 1947

Lassiter and Adams and the rest of aviation were up bright and early this morning. Lassiter took off about 8:00 am and Adams about 8:45 am for the Mobile Oil Base. They landed safely and Chuck began to search that area right away. Lassiter started off for the outer rim and flew up around the plateau and Square Bay area. He was near here at lunch time, so landed to take more stuff and refuel.

Meanwhile Robertson tried to turn over the Beech engines. Finn and Lassiter thought the Beech should be used for stand-by. Ken and Ike thought it should be flown in the search because of today's excellent weather. Ken decided to go home, and asked Finn, who from this Camp should go. Finn decided he would go himself and began getting his emergency gear together. Finn thought they should first fly down as far as Cape Jeremy and take a look at the bay ice and Wordie Shelf Ice. Apparently, Ken had checked out the Beech radios in the morning and according to Robertson, at lunch time the batteries were dead and the engine wouldn't start, nor would the Beech be able to fly today.

Lassiter took off in the Norseman with Tonkin and Owen, who were searching with him and about twenty minutes after he left Base, he excitedly reported over radio that he had sighted the three missing men walking back on the Bay Ice. You could hear the shouting of relief from the cockpit.

The spots at first were taken for seals, but field glasses showed them to be moving slowly. Hopes went up and the men in the plane were rewarded with a burst of red smoke from a bomb set off by the three lost Britishers on the ice. The men had been found! The good news flashed back to Base over the radio and the eight-day search was concluded at 1:45 p.m. on September 23rd. Everyone was elated.

Upon hearing and seeing the Norseman plane overhead, the weakened, weary men were overjoyed. Not realizing Lassiter had seen them, they lit off their only red smoke bomb to identify their position. When the Norseman landed in the iceberg and growler dotted area, Tonkin was so excited that he jumped from the plane forgetting that the headphones to the radio were still on his head. The first remark from Auster pilot Thomson was "Hi Jim (Lassiter), I'll never fly in a plane again". Lassiter took up the jovial comment replying, "OK Tommy, I'll leave you here to walk in, while I take the others back". Shakened, Tommy quickly replied, "Excluding this plane ride that is". In order to give enough room in the loaded plane for the three to be returned, Tonkin and Owen remained on the bay ice and prepared to spend several days there if necessary.

The three men were uninjured, well, but very thin, worn, and weary. They had not been able to sleep for several nights, their boots were frozen boards, and when their sole sleeping bag was dumped from the plane, it thumped to the ground one solid ball of ice.

> *At Base, Terry yelled the good news. Nichols out in front of our camp picked it up and gave a war whoop.*
>
> *We rushed over to congratulate Ken, who was on the radio trying to contact Adams and the field units, as well as inform the Governor. Jennie came rushing in and tried to be all sweetness and light to me, but I was very stilted in my answers. She said there would be a big celebration, etc. and everything would be all right from now on, etc. Finn came out of Ken's radio shack and Jennie spoke to him saying isn't that fine. Finn passed her by and didn't even speak to her. When Terry came out, he threw his arms around Jennie and they danced up and down. I stood on the hill above the British camp to watch the plane come in for a landing. Jennie came down and stood in front of me, suggesting we go down to the plane. I told her I would stay where I was, so she remained at her position also. The three missing men got out of the plane and talked to the welcoming crowd around them for a few minutes. Ken came walking up with Bernard Stonehouse and Tommy.*

Harry was on the other side of them. When they reached the door to the British hut, Jennie yelled, "Tommy, I'll bake you a cake!" I yelled "hello" to the two and Bernard yelled back, "I'm sure glad to see you again, Jackie!" Ken gave Harry and Jennie a royal brush-off, so both of them went back to our camp. As Harry passed me, he said, "They crashed near Mushroom Island." I said, "Yeah?"

After they left, I went down and shook hands with Reg and walked up to Base with him. Ken called to him to come inside and I insisted we come back to camp and leave them alone, which we did. I wrote a brief story on the information I had and Finn took it over for Terry to send out, which he did immediately.

John Tonkin came in to thank Finn for all he had done and how much he appreciated it and how understanding it was of Finn to let Butler run everything as he saw fit. Finn thanked him and said that was all right and then brought up the question of the nasty British broadcast saying an American plane had flown over the area for thirty minutes, etc. John was most embarrassed and apologized saying some of the dumb things the Colonial Office did and hoped Finn wouldn't get into trouble with NANA over it and saying he would suggest to Ken that they request the Colonial Office to release a story, which they would write of the whole affair. He said Lassiter and Adams flew on days that he wouldn't even take a sledge team out. He also said Bernard Stonehouse was a walking testimonial of the alpaca suits.

While refueling the L-5 at Mobileoil Bay, Adams was informed by radio that the lost men had been sighted and were being flown back to Base. The Mobileoil Bay camp was made ready to be flown out immediately. After Lassiter had deposited the three British flyers at their Base, he took off and with Adams returned all of the field units that same day, while the good weather lasted.

Finn invited them all over for dinner and John left saying he would be back in forty-five minutes. Both Ken and John came back then and Ken gave Finn a very nice note of appreciation and thanks from the Governor on behalf of the Secretary of the Colonial Office. Ken then said he would endeavor to help Finn straighten things out with the Colonial Office and get recognition for what he had done. We had a nice dinner with a full table and a group of happy people there. Finn read the Governor's telegram.

> ***"I am directed to convey to you the grateful thanks of the Secretary of State for the Colonies for the unstinted help you have given in the search, so aptly rewarded, for your three British colleagues. May I add my own most sincere appreciation and good wishes to you all.***
>
> ***Clifford Governor, Falklands"***

Ken got up and thanked the whole camp, particularly Finn, Lassiter, and Adams. John echoed this thanks. We came in here briefly and then they left to see a movie, "The Flame of the Barbary Coast", while I listened to the BBC and US broadcasts, but nothing was on.

I wrote a long article, on what I had gotten about the three men from John and Ken. Ken, John, Ike, Lassiter, Adams, and Robertson, Sig, Finn and I all had a glass of champagne after the movie was over and chatted for a while. We listened to BBC at 11 o'clock and US at 12:00, but no news was on.

Lassiter and Adams had done a most outstanding job of polar flying under appalling conditions. These two officers had the opportunity to show their excellent training under the U.S. Air Force, and in a determined, modest, efficient manner, carried out a thorough and successful searching program, when the lives of three men were at stake. They conducted themselves like veteran polar pilots under extremely hazardous conditions.

Within a few days, the three men felt well enough to receive visitors and we were able to hear their side of the story. On the fateful day of September 15th, when the Auster realized that NANA had taken off from our Base, Thomson headed for Keeler thinking she would easily catch up. They landed further inland than had been agreed upon and began staking out a landing field with orange colored trail flags for NANA. The Norseman flying high did not see the Auster, whose colors blended easily into the Antarctic snow-covered landscape. The three Britishers lit a red smoke bomb, but NANA had already passed over the area. When she returned, the Britishers believed that the Norseman personnel had sighted them, but when she flew in a direction signifying she was returning to Stonington Island, they realized the overcast was closing in and within ten minutes, 6:25 p.m., they had their plane ready for a take-off. The overcast caught up with them almost immediately. As most of his flying was being done blind, it was not surprising that Thomson became slightly turned around while flying in the overcast. He picked up two well known Nunataks, mistook one for the other and realizing the mistake too late, decided to get over the sea ice in order to land the aircraft as soon as possible. By this time it had started to snow and his landing visibility was one hundred yards. Actually, the sea ice was not seen until a fraction of a second before the plane touched. The right ski of the plane hit a growler in the ice, broke, and snapped off, throwing the plane on its back. No one was hurt. Inspection revealed that the crash landing had ripped off a wing and broken the back strength members of the plane in three places. The Auster was written off the books and the three men pitched their camp nearby the first night. They tried to work their radio, but found that the transmitter was damaged. However, on their receiver, they heard their Base calling them until the following morning, at which time the batteries went dead. They attempted to get some message through, but it was impossible.

Upon the dawn of the new day, they broke camp in a strong wind. By removing the belly fuel tank from the plane and attaching a climbing rope to it, a man hauling sled for pulling their emergency gear was provided. A snowy petrel flew overhead which they decided was a good omen. They knew they were south of the Base, but didn't know how far because poor visibility made identifying landmarks impossible and they feared searchers would never find them so far off their course. Food rationing began immediately. This meant a little more than five hundred calories per man per day. Drift, poor visibility, and a wind of forty-five miles per hour necessitated making camp after traveling three and one-half miles along the ice cliff.

During the days and nights that followed until they were rescued on the 23rd, they traveled short distances when the weather permitted. The surfaces were bad, and going was slow. At times they plowed through knee deep snow at the bottom of which was slush. Their boots and clothing became wet, froze, thawed, and froze again at various times. Camping was more miserable than traveling. Their mouths became raw and sore from eating snow because they dared not use their fuel for melting drinking water. All three emphasized that during the whole horrible time, everything went smoothly between them. No one asked for more pemmican than he received, or said lets go farther today, and they never felt once that they wouldn't make it. Their greatest worry was that the men back at the Base didn't know that they were safe. They were so dehydrated (a certain amount of which is only natural in returning from the trail) that each gained back ten of the twenty pounds lost the first twenty-four hours after their return. Cases of trench foot from their feet being constantly wet and cold confined them to bed for the following two weeks.

Whether the men would have had difficulty making their Base under the conditions is a hard thing to say, for the five days which followed their return were some of the most miserable we experienced during the whole year. Winds blew continuously with only a few hours respite now and then. The general feeling held by the men themselves was that traveling in their condition would have been impossible. Indeed we were all much more than happy that things turned out so well and that they had suffered no more than they did.

The Norseman and the Beechcraft planes land at field camp

XIII

Field Programs

The following day, Finn called an aviation meeting to assess the remaining supply of high octane gas. Originally, there were 135 drums of #86 octane for the Beechcraft and Norseman. The latter had consumed 850 gallons, or 16 drums, working to keep three names off the Antarctic fatality list.

It was still necessary to establish an advanced weather base at Cape Keeler, on the other side of the 6,000-foot high plateau, which bisected the Peninsula. It would not be as far south as Finn had hoped, but it would be a move one hundred and twenty-five miles in the right direction. Smith and Fiske were assigned to the project. Once the men were there, we would have access to sufficient weather information to fly a stockpile of gas and other equipment to the other side. Then additional flight personnel could move over and operate further south from there by coping with weather conditions on one side of the Plateau only.

The following four days brought bad winds, but Robertson and others braved them to get the planes loaded and ready. This same bad weather also held up the departure of the Geological Sledge Party. It was at this time, too, that Jorge apologized to Finn and resumed his mess duties.

Sunday, September 28, 1947

Lassiter and Adams got up ready to fly, but didn't say anything to Ike, which made him mad. He blew off at Finn and said Finn didn't back him up, which Finn denied. The weather got progressively worse and when the final one of Fiske's one million bags was stowed in the plane, Jim decided it was too bad to take off. Finn caught two Army folding cots, weighing thirty pounds apiece, which he had them take out of the plane. Adams made a trip up to the Plateau with kerosene, butter, etc., for the fellows there. Woody was writing a story about "Life on the Plateau."

Ken came over in the afternoon and took a look at the Radio Room. He found several things wrong with the equipment and fixed them. Finn and Ken drew up a new arrangement for the radio room. In the afternoon, Ike, Latady, and Jennie were frying liver over the bunkhouse stove. Finn called them down for it. Ike said, "he started it." Finn said, "well its up to you to change things then, its just too great a fire hazard."

Also on September 28th, Nichols and Dodson started out toward the Sound on their second attempt at sledging over the ice of Marguerite Bay. Chuck Adams in the L-5 said they were about one mile from Red Rock Ridge at noon. A fifteen-dog team carried the supplies and equipment. Hopefully this would allow them to stay in the field until Christmas with one additional 500-pound load of man and dog food flown to them when they reached the head of the Sound.

The dogs never ceased to supply challenges. One red dog in the team named Prancer suffered pain from a loose tooth, which had to be pulled before he could consume his daily dog pemmican rations. Another, a black and white Malamute named Spot, noticeably reneged on his pulling ability, so they tied him to a rock on Red Rock Ridge and placed food for six days beside him. Bob Dodson intended to inform Base by radio of his whereabouts and have some go out to pick him up, but before this was done, Spot managed to bite through his tethering line and found his own way back to Base. He paraded through camp obviously showing off his achievement and had not suffered in the slightest.

Meanwhile, at the Base, the aviation part of the geographical exploration program was gearing-up. On September 29th, a sudden break in the heavily overcast skies marked the end of fourteen days of equinoctial storms. NANA took the first plane load of personnel and equipment to establish the Cape Keeler advanced weather base. With Lassiter as pilot, Fiske and Smith as passengers were all in good spirits as they climbed into the plane around noon. "Before take off, Finn took Lassiter's food to him in the plane. Onlooker Mac made a crack about the curb service and how he didn't like the bellhop. Lassiter's plate still had some jam on it and later someone moved it to Finn's place at the table and put a sign on it "Example." The flyers strapped their parachutes in place, gave the onlookers broad grinning smiles, as the powerful plane taxied onto the snowy bay ice. Besides the three men, NANA took an unusually heavy load of 2,400 pounds cargo. In order for Smith to get in, he had to back into the cargo compartment from the pilot's seat and succeeded in wedging himself on a sleeping bag on top of the load with barely enough room to get a glimpse of the passing scenery. The plane taxied for quite a long time. At the very end of the island, the plane bogged down and Finn quickly drove the weasel out to help Lassiter get going again. Mac, making absolutely no attempt to help, made a dirty crack about Finn's driving the weasel. Fortunately, Finn was not aware of these remarks at the time.

Adams in the L-5 rendezvoused with Lassiter in NANA at an altitude of 7,000 feet and together the two planes traveled on. Adams made the initial landing at Keeler and staked out a field for NANA. Smith was out of the plane immediately to stretch his legs after an hour and a half in his cramped position. His first remark to Lassiter was "Hey, its certainly nice to be on the ground again". When the cargo was unloaded, Lassiter and Adams made two flights in NANA to the recently abandoned Mobileoil field base to collect and move to Keeler all supplies which had been left there. The L-5 remained temporarily at Keeler and both pilots returned to the main Base in NANA after helping Fiske and Smith set up their large command tent. Upon completion of the day's operations, it was estimated that NANA had moved in excess of three tons of equipment to the Cape Keeler advanced base. This included man food, tents, sleeping bags, cooking equipment, navigational equipment, plus the scientific equipment for Fiske in meteorology and Smith for taking recordings in refraction and terrestrial magnetism.

With the establishment of the advanced base, we were able to obtain regular weather reports from the other side of the Peninsula. A shuttle service was set-up to transport gasoline over the Plateau. Both pilots were anxious to start on this work without further delay.

Tuesday, September 30, 1947

Lassiter and Adams were up early to take off at seven o'clock. Ike didn't want to fly over this morning. I think he knew the Beech would be test hopped today, so decided to stay and go with it. Lassiter waited until after ten to take off, when a weather report was received from the Plateau. The day started out beautifully clear, but after they took off, it clouded up. Ken covered the radio schedule and heard Larry fine. The Bunkhouse radio also heard Larry, but not Kelsey.

Their cargo consisted of four, fifty-five gallon drums of gasoline and four empty drums. Upon their arrival at the Cape Keeler base the four empty drums were filled with gasoline from the surplus supply carried in the plane's own fuselage tanks. By the time the cargo had been unloaded, the weather had closed there as well as here, so a return flight back to Base was impossible. Therefore, the two pilots settled down as guests of Fiske and Smith to wait it out until the weather cleared.

They didn't see Nichols' party this morning. We feel that they have purposely not kept their radio schedules, for they haven't been heard from since they left.

Harry test hopped the Beech with Ike at 1:00 o'clock today. Ken was on the radio and told Harry the wind was from the North. Harry asked, which direction was North. The Beech's one motor was burning, so Harry landed. Jimmy Robertson fixed it, after about three hour's work. He then came in for a cup of coffee and said he didn't want to fly with Harry, he was too casual and vague about what he was doing. Harry didn't even know how to start the engines, so Jimmy had to start them for him. Earlier Harry was in Ken's radio shack listening to Lassiter's flight. Finn and Ike walked in and Finn said to Harry, what are you doing here? Harry said he had asked Lassiter to tell him about the weather and he was standing by, covering Lassiter. Ike said he knew nothing about that and Finn told him in no uncertain way, he was to take orders from Ike only. Harry wanted a 10,000-foot ceiling to test the plane.

Saturday, October 4, 1947

Another dull day, it was snowing. Planes couldn't fly, and still no word from Nichols. We stayed in the shack most of the day. Finn got mad at Peterson because he built a window in the Science Bldg., without consulting him, but it was patched up and Finn talked to him about better radio with Kelsey. Pete said don't yell at him and don't push him, he just gets obstinate.

Ken came in and Finn unloaded his troubles. Ken who of course was a radio engineer, offered to let the trail party go on, if Finn would fly him out in two weeks, Ken would fix the station up and get the radio photo working. Ken also said, that Harry knew my article had gone out on flying, that he told Tommy and Tommy told Ken . Ken and Finn went into Kel while he was trying to make a schedule. They stayed about two hours and got Kel through to WEK on voice loud and strong. We rejoiced. Kelsey wanted to send his traffic by voice, but WEK said go back to key. We were up until 3 am.

Sunday, October 5, 1947

Didn't get up until noon and after breakfast, Kelsey, Ken, Ike, Pete, and Finn had a conference about radio. Kel was told that Ken would set the station up. The next thing was to get him off the early morning schedule and cut off all broadcasting after 12 o'clock. Kelsey agreed to all these things. The next thing was to get the trail schedule straightened out as to what frequencies to be used by which Base. Everybody had something to say about the schedules and then they were worked up satisfactorily to everybody. Ken worked them up and I typed them up and gave copies to everyone. There was much talk about a new antenna and Pete and Ken discussed it at length. It was decided to work on the rhombic again, Ken and Pete to work it out.

Lassiter and Adams received a report of good weather from Terry and started back.

While they remained at Keeler for five days, they spent their idle time building two igloos. After the igloos were completed, they lit a small primus stove inside. The heat melted the snow enough to give the shelter a glaze that cemented the snow blocks together. In addition, they helped Fiske and Smith to fix up the camp by digging the command tent down into the snow until the top was level with the surface. Fiske set up an excellent radio station and began maintaining three daily schedules for sending reports to the main Base. Smith took sun sights with his transit and established the correct location of the outpost. He created a great stir with the announcement that they were not at all where everyone thought they were. The advanced base was becoming a very comfortable home and a very busy place.

It was minus 25 degrees F when the two pilots left Keeler and landed without difficulty at the main Base.

> *Finn and Ken decided to take a flight to look for Nichols and when Nana and the L-5 landed, Lassiter asked me to go along. Finn insisted and I got ready. We had a wonderful 1 and ½ hour flight down to past Cape Berteaux. It was very thrilling. Weather turned us back then. We circled above the crashed Auster plane. On the way back, Finn spotted Kevin and Dick Butson about three miles east of Terra Firma Islands. We circled them and Finn dropped a note. They were, obviously, on their way back and, therefore, it is felt Nichols was much further down the coast. There was not too much bitching about my flying, but Sig says Robertson asked why did they take a woman along. Jim said neither he nor Chuck told anyone about my previous flight story going out, so that only means that Kelsey told because no one else knew. Jim told a funny story about the empty gas drums in the plane popping their caps off, when the pressure became too great, because of the altitude.*

From then on, each time, he took some empty drums in the plane, he loosened their caps to prevented them from popping and frightening him when the air pressure inside the drums became greater than the rarefied air outside.

> *Kelsey got a ten o'clock radio schedule and sent the weather, then got some sleep for the night. Bill Latady worked until after twelve, getting pictures ready for Ken to transmit. Lassiter said Ken had asked him, to ask Finn, to send someone from here down to replace Butson and*

bring Butson back to go in Ken's place, on Wednesday's trail trip departure.

Monday, October 6, 1947

The fellows got up early this morning to fly, as it was a good day. It was still very cold, -12 degrees. After the struts were pumped up and the gas loaded, it was eleven-thirty before Lassiter took off, with Dougie Mason. Kelsey, the Plateau station, and Fiske at Advanced Base at Cape Keeler, covered the radio guard. Ken and Pete worked on the V antenna and re-fixed it. Jim in the plane had a great deal of trouble getting Kelsey. When Ken came into the radio room, he found out why. Kelsey had no power on, except for his tuning device. When Ken switched the power on, he boomed through to Lassiter. which proved to Ken, that Kelsey did know what he was doing and was just pretending to be dumb.

Lassiter made two trips to Keeler with gasoline and landed finally, back here at 8:05 local time.

Meanwhile, during the afternoon, Robertson fixed up the bad wing from the Plateau trip yesterday and Chuck flew over to Kevin and Dick Butson with Hassage. Finn gave Hassage the chance to take Dick's place to bring the dog team back to Base, with Kevin. Hassage was hesitant, but glad to go. Finn let him understand that there was no danger flying in these planes, with Lassiter or Adams. Dick was to come back and replace Ken on the trail trip, while Ken continued to work on our radio equipment, until we could get a radiophoto out. Chuck traced their ski tracks from Terra Firma Island and found them, about two miles from Refuge Island. They had been traveling since five o'clock and had made almost thirty miles that day. When Dick got back he came in and gave me all the information on their trip, for a story. Dick seemed tired and was concerned about rushing into the other trip. Dick said they really gave Nichols and Dodson a work out and he figured the maximum they could do was eight miles a day.

Tuesday, October 7, 1947

Intended to work on news articles, but Dougie Mason asked me to go on a dog team trip, in the afternoon. Apparently, McClary took Don McLean and Jennie out with our dog team and I think Ken asked Dougie to take me. It was a nice sunny day, but no good for flying because of complete hazy overcast half way up the mountains, with the sun shinning beneath. Latady took pictures during the morning, for the radiophotos. I went over to the British Base and spoke to the three found men, who are still in bed recovering from trench foot. Just as we were about to start, the four dogs already harnessed to the sled took off, without anyone driving. Dougie and John took after them, but before long, they were a mile in front of their chasers, heading around Neny. I went in and had tea until the fellows recovered them and then Dougie took me for a nice eight mile run around Figure Four in front of Neny Fjord. We saw four seals, apparently pupping. On the way back, the temperature dropped considerably and I was about frozen by the time we got back.

After dinner, Ken got a very good radio voice contact with WEK in New Orleans and asked to send a radiophoto, to be received by them on a wire recorder. WEK only had a Dictaphone, so asked us to wait until tomorrow night, when they would have a wire recorder available. Then I talked over the radio to Mr. Barrett, being the first woman to broadcast from the Antarctic. Mr. Barrett complimented me on my broadcasting voice and offered me a job there in the future if I wanted it. Finn said a few words and then, we left to let Kelsey work CW. Ken, Finn, Sig, and I celebrated the broadcast by a bottle of wine. Ken discussed with Finn the advantages of the Beechcraft for a long flight to the pole. It has better equipment and two engines.

The possibility of a long flight to the Pole was discussed from time to time. Finn had no previous plans for one and it certainly was never his major objective, but Lassiter thought it could be done, was anxious to do it, and promoted it often.

Wednesday, October 8, 1947

I worked all day on writing a broadcast for Finn to make to the States tonight, at the suggestion of Ken. Lassiter introduced him and Finn made about a twelve-minute speech. It was excellent. They made three recordings on the wire recorder, selected the best one, which was broadcast to WEK. Then Finn broadcast it again, directly into the microphone. They sent a radiophoto first and followed with some afterward.

Thursday, October 9, 1947

The Joint British-American Trail Party, with two Britishers and two Americans, Dougie Mason, Dick Butson, Nelson McClary, and Art Owen, left around ten this morning, for the top of the Plateau, as a first leg.

Our two trail parties and two advanced weather stations all were to be supplied with food and equipment by plane. This had never been done before, as previously trail parties had to be self-sufficient, or depend upon additional support dog team parties to advance their supplies.

Meanwhile, the Geological Party heading for George VI Sound along the sea ice of Marguerite Bay had been failing to meet their radio schedules. Knowing that their future field supplies via plane depended upon good communication, Finn thought it safest to fly them down a new handcranking trail radio set. Adams flew Finn down in the L-5 and spotted the two men twenty miles south of Mushroom Island. They were busily relaying their load over very poor surfaces. At the end of the day's work, they would have advanced only four miles after actually traveling twelve miles. The dogs just were not able to pull the load over such surfaces. The men were not too happy to see the new radio in place of the broken one they had abandoned. All it meant to them was an additional weight with which to struggle.

Bob said Mushroom Island 140 feet high contained more minerals in the rock than any rock he had seen yet.

Jorge has been agitating all over the place to go out in the field. He wants to do some drawing or fly co-pilot with Lassiter on one trip. Hassage told him off, saying he had done nothing but talk about Finn for six months and now he wanted a favor from him. Hassage also said, Finn, although an adopted American, was a much better American than many men on the expedition. Lassiter talked to Jorge for a long while, pointing out how he had hemmed and hawed about taking care of the puppies this morning, when Finn had asked him. Lassiter told Jorge he had better agree to everything that Finn asked him to do after this. Jorge said he would.

Friday, October 10, 1947

The wind was blowing hard today, a steady 43-mph, and it was still cold. There was no flying and most fellows were just sitting around. Ken came over shortly before lunch and asked Finn to get Kelsey out of the radio room. Finn did and Ken worked there for a while. He then came back for a cup of coffee and told us some very amusing things about the Argentines and Chileans, who were down last year. He thinks, very definitely, they will be here again this year. Ken said the Argentines were very good, only the Captain and a Chilean observer came ashore, walked around the Island and left again. Later two Argentine gunboats came in the cove, steamed around and left again without anyone coming ashore. Then the Chileans came, first the "Iroquois" and then the "Argonamous". They went through our Base like a dose of salts and nothing Ken could say stopped them. The officers seemed to have no control over the men. It was a disgusting, horrible thing to do.

I knitted and finished the back of my sweater. Received a nice message from Betty Earle and one from Wheeler, saying I could write the Saturday Evening Post story. After dinner, Finn held an aviation conference in here, which accomplished a great deal. Harry was questioned by Robertson, as to why the Beech couldn't carry more. Harry, in a mushmouth way, explained it incompletely, as usual. It was decided to move all aviation personnel over to Keeler, as soon as possible, and then go operate south from there. Ken had a good contact with WEK and got out eight pictures in two hours, before they faded, making a total of fourteen pictures that have gone out.

Saturday, October 11, 1947

The day was still a blowy one and the drift outside our window, caused by the L-5, is getting higher, just about cutting us off from any view at all. Robertson went outside to get something and walked right off a hill and fell flat on his face, the depth perception was so impossible, a true whiteout.

Latady said he had received some requests from the fellows to see the pictures that had gone out, so Finn foxed them by announcing at dinner those persons wishing to see the pictures, could come in to see him and he would be glad to show them. Chuck and Lassiter came in, but no one else. Jennie went down to the galley after lunch and filled up a whole bowl of salmon for Chinook. This made Finn so mad, he wrote a memo prohibiting consumable food to go to the dogs, sending a copy to the Darlingtons. The show was, "Spawn of the North" and was very good. Ken came in later and we talked about the lay out of Washington until late. Ken found out tonight that Kelsey had accidentally cut a bunch of wires over the transmitter and they all fell into the transmitter.

With the exception of some little extra touch, such as cake, an especially good dinner, or a special movie, birthdays and anniversaries went by almost unnoticed on the expedition. Our program was a large one for our small group and on nearly every such occasion some vital portion of the day required the attention of all or a few. When it was convenient to celebrate holidays, we did so, otherwise they were looked upon as just another twenty-four hour period in which we could further our objectives.

Monday, October 13, 1947

My birthday – twenty-eight years old today. It has gone by just about unnoticed. I hope I never spend another one under such general unpleasant circumstances. It is true that everyone is out to get the Leader – just as Sir Hubert Wilkins warned. Each person has his own individual agenda and when he doesn't get what he wants, he becomes antagonistic against the leader.

At dinner I told Finn it was my birthday and he was terribly embarrassed that he had forgotten it – understandable with all he had on his mind. He asked Lassiter, Adams, and Robertson to come in for some champagne at 10 o'clock. They came in, suddenly, at nine and Lassiter brought a bottle, which we killed at once. It was much cherished wine, which they had been saving a long time for the proper celebration. It did suffice to celebrate the anniversary of the first woman to celebrate her birthday in the Antarctic. Finn, Ken, and Ike came in about ten and we had two more bottles and a good lively chat until 12:30, or so.

Tuesday, October 14, 1947

It was a fairly good day here with continued winds now and then. The weather report from Larry was still bad, with continued wind, and bad drifts all over the place. I received messages from my aunt and from Ruth Hughes on my birthday. Wheeler wants an article for the Times Magazine Section, probably Russ Owen is responsible. Russ was a well-known writer who had been with Finn's father on the First Byrd Expedition 1928-30. Lassiter and Finn were discussing weights and plans, when Ken and John came rushing in saying that Dougie and Art Owen were back from the top with news that McClary had broken his collarbone by being thrown forward over the sled when it stopped suddenly, after hitting a high piece of sastrugi. Finn was pressed by John to make an immediate decision, as to whom from this Camp would replace him tomorrow. Finn would not be pressed and said he would think it over for a few minutes. The Darlington gang showed little concern over Mac's accident. After dinner Finn called Ike in and got his advice. It was decided, it would be best to send Andy as far as Keeler and then probably send Smitty from then on. Don would go up tomorrow to help bring Mac back. It would take at least six weeks for Mac to be well again. Don jumped on his ankle a few days ago and restrained a muscle. He asked Finn if it would be possible to have him join the party with Ken at Keeler. Finn said he would have to think it over. Andy was eager to go.

Jorge rushed in and wondered if Finn wanted to send him. Finn said no, it was all taken care of. He was too funny, saying Don was still limping and Lassiter and Robertson said it would ruin the flying program if Smitty went. Finn said he would take care of that and dismissed Jorge, who was completely tongue-tied. Minutes later, Hassage came in raving mad saying, "I understand you are sending Smitty down, have you ever considered me". Finn said, "Yes, Chuck I have considered you, won't you sit down". He began to calm down. Finn said, "First, I have got to get the party to Keeler and I think Andy can do that and it saves flying him and his equipment. After Keeler, I don't know for sure. Mac may be well then. I need a navigator, are you one?" Chuck said, "No"! "Are you a radio operator? No! Well why do you let that crowd in there work you up, as the right man in my faulty decision?" Hassage admitted they had needled him and that said Smitty was not a strong man and predicted Finn would have trouble, if he sent him. Finn said, it was easy for people to criticize him, but he took everything into consideration before he made a decision. Finn calmed him down and said there might be a chance for him to fly down and help man the Cape Keeler Base weather station. He said he understood, etc., etc. and left. Ken got five pictures off and came in for a short chat.

Owen and Mason had sledged back to Base to inform us of the accident. The following morning, October 15, the day dawned clear, but by noon the Base was covered with mist. McLean departed with a dog team to bring Mac back. At the same time, Owen and Mason returned with the new sled and took with them Geophysicist Andy Thompson who would replace Mac as far as Cape Keeler. While Thompson was away, I would take care of his programs in both seismology and tidal measurements.

Wednesday, October 15, 1947

The day was fairly clear here and warm, but Fiske reported bad weather, so the planes were grounded and by noon time, the Base was clouded over with mist. We worked around here in the morning. Sig and Lassiter went fishing in a tide crack in back of camp and caught twenty small fish. After lunch they went back again and Finn and

I skied over to take pictures of them. We took Kasco with us and that little devil pulled me right along. We then went over to look at a very large (approximately 11 feet) Weddell Seal. She was about ready to have a pup and Finn got some very good movies of her.

Ken came in and didn't have any luck with pictures for WEK. He left around twelve o'clock. Harry caught Finn and came in to tell us Jennie's diamond ring worth $4,200 had been stolen about three weeks ago and it was his fault for not having the stuff put in the safe, but he wanted Finn to know for Insurance reasons. A half of a gold bracelet was also taken, but three days later it was put back in a box on the windowsill, containing earrings and the other half. Harry said he had his suspicions, but would accuse no one. He also said Chuck Adams was missing an $80 watch left at the wash basin last week.

Mac was brought back to Base by a bumpy dog team ambulance sled. His T shaped back splint worked loose so that his collarbone had to be reset after his arrival. The break was the final mishap that prevented McClary from participating in a long sledge trip, which he had looked forward to with great anticipation. His misfortune at not going on a sledge trip colored his attitude toward the expedition for the duration. Thus far he had suffered a broken bone in his hand aboard ship, a nearly fatal fall from the ice cliff, and now this. He was not a "happy camper".

Summer was approaching. The sun was above the horizon eighteen and twenty hours a day with twilight periods around midnight. We were anxious to get the gasoline cache at the advanced base at Keeler built up so that our flying activities could be moved to the other side of the peninsula, but three weeks of unsuitable weather kept the planes grounded. Peterson was one of the busiest men in camp, with his many weather checks and balloon runs, his answer was usually the same – no good weather in sight. When the main Base remained at ceiling zero, blue skies often appeared one hundred and twenty-five miles away on the other side of the Peninsula. Then at Base, we occasionally had a beautiful clear day, but on these days, the weather schedules from Keeler reported overcast, or blizzard winds. Not once had the weather been good on both sides of the Plateau long enough to make a flight.

With no let up day after day, members of the aviation group became frustrated and irritable. The weather began to tell on our nerves. These delays were putting us behind schedule in coordinating the exploratory flights with the needs and progress of the two trail parties. There was just nothing to do, but be patient and wait it out. During this time, Finn worked and reworked the loads to be carried in each of the several stages of flights by the planes. The pilots became despondent and thought the sun would never shine again on this part of the world.

They looked for other ways of occupying their time. This was when Lassiter and Sig Gutenko located a thinly iced tide crack in back of camp. A sled was set across the crack, a hole was poked through the ice to open water and they spent several days fishing. They managed to catch about forty small two to three inch fish. One day while Finn was exercising our snow-white dog Kasco in the art of skijoring, he stopped to chat with the fishermen. One of the small fish from their catch was flopping around on the ice nearby. Kasco being the inquisitive sort, pawed it a bit, then devoured it alive, to the disgust of the cold fishermen. He showed no ill effects, but could never be persuaded to try another fish dinner.

That evening Sig prepared the meager results of their outing so that all of us had a chance to try a French fried Antarctic species of fish. It was a change from our usual fairly inflexible diet, and we sampled them with great relish. A few minutes after the last fish had been consumed, the British biologist dropped in for a chat. When he found out what we had been up to, his jaw dropped. Honesty compelled him to tell us that his recent study of these fish revealed they were the egg carriers of the millions of parasites found in the stomach of the Weddell seals. Fortunately, no one became ill, but from then on we respected Kasco's intelligence, although the fishermen continued to persevere. On one occasion, Jim caught a very funny looking octopus which we put in alcohol to take back to Dr Alexander Whetmore, director of the Smithsonian Institution in Washington.

Sunday, October 19, 1947

Awoke and had breakfast late in the Bunkhouse. Ken came over in the early evening and we chatted all night. He reiterated his belief that Finn should not fly with Harry, that Harry was extremely dangerous, that while he felt like punching McClary in the nose, he did not think he had enough drive to be the leader of the group trying to ruin the expedition, that he felt Don McLean was the one who kept the bitching going. Ken was interested in coming to the States, inquired about opportunities for jobs, living expenses, etc. and how to take out citizenship. I am sending a wire off to my friend Bettie in the State Department to get the dope.

Finn had an aviation meeting in here all afternoon, to discuss ways of making the main flight quickly. Result was to take all three planes, fully loaded, to Violente Inlet and then pick the plane to make the trip. Lassiter was willing to carry everything. Harry willing to carry nothing. It was decided to have Chuck Adams get the cache to Nichols and then go to Keeler with Robertson. Lassiter and Finn would go in the Norseman and Harry, Latady, and Ike in the Beech, on the first clear day. After Jennie heard the news, she said I'll bet anyone $100 the Beech will never fly trimetrogon. McClary said, I wonder if all this rushing around at the last minute will be worth it. Hassage is sour and McLean bitter. The Joint British-American Weddell Coast Party has not reached the meteorological station yet. The weather was bad still, snow and blowing, temperature high and our shack is leaking badly.

Monday, October 20, 1947

Harry came in and said the Beech would not be able to carry full tanks of gas to Violante Inlet because with his weights, he would be landing with 1400 lb. over weight. He talked for an hour and then left saying, don't count on anything he had said, because he didn't know what the plane would do. After Harry left, Finn discussed it with Ike and decided the Beech would be the plane to use, but that he would not fly with Harry. Ike said he felt something like that was up and he didn't dispute Finn's decision. Finn spent the evening sending pictures to Press Wireless. Britisher David Jones and Lassiter gave the Norseman a thorough check today. The weather continued to be bad, sun coming out now and then, but overcast following a few minutes later.

Tuesday, October 21, 1947

Don wasn't up at ten o'clock and was Mess Cook. Finn called him and got him up. David worked with Lassiter on the Norseman. The weather was still very bad and both last night and today it was snowing heavily. Finn took pictures of me digging myself out of the passageway. Ken was over here working on the radio, still trying to get these pictures out to Press Wireless. Finn had a talk with Ken about what to do in aviation, relative to Harry. Ken said, if you get that coastline in trimetrogon photography, it would be the greatest thing ever done here. Finn agreed. Harry does not fit into this program. He is in a position to cause trouble. Finn, unfortunately, still feels sorry for him. Finn called in Lassiter and talked to him about flying the Beechcraft on the main trimetrogon mission. It was fine by him. Ike came in and he said, it would come as a blow, but he would tell Harry and inform Lassiter, who already knew, that he (Ike) also knew about it now. Finn then talked to Latady, who was most agreeable and said little about the Harry angle. Robertson was next and he agreed. He also told us that Harry had the heaters going in the Beech, when the gas tanks were empty and condensation formed inside. He ran the motors for forty-five minutes yesterday. Harry was in the plane. The switch on the inter-communication system was also on and when Jimmy went in, Harry was in there with fumes all around him. Jimmy felt the motors and they were red hot. One spark would have burned up the whole plane. The question is, is this what Harry wants. We all saw a movie, "Henry Aldrich", which was funny in a way. Ken came in and we chatted. Ken feels Finn should crack the whip with these guys and lay down the law. They get away with one thing and then try something else.

Wednesday, October 22, 1947

Last night was the first night I noticed how light it was, practically the whole night through. We went to bed around twelve and the twilight shown through our upper windows. I didn't sleep well and it seemed to be getting lighter all the time. It is, of course, the first time I have ever experienced this. From all reports, Harry took the news that he would not fly the Filchner Ice Shelf hop with the Beech very calmly. He seemed to be relieved and probably in his inner self does not have the nerve to do the job. He went around with a long face pretending to be unhappy, but there have been practically no repercussions over the incident.

Finn talked to Chuck Adams about the program and then had a long talk with Lassiter about weights. Finn got Robertson up and he did some work on the Beech. Finn gave McLean hell for not washing the dishes, but just sitting by the fire. Lassiter said that Dave had told him Ken might go back with us. Lassiter is very anxious to fly back to Punta Arenas, if he isn't needed on the ship. Ken didn't come over today, as the contact with Press Wireless was not strong enough with bad interference. I revised the N.Y.Times Magazine article. McClary is working on a model of the British sled. The gang was pretty quiet tonight; there must be something brewing. It continued to snow and the visibility was down to the deck. Some of the fellows brought in coal and diesel oil from the ship during the day. Lassiter is finished checking the Norseman and is looking over the Beech. Latady is working on some bags for the plane.

Thursday, October 23, 1947

I finished typing up the article for the Times Magazine. Finn worked on a map for plotting in his courses in flight and made a plotting board. Latady came in saying the weights of the cameras had not been calculated in the weight of the plane, which Robertson had given Finn. He had obviously come from Harry. Finn said, they had been accounted for and upon checking with Robertson, Bill and Finn both found this to be so. They discussed extensively the different things to be taken along and Bill intended rounding up much of it. It looked as thought it might clear all day, but never did. Finn called Hassage in and asked him to take over the charge of the camp in his absence. He screamed, "Hell no, not me – never, you just do all the work that way, why not get Sig, how about

McClary? I'm not good enough to do anything else, now you want me to do this". Finn said, " You try to run your own expedition sometime Chuck and you'll find out how hard it is". Hassage said, "Harry won't do anything". He thought for a few more minutes and said, "O.K., Finn I'll do it, but don't expect too much of me" and then said, "I'll see you later, I'll go out and get a cup of coffee."

Just before the lights went out for the evening, Harry came in and asked Finn if he would please O.K. two messages. I was playing cards on the table and didn't even turn around to look at him. Finn said suddenly, "What is this message to Admiral Byrd about your no longer connected with the aviation program". Harry said, "I talked that all over with the Admiral before I left and this is a personal message to him". Finn said, " Admiral Byrd has nothing to do with this expedition and I think he will sleep even if he doesn't get this message from you". Harry said, "But that's a personal message, you aren't going to let it go out"? Finn said, " No, I'm not going to let it go out". The message to Harry's mother Finn let go. After thinking it over, Finn called Harry back in and asked him, what Ike had told him. Harry replied, "That I was not going to fly the trimetrogon hop". Finn said, "On this operation you mean". Harry said, "Yes, but so far as I am concerned that means I'm through with aviation". Finn said, "I should like to have that in writing Harry". He said, "O.K. I'll be glad to". Finn said, he was sorry it had happened as it had, but that Harry had brought it on himself. Harry said, he would rather not discuss it. Finn said, "You realize that the messages which go out of here are my prerogative and your sending information like that in a message is a slap at me, which I just don't stand for". Harry replied, that he just didn't want his mother, or anyone else, to think that he had any connection with, or was responsible for, the aviation unit in case anything went wrong. Finn said, "I can assure you your name has not been mentioned in that connection for sometime and will not be in the future". Harry said, "Fine". Finn said, "I want that message to your mother reworded before it goes out". Harry said, "O.K.". Finn said, "You can tell the Admiral anything you like when you get back". Harry said, " I certainly intend to". Finn said, "Do you mean that you intend to have no more connection with the expedition"? and Harry said, "Oh no!" "I intend to do my share of the work around here as I always have before". Finn said, "Ike, tells me he can't get you up in the morning". Harry said, "When Ike wants me for work, I'll be there". Then he asked Finn if he could train the rest of the dogs here and work on a project he started for school sometime ago. Finn said, "Yes, go ahead and do that, after you have completed your expedition duties". Harry left.

Friday, October 24, 1947

Another bad day. Bill worked on the weights and stuff to go in the Beech. Robertson and Jim worked on the Beech. Inexplicably, they found three quarts of water in the gasoline tanks recently, but definitely, after Harry knew he wasn't going to fly it. Ken came over in the evening with the big news of the day. Kelsey told Ken, that Harry had tried to bribe him to get those two messages out. Kelsey refused and Ken told him, he had better not try to send them, or he would easily be caught up and it could mean nothing but trouble for him. Kelsey tore up the message and burned it. Kelsey also told Ken that Harry was making no secret about the fact that he planned to spend $10,000, if necessary, to wreck Finn and the expedition. Ken said, that Harry had come over to him today, bitching about Finn. Ken stopped that and said, it was none of their concern. Harry then asked Ken, to send the messages for him and he refused, saying no message would go out from there without Finn's signature. Ken also said that about six weeks to two months ago, Harry had asked Ken to sell him some liquor, that he was willing to pay for it. Ken refused saying they did not have much and that he couldn't sell it, because it was Government stores. Ken said, Harry started in on Finn again and finally, Ken said you know Harry I think the best thing for you to do would be for you and Jennie to get clear out of this and go live at the Debenhams. Harry thought that was a good idea, but didn't think Finn would let him have the food. Ken said, *if he wished, he would talk to Finn and he felt sure Finn would let them have the food, but if not, he would let them have some of his stores. Harry said fine, I'll have to talk to Jennie about it.*

When Ken later told his group that he had offered the Debenhams to the Darlingtons, they all cheered and thought it was wonderful to get them out. Harry later asked Ken, if he could arrange to have them get passage back on a British ship. Ken said, he didn't know as that was out of his hands. Ken said, he thought Harry should be made to work his way back with the expedition, instead of going back in style and being able to start trouble two months ahead of Finn's return. He was also afraid of the lies and trouble he would cause in the Falklands, while being entertained there as a guest. Finn agreed. Ken strongly urged Finn to submit a report to the Navy Dept. in code on Harry to forestall the trouble he knew Harry would try to cause. Ken left late and we couldn't sleep for fear Harry would try to sabotage the planes. Finn called in Lassiter and told him the whole story. Lassiter said, he would have Robertson and Dave check for the obvious. He strongly suggested sending McLean south with Nichols and Jorge to the Plateau, to get them out of Camp. Lassiter also said, Harry had told him that if he had gone back on the Fitzroy that time, he would have felt he had let the expedition down, but now he felt no responsibility for the success of the expedition's program, whatsoever. Finn had a talk with Latady this morning. He said Harry was extremely difficult to get along with and that Harry had tried to persuade him to drop out of the aerial program and not take the pictures. Bill said he couldn't see why he should do this, at all.

The never ending contention was extremely depressing, keeping our nerves on edge, much like walking a tight rope, wondering day and night what would happen next.

Saturday, October 25, 1947

Of course, we didn't sleep much last night. Lassiter said, Robertson had said, he felt Harry was angry enough to sabotage the planes, particularly the Beech, because, if he couldn't fly it, he wouldn't want anyone else to do so. Finn turned off the radio in the Bunkhouse at 10:30 this morning. This made Peterson mad and he asked Sig, what made Finn the way he was and why did he make such wrong decisions. Don McLean and McClary were there. Sig said, so far as he was concerned, Finn's decisions were not wrong, and he personally did not come along on the expedition to question the decisions of the Leader. At my suggestion, Finn brought in Peterson and had a talk with him. He told him, the expedition was at a crisis with Harry, who threatened to wreck it and he needed people who were loyal to back him up and work for him, not question his decisions in public and try to make and stir up trouble and contribute to the general bitching. Pete said, although he had a different attitude from the one shown by Finn, he felt ashamed of himself and would try not to say anything about him in the future. Finn next decided to tackle Don McLean, who was out skiing with Bill, Jennie, and Jorge.

After dinner, Ike and Don came in. Finn asked Don where he stood on the expedition and what he wanted to get out of it and how he felt about things in general. Don said, he would stay in camp, work here on medicine, biology, and camp work. Finn said he had been very angry the other night and just found out that Don and Jorge had been drunk several nights, before he came off night watch. Don was most surprised that Finn knew this. Finn asked Don, where he had gotten the liquor. Don said, from what Andy had brought with him. Don denied he had been the one to do his business aboard ship. Finn said Harry had given him the information and that Bob Nichols had spoken to him about it also, but that he was glad to know Don denied doing it. Finn said he viewed the doctor as a morale building factor. McLean agreed and said, that he had been obstinate in his ways and had over slept and not worked, because he was sulking over Finn's reading him off. Finn brought up Harry and told Don of his threats and that Finn would have to report Harry's behavior to protect himself if Harry attempted to carry these threats out. He also said he would make a report on all Navy people including Don. Don said he didn't believe Harry would carry out his threats. He agreed that Harry was difficult to get along with, but thought he said things in angry tempers, which he didn't mean. He said, Harry felt that he was the better navigator of the pilots and that if they had a forced landing out someplace, he would be the better trail man, in view of his previous experience, but, of course, Don added this was a matter for Finn to decide. Finn said, that if Don showed an interest in his medical work, cleaned up the Dispensary in the Science Building, and gave Finn the reports he had requested months ago, that there may be a possibility for him to join Nichols and his party, providing McClary was in good condition, needed no attention, the same with Andy and if Butson would be back soon. Don was surprised at this and said it was more than he had expected and naturally, he was anxious to go. He said, how glad he was to have this talk with Finn. Finn said, he wasn't a hard person to get along with, if people met him half way. Don shook Finn's hand on the way out. Kelsey told Finn that Harry had tried to bribe him to send out the messages. Finn asked Jorge, if he wanted to go to the Plateau for a while. Jorge was tickled pink and thrilled to death. Right away, he was a changed man. The next person on the agenda was Harry.

Finn called in Ike, Harry, and Jennie. Finn asked them both what their intentions were, that Ken had spoken to him about their going to the Debenhams and did they intend to go. Harry said, he thought it was a good idea, if he got away from it all and go there, but if Finn thought they could live at Base, without a recurrence of the performance yesterday morning, he would try to keep out of Finn's way. Finn said, "What do you refer to about yesterday morning"? Harry said, "Why the way you bawled my wife out for drinking a cup of tea". Finn said, "I told your wife it was twelve o'clock, that lunch would be ready in thirty minutes, that this was no time for breakfast, that if she wanted breakfast, you could get up in the morning when the rest did and carry it in to her the way I did with Jackie, that she knew when meal times were, that if she couldn't read, I felt sorry for her and that I didn't want people in the Galley and I didn't want persons eating all day long, anytime they felt like it". I said, "Harry, if you refer to any rudeness, you have on several occasions overstepped your bounds of rudeness to me, more than Finn has ever done with Jennie". Harry said, "I think it would be better, if we both got out of it and moved to Debenhams. I don't want to argue with you, I'm tired of it all and I just want to get out of it. I sincerely feel it would be better for you and the expedition, particularly, when your big flying program is coming up, if we just left. So far as I am concerned, I have just wasted a year and a half of my life and I want to make arrangements to leave the expedition as soon as possible".

Finn started to say something and Harry butted in. Finn said, "Let me talk, I let you talk". Finn said, "You said you wasted a year and a half of your life by coming, let me say that the reason is all of your own making. You were Third-in-Command and Head of Aviation, in that capacity you were expected to take orders from me and act in the best interests of the expedition. Instead, you disobeyed my orders continuously, after I gave you a chance, along with the rest to leave in Panama, if you felt you couldn't take orders. You disobeyed me by going to the British camp, when I told you not to, you tried to cause trouble between the two camps with your lies and misstatements, you tried to negotiate with the British, after I told you I would be the only one to do that, you tried to cause trouble in the British Camp against the Leader of that camp, you tried to cause trouble during the search for the Britishers between Ike and Ken Butler, you asked Kelsey to inform him when Jackie's flying story went out, that you were sure going to cause trouble about that, that you stated before witnesses that you were disloyal to me, saw no reason why you should be loyal, that you intended to do as you pleased at all times, that I could have no confidence in you". Finn also stated, that he had tried to bribe Kelsey into getting the messages out of camp and that he had tried to get them out over the British station, that he had threatened to spend $10,000 if necessary to wreck the expedition. Harry was furious, he said, he had *given the L-5 a down, when Nichols, Lassiter, and I flew that day. Finn said, "If you had any reservations about the L-5, Harry, it was your responsibility to inform me of it as you were responsible to me alone and you had been on a drunk and hadn't spoken to me for five days." I said, "What connection does my reporting my flight have to do with you, whether you downed the plane or not."*

Harry was cornered and said, I just wanted to know that's all. I said, "That was none of your business Harry". Harry denied that he had said Finn could have no confidence in him and that he had said he had no confidence in Finn. I said I was there and it was the other way around. Harry denied that he had tried to bribe Kelsey and Ken to get the messages out and asked Finn to prove it. Finn refused to call them in now. Harry denied saying he would use money to wreck Finn and the expedition, saying he only wanted to forget it. I said, " Harry you are lying, we know these things are true". Finn said, Harry said, Finn had made all sorts of promises to him in Washington, which didn't exist, particularly about the women not flying. Finn said the women had no intention of going to the Antarctic when we were in Washington.

Harry denied saying about that agreement in Washington and I said, "Harry, you accused Finn of that in this very room". Harry said again he felt he and Jennie should go to the Debenhams and get out of the way, so Finn could run his expedition in the way he wanted to. I said, "It is too bad Harry that you did not feel that way before this". Finn told Harry that he understood now, why Admiral Byrd always stressed loyalty as much as he did, for one disloyal person could certainly cause a lot of trouble, particularly while acting as Third-in-Command, to talk over things with Finn, agree on a solution, then go right out to the men and say, "That's the way he wants it, I wouldn't do it that way, but my hands are tied". Finn promised Harry E rations for food and told him he could make out a list of other food, including steak and give it to Sig. Finn told him to take anything necessary for their health and comfort and that he would speak to Ken about taking them up by a British dogteam. Finn also told Harry, that if he continued his undermining actions, he would have to order them to the Debenhams. He also told Harry, that because of his threats to ruin the expedition, he would have to report his actions and behavior officially, that Finn was thoroughly aware of his influence and connections in Washington and that if he attempted to carry out his threats, he would have to take action, accordingly.

Finn made it understood, in front of Ike, that Harry had been told he would not be flying this particular hop, because Finn wanted to use that plane and would not fly with him. Harry and Jennie said good-bye and left after Jennie had gotten Finn to O.K. a message concerning the insurance on her diamond ring, which she lost. Ike said. "Well that's two down today.

In some respects the showdown had been a relief although very sad to realize that the very close friendship we once had enjoyed had come to this impasse. Things could never possibly be the same again. We all went to see the movie, "Murder My Sweet". Ken came in afterward and we told him the story of the day. He couldn't believe that Harry had the nerve to deny that he hadn't tried to get the messages out through him. Ken again strongly urged that Finn submit an immediate report on Harry to Washington, because he was a dangerous man and would cause Finn trouble, which Finn should try to protect himself against first, before Harry started.

Finn never did make such a report, as he never felt that anything Harry would ever say could ever carry much credence or weight. People would easily see through Harry's lies Finn felt certain.

Just before the movie, Finn went in and asked Harry to give it to him in writing, that he had requested Finn to let them go to the Debenhams, that he chose to do so of his own free will and accord, and that Finn was in no way responsible for their welfare and safety while there.

Sunday, October 26, 1947

Finn reported good feeling in Camp this morning. Everyone including McLean was out helping to get the Beech ready for a flight. I went out on skis to watch them. Don was very friendly.

The Beech performed beautifully. It can turn on a dime and she took off very quickly, carrying about 85,000 lb. Chuck Adams got the L-5 ready to take off with the stuff for Nichols. Finn and I skied up the glacier with Kasco. Kasco pulled me on the level. He is really turning out to be a thoroughbred Husky and really looks and acts like one. Pete was up on the glacier rummaging around. We saw the rhombic antenna was grounded in the snow in two places. Pete said he didn't know this, and didn't know whether Kelsey did, but would tell him.

Chuck took off for Nichols, and Lassiter landed after a successful flight with Bill. They all came in for coffee and sandwiches and a chat. Bill prepared to develop the pictures immediately.

The cameras had been set so that they took one set of pictures every twenty seconds and at a 10,000 foot altitude this gave about the desired sixty percent overlap. The pictures which Latady obtained from this test run revealed that the cameras were in perfect working order and needed little further adjustment before being used on the main exploratory flights.

Chuck was unable to reach Nichols because of bad weather. Sig said, Jennie came out about 12:30 and asked Don if breakfast was over. He said yes, we had it about eleven o'clock. She cleaned her teeth and went back. While we were up on the glacier, Don, Jennie and Harry started out skiing in the direction of the Debenhams. Around 4:30 Jennie, who was back, announced that she was going over to the British Camp for lunch as she was hungry.

After dinner, at which the Darlingtons were not present, we noticed as the door to their room was open, that the room looked as thought it was being torn apart. Finn asked Ike to come in and we read him what we wanted Harry to sign, if he went to the Debenhams.

Finn discussed with Ike, the possibility of making a report on Harry. Ike advised against it, saying they would ask Harry for a statement, after which they would decide what to do, including investigation and court-martial proceedings or merely filing in his jacket. Ike said there was very little Harry could do unofficially except cause nuisance trouble and that he had seen so many others threaten to do thus and so, but people paid little attention to them. He also said, if Harry attacked Finn officially, it was a very serious charge to make against a superior officer and that he had darn well better be right or else he would be court martialed. On the strength of this, Finn decided to make no report to the Navy Dept. concerning Harry.

Monday, October 27, 1947

Finn went over to see Ken, who told him, and later in the day told both of us, that Harry had been over several times bitching for hours on end, to anyone who would listen to him. He told Ken, that Ken should not have told Finn about his wanting to send the messages out over their radio station. Harry said, that was the only thing Finn had ever gotten on him, implying that there had been plenty of other things, but he had been clever enough to cover them up. He then told Ken, that the present situation was all Ken's fault for telling Finn what he did. He again asked Ken to send out the message that he only wanted to tell his mother that he was no longer connected with aviation, so that she would not worry. Ken said to him, that he believed there was more behind it than that, and that this would not be used to harm Finn, if he could help it. Harry then stated that if his mother got that message, she would call up Admiral Byrd and President Truman and there would be plenty of trouble for Finn. He then told Ken, that he intended to resign from the expedition and have nothing more to do with it. Ken told Finn, if he accepted Harry's resignation, that Harry and Jennie would immediately become their responsibility and he wanted nothing to do with him, because he considered him highly dangerous and was afraid of the trouble he would unnecessarily cause them.

He also stated, that he would be obliged to send out Harry's message, when he had no connection with this expedition, because he was operating a commercial station Finn said he didn't intend to accept Harry's resignation. Ken said, as long as Harry thought Ken was not going to double cross him openly, Harry would continue to tell Ken what he was up to, so that Ken could pass it on to Finn. Ken said, on Saturday night, Harry and Jennie had gone over to Dave and bitched all evening. Dave kept saying it was his bath night, but they wouldn't take the hint. He was about to be tied, by the time the rest of the Britishers returned from our Camp. Ken said, he had had no trouble with his group of men up until the time Harry started his actions over there.

Chuck Hassage came in and tried to talk Finn into forgetting the Harry situation because the more he found himself cornered, the more fanatical he became and Chuck was afraid he would employ foul play against Finn. He said, he fully realized how Harry had been lying for months and it took him a long time to find out how much he really was lying, and to what extent he was going with his lies. Chuck said, he had told Harry that he would be in charge of Camp when Finn left and that he expected Harry to pitch in and do his share of the work. Harry assured Chuck that he would do this. Chuck told me about the novel he was writing and it sounded quite good. Chuck tried to tell Finn to stop worrying about Harry, that if he pulled any sabotage the rest of the camp would beat him up. Chuck said he watched the planes at night, that he had already thought about that.

Tuesday, October 28, 1947

The day started out cloudy and overcast as usual. I almost finished my sweater today. Finn asked Bill to come in. Bill brought in the trimetrogon pictures, which he had printed thus far. They were excellent. Finn asked Bill if he would sign a statement to the effect that Harry had tried to persuade him not to operate the trimet cameras or be in aviation anymore. Bill said he would rather not because, he didn't think it would do any good. Finn said, he didn't want him to do it if he didn't want to, but he considered Harry's threats dangerous and he felt he had to protect himself and the expedition in the future. Bill said he was terribly sorry about the whole thing, that he knew both sides of the story and he thoroughly sympathized with Finn. He said he would sign any statement to the effect that he was one hundred percent in back of the expedition and his complete sympathies were with Finn. He said, he hoped to talk to Harry, whom he considered to be very ill advised, and try to persuade him that even if he didn't like Finn, he still had to consider the rights of twenty other people. He said, he hoped to talk to Jennie in the same vein, because she had a great influence over Harry's actions.

Finn and Bill talked about the trimetrogon, and felt that it was ready to go. Sig came in for a short chat and stated that he felt Harry was powerless to cause all the trouble in the States that he was threatening. Finn went out to work on the planes and take some pictures.

The weather began clearing. Robertson was gassing the Beech. Jennie, Mac, and Don were taking a walk. Chuck Adams prepared the L-5 to fly to Nichols. He attempted two take-offs, but got stuck in the soft snow twice. The second time, the weasel had to drag him out. Kelsey hadn't heard from Fiske, the Plateau, or Nichols, with regard to weather.

Chuck decided to give up trying to get off with the heavy load to Nichols and to try taking Jorge to the Plateau. He and Jorge took off, but were unable to land on top because of low-lying clouds right on the Plateau. He reported bad weather coming in from the North. Finn told Kelsey to get Fiske and Nichols both to come up on the seven o'clock schedule tomorrow. Ken came over and chatted. He hopes to leave for the trail party in the Norseman on the first flying day. He seems to think his radio room is pretty secure now and that if Finn gets Harry aboard, ship before other ships come in and gets him back to the States with the expedition, there is very little that he can do. We had a movie, "Bewitched," and went to bed early.

Saturday, November 1, 1947

After lunch Finn called an aviation meeting to discuss the next steps in the program. It was agreed by everyone present, Ike, Latady, Lassiter, Adams, and Robertson, that the best thing to do after getting Nichols squared away was to utilize both planes to carry gas to Keeler, in case the Bay Ice should become slushy, making any operation off of it impossible and thus forcing operations onto the infinitely more difficult glacier. Bill suggested making the Crane Inlet trimetrogon hop before leaving for Keeler. This would give another check on the cameras operation. It was decided to do this, if possible before leaving, but not at the expense of getting the gas over there. Personnel to man the Keeler Base and an Advanced Base was then discussed. Fiske would go to Advanced Base everyone agreed. The question was who would stay with Fiske. Don was suggested. Finn asked Ike if he would like to do this and Ike suddenly started on a tirade against Finn. Ike said, No! he was a pilot. He had it in writing that Finn had asked him to come as a pilot. He denied promising Finn that he wouldn't fly solo in view of Don McLean's medical report on his one eye condition.

Finn knew that Ike had a tendency toward having double and triple vision. On one occasion when he and Finn were outside the buildings, Ike asked who those three men were walking out on the Bay ice. Finn said, "Ike, there is only <u>one</u> man out there!"

He said Don didn't know what he was talking about, wasn't able to judge, was no flight surgeon. He said as long as the younger fellows could manage the program, he was content to sit back, but now Finn was short of pilots, that he may be called upon and he wasn't prepared and had to prepare himself by going on every flight and had to be flying the planes. This, of course, made Finn mad and Finn asked Ike to get Don McLean.

Finn searched for and finally found McLean's written medical report and in front of the group read it. Don was definitely on the spot. Ike asked him to change it saying he was O.K. Ike told Don, he didn't know what he was talking about, and had never told him what he was going to do which wasn't fair. Ike said, Finn had asked Don for such a report. Finn denied this. Don was forced to back up his report, saying it was still his belief that Ike should not fly alone, nor should he land a plane. Ike retreated and said how about co-pilot. Don said he would write a memo to Finn saying, Ike was medically fit to fly co-pilot and relieve Finn of any responsibility in this connection and would give it to him by the end of the day. Don then left. Ike said he would be co-pilot. Finn said, I have never been in any disagreement with you about that. Ike said Don was not his friend, no friend would have done that and Don had been mad at him at the time, cause after Finn had informed Ike of the existence of the report, Ike questioned Don about it and Ike said Don apologized to him for having written it. Ike then agreed that he had previously promised Finn that he would not fly solo and would stick to this promise and act only as co-pilot, when the pilot was responsible for the plane, unless in an emergency when no pilot was available and his services might mean life or death.

Chuck Adams was agreeable to this and said he couldn't see that the situation had changed any from what it had previously been. All in all, Ike acted surprisingly badly and we were both quite surprised. He had threatened Finn with, if I don't fly, I'll have nothing more to do with aviation and go live on the ship. All of which seems to prove that persons will agree with you about most anything, until they themselves are directly affected, then to heck with the good of the expedition plans, or loyalty, or wishes or anything else, they are just out to make you wrong and gain their own ends. I didn't think Ike would do this, but he did, as did many others before him Harry, Nichols, McClary, McLean, etc. The meeting broke up to get the Norseman to look for Nichols. Before they got off, the weather closed in and the flight was canceled. Lassiter and Robertson told Finn they both thought Ike had turned the argument around. Robertson told Finn, he didn't think Finn should let Ike fly even as co-pilot.

At lunch, Finn announced the loss of Jennie's diamond ring. Outwardly there seemed to be no reaction. The rest of the day was relatively peaceful and we saw a movie, "Over 21", at night.

Sunday, November 2, 1947

Finn awoke at 6:30 and saw the sun shining brightly. He woke up Sig and all aviation and the Norseman was made ready to fly to Nichols. Lassiter piloted and against Finn's wishes, Ike sat up front in the co-pilot's seat, although he can't see a thing and couldn't spot Nichols on the ground anyway. Hassage went along to throw the stuff out of the plane. They got as far as Mt. Edgell and had to return to Base, because of bad weather with fog covering the ground.

Finn met Andy this morning who said I hear you have made some changes, while I was away. Finn said, yes, because of Harry's lies, disloyalty and undermining actions, I had to remove him. Andy said, well he is spoiled, had always had his way and wants to always have it. He said, however, he liked Harry and considered him a friend. Finn said he was welcome to his opinion, but that he (Finn) had it in writing that Harry threatened to wreck the expedition and spend $10,000 to do so if necessary. Andy said, do you have that in writing and Finn said, I certainly do.

Monday, November 3, 1947

The day dawned with overcast skies, but by 10 o'clock, the sun was shining and there wasn't a cloud in the sky. Both planes took off for Keeler. The Norseman with Chuck and Ike carried gear and about four drums of gas. The Beech carried gas, but couldn't drain it because the pipe was too short. Both planes came back and Chuck, Hassage and Latady took a trip down to the Sound to look for Nichols and Dodson. They searched the area for over an hour, but couldn't' see them. Lassiter was depressed all day, because they couldn't utilize the good weather to the best advantage on the other side. It was decided by all flight personnel that the best thing to do, was to take both planes down the Sound for another search. Lassiter, Finn and Andy flew in the Beech, Chuck, Robertson, and

Latady in the Norseman. They searched everywhere, but couldn't see Nichols or any trace of him.

Butler had arrived at Cape Keeler advance base via the NANA plane a few days earlier and joined the party. Butson dropped out and was later returned to his British Base. Wood remained at Keeler and Walter Smith took his place as surveyor. The party now consisted of Britishers Butler and Mason; and Smith and Owen from our group. These men composed the British–American Weddell Coast Sledge Party and headed south for the long trip.

I certainly had plenty of time to philosophize about the actions of these men in polar isolation. Hardly a day passed without my thinking that if I ever got home wild horses would never be able to drive me back to Antarctica again. Never! Never! Never! and nothing would ever change my mind about that, I was quite sure!

It hurt me to have Finn critized so much. I wanted to explain his reasoning in every way. His first and foremost motivation was the complete success of every facet of the expedition, but he also very much wanted each member to have the opportunity to look back on a rewarding experience. Despite a sometimes formal brusque exterior, he had a very soft side. In spite of all Harry had done against him, he felt sorry for him – a man he had known a long time. He truly wished desperately that things had turned out differently. At this particular period in Antarctic exploration, the nine-to-five type of man did not volunteer to go. Instead, expedition life had an appeal to the young, brash restless soul who served duty in the Second World War and who had not been able to settle down yet, who was looking for some excitement before doing so. To a few it was either the romantic history and/or their desire to contribute to it that was the compelling factor. I know enough about the history of Antarctic exploration to know that each expedition has had its own peculiar personality difficulties for a wide variety of different reasons. In this case it is remarkable that the endless turmoil did not impede the outstanding successful results of the expedition. In fact it may even have enhanced it. Finn's determination and drive was relentless. But we did realize that we certainly should have paid more attention to what Harry's mother had tried to tell us about her son's unpredictable behavior when she had us down to tea that afternoon before we left Washington.

XIV

One Continent

November 4 dawned bright and sunny. Lassiter, Adams and Robertson had been up very early and the planes were ready for take off. Hassage drove the weasel back and forth across the runway to pack down the snowy surface. The camp was full of excitement and we eagerly awaited the 9 o'clock weather report from Cape Keeler.

> *Jim Lassiter got mad at Larry at Keeler and Kelsey here carrying on a newsy conversation, while he and Chuck were sitting in the planes, engines going, ready to fly, Larry got down to business and sent the weather so that it could be intelligently interpreted. He reported marginal bad weather coming in from the north, but clear in all other directions. We were very disappointed, because the weather at Base was perfect.*

Finn and I skied for a few minutes on the glacier then came back to our shack. After an hour or so of hemming and hawing, Lassiter could stand it no longer. He came in and said to Finn, "if you are willing, I would like to take off. I see no reason why we can't find a way over." Finn's gear already had been stowed in the plane. As Schlossback was also at Keeler, Finn already had appointed Hassage to be in charge of camp while he was away, and in addition, he had made arrangements for the future managing of the expedition to be in my hands in case anything unforeseen should happen to him. I was the only one who knew all of his commitments stateside and in whom he had total trust.

Soon, the Beechcraft taxied onto the bay-ice for take-off, loaded with full tanks of gas, three trimetrogon cameras installed, one hundred and fifty pounds of film and all of Lassiter's and Finn's camping equipment and emergency gear. As they wanted to leave five full drums of the gas at Keeler, they had difficulty getting into the air with their heavy load of about 10,000 pounds. Once off, they were able to fly under the overcast covering the Traffic Circle.

After gaining altitude to cross over the hump, Finn quickly recognized the mountainous features of Cape Keeler and through the haze was able to site our advanced Base. The shelf ice, on which our advanced base was located, extended seaward from the Cape and was about sixty-five feet above sea level. Moving glaciers flowing eastward from the high Palmer Land Plateau, caused heavy pressure areas to the south of the Cape, extending five miles seaward. The camp was located about a half mile from the Mainland and three miles eastward of the Cape. From the air it was very inconspicuous with only the anchored L-5, a couple of poles and the anemometer visible. Regardless of the wind's direction, the shelf ice surface was smooth and afforded perfect conditions for a flying field from all sides. Fiske let off a flare to give the wind direction. After the one-hour's flight, Lassiter made a very smooth landing and taxied the plane to the campsite. Once on the ground there was nothing visible eastward to break the monotony of pale blue sky and level white snow.

> *Lassiter radioed Adams to bring Latady over and to fly under the overcast at the Traffic Circle. We had lunch and they got ready quickly, because the weather here began to close in rapidly. John brought a dog named Monkey over from the British camp to replace a bitch in the Weddell Coast Sledge Party's team who was having pups soon. The dog was just tied securely to a gas drum in the plane and peered inquiringly out of the side window. The take-off surface had gotten progressively worse since this morning. It was very sticky. I was skiing on the glacier and the snow just clung to the bottom of my skis, making it impossible to slide. I had to walk down the hill. Chuck made two false take-off runs and after each one, had to remove some gasoline, a total of seven hundred pounds was taken out. The Beech had carried enough to leave five drums of gas and NANA carried empty drums only. Adams landed at*

Keeler safely with Latady. Both planes tried to come back this afternoon, to pick up Mechanic Robertson, additional gasoline and cargo and but were forced to land at Keeler again because of the overcast here.

When the dog Monkey had arrived at Keeler, she jumped out of the plane and trotted immediately to the three staked out teams where she renewed old acquaintances. The husky which Monkey replaced remained at Keeler to give birth to three healthy puppies, which in her excitement, she unfortunately ate. Much later, she was returned to our Base by plane.

Keeler Base had a full house. However, at midnight the four men on the Joint Weddell Coast Party, who had arrived a few days before, departed with their teams and fully loaded sledges to continue their trip south.

Fiske had inaugurated a rather amusing formal ceremony for greeting all newcomers. He approached Finn with a log to sign and went through his welcoming speech elaborating that he was the magistrate of "Pemmicamp, Lower East-Side Township", and was not responsible for anyone who slept less than ten hours a day or got further than fifty feet from camp. The reason for the latter was that on one day of very poor visibility, Fiske himself had fallen headfirst into a snow excavation, which he had dug right outside the tent door.

After the formal ceremonies, Fiske conducted a tour of the Outpost. The command tent was the assembly place containing the cooking equipment, food and eating space. A tunnel led to the meteorological room, dug out of the barrier. The igloo, which had been built on top, was a dome, second only to that of the Capitol Building in Washington, D.C. Various meteorological instruments, weather log, hydrogen bottles for balloon runs, barograph, and quite an assortment of batteries were stored here. Great care and been shown by Fiske and Smith in the operations and maintenance of their programs. From the Met stations another tunnel led through a smaller opening to a storeroom for unused sleeping and personal gear. From the larger tunnel, smaller ones led to sleeping tents on either side. Continuous drifting snow had gradually buried the small settlement so that much of their life was spent beneath the surface.

Finn moved into the tent set up for him and prepared to spend most of his waking hours underground. Latady was sleeping in a small orange colored tent and Lassiter and Adams in a large pyramidal tent nearby, in which Finn soon joined them. Fiske, Smith and later Wood, replacing Smith, were living in a tent on the other side of the command tent, from which the tunnels radiated. Schlossbach's small mountain tent had been pitched topside. It was only six feet long, four feet wide and less than four feet high. Many a morning they stood convulsed watching Ike trying to emerge from his cramped quarters. He did everything but tear the tent down.

With bad weather at the Main Base, Finn wanted to utilize Keeler's good weather to take a short exploratory flight east over the Larsen Shelf Ice with Adams in the L-5. In 1928, Sir Hubert Wilkins had flown from Deception Island in Lat. 62 Deg. 56 Min. South, Long. 60 Deg. and 34 Min. West, southward along the Weddell Coast as far as Cape Eielsen. He reported the appearance of land off the coast to the East of Keeler, but because of increasing bad visibility, he was unable to verify its existence. In a 1940 flight over that same area, Finn also detected the appearance of land in that direction and our pilots flying to and from Keeler in the last two months, also believed there were low lying islands off the coast. Finn was anxious to solve the question. At two o'clock on the afternoon of November 7th, 1947, Finn and Adams took off on a course of 60 Deg. true.

> *Meanwhile at the Main Base, Chuck Hassage took over the running of the Camp and announced no night watch and no candle burning after lights out and no long walks on the Bay Ice without first informing someone of their departure. Don, Mac, Jennie and Harry sat alone at their end tonight and the rest of the group, Andy, Pete, Kelsey, and Robertson, sat up at my usual end. I sent a story in on the flight departure to the North American Newspaper Alliance.*

Wednesday, November 5, 1947

> *Robertson was in all afternoon. We played cards and chatted. He certainly has no use for Harry and says for his money, Harry is no pilot as he knows pilots, for he is so unconcerned about things. He says definitely that the gang in Harry's room is drinking medical alcohol. He says that Harry had about a case of liquor with him and that he has had about three drinks in there, but that is probably gone now and the medical alcohol is being used. He came in after dinner and we chatted until twelve.*
>
> *Hassage made a facetious remark to Sig this morning saying Sig was tunnel runner #1, Robertson #2 and him-*

self #3. The tunnel runners were those who often came through the short tunnel from the Bunkhouse to our adjoining quarters.

Thursday, November 6, 1947

Sig chopped me some kindling wood yesterday and this morning, the two of us together dug the snowed-in passage way out. The sun was shining bright around noon and there was some local clearing, but before the hour was up, the overcast had obscured all the surrounding mountains. Hassage carried in a bag of coal for me and chatted for a while. Kelsey decided to sleep this morning, so Pete listened for Fiske to come up on the battery set and the generator stayed off all day. Andy came in and had a long chat with me about the possibilities for a job in the Government after he got back and things in general. He made some prints of the men leaving on the Beech flight and will make some to go to NANA.

John Tonkin invited me over to tea. We had delicious chopped egg sandwiches with green cress from the hot house. We discussed Nichols and found that most people felt he had gone to the mountains after rocks, except Kevin, who said Bob was hopeless on the trail, but finally did realíze how dangerous the place was and didn't intend to try any heroics. Kevin left Bob on October 4th, with thirty-eight days of food which, except for caches, would last until Nov. 11th, and longer if they did not eat full rations. He said Nichols had agreed when he got down to six days food, they would start back. Kevin didn't see how anything completely disastrous could happen to them on the Bay Ice and even if dogs and sled were lost, they could still get back with their skis, by utilizing their caches. There were oodles of seals on the Bay Ice. and they had eight gallons of kerosene.

Friday, November 7, 1947

I found out Finn and Chuck Adams took a flight eastward today in search of possible Islands. When I went to read Finn the message over the radio about the two Navy Icebreakers coming down, one to the Bellingshausen Sea and the Other 180 Deg. away on the Knox Coast. I read the message to Fiske when I found out Finn wasn't there.

After I came back to the shack, I turned on the radio and discovered Larry was telling Kelsey that he (Kelsey) was in the doghouse with Finn because he hadn't come up on the radio that morning. Kelsey' reason was that he didn't want to bother the radiomen in the field when it wasn't necessary. This, of course, does not explain away the fact that Fiske had to meet the schedule even though Kelsey didn't. Kelsey acted as though he had been terribly abused. Fiske then asked about whether his messages had gone out and Kelsey said, "No", that the power had to be turned off at eleven-thirty. Fiske went into a rage saying Finn had said nothing would prevent the messages from the men in the field from going through and if this was so, he was really going to bark. Kelsey, who had already stuck his neck out, explained things to him more carefully and ended by saying, "I don't know who is listening, but by golly, I will keep the generator operating after eleven-thirty and get your message out." This chatter on the radio, trying to cause nothing but trouble made me mad, but I didn't say anything.

Around dinnertime, I heard that the two planes were coming back to Base again. Finn and Chuck had gotten back safely in the L-5 from the eastern flight. When Finn learned that the weather here had begun to clear, he decided to return for a few days.

The day was so beautiful, I decided to ski a bit. The glacier was perfect with light powdered snow on top of a hard ice crust. I was there for about an hour before Chuck Hassage, Britishers John, Kevin, Terry, Bernard, and later Pete joined me. We had jots of fun going up and down and finally discovered an extension to our slope by going over the built-up snow ramp down to the Bay Ice. One had to jump over a tide crack, which added a bit to the danger. John was the worst skier among the Britishers. I noticed, however, that they all wore hard boots and cable bindings this time out. Their skis were all shorter than ours. At 9:45 PM., the sun was shining brightly, as though it was twelve o'clock noon. Just then we heard the plane and watched the Beech land, then suddenly take-off again, fly over us and circle the camp for another landing. Jim and Finn got out. Chuck in the Norseman landed minutes later.

Finn and I came into the shack and I caught Finn up on all the news, including the new label of the core people visiting us as "Tunnel Runners". Finn told me about the flight.

They flew over the Larsen Ice Shelf for one hundred miles to where it dropped into the Weddell Sea. About twenty-five miles southwest of their southern turn point, they saw a small unnamed snow-covered domed island about eight miles in diameter and three to four hundred feet high. But, at no time during their three hour and fifteen minute flight did they sight any other islands. The flight was worthwhile as they had covered about 15,000 square miles of that unexplored Weddell Sea area and knowledge of the contour of the Larsen Ice Shelf for one hundred miles.

Finn was not too happy when he found out that Don was suspected of giving out medical alcohol for drinks in the Darlington room. Robertson says that is what they are drinking and Hassage says Darlington has recently asked him in several times to partake. Finn called Don in and requested the alcohol and any liquor he had be turned over immediately. Finn never did believe that alcohol and the polar regions mixed well. He had seen too much trouble it had caused on previous expeditions. He told Don why and asked if he knew of anyone who had liquor on the expedition. Don hesitantily said, "Yes. Andy!" Finn said, "I'm not referring to Andy." Don said, I know Lassiter had some". Finn said he was not worried about Lassiter. Don said, he knew of no one else who had any. Finn told Don he didn't believe he was always telling him the truth, that he knew of one time Don had told him a direct lie in this very room. Don asked what that was and Finn said when he had asked him if he had ever heard Harry threaten the expedition and Don had said no he hadn't when Finn knew Don had been one of the persons present when Harry had. Don tried to get out of it by saying he had been present on occasions when Harry had been angry and had uttered all sorts of crazy ideas, but that he *held no stock in them and felt Harry would do nothing to harm the expedition and believed Harry when he said all he wanted to do was to forget it. Finn told Don he knew Harry had cases of wine and liquor, all of which he had allowed Harry to bring to serve for everyone, just as he had done, but he believed it now to be gone and not one bottle had been served openly. Don agreed that it was all gone. Finn told Don that Harry had lied about Scaiffe giving the expedition $3,500, instead it was $2,500 of which Harry was given $1,000 for his expenses. Finn told Don about Harry's lies to him and to the British camp, about the messages he tried to get out there and that Harry had lied when he said he only wanted to forget the expedition, that he would do everything he could to discredit it. Don said he certainly was in back of the expedition himself and he didn't want to be caught in this argument. Finn told him you only get out of an expedition what you put into it and that Don walked away Sunday on a skiing trip while aviation worked for hours to get these flights off and that is why Don didn't go on one of them and Andy did. Don said he would bring in the alcohol, of which he had gotten five gallons and about 4½ were left. He said this he had used to clean surgical instruments and give some to people to clean watches. He said it could be drunk, but it hurt some people's eyes. When he brought it in, there was only 3½ gallons left. Don said to me, you know I have the feeling that Finn doesn't trust me and I don't want him to have that feeling.*

Saturday, November 8, 1947

Finn had received some information from Fiske, which he hadn't received before, stating that when the two Bobs (Nichols and Dodson) went looking for seals, they were up to their hips in slush. Kelsey had the contact on which Fiske had overheard this statement, but Kelsey denied ever having heard it, or knowing anything about it. Finn also found out for the first time that the cache they referred to was seventeen miles to the north on Alexander Island, instead of seventeen miles back toward Base. Lassiter asked Finn if he considered it an emergency and Finn said, "Yes, I do". Lassiter said, "Then we'll make arrangements to take off right away and if we find them, shall we bring them back to Base"? Finn said, "Yes," and Lassiter said to Hassage, "And keep them all in bed until after the flying season is over."

They went out to start the plane, but the weather closed in so badly, they couldn't take-off. After dinner, they all went up to the aviation cache, while Andy and I took a couple of ski runs down the hill, but the visibility was so poor and last night's wind took all the snow off and the hill was just icy.

Sunday, November 9, 1947

This afternoon, Chuck Adams, Chuck Hassage and Robertson took off in NANA to look for Nichols. They got as far as five miles past Terra Firma, which is approximately 40 miles from Base, and had to come back because of the weather. There were many open leads that the men felt could not be negotiated by dog team. Also we knew that the northern cape of mountainous Red Rock Ridge, around which the party would have to come, was surrounded by open water.

Monday, November 10, 1947

I read most of the day. Finn, Don and I drove over to Neny Island in the weasel to look for the snowy petrels. Finn wanted to take pictures of them. We climbed about 800 feet on snow and then the rock climb began. Finn was ahead and then Don. I had just started, when Finn yelled look out below and down came a rock landing on my back near my shoulder. I thought I had been knocked out and then, that my neck had been broken. It pained dreadfully. I slid all the way back down the hill and waited in the weasel. Finn came down much later, saying that it was a very dangerous place with loose rocks everywhere and that he had broken his camera when it fell from his pocket. Going over we got a huge bump as we crossed over a large open lead. It was good to get back to my book.

Jim Lassiter came in at night to discuss how much more gas needed to be hauled to Keeler. He was in a very bad humor, because of sitting around over here. He told us about the missing Tricorn area pictures. Dick Butson, at Keeler, gave them to Lassiter and said, here are the pictures McClary stole, that Mac had asked him to take them, as he didn't want them but did want them returned as quietly as possible. Lassiter brought them back and told McClary where they were. McClary got them and, of course, had to bring them into Finn saying they were found by mistake in his stuff to go to Knowles. Nice guy, McClary.

Tuesday, November 11, 1947

Armistice Day provided another break in the weather. Lassiter and Adams started to take the Norseman after Nichols. Finn stopped both pilots from going in one plane and Lassiter got mad and stayed mad all day. He wouldn't fly the Beech to Keeler. After lunch Chuck Adams, Chuck Hassage and Thompson took the Norseman and found Nichols at Mushroom Island about eighty miles from Base. They dropped a Walkie Talkie, but it didn't work. The two Bobs stomped out food in the snow, so the plane parachuted man and dog food for another 30 days to them so that they could continue geologizing.

Everyone was glad they had been found even though it is quite impossible for them to return to Base over the ice from Terra Firma on. Finn wrote them a message tonight and Kelsey will broadcast it to them three times a day for a week concerning the ice conditions on their return route, and instead, because of the many open leads, to go over Windy Valley to the Traffic Circle, to be picked up there.

Now that the missing had been found, we could work with freer minds. Scientific observations and general maintenance continued as usual and periodic trips were made out to the ship to shovel the decks clear of snow.

If there is one job all hated, it was shoveling snow. There seems to be no end to it and yet it had to be done on an almost daily basis. Hundreds of cases of food were stored outside, because of the lack of indoor storing space. After successive snows, thaws, and freezes, all were covered and iced together solidly, necessitating frequent digging, only to find a case of peas where a case of tomato juice was thought to be. Occasionally, our evening's meal was the result of the strength, patience and character of the men behind the shovel.

Still remaining in the freezer aboard ship were several thousand pounds of meat. With the days becoming progressively warmer and lack of power to keep a regulated temperature below thawing, presented concern. Sig and Hassage decided to chop out an ice cache in the glacier where the meat could be placed for safe keeping. Several men spent half a day digging the cache when Hassage had another idea. The glacier cache would not be necessary as we could use one of our small generators to lower the temperature of the ship's freezer every three or four days. I was glad I was not around when the cache diggers learned of the new plan.

The next flight out of the Main Base was planned to be the last before attempting the big exploratory flight south and it would include the 1,800 lb. cache of supplies to be laid on the Weddell Coast for the Joint British-American Sledge Party.

Wednesday, November 12, 1947

Another bad day. Hassage put up the work list and McLean, Harry and McClary went off on a walk, paying no attention to it whatsoever. They missed breakfast, which was late and didn't get back until late afternoon. Finn caught McLean going into Darlington's room with an armful of crackers from the Science Building. Finn told him to eat the crackers at the Mess Table and asked him if he had paid any attention to the work list this morning. He said no he hadn't, that he had to exercise his ankle and that he had done his share of work on the expedition. Finn said he could exercise his ankle after working hours and that it was not a question of share of work, it was a question of each day pitching in and doing what had to be done. Don said he came along as a doctor to do medical work. Finn said since you bring it up, you have medical work to do for the Office of Naval Research which you haven't done. McLean said Slesniak in the Office of Naval Research said he had absolutely nothing for McLean to do. Finn said, will you put that in writing to me and Don said, certainly.

This morning Hassage told Finn not to be worried by those guys, to simply ignore them because they were only trying to antagonize Finn and when they did, they were happy. He also volunteered that he would be glad to write up a statement against Harry and what he had done against Finn on the expedition.

Saturday, November 15, 1947

Chuck Hassage and the fellows started to work on getting some of the stuff back to the ship. They took over almost a ton of supplies in the afternoon. Right after lunch Finn and I took a skiing trip to the aviation shack up on the glacier to look for any exposed gas drum. We did not find any, so we had a nice fast ski down. Visibility and depth perception was pretty bad. Finn took Kasco along.

Hassage wrote Finn a good letter supporting him in anything Harry might accuse him of in the future. He backed him up in all things.

We heard from Robertson that Peterson had locked Kelsey in the Radio Room last night and Kelsey had to tear the door down to get out. As a result, right after Peterson changed his sheets, Kelsey put a bag of coal in his bed. Kelsey said nothing and Peterson said nothing. The two are bosom friends now. Lassiter showed, "You Came Along", and the British came over to see it.

In sporadic radio messages, Fiske, at Keeler, told of a raging blizzard sweeping over their camp for five days with wind velocities of sixty-eight miles per hour and zero degree temperatures. Heavy drifts accumulated around the L-5 plane and covered the gas drums and other equipment. The men spent most of their time in their sleeping bags underground, waking to eat and take weather observations. Automatic recording instruments provided other necessary data. Our storm at the Main Base was not as severe as the one at Keeler.

Sunday, November 16, 1947

Finally in the afternoon, the storm cleared on both sides of the Plateau. Lassiter and Finn took off in the Beech, named the "Ed Sweeney" (after a close friend and supporter) for Keeler at 17:30, after Larry failed to come up on Keeler radio at 1700. They landed safely at Keeler and Larry quickly asked Kelsey if he had called him at 17:00. Larry knew he was wrong in not coming up on the radio and hoped Kelsey could offer some excuse that Larry could hide behind before, as Larry put it, "the blitz" came.

Because of bad weather and intermittent heavy snowfalls, the next three days were unflyable. At Keeler Finn and Lassiter settled down to regular camp routine.

Monday, November 17, 1947

I didn't feel well and so slept right through most of the day until about 4:30. I missed Finn and I wanted this darn flight to get over with. I was concerned about it because I knew how much it meant to Finn to have it successful. People were in talking the rest of the day, the tunnel running gang. Hassage said Fiske was the greatest offender of sneaking over to the British when Finn had the ruling that no one should go over there. He would tell them all about how Finn felt toward them, etc. Went to bed fairly early and got a good night's sleep.

Most of the men were always great toward me. They never cursed, nor did they ever tell a dirty joke around me, not ever. If they could help me with anything, they did. On the other hand, I did not abuse this attitude and never made demands on them in any way. When Finn was away, they made sure no one had any chance to make an overt move toward me. Literally, without my knowing it, I was being watched over.

Tuesday, November 18, 1947

The day was a sunny one to begin with and looked every minute as though it was going to clear, although it never did sufficiently for the NANA to fly. Cape Keeler had marginal weather on the bad side.

Hassage said he had a run-in with McClary this morning about fixing the outboard motor. McClary said if anyone thought he was going to fix that small boat, they were mightily mistaken. Later Harry helped Hassage move some diesel oil and asked him about the boat situation. Hassage told him he didn't intend to fix all the boats for the other men, if they didn't pitch in and help too. Hassage continued, "It doesn't matter how you all may feel toward Finn, if you can't see that you are all dependent upon the same things for your safety, you all are pretty dumb". Harry said, "Well, you know it is all a result of poor organization". Hassage told Harry that wasn't true and he knew it.

John Tonkin, Hassage, Robertson, and Adams came in for some coffee. John stayed and chatted and then stayed for dinner. Don decided to learn to run the 35 mm projector and so they showed the Harold Lloyd film.

Wednesday, November 19, 1947

I worked on the book most of the day. The fellows moved some things out to the ship and were in for coffee off and on. Robertson stated in front of Chuck Adams, Hassage and Sig that Harry had proved himself incompetent as a pilot, that when he flew he was all over the field and that he was very nonchalant and indifferent as to what he was doing or going to do. The L-5's airplane wings were given as another example of his incompetence to head aviation. They agreed it was much more than a difference of opinion as to how things should be run, which, of course, would be Harry's excuse, giving him the perfect out to his utter irresponsibility. It snowed a great deal yesterday and today.

Thursday, November 20, 1947

The day dawned lovely, beautifully clear and sunny. Adams and Robertson made immediate preparations to fly and got the Norseman ready. From 8:45 until 10:45 they did nothing but taxi up and down the runway trying to get off with a dead calm and a soft powdery snow runway which, with the weasel packing, did not seem to help. After taking out the two aircraft batteries and the hamburger, and a bag of food, a total of 400 lb., they finally made it. When they got to Keeler, they refueled and when ready the L-5 took-off to lay the Joint Party's Cape Knowles cache, expecting the Norduyn to follow. The plane NANA had engine trouble and so the L-5 came back to Keeler and landed. It took over an hour to fix the plane and finally, when both planes took off, Woody reported to the NANA that she had a gas leak in one of her wing tanks.

John came over very concerned about the Knowles cache, thinking it would have been far better for them to have come back here gotten everything and then flown the Knowles cache. I said, they were lucky they got away from here with what they had, I thought. He asked for Finn's permission to dissolve the Met Station on top of the Plateau, when their party went to meet the Hope Bay Party, and take Mac and Jorge along with them. They hope to leave from here on Dec. 1, and be back the first part of January. I told him I would ask Finn about it. I worked on the book some, talked to Andy and then went up and swept off the roof of snow and water. It was warm out, but steadily getting colder.

Kelsey listened all day for the planes and Keeler. Keeler kept calling him, but when Kelsey answered, they said no more. We went to bed not knowing the whereabouts of the planes or whether they had been successful in laying the Knowles cache.

Friday, November 21, 1947

At ten o'clock Kelsey went on the radio to Cape Keeler and made some excuse and apology for not getting on before. Wood informed him that the Norseman had just taken-off and that the Beech had carburetor trouble but would take-off as soon as it was fixed. Finn was there and came on the radio to receive my message. Finn said to tell John that the Joint British-American Trail Party had received plenty of food yesterday and for him not to worry. He also said it was O.K. for Jorge to go with the British and for John to do as he saw fit in the matter.

Keeler had indicated the weather was perfect with a cloudless sky, 15-knot NW wind and temperature 8 Deg below zero F. It sounded as though they might be off on the long flight, although no one said so.

Woody at Keeler guarded the flight by radio. Kelsey at the home base could hear nothing for a long time, then suddenly he heard Chuck Adams calling and saying he was at Darlington Island. I found out Finn was flying with Jim in the Beech. Kelsey lost Chuck, but heard Jim say he was thirty minutes away from Mt. Tricorn and that Jim had just heard from Chuck, who said he was at Mt. Tricorn. Jim told Chuck to land and that he would be there soon. That is the last report Kelsey received this afternoon and although, he has been guarding them ever since, has heard nothing. He plans to guard them all night.

This afternoon Harry was reading the Mess Cook List and saw that Jennie was Mess Cook tomorrow, he noted that Chuck Hassage had said he would carry out the water as it was heavy. Harry ridiculed Chuck and Chuck said, well would't you do it for your wife? Harry said, Hell No, any man is crazy to volunteer to do a job in this camp. Chuck said O.K., I don't want to do it either then, we will just cross the women off, and he did. Harry said nothing then. I say, good for Chuck!

Don showed, "Algiers" tonightand the British came over. I sat and talked to Reg and John. Afterwards, I came in and did some work. Sig went fishing. Kelsey kept an all night watch over the planes and I got to bed about 3:30, but nothing had been heard from them. Kelsey went to bed about 5:30, leaving Britisher McLeod on the Plateau listening for the planes. It was kind of hard figuring out what they were doing, but I assume they were laying a gas cache at Tricorn and were merely out of radio range. Kelsey did not have any radio contact with WEK tonight because of plane guard and he was not able to report even the weather.

Saturday, November 22, 1947

A very big day today, although I didn't know it to begin with. At twelve noon, I heard Kelsey come on the radio and apologize to McLeod on the Plateau for not being on before, but no one here at Base woke up until noon. Mac said his batteries were low and he had to charge them, so he went off the air. I got up and got dressed and around two o'clock went over to see if Kelsey had heard anything I didn't know about. Just as I walked into the Radio Shack, Kelsey had received a call from Jim, who reported both planes were at Steel Island and would take off practically immediately. They said they were low on gas, both planes, but thought they could make Keeler and be there in about 2 1/2 hours. When they got in the air, the radio contact was perfect and I was surprised when Finn sent me a message, which I could not hear destinctly, but went over to Kelsey and found out he said, "The flight is in the Bag".

I was very surprised and began wondering if that meant they had successfully completed the flight, because Finn was coming back. The next thing I heard Larry say, "Are Congratulations or Condolences in order? You have been unheard of for 18 hours, and we are wondering"? Jim came back with, "Congratulations". So Larry said, "Congratulations, all of you". That made me wonder much more.

Larry indicated that Ike was flying in NANA with Chuck Adams. Jim, in the Beech, asked for the weather at Stonington, as they were anxious to get back to the Main Base. This made me think, definitely, they had completed the flight, but I still wasn't sure. The weather at Stonington was not flyable at the time. Both planes landed safely at Keeler. I asked Kelsey to ask, if they had completed the flight as he didn't know. When Larry came back the next hour, the weather at Stonington had changed for the better and Pete told him the planes could come in. Therefore, immediate preparations were made to fly and guard the flight, so Kelsey still didn't ask about the long flight.

When the Beech was in the air and very near home Base, Jim thanked Kelsey for standing by the way he had and that the Base radio could be heard the entire time, even when they were 1,000 miles south. This practically confirmed the flight and when the Beech landed, Bill Latady jumped out of the plane and I asked him if they got the flight in, he said, yes, I said in pictures? He said, yes. We were wild with joy. Finn got out of the plane and Tonkin and Thomson came up and Hassage. Lassiter got out and everybody was congratulating them. Tonkin told Finn how sincerely glad he was that Finn had made the successful flight. Pictures were taken of the three men by the Beechcraft. They told briefly what they had seen and the determination of the coastline. Chuck landed in the Norseman, with Dick Butson and the dog.

Finn and I came back to the shack and on the way saw Harry and Don carrying out the garbage. Harry made himself scarce immediately and Don said to Finn, "Well that certainly was the quickest trip I have ever seen". Finn said, " Yes, it was, when we finally got a break in the weather". Sig said the Darlingtons disappeared into their room and nothing was heard from them again. Later, we heard from Hassage that the bitchers had Finn and the rest in a plane wreck and everybody killed, etc. Finn and I, immediately, got to work on getting the story out and Kelsey worked WEK until after two o'clock transmitting it.

Finn was very enthusiastic about the flight as he described it. He sat in the co-pilot's seat with the plotting board on his lap to do the navigation and make observational notes of the new terrain and its features. Seaward there was a 20 mile wide stretch of sea ice attached to the land, then came a stretch of open water, beyond which a belt of heavy pack ice to the horizon. As new features were discovered he noted them and later named them for members of the expedition and for people who had helped him get there. The 5,600 foot high new Mt. Andrew Thompson was sighted close to Cape Eielson. To the west of their flight, in the center of the Peninsula, Finn saw several high well-defined mountains south of the previously discovered Mt. Andrew Jackson. These new mountains he named Mt. Russell Owen, Vincent Gutenko Mountains, and Mt. Dana Coman. They rose high above the Plateau, to an estimated height of more than 10,000 feet.

Two hours and fifteen minutes out of Cape Keeler, they heard Adams calling on the radio to report he and Schlossbach were 5,000 feet above Cape Tricorn Inlet with more gasoline on hand than expected. His first utterance was: "where the Devil have you been, I have been waiting for you."

Mt. Tricorn had been the southernmost turning point of an exploratory flight made by the United States Antarctic Service Expedition in

1940 and whose maps they were following. They should not be due at Mt. Tricorn for some twenty to twenty-five more minutes, but already it was beneath them. They realized that Tricorn was actually some forty to fifty miles north and thirty miles to the west of its previously charted position. Since the Norseman had not used half her gas supply and with Tricorn north of where they expected to find it, they could continue further south before picking a landing for their stand-by base. At Mt. Tricorn, Finn sighted and named Wright Inlet, its northernmost Cape Wheeler and the Southern Cape Little.

As they were entering unexplored territory, Latady quickly took the opportunity of taking the Norseman in motion pictures. The two planes flew south along the coastline at 4,000 feet altitude. Numerous new features were sighted, named and recorded, Keller Inlet just below them, Mt. Nash a few miles away, and thirty miles later Cape Fiske, on the northernmost headland of Nantucket Inlet and Cape Smithy its southernmost, with the two glaciers flowing into the inlet from the west, Johnston Glacier and Kelsey Glacier.

About 50 miles south of Mt. Tricorn, they suddenly came upon a large bay, some 55 miles wide, which Finn named Gardner Bay. Near the center was a striking snow-covered dome mountain Finn called Mt. Austin. The two glaciers flowing from the northwest Finn named Irvine and Wetmore and the one from the south Ketchum Glacier. The peninsula between Nantucket Inlet and Gardner Bay he called Isaiah Bowman Peninsula, its southeastern cape, Cape Adams, and Cape Schlossback the southern entrance to the Bay. Mt. Robertson was about twenty-five miles northwest of Mt. Austin.

They landed both planes in surprisingly deep powdered snow at Mt. Austin, since its 3,200 foot height provided an easily recognizable feature for a stand-by base and half the gasoline supply in the Norseman fuselage tanks had been used. When they jumped out of the plane, they sank to their knees in snow, a new experience in the Antarctic, where frequent winds pack the surface so hard you can barely see a heel mark. They were 240 miles south of where any human foot had ever trod before in this area.

With Latady as time keeper, Finn immediately began to take sun sights with the bubble sextant getting a good fix at Lat. 74 Deg. and 48' South, Longitude 62 Deg. and 50 Deg. West., after later being correlated with those he took upon their return to Gardner Bay. The position proved that Mt. Tricorn was 55 miles further northwest than had been thought and that southward from Cape Knowles, in 71 Deg. and 45' South, the entire coastline was about 30 miles further to the west than had been previously plotted and its configuration was considerably different.

When the gasoline drums, weighing 450 lb., were dumped from the Norseman, they nearly sank out of sight. It took all the strength of the five men to haul them to the Beechcraft for refueling. A beacon was made of the empty drums.

By this time Adams and Schlossback, who would guard the next leg of the Beechcraft's flight, had pitched their tent, so they all sat down for some hot chocolate and biscuits. After checking out the handcranking trail radio, Lassiter, Finn and Latady took off in the Beech.

Their first objective was to continue following the Palmer Land Mountain Range wherever it might lead and capture it in trimetrogon pictures. Between Mt. Tricorn and Coats Land to the east, there was an unknown stretch of coastline of approximately 450 miles. The trend and type of formation beneath this area could be the key to whether the Antarctic was one or two continents and was one of Finn's major objectives. A natural assumption would be that the range would swing to the southeast, so they were greatly surprised to find that the trend of the mountains was instead to the southwest.

New features began to appear. Within thirty miles, Dodson Island, the last island discovered, was sighted some five miles off the mainland. The coast along which they were flying, Finn called Orville Escarpment, which turned westward until its trend became 245 Deg. True. Further to the west were mountains dotting the entire landscape, spread further and further apart. Finn named them as they were discovered. Sweeney Mountains with Mr. Edward in the center, Scaife Mountains, Wilkins Mountains, Lowell Thomas Mountains, Mt. Horne, Mt. Brundage, Hauberg Mountains and Mt. Hassage. Approximately 100 miles due west, Mt. Haag estimated at 10,000 feet was the last mountain they discovered on this flight. In the distance, Mt. Mary Louise Ulmer in the Sentinel Range, discovered by Lincoln Ellsworth in 1935 on his daring flight across the Continent to the Bay of Whales, was named for his wife, and now loomed above the horizon.

The weather remained perfect. Finn kept a very accurate account of the magnetic courses, time spent on each and the indicated airspeed. To the right were the mountains and to the left was the unbroken gradually rising snow plateau. Had there been a strait dividing the Continent, here is where it would have been. Finn was excited that they were in a region never before seen and they were to solve the great enigma of whether the continent was divided at this point. All the stumbling blocks, which had been overcome, were all worth this one view.

There was not a thing to be seen southward except that plain. Finn asked Lassiter if he could see anything to the left, where not even a rock stuck its head over the surface. "Only higher elevation of the land", was his reply. Beyond the bluffs that marked the coast, were crevasses and hard blue ice, and a few rock exposures directly beneath them. They were anxious to make a landing, but if anything went wrong, it would have been inexcusable, so they didn't dare.

So far their flight had proved that the mountain axis of the Peninsula gradually swings southwest to 77 Deg., 30 min. South and 70 Deg. West, where it dies out or merges into a higher plateau. They estimated the elevation of this Joerg Plateau at close to 5,000 feet, stretching southward for an estimate of 200 miles, or as far as 81 Deg. South from their altitude of 10,500 feet. They had determined the extension of the Palmer Land Mountain Range, which seemed to eliminate the possibility of any connection between the Ross Sea and the Weddell Sea, at this point. A weighted American flag was dropped from the photo-door, signifying they had achieved one of their two major geographic objectives.

The second objective to explore and photograph the last unknown coastline in the Antarctic lay ahead. As one of the two greatest ice-walls on earth, (the other being the Ross Ice Barrier on the other side of the continent in the Ross Sea), it had balked all attempts to reach it. Shackleton had tried to reach it in 1915. Filchner had tried to get that far south in 1912, and before that, Bruce of the Scotia Expedition had been stopped at Coats Land in 1904. Magnificent and impenetrable, it rises from 100 to 250 feet above the sea and stretches for more than 450 miles from the Palmer Peninsula to Coats Land. Flying comfortably at an altitude of about 10,000 feet, they were the first to see it, continuing to 77 Deg. South and 50 Deg. West, when their gas supply forced them to turn back as the shelf ice continued in the same south-easterly direction. Finn observed open water below and wide leads between the ice floes, suggesting a ship might penetrate as far as the barrier this particular year.

They landed at Mt. Austin alongside of Adams and Schlossback in the Norseman, six hours and forty-five minutes after taking off. Adams had hot bouillon and melted water awaiting the three thirsty and hungry men. They had eaten chocolate bars during the flight, but after a while they became tasteless. On the ground, the temperature was 9 Deg. below zero F. Lassiter did not turn off the Beechcraft motors for fear of restarting them at this temperature. Finn realized another flight would be needed to determine the extension of the shelf ice to the east and its connection with Coats Land. More gasoline would be needed for the Beechcraft, but instead of waiting in the field for the Norseman to fly several loads to them, Finn decided it was more efficient for both planes to return to Keeler and the main Base, refuel, and then make the second flight south.

Although it was 10:00 p.m., the weather was still good for trimetrogon photography on the coast north, the tent came down, radio gear and other equipment stored in the Norseman and after three tries, Adams got the engine started without preheating with a blowtorch. While the two planes warmed up their engines, the pilots tried out the inter-communication radio and within minutes both planes were in the air, maintaining constant radio contact with each other during the flight. At Violante Inlet, 175 miles up the coast, clouds rolled in , but they kept going until a landing was imperative. After flying in thick soup for a while, they found an opening over Steele Island. Lassiter yelled to Latady, "Hey, Bill, get up, we are making an emergency landing". Bill, exhausted from hours of tedious work with the cameras, slowly replied, "What do you want me to do, you're flying the plane?". Lassiter radioed Adams and asked him where he was. "I wish I knew", said Chuck, also lost in the muck. Jim told him to look for a large opening lead on the sea ice off the coast. Lassiter was circling at 500 feet, while Adams was at 1,000 feet, so as not to barge into one another. He came out of the clouds a half mile away and the both landed as soon as they could. The clouds closed tight after them. They informed the main Base 250 miles away their whereabouts via their handcranking trail radio-set.

They pitched a tent and had a good meal of pemmican. As the last spoonful was consumed, Latady, in his slow way, said he had a number of steaks packed in the nose compartment of the Beech, so they wasted little time starting the primus stove again, and the satisfied and happy group turned into their sleeping bags for a rest early that morning.

The clouds did not lift until afternoon. The temperature was 5 Deg. below, but the engines, although a bit sluggish, turned over and an hour and a half later, five tired men sat down to a couple of steaks each that Fiske had ready for their arrival. Since the weather was clear at the main Base at Stonington, they landed here at 6 p.m., just 31 hours after they had left Keeler for the flight south. Adams brought back Britisher Butson and the dog that had produced and eaten all of her pups. That same evening Adams left again for Keeler, carrying another load of gasoline for the next flight south.

After several days of plotting the results, Finn made a conservative estimate that they had covered an unknown area of approximately 170,000 square miles. While, on their return trip from Gardner Bay they had covered an additional 30,000 square miles. With the entire flight recorded by trimetrogon photographs and with the accurate astronomical fix obtained at Gardner Bay, plus running lines of position, it would enable a fairly accurate map to be made. Aerial survey over such terrain had a great many advantages over a surface survey. To cover the same area by a dog team party, would take months of traveling, and prohibitive tons of supplies to maintain a dog team party in the field for such a length of time.

Sunday, November 23, 1947

Finn and I slept until afternoon. Then I fixed him a special treat, the egg, which Sig's chickens had laid two days ago, sunnyside up.

Their new suite in the Met Tower had provided the chickens with the desired freedom of movement and after some straw and hay were strewn about, the happy Leghorns began clucking significantly. About this time Sig ran out of chicken feed. We were used to substituting the next best thing, for the chicks barely raised a feather with mashed dog food in place of their usual diet. From then on until our departure, they outdid themselves in laying eggs. Sig averaged one a day and quietly collected them to feed the men who came back from the trail. When each had two a piece, the rest of the camp received their share.

Finn decided to name all of the new area Edith Ronne Land after me, which I considered quite a compliment. The fellows (Hassage and Lassiter) congratulated me on receiving the honor for the land explored. Finn had promised Lassiter the Barrier, and asked Latady what he wanted. He said, he preferred mountains, a prominent mountain, or a mountain range.

Now that the main flights were accomplished, everyone seemed to have a more relaxed approach. The elusiveness of the much-discussed Charcot Island had captured Finn's imagination and if at all possible, he hoped to take a flight in that direction to establish its definite position in aerial photographs once and for all. It all depended upon the weather, which was not good.

As soon as Finn caught up with the camp's activities, he began work on a large-scale map, which would accurately portray their discoveries. From his flight log, he plotted the courses flown, lines of position, and established the fixes obtained en route. Latady developed certain key rolls of the pictures, a complicated process. When he had finished, Finn went over the ones taken over the ice barrier on the southeastern leg of their flight. After a careful review, and checking with the lines of position, it was obvious that they had not flown as far along this barrier as they should have, as they had not been within sight of the Filchner Shelf Ice. Finn wanted to take another flight due south in this region as far as the plane's range would allow, but from the information at hand, getting the rest of the ice barrier came before additional southern operations. Again we settled down to await the weather. Gas drums were hauled down to the plane and the gas siphoned and chamoised into the Beechcraft. She was ready to go again on a moment's notice.

Monday, November 24, 1947

Andy came in this morning and asked me if I would run the seismograph while he was away. I said yes, of course, but what's wrong with Don. Andy said Don may have a chance to go with the British to meet the Hope Bay Party, in which case, he couldn't take an interest in working it. I said, really, he hasn't said anything to Finn about it yet. I got dressed and went with Andy for several hours learning how to work it. Andy said, I caught on quicker than anyone he had shown yet. I went with Andy to change the seismograph paper at around eleven and then, Andy showed me the workings of the tidal gauge. We came back and had some coffee. We got a nice message from Harry's mother, Mrs. Garrett. Chatted until 1:30.

From now on, I changed the sheets for the seismograph and the tidal gauge daily whenever Andy was in the field, and often assisted him even when he wasn't. While this was more work on top of my own commitments, I thoroughly enjoyed the challenge of participating fully in the scientific work. I soon became adept at changing pencils in the tidal gauge and developing the seismic sheets. It took me out of my room for a change of scene. I could be found shinnying under the floor of the Met Tower in complete darkness daily to change the sheet of the seismograph without exposing either the used one or the new one to rays of light. Then developing them somewhat like a photo negative to reveal any earthquake or other seismic activity occurring in the Antarctic or Southern Hemisphere. I also walked daily down to the shore where the tidal gauge was located. I hadn't often thought about how much work the scientists were doing up until this point. Having to help with some of Andy's work while he was away certainly helped me to develop a greater appreciation of the hard work they were putting into the expedition, particularly on days when the weather wasn't so pleasant or the equipment didn't function properly. I felt empowered by my scientific work and carried out my own experiment in hydroponics: my garden of cress grew very well.

A further excitement to me, and to several others, around this part of the early summer, was the expected return of the Adelie penguins to nest at their rookeries over on Red Rock Ridge. We were anxious to observe as much about their habits as possible. A couple of days after Thanksgiving (which we had passed very quietly) five of us left Finn looking after the base and traveled in the Weasel on the nine mile trip to see the penguins.

Saturday, November 29, 1947

We first sighted a school of penguins swimming and diving through the water on the seaward side of Red Rock Ridge. They look very much like porpoises as they are very fast swimmers and can probably outdistance most fish. Half a mile from the rookery, penguins were propelling themselves over the ice at a great rate of speed using their flippers as balance points. They would walk a few steps quickly, then throw themselves on their white stomachs and propel themselves forward rapidly.

Our noses were our best reminders that the rookery was not far off. Just around the point was their nesting ground of from one thousand to twelve hundred penguins. Each couple guarded a nest containing one or two eggs. Our presence was noted immediately. Each member of the heretofore-quiet contented colony contributed to the outburst, which was a collection of discordant sounds unlike any ever heard before. The continuous uproar obviously was not meant to be a royal welcome, but more like that of highly suspicious dissatisfaction.

We did take time to observe some of the penguin's habits more closely. Their nests were made of small stones and were about one foot in width. Their eggs are about twice the size of a regular chicken egg. Before long they noticed several penguins approaching the rookery from the sea and watched to see what they would do. As they arrived, each went to his particular nest and had a fifteen-minute discussion with his mate who had been keeping the egg warm during his absence. The penguin that had been sitting on the egg, exchanged places with the penguin from the sea. Off the first penguin went for a much-needed bath and search for food. Hassage thought it might be worth while to engage one in an argument and much to his amazement came out on the loosing side. Their surprisingly strong flippers beat large welts on his hand, which proved so painful that he tossed in the white flag. The penguins have no fear of men as a source of danger and Hassage is one man who can understand why. It was not possible to make friends with any of them. Although curious, in their unique way, they avoid all contact, and man is at a distinct disadvantage trying to catch one. After much chasing and jockeying for the proper approach, Lassiter's untiring determination finally enabled him to capture one by approaching from the rear to pull back his flippers. He was carried precariously up a nearby glacier and promptly did just what was intended of him; i.e. slid back down penguin fashion. We spent about an hour and a half taking pictures at the rookery.

Although the day was as bright as when we had left camp, our watches showed that it was eight p.m. We regretfully took leave of the rookery and began retracing our steps. Two hours and fifteen minutes later, we were on the steep glacier where we had left our skis. A few minutes of good down hill skiing brought us back to the weasel, pleasantly tired after a day's strenuous exercise in the great out-of-doors. After a drink of hot chocolate from the thermos, we headed back to camp where Finn met us upon our arrival at eleven p.m. It had been a most enjoyable trip and for me a change from my usual camp routine. I was very tired, however, and after some hot tomato soup, I fell in bed.

This visit to the Penguin Rookery started a life-long fascination for me toward penguins. Ever since, I have been unable to resist acquiring every penguin knick-knack that came my way, to the point where they have completely taken over my house. These compelling creatures have increasingly cast their spell over everyone who comes into contact with them and are fast becoming a cultural icon.

Once the weather cleared several local flights were made by Lassiter and Lataday which significantly increased our knowledge and photographic record of the local Peninsula area. On the return of one flight, both of the engines stopped momentarily as Lassiter drained the last drop of precious gas from one of his seven tanks and shifted to another. He questioningly turned to see the expression on Latady's face. Latady, who was getting quite a reputation for his nonchalance, smilingly shrugged his shoulders and yelled, "Its up to you", and continued taking his pictures. The dedication of these two men was responsible for much of the mapping done of the Peninsula at this time. Finn too, made a flight towards Charcot Island but that prize continued to elude him. He was nevertheless very keen to get there.

Two more of our dedicated team were brought back from Cape Keeler to base on December 1 Woody and Fiske had been two of the first to leave for the field and were the first of our widely separated field units to return. We all met them as they landed and the fellows seemed glad to be back. Fiske had been in the field for sixty-three days and Woody proudly told Finn, as he got out of the plane, that he had been out for eighty-three days. He thought that he had beaten Finn's record from the United States Antarctic Service Expedition when he and Carl Eklund traveled by dog team 1,264 miles in 84 days. He had missed it by only one day. Fiske came in for a chat and obviously was trying to make up to Finn and excuse himself for the many foolish things he had done.

After a hearty meal, a bath, and a shave, they soon settled down to regular camp routine. The thing that seemed to impress the men the most upon return, was how enormous our buildings appeared after becoming accustomed to the confined quarters of a tent.

It was thanks to men such as these that our programs of science and exploration were going considerably better than Finn had ever expected. This was despite the negative efforts of some other members of the party. Jenny was very sick around this period and we were quite sure that she must be pregnant.

Finn and Jackie skiing around the base and on the glacier

The expedition discovered hundreds of square miles of previously unseen and uncharted territory. This photo was taken from the trimetrogon cameras.

Andy Thompson analyzing seismograph sheet for possible earthquakes

Geologists Bob Dodson and Bob Nichols study rocks in the field

Smitty (second from right) and Art Owen (right) at their farthest south on the Ronne / Weddell Coast

Christmas Dinner. The Ronnes invited the Britishers to join the celebration.

XV

The Last Coastline

Anyone working in the out-of-doors this time of the year soon showed the powerful effect of the sun's radiation in these latitudes. Various shades of pink, red, and brown skins put in their appearance. For a few hours during the day, it was possible and not unusual for the men working in the bright sun, either on the trail, or at the Base, to strip to the waist in perfect comfort, although the temperature was far below freezing. Needless to say, I did not strip to the waist, though I did develop a tan. The vast white snowy surfaces reflect the sun's rays and heat from all directions. The complete lack of dust particles in the air, allows the full force of the sun to reach the body and unless proper precautions are taken, a severe burn may result. Dark glasses must always be worn to prevent snow-blindness, which can occur without warning after only a few minutes of unprotected exposure. I began to wonder if my Aunt hadn't been right when she cautioned me about losing my complexion.

Friday, December 5, 1947

The day was a beautiful one. Looked at the tide gauge and changed seismograph paper, both working well. Lassiter and Finn decided to take a flight to look for Nichols. They used the Beech.

It had been three weeks since Adams had parachuted the month's food supply to them, but they had not been seen or heard from since. We knew from flights that there was still open water around the western end of Red Rock Ridge and that the numerous sea leads along their assumed route had been opening and closing with our variable weather. Kelsey continued to transmit them this information daily, but Finn was not positive that their receiver permitted them to hear. Their transmitter difficulty did not enable them to give us any sort of a signal. Finn wanted to be very sure that they had knowledge of the ice conditions before they sledged by other possible routes back to camp. Lassiter and Finn began scanning the surface shortly after take-off. Soon they sighted several black specks on the bay ice, but field glasses proved them to be long shadows cast on the ice by broken ice pressure ridges. Finally, Nichols' camp was spotted about thirty-five miles south from Base, near the entrance to Windy Valley. Lassiter spotted the red smoke from a landing flare and began circling the microscopic camp as he let the plane down. He assured Finn that the ice beside the small camp was suitable for a safe landing. Taking great care to avoid the many crisscrossing sea leads, he made a perfect landing. While taxiing to the geologists campsite two miles toward the ice cliff, the Beechcraft slid across a couple of narrow sea leads.

As they stepped out of the plane, Nichols and Dodson rushed to greet them as the first humans they had seen or talked to in sixty-seven days. They were in excellent health, well bearded, tanned by the sun, and hardened from the strenuous life which a sledge trip in the polar regions affords. They wanted to make their own way back to Base. Finn was relieved to learn that their trail receiver was in good order and that they had been listening to the regular schedules from the Base.

Nichols was very pleased with all Finn had done for him and said, as soon as he got back to Camp, he wanted to take a trip up Neny Trough. Finn told him about the Mac situation and how Mac had said Finn was holding the bag on Nichols by sending an incompetent man into the field.

Nichols cursed him out and said that guy had just better keep out of my way that's all.

Finn told them he had found a pass over the coll which provided a route over the steepest part and down to the bay ice in Neny Fjord. How long the ice conditions would remain so favorable was uncertain; therefore Finn requested that they return to Base by Christmas, as the dangers after that time most probably would increase. Finn offered to return them by plane if they preferred. Horrified at the idea of their party hitchhiking back, in unison the two men spurned the offer with thanks, saying that after traveling this far, they would be quite able to complete the rest of the journey.

Before leaving Finn asked Nichols if there was anything he could take back for him. Without a moments hesitation, he mumbled something about a small bag he would like to get rid of. He rummaged around in the sledge tank and handed over a fairly well filled rucksack. As Finn took hold of it, the surprisingly heavy load threw him slightly off balance. Closer investigation revealed the rucksack contained one hundred pounds of geological rock specimens. Dr. Nichols placed such a high value on these specimens that they were greatly impressed by the honor he conferred upon the plane crew to transport his irreplaceable rocks back to the Base.

Nichols estimated that they would arrive at Stonington Island within the next ten to fourteen days, depending upon the geological work he found on the last leg of their journey. As the Beechcraft soared into the air, they had the last glimpse of the two men waving, with their tent and sleds making a picturesque background. The dogs, outstretched on their tethering line, strained in their chains at the noise of the engines.

While they were gone, Bill, Fiske, Woody and I took a skiing trip up the glacier for more colored pictures with the ship in the background.. Mac and Harry spent all day working on the Ship and Chuck Hassage, who went out with the refrigerator, reported that they had done a good job in cleaning up the fan tail of the ship.

When Finn and Jim got back, Jim took Hassage, Sig, Kelsey, and me for a ride in the Beech. The weather was still good and Lassiter had installed a new trailing antenna on the plane's radio and wanted Kelsey to check it out while the plane was in flight. It was the first time Kelsey had even been in a plane and at first he was scared to death. Once we took off, he got quite a kick out of seeing the Antarctic terrain from the air. He was still panicky whenever we banked or struck a rough spot. One can really appreciate the dangers, when with one sweep of the eye you are able to take in the numerous high mountains, glaciers and huge gapping crevasses. He could better appreciate why his constant radio guard of our flights might very well mean the difference between life and death. Without knowing the exact position of a traveling plane, it would offer a rescuing plane a mighty difficult time trying to locate a downed plane in this vast wilderness. We circled over Nichols and then went over the Plateau Weather Station and while doing so made radio contact with the people there. The British sledging party on their way to meet a British party of five sledging down from their base at Hope Bay had just reached the Met station that afternoon. Their sledges and dogs could be seen below, just spots on the white surface, really the only thing which designated the snow covered tents of the Met station. The two inhabitants of the station, McLeod and Jorge were busy in their underground tents packing the instruments and their personal belongings in order to accompany the sledge party down. The Plateau weather station was being dissolved after over three months of operations.

The Weddell Sea was fogged in so we couldn't see it. I had a marvelous view of all the surrounding mountains. We were in the air for about an hour and the Beech is one smooth plane. Before landing, Lassiter flew low over those who had been waiting patiently on an iceberg to get a picture of the Beechcraft while in flight over the Base.

We had dinner and Jim rubbed Mac and Harry pretty hard when telling them about how well Nichols was, etc.

Mac's ears got as red as a beet, Jim said, since he had no confidence that Nichols could take care of himself.

The next few days remained excellent on our side, but Keeler, and the Weddell Coast Party continued to report bad weather. The men hauled more gas drums into position, chamoised and refueled the plane. Latady was busy repairing one of the trimetrogon cameras which had given him some trouble on the last flight. The group working on the ship, hauled ashore what we estimated would be our maximum needs in coal for the rest of our stay. They had cleaned up the fan tail of the ship and were starting on the forward hold.

Sunday, December 7, 1947

Six years ago today, on a Sunday, was Pearl Harbor Day. The day was a lovely one, bright and sunny, but Keeler still reports bad weather and so does Ken. Latady worked all day, repairing one of the cameras and later, Finn helped him with developing one critical roll of K17, which would reveal how far they had gone on the Filchner Flight. The meteorology gang worked pretty hard all morning, then Woody went off with some others to the Petrel Rookery and Peterson and Fiske out to the seal hole near Roman figure IV Mountain. After dinner, Finn and I drove the weasel out and photographed the two seals, one huge fellow. I threw small things at them and they came after me in their loping fashion. I tended to the scientific work and spent the evening answering some messages to Burr Brundage and Meinholtz, then worked on the Rookery story, somewhat. Mac and Harry are really quiet these days. Harry taking occasional trips over to the British Camp, but they are only short ones. Jennie is pretty sick. Pete asked Harry today if she were going to have a baby soon. Harry said, oh no, nothing like that, she had an operation on her side a short time before she came down and I guess that is bothering her. Lassiter and Hassage were in. Hassage turned in a report on the weasel. Pete and Larry took the weasel out beyond Neny and made some atmospheric refraction measurements.

Monday, December 8, 1947

Keeler and Ken Butler on the Joint Sledge Party reported good weather so Lassiter, Finn, and Bill took off in the Beech after much last minute rushing. Bill Latady's pre-flight preparations always amused everyone. He was a one-man store. Each of the many pockets of his heavy flying suit was crammed to capacity. In addition, he removed the seat attached to his parachute and stuffed that compartment with all manner of useful things. If he ever had to jump, he could just dig in and live for a month in comfort with what he had on him. He bulged so much he couldn't get into the plane the normal way, but had to be pushed in sideways.

They flew to Keeler, where Bill picked up a new camera and the gas tanks were topped off, giving them a total weight of 10,000 pounds. When Adams, Robertson, and Schlossbach, already at Keeler, began preparing NANA for flight they discovered a frozen carburetor and a broken exhaust pipe. The temperatures on the East Coast of the Peninsula nearly always were several degrees lower than at the main Base, giving a certain number of maintenance problems.

Usually, the Keeler runway consisted of hard packed snow and with a slight wind blowing, it helped considerably to obtain flying speed. However, on this particular day, the surface was sticky and the lack of any wind made it extremely difficult to get sufficient flying speed to lift the plane into the air. The Norseman was carrying a load of 9,600 pounds, a 1,600 pounds overload. Adams, with Schlossbach as Co-pilot, made two long runs of two miles, but was not able to get off. They stopped and took out one of the five – fifty-five gallon drums of gasoline and tried again. He still was not able to lift the plane off the ground, so they stopped and took out another precious drum of gasoline. Another try also was unsuccessful, so Schlossbach and all of his emergency gear finally left the plane and after another run of two miles with a total of 1,100 pounds removed, NANA barely lifted into the air. Adams was flying alone and the cargo had been cut to only three drums of gasoline. Their flight would be limited by the amount of gas available.

Unlike the Norseman, the Beechcraft had no difficulty in getting into the air. Their flight track was farther inland than before, so that Latady might obtain an additional set of overlapping pictures. The terrain beneath was highly mountainous, and in places the sea ice came close to its rugged side. The 20-mile-wide belt of sea ice stretched south along the coast for 350 miles, to the great shelf ice (now named the Ronne Ice Shelf). Numerous sea leads ran from the open water toward the mountainous coast, and frequently seals were detected sunning themselves on the ice below.

Both planes were headed for Ken Butler and the Joint British-American Party at Tricorn, where they landed safely around three o'clock. The Sledge Party had reached Wright Inlet at Mt. Tricorn the day before and guided them in for safe landings. Finn had intended to have them stand-by with Adams in the Norseman to guard the Beechcraft long flight. They got out of the planes and congratulated the members of the trail party on their outstanding journey and on being the first persons to reach Mt. Tricorn by surface transport. After a few minutes of exchanging greetings and news, two drums of gasoline were pumped into the Beechcraft's tanks, their emergency gear was checked, and the trimetrogon film was made ready for reloading the three cameras at intervals during the flight. The weather looked perfect, but after flying south for two hours, they were forced to return to Tricorn because of heavy fog and all radio guards were canceled until further notice.

They camped with the Joint sledge party and spent a great time learning more details of their journey than cryptic radio messages had allowed. Finn was invited to their tent for supper and freely admitted that he tasted the best piece of seal meat ever prepared in the Antarctic.

Three miles to the west was the rocky and mountainous coastline of the Peninsula and beyond it rose the rolling surface of the Plateau, reaching as high as 7,000 feet in places. The ground party was very carefully surveying the whole thing, and vital ground control points for the trimetrogon photographs were being established. From the Plateau top, great glaciers descended in tumbled masses of ice with an austere and cruel beauty. Where they met the shelf ice, they caused large pressure ridges and extensive crevassed areas. The trail party had to find a safe way through these areas.

Usually the dogs were driven ahead without a guide, but occasionally in pressure ice or other difficult terrain, it was necessary to have one man go ahead on skis and break a trail for the teams to follow. These remarkable husky work dogs, who actually love their work, can pull a heavier load than a man would be able to manage over the same long period of time. Their only reward was a pound and a quarter of concentrated dog pemmican when their work was through and an occasional friendly pat. A small bell was attached to each dog's harness as a sort of morale factor during the long day's monotonous struggle. This small distraction worked surprisingly well.

Owing to the higher temperatures during the day, which makes for mushy surfaces, the party had been traveling at night when they got better conditions. In spite of sub-zero temperatures, (for the midnight sun gives practically no heat), they got warm enough skiing alongside the sledges. It is while making and breaking camp that the cold really strikes. As a result, they learned to do the outside chores very fast. The tents went up and the dogs were fed with lightening speed, while the ordinary person would still be choosing a campsite. One of their coldest temperatures, they all experienced that night at Mt. Tricorn. The thermometer registered twenty degrees below zero F.

The Joint British-American Sledge Party, as such, had reached its southern destination according to the agreement between Butler and Finn. They were over five hundred miles from the main Bases and had been averaging sixteen miles a day when traveling. From Tricorn, Smith and Owen were to form the Ronne Weddell Coast Party and continue to sledge south as far as their remaining rations would allow. They would establish additional ground control points along their route wherever feasible. While awaiting their return, Butler and Mason were to do work in the general vicinity of Tricorn. However, when our plane arrival at Mt. Tricorn coincided with theirs, Butler asked Finn if he objected to the British accompanying the party south as he and Mason would prefer this to killing time at Tricorn. By doing this, nothing they had agreed upon formerly would be changed, except that the four man party would remain intact. Finn was perfectly agreeable to this suggestion and so the following day, the group packed up their camp, hooked up the teams and disappeared in the overcast to the south.

For the next three days, Lassiter, Adams, Latady, and Finn were weathered-in and spent most of the restless hours in their sleeping bags. Part of the time, a typical Antarctic storm raged with the temperature at zero Deg. F., and winds up to forty miles per hour, causing much surface drift, while at the main Base we were experiencing our fourth consecutive day of perfect weather without a cloud in the sky.

Pete had two chicken-laid fresh eggs and bacon this morning and pictures were taken of him eating them. The whole gang, with exception of aviation, turned out pretty good, also. Turned in about 3:30.and hauled in coal from the ship. They worked hard for three hours according to Hassage. Woody and Mac went sealing and got four. I worked all day on the Rookery story and finally, finished it late tonight. Kelsey sent in part of it and also got off messages to Ward and Ivey, concerning possibility of returning to New York instead of Beaumont. Did scientific work as usual and developed three pretty good seismo sheets tonight. Woody came and sat by me tonight, saying he wanted to get in good with the management. Fiske came in for a chat before dinner, then proceeded to sit in the middle of the table as usual. Pete is very pleased with his scientific program and condescends to say the geographical program is going along pretty well also. Turned in about 3:30.

Wednesday, December 10, 1947

Kelsey was not called this morning and hence did not make the 9:00 schedule with Ken. Robertson at Keeler met the 10:00 one and every hour thereafter. Kelsey came on at 12:00, but nothing was heard from Ken by 2:00. We don't know whether they are flying or not. Around three o'clock, Robertson heard them and they reported bad weather. Finn asked me to make a sensational story about them being weathered in on their long southern flight. This was our fourth perfect day here, not a cloud in the sky. The country is really beautiful when it is like this, but the weather is seldom the same on both sides of the peninsula at the same time.

I worked hard all day, changed seismograph, wrote a story on flight and trail party and two leaders meeting in the field. Then, I made up Christmas greeting list and did some writing on the Beaumont Chapter of the book. Jennie was up and around today, acting as though she had never been sick. Chuck said, Harry and Mac are doing a good job cleaning up the ship. He also said, Woody has been helping him without complaining in the slightest. John Tonkin and Dick Butson were over to dinner. They seemed friendly enough. John kept watching me and when I would catch his eye, he would smile. I washed my hair after dinner. Pete is working hard on his cosmic ray machine. He has the solar radiation working well now. Chuck Hassage was in talking for quite a while. He told me how much he admired me, how swell he thought I was, and how lucky Finn was to get such a good wife. Since he had been against my coming in the first place, I felt redeemed. I checked the tide gauge. Sig and I talked. He had moved the puppy pen with Harry. Harry asked, if Finn was going to take any of the dogs back. Sig said, yes, he thought so. Harry said, I wish he would tell us, so we could start building crates for them.

Friday, December 12, 1947

Larry Fiske awoke me this morning by hollering that Finn had been flying for several hours and they were now at Mt. Sam Houston. I turned on the radio and learned that on the previous evening of December 11th, the southern horizon had finally appeared to clear at Tricorn, revealing the sun in the distance.

Overhead, their skies were still heavy with clouds. A few hours later, there was evidence that the good weather was moving to the north. The three men who were to make the flight turned in to get a few hours sleep before tackling the job ahead, while Adams, always dependable, volunteered to make the plane ready for a take-off. He busily occupied himself with digging the skis of the Beechcraft out of the snowdrifts, completed the loading of the plane, and when he was certain that the weather had improved sufficiently for a take-off, began preparing breakfast. This meal consisted of the usual trail menu, oatmeal, biscuit, bacon, and cocoa. By the time he called the others at 4:30 a.m., he had the plane's motors heated and in all respects had prepared things efficiently for a quick take-off. The plan called for Adams to stand-by at this Base with the Norseman and to guard the flight via the small hand cranking trail radio. As before, this proved to be a highly satisfactory arrangement.

At 5:20 a.m., the engines of the heavily loaded Beechcraft roared for a take-off. After a mile's run in the deep soft snow, she obtained flying speed and lifted into the air. The course was set due south until the Barrier's edge was reached and then changed to southeast. In the three days they had been held up by the bad weather, Finn took stock of their gasoline supply on hand and found out that with the Norseman's cargo of only three drums instead of the five which they had counted on, and as a result of their one false start to the south, they would have to forego their much desired southern flight in favor of completing that last stretch of coastline southeast along the barrier to Coats Land. From there, they would head south as far as their gas supply would permit. Twenty-five minutes after take-off, at an altitude of 2,000 feet, they passed over the Ronne Weddell Coast Sledge Party traveling at snails pace along the sea ice below. They were taking advantage of the hard crusty surface found on the sea ice when the sun was at its lowest. Finn had arranged for the Sledge Party to stop and make camp when the plane passed over them, in order that they also might stay in radio contact with the plane. Less than twenty minutes later, the first contact was made with them as the plane headed eastward along the edge of the ice barrier.

Since the first part of the barrier had been covered in pictures on their November 21st flight, they did not start the cameras before they were at their previous turning point. To save gasoline, they flew low, and by the time they reached the thirty mile stretch of crevasses running parallel to the barrier, they were not more than 1,000 feet over the snowy surface beneath. They checked the radio altimeter on the inside of this broken area and it registered two hundred and fifty feet. Lassiter wanted to swoop down close to the surface to check the reliability of the plane's altimeter and Finn highly favored this. Slowly, they descended to within a few feet of the surface and noted that the plane's altimeter read two hundred and fifty feet. They were very pleased with the result, and the additional gasoline spent on this maneuver was justified. They also checked the outer or seaward side of the crevassed area and found the elevation there to be only one hundred feet high.

The same course of 130 degrees Magnetic was maintained generally during the flight to Moltke Nunatak. Moltke Nunatak, discovered by Filchner in 1912, was the last known feature on the other side of the Weddell Sea. On two occasions, Lassiter flew over large patches of overcast, but as the visibility ahead was unlimited, they continued. Because of this overcast, their altitude varied slightly from time to time. However, during the entire time the cameras operated on the flight, Latady noted the exact time of each exposure, the altitude of the plane at the time, the magnetic heading of the plane, and the drift from a meter, so that this information would be available in the future and the exact flight track of the plane determined when the photographs were being plotted for making a map.

Below, the sheer wall of the barrier, dropping off into the azure blue waters of the open sea, presented a splendid sight, as the sun's shadow from the east cast its reflections upon the pack ice nearest the ice wall. Finn noticed that the area of open water to the north had increased considerably since the flight of November 21st. The looseness of the pack ice as seen through field glasses seemed to indicate that a sturdy vessel could have sailed right up to the shelf ice, if conditions to the north were similar.

In Latitude 78 degrees, 25 min. South, Longitude 44 degrees, West, they crossed a deeply indented bay, about twenty miles by twenty miles, which Finn named Gould Bay. Dr. Lawrence McKinley Gould. a mentor had been on First Byrd Expedition 1928-30 with Finn's father and currently was President of Carleton College in Northfield, Minnesota. At the head of the bay was an ice fall, heavily crevassed for a width of about a mile or more inland. Tongues of ice protruded into the head of the bay and the bay itself was partly filled with small tabular bergs, cemented together with sea ice. It reminded Finn very much of the Bay of Whales, in the Ross Shelf Ice in approximately the same latitude on the opposite side of the Continent. Gould Bay would seem to offer a suitable place for landing a wintering party. (Ten years later during the International Geophysical Year 1956-58, Finn became the Commanding Officer and Scientific Leader of Ellsworth Station established here).

Shortly after crossing the bay, overcast skies appeared straight ahead. To the north and northeast, practically ice-free water could be seen to the horizon. There was, however, some loose pack ice next to the shelf ice. By taking a sun sight to obtain lines of position and by dead reckoning, Finn estimated they were at Latitude 78 degrees, 40 min. South, Longitude 40 degrees, West, and about fifty miles west of Moltke Nunatak. Through a light haze, they could see the easterly trend of the shelf ice.

Three hours and seven minutes after they had taken off, black clouds covered the surface beneath, and they were forced to change course to 218 degrees, True. Through a distant clearing beyond the clouds, they could see a snowy surface without visible rock outcrops. They were unable to see either Moltke Nunatak or other mountains, and felt if any exist, they either are small in size, or were obscured by the clouds. Their new course took them south along the edge of the overcast. As this was a most important leg of the flight, Finn scanned the horizon with field glasses for a break of surface, but none was visible. At 8:50 a.m. Lassiter informed Finn that one of the fuselage tanks might run dry at any minute, and Finn knew that they had to return soon. Just then the engines missed for an instant, and Lassiter switched to a full fuel tank. Latady again dropped the American flag in the name of the United States, and Finn made this area part of Edith Ronne Land, which name he had given to all the newly discovered land from the farthest west seen on the November 21st flight to the farthest east seen on this flight.

Finn obtained a sight with the bubble sextant, which gave him the approximate position of their turning point. About twelve miles from the edge of the shelf ice, Latady obtained a reading from the radio altimeter, which indicated that the surface beneath was seven hundred feet above sea level; a few minutes later another reading from the radio altimeter indicated that the surface was now three hundred feet above sea level; and a final reading, at the edge, showed only one hundred feet. The gradual southward increase in elevation of this huge ice mass was their second important discovery. These observations, together with the observations made on the November 21st flight, the obvious obstruction which accounts for the indentation named Gould Bay, the lines of crevasses which they saw at some points extending parallel with the Lassiter Shelf Ice fringe over a width of fifteen to twenty miles inland, and the fact that as seen from their most southerly position, the surface of the ice seemed to rise steadily, led Finn to believe that the Antarctic Continent was a single unit and not divided by a frozen body of water extending from the Ross Sea to the Weddell Sea. The whole area had now been covered where a possible strait might exist. The line of position obtained at the barrier when the sun was 90 degrees, off the plane's heading fixed its location precisely. Later explorations during the IGY revealed this rising area to be an island, later named Berkner Island, and located within the Ronne Ice Shelf.

While flying over the ice shelf more than 900 miles away, Finn heard Kelsey come in on the radio stronger than ever. They also had contact from time to time with Cape Keeler and with Chuck Adams at Cape Wheeler. At one point, they heard Robertson at Keeler tell Kelsey at the main Base, "Gees Kelsey, I ain't heard a damn thing".

Approaching Mt. Austin, the mountainous coastline loomed ahead once more. New features, the Scaife Mountains stood out over the otherwise snowy scenery to the south, and as they passed the foot of Wetmore and Irvine Glaciers, the dark isolated, but massive Mt. Robertson and Mt. Wood appeared above the terrain. The two glaciers looked like smooth thoroughfares leading from the bottom of Gardner Bay to the higher elevation westward. About twenty-five miles south of Mt. Tricorn, the sharp Mt. Nash was close to the right of their flight track. Latady was eager to obtain a second set of trimetrogon photographs of the coastline as they continued northward, so they radioed Adams to take-off at once for Cape Keeler.

As Finn looked southeast for the last time, the one hundred foot barrier disappeared over the horizon. Behind lay their most important discovery. For four hundred and fifty miles, they had followed the ice barrier that bounds the Weddell Sea on the south. They had found that it connects with Coats Land some distance south of Latitude 77 degrees, 50 min. South, Longitude 36 degrees, West, where Filchner found the ice wall in 1912.

As they approached Mt. Tricorn at an altitude of 10,000 feet, Adams, who had been guarding the flight by radio, prepared to take-off. Through field glasses Finn saw him taxi to a take-off position, but he did not see them. The speedier Beechcraft outdistanced him, but good radio contact between both planes was maintained. There were some patches of overcast beneath. Adams, with less elevation flew through them. The overcast made it difficult for the Beechcraft crew to locate the Gruening Glacier gas cache, so they landed on the sea ice to the east of some rock outcrops which they were unable to identify. The sun was practically due north, so Finn took a sun sight and determined their position was about thirty-five miles too far north. They flew south again, beneath the light haze overcast and had no difficulty locating the cache.

At 12:55 p.m., they landed safely at Cape Knowles and the Gruening Glacier cache after a seven and a half-hour flight. It was a relief to stretch their legs and walk on the snowy surface while refueling. Thus far, they had covered a distance of 1,200 miles with an average speed of one hundred and fifty-eight miles per hour. While they pumped the one hundred and thirty-eight gallons of gasoline into their nearly empty tanks. Adams in NANA passed overhead flying directly for Cape Keeler, even though Keeler reported marginal weather. On the radio Kelsey asked Chuck Adams, "Have you any clue as to what you are going to do?" Adams replied, "No Kelsey, I haven't a clue."

By 3 p.m., the Beechcraft was air borne again and headed for the main Base. About thirty miles north of Cape Eielson, Finn sighted the low snow covered dome shaped island which he and Adams had sighted on their November 6th flight east to the edge of Larsen Shelf Ice. There was still open water close to the eastern side of the Island. There were many patches of clouds and for a while they discussed the possibility of having to land. Since Keeler had reported marginal weather, while the main Base reported excellent weather, Lassiter ducked through the rough places and flew into brilliant skies with ceiling and visibility unlimited by the time they were a short distance south of Keeler. They had successfully completed the most extraordinary flight. Finn had also found that there were many discrepencies in existing maps, particularly in the area along the east coast of the Peninsula as far south as Mt. Tricorn, clearly illustrating the desirability of having ground control parties in the field.

At 6:05 p.m., after covering more than 1,600 miles of terrain during the day, with only one stop for refueling, they came into the main Base for a safe landing on the bay ice alongside of our ship. One of their engines had been acting up for sometime. Later it was diagnosed as a burned out valve.

I had been following the flight as best I could and anxiously waited for news during the times that they were out of contact. For most of the time that Finn was out doing his exploratory flights with the team I was too concerned about him to concentrate on reading or knitting. I could therefore usually be found writing in our shack, carefully distracting myself from becoming too agitated about his whereabouts and hoping for the best. It was always a great relief to me to have him safely back at base, particularly when it had been a succesful flight. This especially in view of the fact that there were Mac and Harry's group at the base who were actively postulating their destruction every time that they went out of radio contact. Such awful suggestions really made life very difficult indeed for me at these times.

Meanwhile, Adams had landed safely at Cape Keeler, refueled and made preparations to abandon that base and return the remaining personnel, Schlossbach, Robertson, and Thompson to the main base that same day. The base had served a worthwhile purpose. Our main southern flights from there had been concluded, and our men were only too anxious to pack their belongings in anticipation of more comfortable quarters, a change in diet, and a bath. On the way back from Keeler, Adams informed Kelsey, "I'm in Neny Trough, coming down to 3,500 feet and going to land". Kelsey, "Are you going to land at the main Base?" Adams, "Well I suppose so, is there any other place you had in mind for me to land on?"

At the main Base that evening, we had a full table at dinner, and everyone was in a good mood, but the flyers were very tired. Now, we had only six men out of camp; two on each of the three trail parties in the field. All agreed it was a good flight, but Finn says the flying is over for him and that the other guys can do the rest! We'll see.

Saturday, December 13, 1947

Finn was tired, but we were up fairly early and spent the rest of the day working hard. I did much writing on the book, while Finn worked out his sights and plotted the flight track. In the afternoon, the aviation gang dropped in for some coffee, minus Ike. They had been working on fixing up the planes for flying again. They wanted to discuss with Finn further aviation plans. Finn thought another trip further south would be beneficial, but the ensuing discussion made him decide that this was not wise. Our gasoline supply is now low and there would be no reserve, in case any rescue work was necessary. The planes had taken a beating and need some work done on them. The planes don't have sufficient range to go very much further south than they have already been, without laying another long distance cache of gasoline at least one hundred miles south of Gardner Bay. Providing things went as well as they had on previous flight, it would be barely possible, but our supply of gasoline would not allow this third flight with an adequate safety margin were any unforeseen trouble to occur. We had accomplished what we came to do and more, so it was deemed foolish to stretch our luck too far. They could not safely make the Pole and the territory, between where they have been and the Pole, looks like nothing but a vast expanse of whiteness. Therefore further penetration into the terrain due south toward the Pole would be left to a future expedition based in closer proximity to the area, or have longer range planes, more advanced mapping equipment and sufficient gasoline resources at its command. To have attempted this job under the circumstances would have stretched safety precautions.

Sunday, December 14, 1947

Chuck Hassage said Ike had told him he didn't want to run the camp anymore, so Finn asked Chuck to continue running it. After breakfast, Finn called all of aviation in and told them they had done an excellent job and of his decision with regard to future flights. Ike spoke of loading the planes back on the ship and Finn told him about the proposed Punta Arenas trip. Ike said that would eliminate the problem of the Beechcraft, that he would like to make the flight himself and that anybody could run the ship back. He stated he did not want to run the camp, that everybody had gotten things done on the expedition except him, and that he wanted to work on his navigation on the ship. Finn said he could understand this. Ike said let some of the criticizers and bitchers take a crack at running the camp and see how they like it – that he had never heard so much bitching before in his life. Finn asked Hassage and he said, of course he would run it and do the best job he could. Ike is anxious to get home as soon as possible and wants to start working on the engine room. Finn told him about Mac during his absence. The meeting ended with the decision that after the planes had been given engine checks, we would continue our aerial photographic program over areas which were within the range of our main base. In addition we would utilise our planes for some scientific projects to round out our program until such time as our gasoline had been exhausted, or our climatic conditions forced us to discontinue our flight operations.

Robertson came in for a long chat in the afternoon and got caught up with all the happenings, while he was away.

I worked on an article about the last flight, the winding down of the exploratory program, and a summary of its accomplishments. It was a good article, I believe. Kelsey got it all out, three pages. Sig made us some French toast and we went to bed around two o'clock. Jennie was in her room all day. Mac and Harry moved the dogs over by the British hanger. Finn had them move them back again. Chinook was running loose twice today and Finn had Hassage get Harry to chain him. Sent more information to Dana for Encyclopedia Britannica.

Wednesday, December 17, 1947

Mac and Harry spent the day taking the dogs out. Mac came in at dinnertime in the funniest costume I have seen. He had a Chilean tam on the side of his head and a 15-foot British whip wound around his shoulder. He really was comical trying to look like the great explorer and only succeeded in being ridiculous without realizing it.

Saturday, December 20, 1947

Finn's birthday. We decided to rearrange the shack a bit. Finn brought in a new table for the typewriter and we held a general house cleaning. Finn went out and took some pictures, while I tried to do some writing, but there were so many interruptions, that I didn't get much done. Andy had a message for Professor Ewing to receive his seismic and all weather data by radio at Columbia for him, after we leave. Finn agreed and approved it. Kelsey had a message from Jennie for Finn to sign, but Finn told him to take it back to them and get them to bring it to him themselves. Kelsey told a funny one about someone asking him to keep a bag of laundry for him and when he stored it away, he heard something hard bang. When Lassiter was looking for the Astro-compass, Kelsey remembered this and sure enough, Lassiter got all three of the astro-compasses back in the same manner. After dinner, we had a movie, "The Falcon in San Francisco". Robertson announced a meeting of the Tunnel Runners Society and we all had a glass of wine, coffee, and cake and chocolate and peanuts and some Chilean fruit drink. Ike, Pete, Bill, Larry, Hassage, Robertson, Lassiter, Adams, and Sig were in attendance, to wish Finn a happy birthday. They left early and we went to bed. Wind blew hard all day.

There was one rather complex problem confronting us. The bay ice was sufficiently strong still to use as a flying field and at the same time, move heavy supplies over it to the ship to be hoisted on board. When the bay ice became unsafe, or broke-up completely, the planes could move their runway up to the glacier, but we would no longer be able to transport heavy equipment to the ship via the weasel. Should this occur before the aviation program had been completed, we would not only have to contend with the danger of the planes operating from the crevassed glacier, but it would be almost impossible for us to load them on the ship without the aid of the bay ice. The difficulties involved in loading the two large planes on anything we could construct, would be about impossible. For the next few weeks, we prayed that the bay ice would hold until the flights were finished and could load the planes aboard ship.

Robertson gave the Norseman and Beechcraft a thorough going over and gassed them for flight. On December 19th and 20th, strong steady winds lashed over camp, but on December 21st, the wind subsided, although the temperature was very low. Several exploratory flights were made over the Peninsula during the following days and covered by trimetrogon photography.

Sunday, December 21, 1947

We were up at twelve. Finn took some pictures of the fellows loading the plane to fly as well as of me with the blooming pansies I had carefully grown with hydroponics, which, so far as I know was another Antarctic first experiment.

Tuesday, December 23, 1947

The weather was good again today, although the wind was strong. Finn decided to go with them, on the hop south beyond King George VI Sound area, so much for Finn not flying again! They gassed the plane and took off at 2:00 o'clock. Thirty minutes later, at the Wordie Ice Shelf, Kelsey lost radio contact with them for over seven hours. We were all beginning to get worried. Mac, Ike, Harry, and Chuck went aboard the Ship. Chuck worked on pumping out the center fuel tanks and he told me the fellows had cleaned up the Crew's quarters today. Robertson was in and gave me a report on the L-5, which was quite good. He was a little concerned about the flight, as it was five hours since they had been heard from and they only had eight hours of gas before running on emergency.

After dinner, the weather began to get bad. Kelsey kept broadcasting the weather blind. Finally, he heard Jim and kept telling him the weather at Base was deteriorating rapidly. Jim finally, gave his position at Cape Berteaux. It was obvious, he was going to try to make it back. The ceiling was 3,000 feet with visibility to five miles and wind 20 mph steady, with gusts to 30 mph. The weasel went out on the British side of the Bay Ice and finally, after an 8 1/2 hour flight, they landed off Figure IV Mountain, about four miles away from Base. The fellows had to get on the wings and ride back to keep the plane from being blown over.

That eight and one half-hour flight proved to be one of the most exciting, successful, and dangerous ones of the expedition.

Upon reaching George VI Sound, they followed its Eastern Shore to its southern extremities, at which point they lost all radio communication with the main Base and deliberately went off of their planned course. Down below the end of Alexander I Island – that huge island that nestles in the crook of the Peninsula where it turns west to the mainland – they also turned west, south of George VI sound. It certainly was not the wisest thing to do, for if they had come down on this westward leg, or anywhere between there and home they would have been lost. Still Finn considered it would be well worth while to tie-in Alexander I Island with the area south of the Batterbee Mountains and then connect this with the Robert English Coast. These areas had not been photographed previously with trimetrogon cameras.

They passed Eklund Island about ten miles to the north. Farther to the northwest, they could see where the Sound ice terminated in Ronne Bay, named for Finn's father. Carl Eklund and Finn had sledged all over this area on the United States Antarctic Service Expedition in 1941. Isolated mountain peaks lay to the south. Had the weather been more favorable at the time of his flight in 1935, Lincoln Ellsworth certainly would have seen them. Fifty miles to the south of Ashley Snow Nunataks, a snow-covered mountain rose to a height of more than 10,000 feet and Finn named it Mt. Rex. Sixty miles west of it was Mt. Peterson, tabular and about 9,000 feet high, with six smaller peaks nearby. Ahead was completely unknown territory. Visibility was not less than 200 miles. Due west, Finn sighted Mt. Tuve, and the last mountain seen to the west of Ronne Bay, Finn named Mt. Combs in about Latitude 72 degrees, 30 min. S, Longitude 84 degrees W. The terrain gradually rose toward this mountain and terminated in the prominent cone shaped peak.

The surface appeared level and uncrevassed, and they decided to land to take a sun sight. Lassiter had no difficulty whatsoever in setting the plane down for a landing in the deep soft snow. From the air, they had commanded a wonderful view over miles and miles of unknown terrain beneath and to the west, but on the ground, they were merely a few microscopic figures in the middle of expansive whiteness over five hundred miles from any other human being. It was a lonely feeling. With only the softly coughing plane motors, and the suggestion of a mountain in the distance, Finn said he didn't believe he had ever felt so helpless before in his life. Even big Jim Lassiter, who ordinarily had no nerves, was a bit on the edge, and said "Hurry, Commander, let's get going".

Twelve minutes later, they were airborne again, following a course directly toward the main Base. Half of the gasoline supply had been consumed by the time they flew over Ronne Bay. Finn had an opportunity to observe closely the open water where the shelf ice terminated in George VI Sound. Having already penetrated the outer pack ice here, he felt there was no reason why a vessel could not have sailed to the coast at that time. An impressive snow covered range was observed stretching in an east-west direction for about forty miles, and sixty miles to the south, a dark massive range loomed majestically above the surround terrain. These two newly discovered mountain ranges he named the Colbert Range and the LeMay Range respectively.

Their course back to the Base took them close to Charcot Island, and as the visibility in that direction was excellent for a change, they changed course to due north, then northwestward across Wilkins Strait to the Island. In approximately Latitude 71 degrees, South, Longitude 75 degrees, West, Finn observed an ice cliff extending south from Charcot Island to the north coast of Alexander I Island. It appeared to be a connecting link between the two Islands. Finn had been very keen to get to Charcot Island for some time and now he had a golden opportunity.

Charcot Island was first sighted by the French Explorer, Jean Charcot, from the deck of his ship the "Porquoi-pas?" in 1910. It remained unseen for the next eighteen years when Sir Hubert Wilkins flew over the Island in 1929 and determined its extent. Although the Island is of fair size, three small mountain peaks rising to only two thousand feet, are its only conspicuous features. Surface vessels have, from time to time, made vain attempts to penetrate the heavy belt of pack ice which surrounds its shores, but nature's forces thus far had held at bay the civilized world's inventions in steam or diesel. From the view of the icefields it is doubtful if vessels ever will be able to set men on its shores.

Finn recognized the three peaks of Charcot Island from the pictures that Wilkins had taken in 1930. They were quite a contrast to the loftier peaks, which surround the Peninsula, and were the only visible features of the Island. "How would you like to land?" questioned

Lassiter. "Did anybody ever land here? "Nobody ever has", answered Finn, "but go ahead". He set the plane down just south of the center of the Island and about twenty miles south of the peaks. They were the first ones to set foot on that lone outpost. At their position the surface was 900 feet above sea level. Finn took four sights. The sun was due west, and the line of position was good. They stayed about five minutes. The sloping terrain to the south made it easy for the lightly loaded plane to take-off on the last leg of their return flight. There was much open water to the west and north of Charcot Island. Finn felt it would have been possible, but difficult for a ship to force its way to the Island. To the east, they saw many sea leads, though huge tabular ice bergs were still frozen-in the sea's icy grip.

As they flew over the north end of Alexander I Island to cross the 10,000-foot Douglas Range, the sun still shone brightly in all directions except the east – the direction of their flight – where there was a heavy overcast. At the same time, Kelsey at the main Base gave them the first of a series of warnings on the sudden and rapid approach of bad weather. They crossed the island by following a deep and wide valley for forty miles. Tufts Valley, as Finn named it, contained a crevassed glacier that terminated on the Marguerite Bay side of the island. A twenty-mile-long glacier, Nichols Glacier, is a north branch of the tributary.

By the time they reached the entrance to George VI Sound, they were flying in overcast. Lassiter descended below the heaviest cloud formations to an attitude of 3,000 feet, and they managed to continue northward. The closer they got to the main Base, the worse the weather became and several times thought they would be forced to land until the storm had passed. Kelsey continued to warn that within twenty minutes the Base would be covered completely, making a landing there virtually impossible. He also informed them of the existing high surface winds of a steady forty miles per hour. Near Cape Berteaux, Lassiter went down to an elevation of 400 feet, and by the time they reached Red Rock Ridge, ten miles from the Base, the weather had closed completely. Fortunately, Lassiter was familiar with the terrain, and he guided the plane around the barely visible outlines of the high cliffs. At 250 feet, they skimmed over icebergs floating in the open water off the Ridge. Once a sudden downdraft caught the plane and forced it violently to within fifty feet of the icy water beneath. Finn thought his time was up, but Lassiter maintained his usual steady control, and a few minutes later landed safely on the bay ice in Neny Fjord, four miles from Base. The geologists Nichols and Dodson, who were camped on the sea ice with their dog teams south of the Base, heard the plane go by at it low altitude and not expecting anyone in any such storm, they thought the roar of the engines was an earthquake.

The weasel, summoned by radio before landing, helped to bring the plane to its mooring. Gusts of wind of as much as seventy miles an hour made taxiing the plane extremely difficult. However, with two men riding on each wind to break the wind stream, they managed to get the Beechcraft moored in its usual position. I know of three men who were mighty happy to be on the ground that night! Finn said never did food taste so good, for there were times on the way home when he thought he would never have another meal. The contrast between the weather at departure and that on their return, after more than eight and a half-hours of flight was striking. Later, Finn commented, "Once again I was deeply aware of the respect one must always hold for the sudden dangers mercilessly lurking behind the white veil that wraps this vast Continent".

On this flight they had made two landings in the field on completely unknown terrain, one at their furthermost southwesting turning point on the Robert English Coast, south of the Bellingshausen Sea, and the other on the heretofore unattainable Charcot Island. They had discovered many new mountains inland from the Robert English Coast and two new mountain ranges on Alexander I Island. About thirty miles to the east of Charcot Island lies Dorsey Island which is much smaller in size, but similar in shape and contains three small peaks resembling those which distinguish Charcot Island. Dorsey Island, rather than Charcot had been the one seen by Lassiter and Latady on a previous flight and mistakenly identified. All were gratified that some of the mysteries in this area had been cleared up at last.

The following day, they checked the high-octane gasoline remaining. Lassiter, despite being very temperamental at times, really was extremely anxious to do his utmost for the maximum success of the expedition's mapping program. He informed Finn that he had enough gasoline on hand to make one more flight, providing he used the high-octane gas only for take-off and landing. He felt it was safe to fly on the lower #73 while they were in the air after they had obtained the desired altitude. Accordingly, the Beechcraft was loaded for its final flight with the next break in the weather.

The next two days were devoted to preparing for Christmas.

Wednesday, December 24, 1947

It was a cloudy day with strong winds blowing. We kept hoping that Nichols and Dodson would come back, but they didn't. We knew they had reached Red Rock Ridge and were camped on a narrow rock beach of the Ridge's seaward side. They would be lightly loaded now, with the exception of rock specimens, and would be able to find some way up and over the high coll, then down to the bay ice on our side of the Ridge. The day passed, however, without any word from them.

No one did much work, as they were in the Christmas mood, more or less. We decorated our hut with red and green crepe paper and a few paper bells. Sig baked all day, however, and we ate 10-in-1's to help him out, while anticipating better things to come on the morrow. Harry and Jennie cracked some nuts for him, but still Jennie doesn't come to chow and has all her meals in her room.

Had a long and good conversation with Bill. Most of the fellows were in and out of here all day. I worked on a good story combining Dec. 21st and 22nd flights and Kelsey got it out tonight. It was the first radio contact we had in two days. We got many (15) personal messages and one from Larry Gould. We listened to the news and the lighting of the Xmas tree in Washington by the President, many Christmas Carols. It made me homesick, I would like to have been there. I am sure more than one of us felt a few pangs of longing for the comforts of a home and family life which this time of the year particularly symbolizes in civilization.

After twelve o'clock, Ike, Chuck Adams, Hassage, and Robertson came in and had a glass of Rhine wine with us. We went to bed late, after a very pleasant evening.

Thursday, December 25, 1947

Breakfast at noon consisted of bacon and frozen scrambled eggs, which was quite a treat to all. In the Bunkhouse, they were decorating with crepe paper and Pete's met balloons. Andy was taking on several of the fellows in a boxing match. I watched him take a good poke at Mac. Finn also watched them for a while. Andy took on Ike and Hassage also. Finn and I got dressed for our Open House. Finn wore a blue shirt and his dark blue ski pants. I wore gray slacks and my clean yellow sweater. Robertson, Adams, Kelsey, Sig, Andy, Larry, Woody, Pete and all the five Britishers were in for champagne. We had a goodly amount of it for all and we had nice chats with everyone. Andy was particularly funny in telling about the Miramar Hotel fight. Ike, Hassage, Lassiter, Harry and Jennie were not there. We went into a wonderful dinner with nice menus, which Pete had made. The meal was delicious and all had a good time. The menu consisted of: Tomato cocktail, Home made chicken noodle soup, Fried chicken a la Lord Baltimore, (both Sig and I were Baltimorians), Candied sweet potatoes, Buttered cream carrots and peas, Buttered Forkhook lima beans. Country buttered milk gravy, Hungarian strudel, Mincemeat pie, Cranberry sauce, Mixed nuts, Green Queen olives, Sweet mixed pickles, Whole wheat bread, Parker House rolls, Cafe Nora, and Tea.

Kelsey dressed in white summer shorts, with a Navy coat on, was a hit. He was dressed so, for Fiske's benefit and sat directly across from him. Lassiter and Kelsey had cooked it up. We chatted for quite a while after dinner. Jennie was the only one not present. After a leisurely dinner and much animated conversation enjoyed by all, we thought it would be nice if Adams flew some chow over to Nichols and Dodson in the L-5. Sig packed up a full size Christmas dinner and in a few minutes the plane was ready to go. Adams landed on the bay ice right in front of their camp. Although the geologists had just finished a hearty meal of pemmican, they were glad to have it and dived into the feast enthusiastically. We sent them a note with Chuck. They had remained at the Ridge to complete the geology there while it was still possible, but now they had finished and were ready to come back to Base the following day.

Friday, December 26, 1947

Another eventful day! The weather was good, a cloudless sky, so Lassiter and Latady decided to make the last flight. Woody wanted to go, but Finn said, no, Sig should have the first chance, since he had not been out before. Sig was pleased with this, so off they took, the three of them in the early afternoon. This flight was scheduled to go right down the center of the Plateau to tie-in all the pictures we had taken both on the West Side and the East Side of the Peninsula, in case such a record would be useful for making future maps. They headed south toward the Traffic Circle climbing for altitude as they flew. When they were fifty-five miles away from the Base, at five thousand feet, Lassiter suddenly saw the left engine vibrating and throwing our bellows of black smoke. As he circled in descent, he hurriedly managed to pick out a suitable landing field on one side of the Nunatak in the center of a large crevassed filled area in the Traffic Circle.

I was talking to Larry and Pete in the Science Bldg., when Lassiter came in on the radio that he had landed with one bad engine by the Nunatak at the Traffic Circle. He requested Chuck to bring Robertson in the L-5. The L-5 had already landed Hassage over by Nichols and Dodson to help them over the ridge and back home to Base. When Adams came back, he took Finn over to the Rookery for some pictures. Chuck and Finn were back soon thereafter. The L-5 was readied with the necessary repair and emergency gear and Adams and Robertson took off within an hour.

Ike kept bitching about the fact that Sig, the cook, was along. Finn told Ike, Sig had just as much right going along as a passenger, as did Woody, that he intended to give as many chances to do things, as he could possibly do. Chuck landed and brought Sig back to camp. The weather closed in then, so the rest couldn't get back.

Robertson took off the cylinder head and got the plane fixed by late evening. The trouble was diagnosed as a stuck valve, probably caused by some of the #73 octane gasoline. We had used this #73 octane for a short time in the Beechcraft on only one other occasion, at which time they noticed a little of this difficulty, but on the whole they thought it had performed fairly successfully. Now the intake valve on number two cylinder had stuck in the open position and the cylinder had to be removed to repair it properly. A new valve was installed and ground in. The exhaust valve was removed and inspected to insure that it was all right. This required five hours of work under field conditions and a near zero temperature.

When the Beechcraft was ready to return, our weather at the Base again began playing tricks at the wrong time. The previous ceiling and visibility unlimited quickly changed to ceiling zero. Lassiter, Latady, and Robertson began making good use of their emergency equipment. They pitched their tent beside the plane, and made preparations to camp in the field until the weather permitted their return.

Nichols and Dodson arrived around eight o'clock and practically everyone in Camp was out to greet them and take their picture. They enjoyed their trip, were enthusiastic about their accomplishments and were anxious to get out again. Nichols came in here after dinner and we caught him up on the domestic news as well as the home news. He requested a berth in Ike's stateroom on the Ship going back and Finn agreed. Bob wants to get as much work done as possible and assured Finn the preliminary report for the Navy Department would be no problem so far as he was concerned.

Saturday, December 27, 1947

When there was good weather here, there was bad weather over in Neny Trough so that Lassiter could not get back with the Beech. We had a long chat with Dodson in the morning about his trip. He was most enthusiastic and pleased with it. Hassage came in the afternoon and told Finn that Lassiter had been nice to Finn's face, until he had gotten everything he wanted and now was going to double-cross him by writing a report to the Army that Finn had neglected their property. Hassage said Lassiter kept a log on what Finn did and said. Hassage, has never liked Lassiter and Lassiter, of course, always talks loud and big when he gets temperamental. I told Finn to ignore it, as though nothing had happened. Adams made one trip up Neny Trough in the afternoon, taking Dodson with him to look at the weather for Jim to come back. The weather was bad, so he returned.

Bob was greatly pleased when Finn suggested naming the Valley on Alexander Island after Tufts College. He kept talking about it and saying how much it meant to him and the college. They showed an excellent movie, "The Valley of Decision", we all enjoyed it. Jennie was there and afterward asked Finn to approve two messages for her. Finn asked her in here to read them and O.K. them. She hadn't been at dinner, however. Adams took another flight in the L-5 to look at Neny Trough, the weather was still bad. He came in for a chat. Ike, Bob Dodson, and Sig were also here. We chatted about things in general and went to bed around one o'clock.

Sunday, December 28, 1947

The weather was excellent here today, but Lassiter reported being snowed in. Finn went around taking pictures. Ike began to ridicule him, saying, oh, this and that guy wanted their picture taken. Finn called him for it. Later, Hassage indicated he was in a bad mood and refused to have his picture taken.

Nichols came in with some typing for me. He had written a very nice letter to Finn, thanking him for his interest and cooperation in his trail trip. He had also written an article announcing the naming of a geographical feature after Tufts College.

Adams decided this was the day to take Pete on his last Cosmic ray hop in the Norseman's last flight. They were up for over two hours. Nichols went along to do some geology from the air, getting the lay of the land. Woody also went along, just for the ride. Mac went out for a dog team spin. Hassage did some work on the battery charger and then went aboard the Ship, as did Ike. Andy came in for some coffee and we had a nice chat and discussed the future British operation of the seismograph and tidal observations. After dinner, I watched Bob Dodson take several pictures of Mac's hand right outside our shack window. Larry Fiske was standing there too. I tried to figure out what was up, as the hand, which Mac had injured on board ship on our way down, was supposed to have been completely well shortly after we all came ashore. Larry had sledged with Mac and Harry this morning and shortly after went sledging with the British. He forgot entirely to make weather reports. He knew he was wrong and came in here to ask me if I had ever seen a Skua Gull's Egg and if I wanted him to give me enough shells to make a necklace. I thanked him and said, yes. We got the announcement out concerning Tufts College Valley naming and sent a copy to President Carmichael of the College.

Tuesday, December 30, 1947

Lassiter came up with good weather this morning and indicated that he planned to take-off and come back shortly. Finn told him it was O.K. to take pictures on the way back, but come straight back. Nothing was heard from him for sometime and Adams became worried and asked Finn if he could take off in the L-5 and go after Jim. Chuck broadcast to Kelsey just before he took off and Jim hearing it, came in on the radio and said he intended to land in five minutes for Chuck to return to Base. Jim landed fine. He wanted to fly Bill to Crane Inlet again for more pictures, saying that the Beech's engines were operating perfectly now. Robertson told Finn that in his opinion, it was the #73 octane which had caused the valve trouble twice now. Finn spoke to Bill Latady about the pictures and Bill was perfectly agreeable with Finn's decision not to fly either large plane again in view of the above and because the bay ice situation is becoming critical. If the planes are not on board before it goes out, it will be almost impossible to get them on board in a safe manner.

This then was virtually the end of the flying program. The three hundred and twenty-four hours of flying which had been done thus far by the three planes, this was the first and only serious mechanical difficulty experienced. It spoke very well for the maintenance work done by Mechanic Robertson. It was no easy job to maintain three such planes under Antarctic conditions. The proximity to the main base of the forced landing had been fortunate indeed, considering the fact that at the height of our aviation, program, flights had been made as far afield as nine hundred miles from our main Base. The alertness of Lassiter in picking a landing in such a hazardous area, the efficiency of Adams in his flight to the downed plane, and the comparative ease with which the engine trouble was corrected, are good examples of the cooperative spirit which existed among the aviation men.

But now was the time to call a halt – our hourglass of luck had run out. The aviation group admitted that they had had enough for this time – the constant strain of coping with Antarctic conditions was beginning to tell on everyone's nerves, including mine. The supply of high-octane gasoline that remained was not worth mentioning. The bay ice was weakening and we feared it would be in a critical condition soon. Already there were numerous open places close to the sides of our ship and she actually was floating free in the water. A loading dock in that part of the world is non-existent. We had to make use of the things nature provided, so immediately work began to dismantle the Norseman and the Beechcraft preparatory to loading them for their return journey to the United States. The smaller L-5 would continue its operations, as it easily could be loaded aboard ship via a boat ramp at a later date.

Wednesday, December 31, 1947

New Year's Eve. Robertson worked on dismantling the planes. Ike and his crowd were on the Ship. Hassage got the main diesel running yesterday. Today he hurt his back and could hardly sit up. Lassiter and Adams worked on the antennas. Peterson wrote a good review of his scientific programs' accomplishments. Finn and Larry worked all day on navigation. John Tonkin forgot for the fourth time to get the fixes of the geographical features from Ken and this disgusted Finn considerably. I worked on an article about the forced landing in the field of the Beech and read it to Lassiter, etc. It went out tonight.

Just before the movie, Kelsey came in to ask Finn about the generator aboard ship. Finn asked him to get Ike and Kelsey went out to get him. In ten minutes or so Kelsey came back saying Ike didn't want to discuss it with Finn and had yelled all over the Bunkhouse about it. Finn asked him to get Ike again, which Kelsey did over his better judgment. Ike came in and shouted around quite a lot for a while not letting Finn talk at all. Ike said he was only trying to help, that he wasn't working against the expedition by wanting the Beech motors below, that it wasn't the question of topside weight and the generator should be there, but even if the generator were not he would still want the engines removed, that no one could give him a good reason for not taking them off, that would be the first thing the Army would do, the Army would thank you for removing them, that he could take them off and hang them on mounts so they wouldn't be sprung. That had been his work, Ike said, and he would sign a statement taking full responsibility for any damage incurred. Finn told him Robertson couldn't get the props off. Ike didn't believe it and said get Jimmy to sign a statement saying he couldn't get the props off. Finn told Ike, so long as he signed a statement for full responsibility for any damage to the engines, that he (Finn) didn't care whether the engines were removed or not and he wanted everything for the good and safety of everyone concerned. All of this was no big deal, but Ike was edgy, anxious to get started back and just showing off about minor matters.

Finn then discussed the watch list going back. Ike said, none of the men were any good to him, but that if Finn could replace the scientists with other men, they could be free so far as he was concerned. He said, if Nichols can get someone to do his work for him that would be O.K. by him. He also said Nichols had moved in his room without asking him. That ended the conversation just about.

They went to the ship and got Sig's Ballentine's Scotch and after the movie had the fellows in here for a drink, Latady, Adams, Robertson, Woody, Peterson, Fiske, Thompson, and Kelsey. Hassage was in bed and Lassiter talking to him. Finn opened a bottle of champagne after cake, pie and coffee. We had a nice New Year's Eve.

Thursday, January 1, 1948

The first day of the New Year, just about like every other one down here. It was a very beautiful day. We had scrambled eggs and bacon for breakfast. Latady wanted to go mountain climbing but canceled it because they decided to load the Beech on board.

For the last few days the men were kept busy with the two larger planes. They removed the wings and tail sections from both planes. On New Year's Day 1948, the Beechcraft and the Norseman were towed by the weasel over the bay ice to the ship, and the Beechcraft was hoisted up over the side and placed on the after deck with the aid of the ship's boom and winch. Its position was lengthwise on the ship's centerline, under the overhead of the boat deck aft. The following day, the Norseman was hoisted aboard and placed after the Beechcraft on the ship on the after deck. Robertson pulled the Norseman' engine and secured it in the hold to get rid of some of our topside weight and at the same time offer the engine better protection from the salt spray and weather. Then he taped all the openings on both planes to prevent any weather and spray from damaging any of the parts. The Beechcraft's wings were stored on one side of the plane and suspended from the overhead of the boat deck so that they would ride with the ship, thus avoiding strain in rough seas. The Norseman wings were stored on the other side of the Beechcraft.

The L-5 was flown up until the very day we sailed from the Antarctic, although it had been loaded aboard ship briefly for a while. As the men had worked hard to load the planes on New Year's Day, the first good day that week was declared a holiday and everyone who as yet, had not had an opportunity to get over to the penguin rookery on Red Rock Ridge, was flown over in the L-5. Lassiter and Adams took turns carrying two men at a time. By this time the penguin chicks had been hatched and they afforded good entertainment for those who were visiting the rookery for the first time.

When the aviation program had been concluded and we finally left the Antarctic, our three planes had flown a total of three hundred and fifty-six hours in the air, covering 39,000 miles of Antarctic terrain. The accomplishments actually were greater than Finn had hoped in making his original plans. The planes had been utilized extensively for reconnaissance work, cache laying missions, both for advanced aviation flights and in support of the two dog team parties, (one of which was supported three hundred and fifty miles away from the

Base), searching for the lost British flyers, transporting personnel and equipment to advanced field bases, geographical exploration over the unknown, and trimetrogon photography. The planes had made no less than eighty-six landings on skis in the field away from the main Base in order to accomplish our program. Thirty-six of these were made by the L-5, thirty-two by the Norseman, and eighteen by the Beechcraft. Over half of these landings had been made completely unsupported i.e. the plane was dependent upon itself for its safe return. This was by far the greatest number of landings ever to be made in the field by any expedition which had visited the Antarctic up to this time. Previously, it had been considered extremely dangerous to land in the field away from the Base. The magnitude of our program had forced us to establish a new technique in polar flying and we found that, providing the landing spot is chosen carefully to avoid possible hidden crevasses, surface sastrugi, and other irregularities, it is possible and feasible to land almost anywhere within reason. The expedition was indeed fortunate, and most successful.

Our program had netted a conservative total of approximately 250,000 square miles of terrain discovered for the first time and photographed in trimetrogon photography. In addition, approximately 450,000 square miles of previously discovered terrain was covered in trimetrogon photographs for the first time. 14,000 trimetrogon aerial photographs recorded our findings. Ground control points were obtained by the surface parties as well as by us when we had been on the ground in the field. Our flights ranged from Longitude 40 degrees, West to 80 degrees, West. It just so happens that this is the east-west segment which is claimed by Great Britain, but which claim has not been recognized by the United States and is held in abeyance under the Antarctic Treaty. The flag of the United States and that of the Explorers Club of New York were carried on all of our flights. This was our geographical exploration program by plane and we could not help being proud of the fact that it was more than any other single Antarctic expedition had flown in the exploration of the wastelands of the world.

Through the splendid cooperation of the Aviation Staff, which included Schlossbach, Lassiter, Adams, Robertson, and Latady; in addition to the indispensable aid given to the Aviation Department by men like Fiske, Smith, Wood, Jorge, and Thompson, who for many weeks efficiently manned the advanced bases; and the countless hours which radio operator Kelsey had willingly and continuously spent guarding our flight operations; plus the enthusiastic aid contributed by Meteorologist Peterson, Chief Engineer Hassage, and Chief Commissary Steward Gutenko; and Walter Smith and Arthur Owen, the men still in the field on the Weddell Coast Sledging Party, and Dodson and Nichols when they were giving us weather information from the field, the exploratory flight program of the expedition was brought to a most successful conclusion. Both our trail parties and our scientific programs had all gathered priceless information. They had worked as a team with one common goal in mind and the obstacles they met were many.

As to the United States Air Force Pilots we were fortunate to have with us, they were unexcelled for their knowledge of flying under Antarctic conditions. They learned about Antarctica the hard way and became veterans familiar with polar methods and techniques in short order. They were great fellows. To all of these men, we were most grateful for the scientific and geographical achievements of the expedition.

Chuck Adams, Jimmy Robertson and Chuck Hassage celebrate New Year's Eve

XVI

Preparing to Leave

Upon the arrival of the New Year, we began to realize that our year in the Antarctic was drawing to an end. As the major portion of our results had been obtained now, the time was spent collecting and rounding out the scientific data and in trying to get this information into a more usable form. Those members who were not involved in this work spent their time in the general care of the camp and, under the direction of Skipper Schlossbach, in making preparations for our departure. The ship had been cleaned out thoroughly, including the decks, the holds, and the sleeping quarters. All of our no longer needed miscellaneous gear, both heavy and light, was taken on board.

Friday, January 2, 1948

This morning Ike and McClary got up and began to discuss the fact that very few people were helping them on the Ship, saying that perhaps the guys considered themselves too good to work, and mentioning Lassiter in particular. Lassiter heard them, got up and slowly got dressed, when he was fully dressed he went up to Mac and said, "Look here, you and I have been getting along fine together, because we haven't had anything to do with each other – lets keep it that way. I came down here to do a job and I have done it without your help. I will do and have done in the past anything around camp that I have been requested to do, which is more than some of you can say. When the time comes to go aboard ship for our return, I shall stand my watch and do anything you or Ike order me to do, but until that day comes, I don't intend to go aboard that Ship and help you in anyway, unless I am ordered to do so. I don't think you have done anything to contribute to the success of this expedition. I'm just telling you, unless you want trouble to keep away from me. You can say anything you want, about anybody else, but keep your mouth shut about me", McClary said nothing and Ike said nothing.

After breakfast Ike, Mac, Harry, Robertson, Woody, Adams, and Latady took the Norseman on board. It took them the whole day. Jimmy Robertson says they have the generator aft hemmed in so that it is impossible to move it any place now. The planes are placed so that they can't move the wings around, without taking them off the ship and putting them on again. Jimmy Robertson said, "Ike didn't have a harsh work to say to me today." Jimmy Robertson told Woody, just before he lifted the winch, to ask them if they were going to put a safety line around the planes, so that they would be protected. After Ike and Mac hemmed and hawed, they finally put a safety line on the planes. Jimmy took the Nordun's engine out, but I don't think anyone will take the Beech engines out now.

Sunday, January 4, 1948

The fellows, Adams and Lassiter, held a taxi service to and from Red Rock Ridge this morning for Pete, Woody, Kelsey, Robertson, Thompson, and Fiske. Lassiter told Finn Ike was bitching, because McClary and the Darlingtons couldn't go. Finn took his large box out to the ship and there saw Hassage and Ike. He had a talk with them. Hassage understood Finn's point of view, but Ike said Mac's bitching was worse than ever and as Mac had worked hard recently, he felt a consolation prize was in order. I worked on the book and got Robertson's article out. Ike came in the afternoon for a long chat on Mac, whom Ike agreed was a complete misfit and maladjusted. Ike said, he even turned on him. Ike literally hates Robert-

son and says he is the only one in camp he can't work with. Both Ike and Hassage were mad with Lassiter, because he wouldn't help load the plane he flew and which brought him all the glory.

Our warmer weather and resulting thaws began revealing many things that we hadn't seen for many months. Among them were a few odd pieces of equipment, such as shovels and hammers, which their owners had given up as lost long since, or accused their campmates of having confiscated as personal property. Even an old food cache left by the 1941 expedition put in its appearance. After a few hours of picking and shoveling, Sig brought forth several cases of cookies and they were soon pronounced as delicious as the day they were baked. Immediately, Sig and Ike had an argument over the cookies (about when they would be put out) which Sig had dug up after fifteen hours of work.

After the two larger planes had been loaded on board, the ship's boom was moved from aft to the forward deck. Then the forward hold was opened and a heavy galley range, which had been brought as a spare and covered by canvass and left topside during the winter, was lowered into the lower hold. Some of the radio equipment, including one of our heavy transmitters and several generators, were stowed there. A few weeks later, one of our two weasels was hoisted aboard and also placed in the lower hold. Peterson's three hundred pound cosmic ray machine was placed on the boat deck aft and he set it up and made necessary adjustments for taking recordings on the voyage northward.

After Hassage made a probable estimate of the oil which we would consume before leaving and allowing sufficient to cope with any bad weather we might experience out to sea, it was evident that we would not be able to lay a great circle course directly to Panama as Finn had hoped. Instead, we would have to stop at Valparaiso, Chile, to take on some diesel oil. In addition to his work on the ship, Hassage continued to putter around the Machine Shop, maintaining our temperamental and worn diesel generators, of which we lived in constant dread would not hold up for radio communication until our departure. He also made up and turned over to Finn some very valuable reports on the operation and maintenance of our two Army supplied weasels, our Base generator system, and the ship's machinery. Up until the time his work on the ship became too great, he handled the general running of the camp and finally, at the very last, was relieved of this rather thankless job by Fiske. Around the middle of January, the two engineers,

Hassage and Wood, temporarily moved aboard the ship and shortly thereafter were able to get the kinks out of our port anchor windlass so that it operated freely.

Fiske continued to aid Peterson with the meteorological program and in assembling and organizing the mass of data. Robertson made up a report on the maintenance of the planes, and their related equipment, such as heaters, etc. Lassiter and Adams turned in reports on the operation and performance of the planes and then turned to and helped in innumerable ways around the camp. One day Lassiter surprised us by bringing in a plan for another expedition which would utilize some of the new larger planes, and from his hurried calculations would be able to map the entire Continent in twenty-five good flying days. All we would have to do was to wait a year or two for the twenty-five good days. We had only eight excellent, twenty-four hour flying days during the whole year. These flyers certainly were enthusiastic about their work and were genuinely sorry about the conclusion of the exploratory program. But they were not the only ones who were sufficiently interested in their work to advance plans for staying or returning to the Antarctic. Woody's sojourn at the Plateau Met Station had made him interested in continuing our meteorological record and Thompson also was anxious to maintain his unbroken records in seismology and tidal observations.

Monday, January 5, 1948

The Hope Bay party and the five British teams arrived this morning bringing back Don and Jorge around nine o'clock. Don and Jorge said hello to everyone and hot tailed it into Jennie's room. They were in there for several hours and then came over here for an hour. Lassiter wanted to get all the ice to melt for water for the rest of the expedition with Adams and Robertson and be relieved of all further mess cooking. Hassage suggested Fiske to run things. Fiske came in and Hassage asked him. Fiske said he would put up the mess cooking and ice detail list, but would not be responsible for having it carried out or running the camp, as he had friends and he didn't want to lose them. It was dinnertime so Finn let it go at that. After dinner we had a movie, "The Flame of the Barbary Coast", and the new British arrivals came over. I met a couple of them, but they didn't seem to have much to say. Jennie, of course, was all dressed up in a white sweater, sitting right up in front and talking her head off after the movie. Just let some new men come around and she is right in the middle of them, even though she seems to be too sick to come to meals.

We received a good message from Sir Hubert and from Ivey concerning coming to N.Y. on return. Another very weak one from Ward about returning to Beaumont. Finn told Mac not to dissect penguins on mess table, to do it elsewhere. After Finn left, Mac said, "Oh, he is just trying to antagonize me."

Tuesday, January, 6, 1948

Thought all night about the New York deal and decided to send messages to Dana and my aunt and uncle asking them advise after explaining situation. Wrote messages also to Sir Hubert and to State Department making a claim for the record in case it ever wanted to be used. Finn spent all day yesterday and today working on new map.

The two pilots continued to fly the L-5 from time to time for local transporting, observations of ice conditions and reconnaissance work. Adams flew Latady over to the penguin rookery to spend a few days studying the nesting habits of the young penguins, now carefully being guarded by their parents. It was no longer possible to land on the bay ice in front of the rookery as it had disappeared a few days before. These flights served to keep us periodically informed about the conditions of the bay ice in both outer and inner Marguerite Bay. Adams reported additional seepage of water on the landward side of the Ridge. Later that same day, Lassiter and Finn flew some additional food rations to Nichols and warned him to get as much work done as soon as possible so that he could move on to Neny Trough, where, if it became necessary, he would be able to get back to camp overland.

Thursday, January 8, 1948

A red letter day! We had bacon and eggs this morning and they were certainly good. Finn worked all day on the map, continuing to name things. I worked all day on the book and really feel as though I am getting someplace. I have completed about fifty thousand words now. Woody, Hassage, Ike, Harry, and Mac all worked on the ship for a long while today and apparently, got a lot done. I don't know what the rest did around here, but apparently, nothing much as it was wet and rainy practically all day. Don brought me in his article tonight which was fairly good, but too late to send in tonight, so I sent Fiske's instead.

We had a movie, "Kiss and Tell", and the British came over. The newcomers are very quiet and we haven't said more than two words to them. Understand that Mac's hand bothers him after boxing with Andy. Don't know whether it is the one he had broken aboard ship or not. He shouldn't be boxing with his brittle bones. Understand after we left the movie the other night, Jennie and Harry entertained two of the new Britishers in their abode.

Friday, January 9, 1948

The fellows worked on the ship and the musketeers made water. The bay ice has more and more water on it. Adams flew over to Latady, landed on the top of the second coll. He took Latady to Nichols, then went back and picked up Britisher Bernard Stonehouse and brought him back. Robertson and Adams came in for a chat and some coffee. Hassage came in later. He said Jennie was better, but still not feeling well. He said, he thought Harry had gone a little batty. He doesn't have much to say to anyone, but talks to himself all the time. Finn with Lassiter flew over to Nichols to take some pictures and some E rations. I tried to work on Don McLean's article. Kelsey came in right after dinner and talked so much he forgot to keep his 7:30 radio schedule.

Today, the thermometer rose to 47 degrees F., for the warmest temperature we experienced during the year. Each day more of the rocks around our Base became exposed. Daily tests revealed that the temperature of the sea water in Back Bay Cove had risen to 36 degrees F. at the surface and in the lower thirties some four feet beneath the surface. As this was much above the 28.6 degrees F. freezing point of sea water, the high temperatures were accompanied by a gradual melting and rotting away of the bay ice all the way to Red Rock Ridge. While the overall ice sheet was fairly solid still, there were pools of open water everywhere. We had to pick our way out to the ship around large patches of water and numerous soft spots. Occasionally a man walking over a soft spot would go through into the icy water up to his knees or hips before being stopped by a layer of solid ice beneath. After a few such incidents, everyone learned to use skis for greater safety when traveling over the ice. The ship itself was surrounded by a seven foot wide lead of open water, was floating completely free, and even swinging from side to side. In order to get aboard her, one of the tide rifts had been rigged so that men could step on it from the bay ice and by a line pull themselves across the patch of open water to the ship's side. The ice really was in such poor condition that we felt one good strong southeasterly wind of a few days duration would break it up and carry it out to sea.

Saturday, January 10, 1948

The fellows went out to the ship again today. I worked hard on Don's story and two other messages. When Don came back from the ship, I got him to read it. With minor changes, he approved what I had written and I got it ready to go out tonight. Finn has just about finished working on the naming of the southern discovered features and is now writing an article for the publication of them. After dinner Finn and I skied out to the ship where we saw pools of water all around it. The musketeers had five barrels of snow melting for water. We had a movie, "God is My Co-Pilot". The British were over. Finn told Lassiter, he was naming the barrier coastline for him. Jim was very, very pleased.

Wednesday, January 14, 1948

John came over this afternoon to tell Finn that Ken was at the top of Bill's gulch and as soon as the weather improved, it would take them two days to get back. He spent the whole afternoon chatting and seemed to be enjoying himself. I worked on messages the rest of the afternoon.

Bob Dodson and Latady came back this evening with the British five dog team. Latady wanted to make up a message for the Photogrametric Society's Annual Meeting on January 21. Larry Fiske came in for a chat. After we had some cocoa, Don came in fairly late. After Larry left, Don started on the business he had obviously come in to transact. He said he and Jorge wanted to go out to the penguin rookery for a few days. After Finn discussed the safety of the ice conditions with him for a while, Don said, he thought that for the good of the man, for Finn's good and the good of the expedition, it would help if Mac could go out in the field for a few days with the dogs he had trained. Finn very logically and diplomatically discussed Mac's situation with Don. Don agreed that Mac had a sarcastic tongue, but said he was anxious to stay out of the whole thing, that he knew Mac pretty well and his opinion was that if he got out, it would benefit everyone. Finn said, he would think it over, talk to Ike and let Don know tomorrow.

Thursday, January 15, 1948

Ike came in at Finn's request this morning and was in his usual morning's foul humor. It was almost impossible to talk to him. He tried to argue with Finn about everything. He said the ice may not go out this year. Finn had been wrong about the Weddell Coast trend, so why shouldn't he be wrong about this. Of course, this was silly because Finn made no predictions about the trend of the Weddell Coast, except to Ike in fun. Then they began arguing about previous ice conditions here and whether the Bear could have rescued them last time. Finn finally, got him to the point and asked him if he could and wanted to spare Don, Jorge, and Mac to go over to the Penguin Rookery for a couple of days. Ike said, yes, he could do that as the fellows had been working hard on the ship. Finn said, before they went he wanted the rest of the airplane parts taken on board and the ship finished up, that was Mac's job and the reason why he had been brought along. Ike said, he saw the whole thing and that other people hadn't worked beside Mac, etc. Ike agreed that Mac had a bad tongue, but there was something wrong with them all, as they all did nothing but show passive resistance. He said, Latady was just fooling around with Nichols so why couldn't Mac. He said, if Finn had a reason for sending somebody someplace it was O.K., but if anyone else had a reason for something, it was wrong. Ike seemed to have forgotten Finn was leading the expedition and his reasons were the ones that counted. Ike said, the aviation gang wouldn't even help load their equipment aboard ship and if they ever complained that the Ship's crew wrecked anything, he would write a letter to the Army explaining it and calling Lassiter down. Now only a few days ago, Ike said he wouldn't have them around, that they could take care of the stuff, but he wouldn't be around the ship when they were there and he just wanted them to bring the stuff out to the Ship's side and the ship's crew would load it. Now, of course, he has changed his mind. Finn asked him if any lugs had been broken off the Norseman engine in loading it. Ike said, no, who told you there had been. Then he blew up at Robertson saying he was nothing but a troublemaker and he would punch him in the nose as soon as he got off the Ship, if he ever had the opportunity. The conversation didn't get very far. Finn went out to see if Lassiter's selected landing place for the L-5 was crevasse free and safe enough.

By this time, the L-5 no longer was of much use. The bay ice take-off field was broken-up sufficiently to present a risk of the plane's skis going through the leads. Finn and I went up on the glacier to investigate a possible landing field, but there too, the melting had brought to view the numerous huge gapping crevasses which we knew existed, but which the winter's snows had covered. Furthermore, the summer weather had broken many of the snow bridges across these crevasses and the whole area was extremely dangerous for traveling over, even with a dog team, let alone a plane.

Finn decided the safest thing to do would be to take the plane on board ship and secure it and call the flying program over with. The fellows stored the airplane parts aboard ship.

Finn called Don in and told him that after the ship was squared away and he wrote the second article on health, he could go to the Rookery for a few days. He also told him to tell Mac if he wanted to go to come and speak to him personally about it. This took Don back a bit, but he said he would.

Woody, Robertson, Lassiter, and Adams came in for some coffee. Woody started to bawl Robertson out for not cooperating, saying that he was only doing harm to the expedition. After dinner, Lassiter and Woody finished filling the ship's third tank and then filled the snow melter with water. Finn, Sig, and I skied about a mile from the end of the Island with Latady and Dodson on their way back to join Nichols. The ice is certainly rotten and we went through to slush in several places. The generator was knocking so Kelsey stopped working early.

Friday, January 16, 1947

Mac still hasn't come to ask Finn if he can go with Don. If he does Finn plans to ask Mac for a written apology for his actions on the expedition, before he lets him go. Finn told Robertson to take the L-5 out to the Ship and ask Ike to see that it was taken on board. Finn went out to take pictures of its being loaded. Everyone was bitching at the other fellow, but mostly everyone was bitching at Robertson, because Ike had sent McLean to ask Robertson to take the ailerons off the Norseman. Robertson said, he would only do it if Ike asked him personally. Woody gave him hell saying he was holding up the work of the expedition by worrying about technicalities. Robertson refused to work. Lassiter did pitch in and help. Finn feels that the wings are placed in the wrong position and Lassiter says they might as well be thrown over board, for they will be ruined.

I worked on a dog story and Dodson's story of a typical day on the trail. Larry came in for a chat in the afternoon and then Jorge to explain to Finn why he had not been out on the ship. Lassiter was mad, because Finn asked him not to send a message to his mother saying he didn't want her to meet him and ride back on the ship from Panama, because we had a faulty steering gear which Finn didn't think was appropriate to advertise. Hassage refused to have anything more to do with the diesel generator at the Base, said he would work on the ship from now on. There is definitely something wrong with the generator and Finn is worrying about how long it will last. If it goes, we are completely without power. Hassage says, he doesn't care about any radio publicity, he doesn't realize the weather and all the business arrangements which go through as well and the money to finance the expedition is coming from that source.

Larry brought in the first flag which was flown on the ship and during our voyage south and the first one which was flown at the Base. I took a walk with him up to the flagpole to change the flag, which he does every three weeks. We saw the British dogs from Hope Bay, funny looking brutes. We received a lot of messages from the States tonight, one from my aunt.

Saturday, January 17, 1948

Finn called Don over and asked him if he was still planning to go over to the Rookery. He said, yes indeed, he certainly was. Finn asked him if he had inspected the ice conditions. He said, no, but he thought they would be all right. Finn advised him to take a good look at them and pick out his route before hand. He then asked him who would be going along. Don said the thought Jorge and Mac. He said, Mac intended coming in and speaking to him this evening. About that time, Mac came walking over and told Finn he would like to go. Finn said that would be all right, but first he wanted Mac to give him a written letter of apology for his actions during the expedition against Finn and against the best interests of the expedition and that all would be forgotten and he could go. Mac said to Don, "I guess you and Jorge better plan to go alone."

Mac said to Finn, "You are not serious are you, you must be nuts".

Finn said, "Yes, Mac I am serious. If you were in the Navy and acted the way you have, you would have been thrown out long ago and you know it."

Mac said, "Well, I'm not in the Navy now and neither are you, that's what's wrong with you".

Finn said, "There is nothing wrong with me, Mac".

Mac said, "I don't know what you want me to apologize for, I haven't done anything".

Finn said, "I want a written apology from you for everything you have done and your vicious tongue has said, since you first tried to start a mutiny on the ship up to the present time. Even after you came to speak to me the last time, you still couldn't keep from bitching about me behind my back, about those pool table slabs on board. Even after I told you to stop it and control your nasty tongue, you still had to bitch behind my back".

Mac was surprised at this. Mac said again, "You must be nuts to really ask me for an apology".

Finn said, No Mac, I'm not nuts, but I'm inclined to think you are," and skied away.

Woody, Chuck Adams, Lassiter, and Robertson came in for a chat in the evening. They stayed until pretty late and we had a good time.

Sunday, January 18, 1948

We got up late as usual. Finn discussed Don's trip with him at breakfast. Mac sitting nearby had a long face. Finn wrote a memo to Don telling him to go prepared with trail equipment and a radio and, if the ice was bad to join Nichols and come back with him. He called Don in to give the memo to him and discuss the trip. Don said, he fully agreed. Finn told him it was too bad Mac didn't come to his senses and meet Finn half way. Finn said, "You know Don I have met you half way". Don said, yes, he was very glad their difficulties had been straightened out, but he said you are asking Mac to meet you more than half way and say that he is all wrong. Finn said, with his attitude, his very vicious tongue criticizing everything I have done, talking against me and trying to get others to go along with him and against me, he is all wrong. Then Finn told him about the incident concerning the Tricorn pictures that Mac had taken and concealed, and I recalled to his mind the things Hassage reported to me. Don raised his eyebrows about this and said no more about Mac.

Finn told him the history of the Bear, in which he was interested and Don left soon after. Finn skied out to the ship to take some things on board. Hassage has moved on board and has asked for Woody to help him. Finn told Woody to move on board too.

Monday, January 19, 1948

About the same thing today – nothing unusual except the weather was pretty chilly. Finn went aboard ship and found Pete working on his Cosmic ray apparatus. They got into a discussion and Pete told Finn that a group of them came into the Science Bldg. the other night and began discussing Finn's inconsistencies. Pete said, "For instance, why did you tell Mac he could have Kasco and then three days later you took him away?"

Finn said, "If I tell you I saw Mac using a 35 foot, 14 lb. dog whip on that six month old puppy, would you think it logical that I told him not to use that puppy?"

Pete said, "Yes, that certainly is logical. They didn't mention that when they told me about it."

Finn said, "No, of course, they didn't. They only give you their side of the story, naturally." Everything Finn said to Pete he had to admit was true. Then Pete told Finn that he knew that Harry had a lot of Finn's stuff in his possession. He said, the Philosophical Society Publication, the Antarctic Pilot and some of Finn's maps.

Tuesday, January 20, 1948

Late this afternoon it began snowing. Everyone halted to see this as it is not good for the melting ice. The fellows had a movie, "Murder My Sweet", but we didn't go, as I was working on a message to Burr Brundage in answer to the nice one we received from him last night, thanking Finn for naming the mountain and requesting some information from Finn for the publication of his article. Received a message from Dr. John K. Wright of the American Geographical Society tonight requesting an article from Finn for the Geographical Review.

After the movie, John Tonkin came in to tell Finn that the Joint Trail Party was near the Met Station on the Plateau waiting for weather to clear, before they came down on the next clear day. John opened up with us more than he has ever done before. He said, that Fiske had given each of them an American flag that they didn't know what to do with, and the one he gave to John, he said was the one flown on the Port of Beaumont on the way down. We laughed heartily.

John told Finn that he could certainly be thankful that he had a thoroughly and highly successful expedition. Finn said, yes, but I've had to fight every inch of the way. John said yes, I know you have, but if you ever need it at any time, I want you to know you can always count on me to make a statement on your behalf and there are many of us over there, who feel the same way about it. He also said, he thought their statements would mean more than anything anyone could say against Finn. John also said, that the British Government was seriously considering decorating Lassiter and Adams for their work during the search.

Wednesday, January 21, 1948

It snowed hard all last night. The clear rocks were completely covered again. We were all wondering, if there was a chance the ice would not go out again this year. The day was clear and sunny, but the temperature was down to 22 degrees last night. Finn and I took a ski trip on the glacier and looked at the crevasses. The top of the Plateau looked clear, so we thought Ken would probably be in tonight. After dinner, I sent out a good story on the naming of the Alexander Island features.

Mac, Harry, and Jennie went out to meet the returning Don and Jorge. Sig made Finn and me some fresh eggs and about one o'clock we went over to the British side to count the coal bags. Finn estimated them to be between 125 – 150. Sig said, at least 250. The temperature stood at 17 degrees and everything was freezing. All the water holes in the Bay Ice had thin coats of ice formed over them. The matter is beginning to get serious. During the day, Lassiter brought in a telegram he wanted to send to the Army for him to stay down here for another year. We postponed his sending it out until Saturday.

Thursday, January 22, 1948

Ken, Dougie, Art, and Smitty on the Joint British-American Sledge Party got in at 7 o'clock this morning. They covered about 1,005 miles. Smitty has been out for 115 days and has done an excellent job. Right away, Mac took Art to the Blubber Shack to talk to him. Then Don McLean got hold of Art. Ken and Dougie came over around 2 o'clock and then Art and Smitty came in. Finn took them out by the dog team and took their pictures. Then, they came back and we had some champagne, coffee, cookies and nuts. We had a nice chat exchanging information. Ken doesn't like trail work too much. He lost way over 20 lb. After they left, Smitty stayed and we caught him up, on some of the news of happenings while he was away. Smitty was happy that he had a chance to prove himself. Robertson came in for a chat in the afternoon. He said, the opposition was making a strong attempt to get Art Owen on their side and it would be too bad, if they did. He said Mac took him out to the Blubber shack immediately, for a long while. Then Don got a hold of him. He said he and Lassiter and Adams would talk to him as soon as possible and try to set him straight. He said, Smitty was O.K., of course, and hoped Finn would make him Mate on the way back.

Around 10:30, Lassiter, Adams, Pete, and Larry got back from their atmospheric refraction trip to Neny. Lassiter told us immediately, that they had followed Don's advice and, of course, climbed the mountain the wrong way and met a dead end at about 700 or 800 feet up. He thought Don had done it purposely to mislead them. They met many rock slides and had a hard time, generally. Pete was very pleased with the refraction measurements he and Larry had taken before the clouds came in. All of them laughingly agreed, that they would not let the rest know that they didn't reach the top.

Friday, January 23, 1948

Finn got up early, had Art and Smitty in for a nice chat about their trip and told them to take a week off and write a report of their trip. They were very pleased with this. Finn took their pictures with the sledge wheel and meter and had a long chat with Ken. I started to work on the book and then Kelsey came in. He got on the subject of Harry and wanted to know his background, so we had a lengthy discussion. He said that Jorge knew one of the men, who had signed a paper against Harry and wondered how he knew. He said, that he had underestimated how dumb Harry really was.

After chow, Finn and I went with Lassiter, Adams, Robertson, Smitty, and Woody out to the Ship. They blew off some more charges of RDX to loosen up the ice in front of the Ship. Finn and Robertson took pictures. Woody didn't have much to say. After we came back, Smitty came in with a message for Finn to sign. We got to talking and he stated he was going to try to find out what the Darlingtons planned to do to cause trouble in the States. He said, he thought they would leave the Ship at the first port we hit, probably Valparaiso. He said, they would fly back and try to cause trouble before we arrived. He said, that before he left the Base 115 days ago, that he was present when Jennie said, "I'll run those bastards out of Washington," referring to Finn and me.

In this sort of atmosphere, it goes without saying why I hadn't had much traffic with Jennie in recent weeks.

Smitty gained about 5 pounds on the trail. Art and Dougie stayed about the same and Ken lost 25 lb. They ate 63 lb. of butter. Smitty said, he was very serious about his work and that he put up with an awful lot with Ike coming down aboard Ship. He said, "Jennie and Harry are the worst of the worst, totally impossible; that Jennie is worse than a bar fly." He said, he found out from Ken that the Grenfeld Mission in Labrador, where Harry has been, was a place where rich people send their wayward sons at great expense, to be straightened out and have some sense knocked into their heads.

Sunday, January 25, 1948

Art Owen and Don McLean left around 5:00 o'clock this morning to climb Figure IV Mountain. I have been working pretty hard on the book and Finn has been working on the American Geographical Society's article. I spent all afternoon and evening typing numbers for Harcly Peterson, on his atmospheric refraction measurements taken since he left. The fellows did a lot more blasting of the ice – Lassiter, Adams, and Robertson. Ike didn't think they should use the dynamite, because we may need it later, actually, to get out. Someone put up a transit or the odolite and we could see the camp of McLean and Owen on Figure IV. Harry, Jennie, Mac, and Fiske went out on a dog team ride. They were gone for nine hours and Fiske came running in afterward, to tell Finn about the ice conditions and see that he was still on good terms. Lassiter got very steamed up about all the guns and ammunition, which is missing. He was particularly concerned about his carbine ammunition issued by the Government. He was the only one who had a gun along, which could use that kind of ammunition. A long time ago this ammunition was missing from his baggage. Fiske turned up with some, saying he had brought it along. This didn't make sense. Lassiter got Finn to write him up a memorandum saying that a recent message from Army Supply at Dayton had requested Adams and Lassiter to hold an inventory of all Government property on the expedition and each man was to list the Government property in his possession, copies of which would be turned over to the Army. Finn did this and Lassiter started in on it. There was a great deal to do for several hours, Jorge saying he would write a nasty letter to the Army Air Force upon his return, but the missing guns and ammunition started to come in. Fiske turned over the carbine ammunition saying, he had gotten it from Swadell, who must have taken it. Everything now is blamed on Swadell, who was sent back from Valparaiso,Chile. Today was the one year anniversary since we left Beaumont.

Monday, January 26, 1948

We worked in shack all day. Hassage and others on Ship worked on port windless and got it operating. McLean and Owen were supposed to come back from Figure IV. A light haze was around the mountain most of the day, but plenty visible for them to come back, had they so desired. Around dinnertime or after, it began snowing and the visibility to the mountain became completely obscured.

There was a movie at night and Ken came over for it. He came in here afterward and we had some fresh eggs, which he greatly enjoyed. He told Finn, he would have to go back to England first and then, if he could use Finn for a recommendation, he intended to immigrate to the States, as soon thereafter as possible. He said, he thought the British-American cooperation down here was the greatest thing yet. He said that 13 Chilean and Argentine ships, 3/4 Argentine, were all over the Peninsula to the north of us and building bases alongside all of the British Bases. On Deception, they are building a huge runway. They have a four-motored Douglas and a smaller sea plane. One flew within twenty-five miles of this camp and dropped flags. They are apparently bent on causing the British trouble. Because both the U.S. and Britain are here, they evidently think something worth while is going on and want to get in on it. Ken doesn't think Harry or any of them can cause Finn any trouble whatsoever on his return. Ken stayed until about 2:15 a.m. We had a nice chat. The "John Biscoe" arrived in Port Stanley, Falkland Islands, on the 25th and will probably be here by the end of February.

Tuesday, January 27, 1948

The most outstanding thing of the day was that after dinner, Jorge came in to have a talk with Finn. He began by saying that he would feel pretty low, if he could not come in and tell Finn how appreciative he was to Finn for giving him the opportunity to go to the Plateau Weather Station and on the sledge trip. He said, that he was glad of that opportunity and felt he had done something on the expedition in the Antarctic. He said, he had wanted to come in for a long time, but that Don had told him not to and had threatened him that, if he came in to talk to Finn, things would go worse for him. He said, he was just beginning to realize how wrong that group of Harry, Don and Mac were, that he had told them so, and didn't want to be a part of their intrigue any more. He said, that when Finn had asked him if he wanted to go to the Plateau, Harry had tried to persuade him not to go, saying there was nothing up there, the weather was miserable and all he would be doing was to keep uninteresting records. Harry told Jorge not to be loyal to Finn, or the expedition that it didn't pay to be loyal. He said, that Harry wanted him to go back on the first Chilean Ship that came in here and to forget about the expedition. He said, Harry intended to send Jennie back with Chinook on the first ship. Jorge said, he realized Harry was trying to work against the expedition to hurt it, that he realized Harry hadn't told him the truth. He said he (Jorge) didn't want Harry to wreck the work he had done, or what the expedition had accomplished. He said, he wanted to go back to Chile with the expedition and that he would even like to go back to the United States with the expedition. He said, his father would be plenty angry with him, if he ever found out that he hadn't supported Finn as the Leader. He said, Harry was fast losing the supporters to his bad aims and he was trying desperately hard to keep them, or get others. Jorge said, Harry had offered him everything except an introduction to a banker on Wall Street, to stay on his side and work against the expedition. He said, he realized it would do him no good and that Harry just wanted his support, for Harry's own personal bad aims. He said, he didn't realize at first that Jennie was involved, that he had asked her why she didn't come have dinner at the table with the rest of them. He said, she said she wasn't feeling well and had to stay in her room. He said, he realized that she was as bad as the rest of them, when they held their conferences in her room and bitched against Finn. He said he had been under a great deal of pressure from Harry, Don, and Mac to be on their side. He said, they had also talked to Art and Smitty, as soon as they got back from the trail, but that he didn't think Harry had any chance of getting their support to his bad aims. Jorge said, that Latady was no longer welcome in the Darlingtons' room as their friend, because Bill had done such good work for the expedition. Finn thanked him for all this information and asked him, if he was man enough to remain loyal. Jorge said yes, Don would probably do something to him, but he could take it. Finn said fine, you do a good job and go your own way, Lassiter is a good friend to you and he will tell you what is right.

Wednesday, January 28, 1948

I spent the day working on Finn's article. We got a request from Town and Country to do another article. After dinner, Finn went in to get a bucket of water and found McLean showing a movie to Harry, Jennie, Mac, and a few others, Hassage, Jorge, Smitty, and Chuck Adams. McLean had not asked Finn's permission and had not even told him about it. Finn was furious. He said, Don should have gotten his permission, because only he knew how much work Kelsey would have before the generator was turned off. Then the movie should be open for everyone, including the British and not to just a private showing. Andy was in here working on a earthquake article with me. Pete came in to find out why Finn had taken such a strong stand on the movie question. Both he and Andy agreed that group didn't like Finn, but Pete tried to convince him not to let it worry him and to just tolerate them until the expedition was over, that they could do nothing because the expedition had been a great success. Lassiter and Adams came in later to get Finn's opinion about whether they sould accept the offer of a Commission in the Active Reserve Corps.

Thursday, January 29, 1948

I worked all day getting an article out on the sledge trip's return based on notes written by Art Owen. Finn invited Ken and John for dinner and then a movie afterward. I was still working on the article during the movie, when Bob Nichols, Latady, and Dodson got back from the trail. Nichols came in very pleased saying, in the 29 days he had been out this trip, 13 were spent completely on geology, whereas, before he had spent 90 days and only 28 on geology. He said, he wanted to go out for a few more days to Neny and Figure IV and finish up his work. He said, he was going to write a strong letter to Aldrich of the Geological Society and tell him how wonderful Finn had been to him and how much Finn had done to help him in his work. Bob got caught up on the news. He was anxious to go back into New York instead of Beaumont, was pleased with our publicity, was sorry to hear about Harry's malicious attitude, but said he couldn't hurt Finn. He was surprised at how funny Ike turned out to be and couldn't understand why he was so evasive, when Bob asked him to go on a short trip with him. Bob left and Ken and John came in again. We chatted about things in general until midnight, then they left. Received a good message from Wilkins. Larry said, the Armed Forces Radio Programs "Here Are the Answers" announced that next week their topic would be, "What is the Finn Ronne Expedition Doing in the Antarctic". Good News!

Friday, January 30, 1948

Smitty came in this morning to read the article on his trail trip, which went out last night. We got to talking and he said, the other night Harry had come over to his bunk and talked to him for four hours, trying to get him to see his side of things, but Smitty said, "As you know, he didn't convince me." Smitty said, he was convinced that Harry was going to make every effort to leave the expedition as soon as possible and get back to the States, to start trouble for Finn. He said, "Harry was very bitter and very hurt and was going to get even with Finn." Smitty said Harry told him, "You know Smitty, wars are won and lost at cocktail parties", and that Harry had also said, "You know it entered my mind that if I was caught by Finn, he might do what he did to me, but then I decided, oh!, he couldn't, 'cause my name is Darlington. But I'll be god damn if he didn't do it anyway." Smitty said he couldn't believe his ears, that Harry actually had the conceit to say such a thing. He said the whole damn thing was childish, but that Harry was very dangerous and that he hoped he would cause no trouble, but if he did, Finn could count on Smitty to be 100% in back of him.

Saturday, January 31, 1948

The usual thing. I was quite tired and disgusted. Nichols came in several times and we had nice conversations. He is quite enthusiastic about all that the expedition has accomplished. In the afternoon, Nichols, Finn, and I took a ski half way to Neny. The ice looked rotten, but when you actually get out on it, you can easily see that it is thick and strong still. It would be hard for the ship to get out now. What we need is a strong wind from the N.W. and then one from the S.E. It is more solid now than it was last year this time. On the way, we saw John Tonkin and two of the new Britishers raising a pole on one of the high rocks up from their camp. By dinner time, we noticed that the British flag was flying from it. They must have some news that some of the Chilean or Argentine ships are coming in soon. The British ship, the, "John Biscoe", is ready to leave the Falklands.

Sunday, February 1, 1948

Kelsey was in for a while in the evening and later Jorge came in. He is trying awfully hard to be nice and to show he is sorry for the way he has acted, in the hopes Finn will take him back to the States. Everyone is trying to find out our port of entry, but Finn can't say anything yet.

Monday, February 2, 1948

I tried to work on the Town and Country article, but I have run out of ideas. After a page, I gave it over to Finn, who is fresher in his imagination. I started on my article for the Saturday Evening Post. Bill Latady did lots of work yesterday with Woody. He was in for a brief chat last night and today for a while. Robertson is working on the Beech report. Pete wanted to go camping at Figure IV with Dodson for three days, but Finn discouraged him. This put him in a bad humor for a few hours, but after dinner he came around and gave us a long chat on the weather and when we could expect winds to clean the ice out. Briefly, he can't see any in the near future as the barometer is remaining pretty steady. Bob Nichols left for several days at Neny with the British Geologist. Dodson will ski over to Figure IV daily to do some work on his own. Pete will go with him one day and Art Owen came in to ask permission to go another day. Ike does not want to go with Nichols. He seems pretty well fed up with the whole bunch. We see little of him these days. Everyone seems to be in a pretty good mood.

Wednesday, February 4, 1948

Smitty, Kelsey and Ike began work on the Radio Direction Finder again. We had a stream of traffic in here all day, Lassiter, Robertson, and Kelsey. Robertson said, that Jorge had come to his bunk last night and told him, that Mac, Don, and Harry had jumped on him and accused him of being a Tunnel Runner and told him things would go hard with him, if he continued. Jorge said, Harry still threatens to use money to wreck the expedition. Harry does not want Jorge to go to the U.S. Robertson said again, that Harry tried to get him and Latady to drop out of the aviation program, if he (Harry) didn't run it and make the expedition a failure. Received a message from Dr. Wright, that the article could be published in the July issue of the AGS review. Kelsey was in here all evening. Later, Bob Dodson brought Britisher Ray Aidy in, who had just come back from Nichols. Ray is from South Africa and we had a most interesting chat with him. Finn got a message from Norway that they were trying to contact him every day. Kelsey went on the radio at 3 o'clock trying to get them, but didn't succeed.

Thursday, February 5, 1948

Finn, Kelsey, Bill, and I skied over to Neny to say hello to Nichols. The ice was firm and hard. Kelsey had a great deal of trouble on skis, but enjoyed the trip. There were large leads around Nichols' camp, but we managed to get over them. There we found Fiske, Adams, Woody, and Hassage. Nichols was overwhelmed with guests. Finn was upset that they were eating up all of Nichols' food.

We didn't stay long, but came back for dinner. That night, we heard the radio station WOL broadcast program "Here Are the Answers". They spoke for a few minutes on what the Finn Ronne Expedition was accomplishing in the Antarctic. They gave a good boost to the scientific program, but had the aviation program wrong. They mentioned the two women being here for the first time and that Mrs. Harry Darlington was the wife of the Chief Pilot. They had the mileage flown wrong. Kelsey came in for the evening's chat. Kelsey was to work the States amateurs and try to get Norway. We sent a message answering Beaumont tonight.

Friday, February 6, 1948

Finn and Bob Dodson went to the Ship this morning to clean out a locker in the after hole. When they came back, Finn said that the locker room had been broken into and that his box, which contained a pad lock, had been opened. The lock had been broken off and thrown away. There was an empty space in the box where things had been taken out. The box contained photographic material for albums to be made up for expedition members. Finn was so disgusted, he will not have that done for everyone now. He had some of the books, which Steffanson had given him in there and he thinks some of these are missing. But, the worst part is that, he found only one, one hundred-foot roll of exposed 16 mm colored film marked Tricorn. He knows he had additional rolls in the box, but is not sure of how many. Chuck Adams, who helped him pack the box, thinks there were six or seven rolls. Everyone we told about the loss was amazed and thinks it is the most serious and despicable thing, which has happened yet. These persons are: Robertson, Sig, Lassiter, Adams, Thompson, Fiske and Kelsey. I was most discouraged about the thing and very bitter. The sad part is that nothing can be done about it. We got a very nice message from Tuve this evening. Fiske said, his box had been opened too, everything was in shambles and the hinges crudely put back on. Robertson is completely unable to find the sewing machine tables he took on board and thinks they were thrown over the side by accident or design. I cer-

tainly will be glad to see the last of this bunch of thieves. I could not believe that grown men could act this way. It was indeed a revelation.

Sunday, February 8, 1948

Bob Nichols came back early this morning. He has 146 days in the field now and 51 days on geology and is very pleased. It was snowing all day.

Wednesday, February 11, 1948

It blew hard again all day. Finn called Don in and asked him for the medical report, now one day overdue. He said, he didn't realize how the time had passed. Finn told him not to use the limping dog, but he said in his medical opinion, it was all right as the dog was in no pain and would get no better. Finn said, it was a cardinal rule of the Antarctic not to use a limping dog and he did not want that dog used. Don said, in other words, you don't have confidence in my opinion as a doctor. Finn said, that was not the question, but that he did not want the dog used.

Finn spoke with Latady again about the British and they chatted with Jim and later Larry. Lassiter said, he had talked with Tommy last night and that it was his (Lassiter's) opinion that the British did not intend to give Finn the material, pictures and astronomical fixes apply to all the discoveries on the Joint British and American Sledge Party along the Weddell Sea Coast. Larry said, that conversations about getting the pictures began at Keeler with Dick Butson. He said, Ken had asked him the other day, whether Bill had developed any of the pictures. Larry said, he didn't know and asked Ken, if it was in the agreement that Ken receive the pictures, as he thought they belonged to the U.S. Air Forces. Ken said, he had forgotten and that he would have to read the agreement, but that he intended to abide by it. Larry also said, that Bill had spoken to Dougie last night about the fixes, but that Dougie said, he hadn't had time to work on it. Larry thought Finn should talk to Ken and Finn agreed. Larry was just about ready to call Ken, when Ken himself came over. Finn told him immediately, that rumor had it, they weren't going to give us the information in the agreement, until they got the pictures. Ken apologized for not coming over sooner, they had been awfully busy, but that he would certainly give Finn all the information he wanted and what they couldn't work up now, they would send to him from the U.K. He said, he was sorry for the rumors, but they would get the information over, immediately.

Ken and I went into see the movie, Fred MacMurray and Claudette Colbert in, "Practically Yours". Jennie was there. When we came back Ken spoke to Finn saying that, from what he was able to observe, he thought the two camps were not as friendly, as they had been before he left and that he wondered, if John had caused the difficulty while he was away. Finn explained John's attitude to Lassiter and himself and Ken apologized saying, John was immature and didn't know what Finn and Ken knew. Finn said, our group was more of a unit now, but that he didn't think anything else was up. Ken said, above everything else, he wanted both camps to leave with a friendly feeling toward each other and wanted to have a little get together before they left. Finn said O.K. and questioned about their ship coming in dispensing liquor to the fellows. Ken said, all liquor and cigarettes would be bonded, as soon as the ship hit this port. Everything was straightened out 100% and it was the friendly old Ken again. We had a nice chat and he left about 2 o'clock.

Loading planes onto ship for return journey

XVII

Ships Ahoy!

Thursday, February 12, 1947

We were just getting to sleep after Butler left, when Kelsey, who was still transmitting, picked up the first of a series of messages received from Comdr. Gerald Ketchum, Commodore of Task Force #39, which consisted of two United States Navy icebreakers, the "U.S.S. Burton Island" and the "U.S.S. Edisto", at the time operating in Antarctic waters to the west of us:

> *"Due your vicinity in about two weeks. Can we be of any assistance?"*
>
> *Signed, Ketchum*

Finn replied that same morning and stated,

> *"Greatly appreciated your message. Hope to see you soon. Strong winds now blowing might clear Marguerite Bay ice now extending a couple of miles from Camp. Expect depart for U.S. approximately 15 March. Job done and all well. Trust you had excellent success. Let's keep radio contact. Regards."*

Finn announced today that the message had been received from the "Burton Island" and that he had answered it. This relieved everyone a great deal. Before he announced it at dinner, he had a talk with Ike. It was a very nice talk and Ike seems to have regained his equilibrium.

Dougie spent the whole afternoon giving Finn the information on the fixes and mentioned that he was very annoyed, that any rumor had started that the British weren't going to provide us with the information. He said, the rest would be sent to Finn, as soon as he returned and could work up the final information. After Finn made the announcement about the icebreakers at dinner, he called up Ken and told him about it. Ken was very pleased and said he would be over tomorrow for a chat.

Friday, February 13, 1948

This was a big day. We worked all day in here.

Although the message indicated the Breakers would be in our vicinity, we were not certain that Ketcham definitely planned to pay a visit to our Base. If the Breakers were coming in regardless, their presence would offer us an excellent opportunity to follow in their wake to the open sea, even if it had to be a few weeks ahead of schedule. However, if we adopted this procedure, we would have to step up our plans to evacuate and so on the following day, Finn sent him another message:

> *"Am interested in knowing whether you definitely plan to make stop in Marguerite Bay. Winds which are still blowing intermittently seem to be helping remove ice now a few miles to open sea. Height of warm spell here is over and freezing weather might overtake area before ice has a chance to go out. Thickness of ice varies from one and one-half to three and one-half feet. I feel there is a possibility that ice will not go out. Should this be the case, I would be most appreciative of your valuable assistance, and would be interested in knowing the latest date you could remain in this area, so that we can prepare to move up our departure date according to your schedule if necessary. Regards."*

Finn called Ike and Hassage in and discussed it. He told them to have the ship ready to go by March 1st. At dinner time, he received an answer to the message. His reply was as follows:

> *"Definitely intend to visit your area arriving about 23 February and departing not later than 1 March. I am committed to being in Callao, Peru on 12 March. Will be glad to render any assistance possible during time available. Ketchum."*

That fairly settled the matter. The possibility of having to remain another year in the Antarctic if the bay ice did not go out for the sake of a few more weeks of recordings, important as they were to our scientific program, was too great a risk to take. We would depart with the Icebreakers. From then on, we exchanged weather information on daily schedules. Up until the day the Breakers arrived, our winds continued intermittently but in the wrong direction and our weather was generally bad.

When Finn announced the news of our impending departure, the camp was electrified and buzzed with activity and excitement.

Everyone got to work immediately. Don even handed in his medical report. It was a dreadful thing. He had not given one examination, but just wrote it up. He had a regular bitch session in it, about the Bunkhouse. What a disgusting guy.

Ken came over and planned to have the "Biscoe" take advantage of the icebreaker too. He told us quite a great deal about the Argentines and Chileans moving into their territory and establishing bases, north of here. The Chilean President is to come down and open one of the bases tomorrow. The British have protested and asked the Chileans and Argentines to discuss it, in the World Court, but they refuse to do so. We heard two broadcasts over the BBC. We also received, an unsigned message from the State Department, regarding British thanks for assistance. Finn told Ken the story. We got another message from ONR (Office of Naval Research) requesting a one thousand word story for the "Fleet Magazine." After Ken left, Jorge came in to sit and chat. He wants to go to the

States badly. After he left, I worked on the story for Navy's ONR until four in the morning.

There were innumerable things to be done. We had to finish loading our ship and in all ways make her ready for sea. We were very fortunate to have started this loading process some weeks before, as the job is one of enormous magnitude.The scientists were the group most effected by the hurried change in plans trying to keep up with their observations and at the same time get their gear packed and crated.

The British were as excited as we. They felt that unless their ship were able to get down in time to utilize the path broken by the Icebreakers, there was a good possibility all of them would have to remain another year. That they took a dim view of this prospect, as they so aptly expressed it, was putting it mildly. Butler had been in constant radio communication with the Governor of the Falkland Islands and strongly urged him to order the *"Biscoe"* to this, their southernmost outpost, without delay. The "John Bisco", a sister ship to the "Port of Beaumont", had been acquired recently from the United States Government by the British Government. We knew that the Icebreakers would want to leave as soon as we were ready, but Finn offered to take the British personnel out on our ship. Butler, of course, would have to remain until the new leader took over, even if it meant staying for another year. We would plan to rendezvous with the "Biscoe" at some one of their northern bases, preferably Deception Island. Butler accepted and for a few days that was the Plan.

Saturday, February 14, 1948

Dick Butson came over this morning to say that his wife could not get enough money together for the Stateside journey, so that he would not be going back on the Ship with us and thanked Finn. Finn asked him, if he had tended anyone in this camp medically, while Don McLean was on the trail. He said, yes, he had treated several people. Finn asked if Mrs. Darlington was one of those persons. He said, that Harry had asked his advice about the case and he had treated her, but that Harry had asked him to keep the matter confidential, which he agreed to do. Finn said, he already knew that she had been pregnant. Dick said yes, well if you know it, it doesn't seem to much matter. Finn said, he wanted Dick to give him a medical report for that period and that he assumed, if Jennie was pregnant then she was still. Dick said, he supposed she was and said. he had quite well been prepared to say that she should leave the Antarctic, as soon as possible in her condition, on the first ship, even if it were a British ship. He said he would like to speak to Harry first, but that he would give Finn a medical report for that time.

All the fellows were working today, trying to get things squared away. It blew most of the day off and on. The Burton Island asked us to give them daily weather reports, which we did. They are off of Cape Dart today. At dinner Finn read McLean's recommendations with regard to camp. Everyone was silent but Harry, jaw lagging, muttered and mumbled something nasty at his end of the table. We had Robertson, Lassiter, Adams, and Fiske in for coffee in the afternoon. Listened to nice radio music during evening. Kelsey got off the ONR requested article I had written for the fleet magazine.

Sunday, February 15, 1948

We worked here hard all day, Finn on the final map and I wrote a dog story, a message from Finn to Spun Sun and a weather story. Bill went through the pictures for NANA and Andy got me to send out a seismograph code. Don came in and wanted to go out in the field with Nichols, saying Bob had been pressing him. Finn told him he couldn't go as he had too much to do. Nichols then pressed for Latady, who knew some geology and could take some pictures. He is held up here because of lack of water for working on photography and so Finn let him go for a few days. I heard a good one on Andy last night. Sig was cooking some leftovers for the dogs and Andy came in, saw it on the stove, helped himself to a bowl, ate it and was on the second bowl, when Sig stopped him. Icebreaker was at Peter 1st Island, just some 400 miles away tonight at six o'clock.

Monday, February 16, 1948

I tried to work on my article today, but was not very inspired. It continued to blow. The icebreaker was sixty miles north of Peter 1st Island, heading this way. Jim Lassiter was funny at dinner tonight. He had to sit way down in the middle of the table, because Art Owen and Jorge were up where he usually sits. He said, three months ago, only three of us were sitting down at that end, but the ship is leaving soon and now, I can't even get a seat down there. I had to laugh, because it was too true.

Tuesday, February 17, 1948

At dinner, Finn received a message that the Icebreaker would be in the vicinity tomorrow evening and that everyone had to be ready to leave immediately. This was a few days earlier than we expected. Ken was at dinner, so he decided to get the Biscoe down here immediately. Finn said, he would take them up to Deception, if they didn't make it in time. Ken was very grateful for this, with regard to the others, but he felt he would have to remain until the new leader arrived, if he could. It was decided that the others would go. Ken went over to make a radio contact with the Biscoe and John came in for a chat – then Butson with the medical report. Dick said, he would discuss it with Finn confidentially, so John left. Finn read the report. Dick had just written, that he had been consulted confidentially and that he advised Mrs. Darlington to leave the Antarctic, as soon as convenient. Finn said, why, you have not stated the reason. Dick felt, he was in his legal rights, not to do so on a confidential examination, according to British Civil Law. He back tracked and said, it was not necessary for her to leave in a matter of days, but that she should be back in the U.S. in a matter of three months. He said, when he examined her, it was difficult to make an accurate diagnosis and he couldn't say definitely what was wrong. His story the other day was quite different. He said, he realized Finn's position and told the patient at the time, he didn't see why the examination should have been confidential, but she would hear of nothing else and he felt that being in the Antarctic, it was his moral obligation to treat her. He said that Don had told him nothing of the case before he left and that when Don came back, he discussed the case with Don and gave him the full particulars of his findings. He said that according to law he would not have to tell Ken the particulars of a confidential examination, even if the patient had been under Ken's leadership and that he wouldn't even be compelled to reveal a confidence to the Colonial Office. Finn's position was that as Leader of the expedition, he had provided the medical care to the members free of charge and that he had a right to know the full particulars about any illness on his expedition. Finn said that Dick had taken the place of McLean and he was obligated to give Finn a report just as McLean was. He said, Dick's report was worth nothing, if it didn't give the reason. Dick would not give in, said he was sorry and didn't want to cause hard feeling, etc. When Ken came back, Finn told him and Ken was furious, saying Dick certainly would have to tell him the particulars of any of his men. He continued, that he would never let anyone go home without knowing a doctor's full reasons for sending the person home. He said, if the examination was so confidential that he couldn't reveal the results then his suggestions for her going home should be kept confidential, as well. He intended to speak with Dick. His conversation with the Biscoe revealed they were going to drop everything and get down here within four days. We chatted for quite awhile. He still feels Harry highly dangerous and that Finn should do everything to protect himself against his threats.

Wednesday, February 18, 1948

Everyone was preparing to evacuate today and packing like mad. Finn had several messages from the Icebreaker and finally, she said she was fifteen miles off Neny Island and would wait until tomorrow to come in.

Finn had Ike and Hassage in to discuss watch lists. Ike started to protest this and that, so Finn said O.K. here are the men who are available, you make up the watch list. Kelsey came in and by mistake started an argument with Ike. Everything anyone said to him Ike argued about. Finally, when he was ready to leave, Finn said, well Ike tomorrow morning Ken will have a dog team ready to take us out to the Burton Island, so dress well, cause it will be cold. Ike flew into a rage and said he knew more about the Arctic and Antarctic than Finn did, that he had been on more expeditions than Finn had and if he wasn't dressed well enough to suit Finn. Finn said, "Good grief, Ike! All you want to do is start an argument. I'm not interested in arguing with you. You froze your toes once this year and I just wanted to comment, that it would be cold tomorrow and for all of us to dress warm." Ike calmed down, said he thought Finn had told him to dress up in clean clothes to meet the Navy and asked Kelsey and me if that wasn't what Finn had said. I said, no, it wasn't in a very disgusted manner. Ike apologized for what he had said and left. Ken came over and said that their ship Biscoe would be there in three days, that they left the plane at Deception Island. He said he had not spoken to Butson about the medical report. Finn was tired and we went to bed early. After we were in bed, Jorge came knocking on the door to say that there were two Icebreakers lying-to on the outside. This was the first time, we were definitely sure that the two breakers were traveling together.

Thursday, February 19, 1948

Finn didn't get any sleep to speak of. In fact, little sleep was had by any of us. Finn was up very early at 5 AM and off they went with the dog team to meet the Icebreakers and guide them into Back Bay Cove.

After traveling about three miles, the team stopped alongside the Breakers already plowing their way through the approximately three and one-half foot thick ice. They climbed aboard the slowly moving "U.S.S. Burton Island", and greeted Comdr. Ketchum, whom Finn had last seen in 1946, when he was the Commanding Officer of the "U.S.S. Beltrami" on the Nanook Task Force to Northern Greenland. They had breakfast aboard and were struck by the appearance of snowy white tablecloths and starched linen napkins, the first they had seen in more than a year. The number of persons on board and the immaculate neatness of the two Navy vessels contrasted greatly in appearance to anything we had to offer. Our number was small and our program large. We had neither sufficient personnel, nor time to keep things shipshape to Navy standards.

I waited until around ten o'clock and then got up. Sig kept telling me how close the breakers were getting. The fellows got up and began moving to the Ship as Finn had ordered them. I went up on the Met Hill and saw both breakers moving slowly through Neny Fjord. I cleaned up the shack quickly and walked alone down over the rocks to watch them come in. Sig tried to catch up with one of the breakers on skis, but it passed him.

The two ships advanced slowly, one behind the other, and from a short distance away they gave much the same appearance as our weasel when it traveled along on top of the ice. Their wake was a path of broken floating loose ice. As the *"U.S.S. Burton Island"* approached the bow of our ship, she swung to our port seventy-five yards away, with the *"U.S.S. Edisto"* right behind her. All of our personnel, who were moving aboard ship that morning, stopped to admire the perfect maneuvering of highly experienced sailors.

When the "Burton Island" had stopped, Finn and Ketchum got off. Ketchum, whom I knew, came over to me and greeted me. We started to walk ashore when Arco Boyd came up and said, "Hello." Finn had known him for years. The three of us walked to camp. Ketchum came in the shack and sat down.

We discussed the arrangements for our departure. He said that they had circumnavigated about one half of the continent in a little over two months, stopping off here and there to visit the base sites of previous Antarctic expeditions, including those of Shackleton and Scott. This was their last stop – their mission was over. As soon as we could finish our loading, they would be ready to leave. Finn estimated we could get ready by the following day and so our departure was set for 6:00 p.m. on February 20th.

Finn had already told Ketchum about Harry and I read the letter which I had written to his mother.

Within minutes after the Breakers were in, our aviation group had hoisted the L-5 over the side of the *"M.V. Port of Beaumont"* and ran down the bay ice for a take off. Each Icebreaker had a helicopter and an aviation group just as eagerly preparing for flight.

Soon, the two planes were in the air and not long afterward, the helicopter from the "Edisto" began to fly as well. We watched them. It was a gala occasion for all of the aviators.

One of the photographers came in and took several pictures of us, which they wanted to send back to the Navy tonight by radiophoto. The men from the two ships began coming ashore. Cameramen were shooting pictures right and left. Finn and I chatted with Ketchum for quite a while, then Finn showed him around Camp and he went back to his ship, after asking us to dinner that evening.

We were busy packing all day, but handled a stream of visitors in and out and around camp.

It was certainly good for all of us to see new faces again and meet people with new interests. After a group spends a year together, they have about run out of subjects for conversation and toward the end, there is little to add to what has been said already. But it was difficult to say whether we were more interested in seeing the newcomers, than they were in seeing us. They had visited several other polar camps along the Antarctic's coastline, but this was the only one occupied. Navy camera men were all over the Island shooting everything in sight. The total compliment of the two ships was probably in excess of five hundred persons, and In the two days they were at anchor, I believe every one of them was ashore at least once. In its existence, the Island had never seen so many people at one time. While passing by the British camp in the afternoon I noticed a large crowd of American sailors around one end of the British hut. There was Thomson, the British pilot, setting up a Post Office and selling stamps. They went as fast as hot dogs in an American ball park.

Malcolm Davis and a man by the name of Mr. Nutt came in and we chatted for a while. Nutt had wanted to go along on the expedition and had been recommended by Waldo Schmitt. He brought me a letter from Barbara Schmitt, a friend from College days telling me of the birth of her baby. They left and a couple of hours later, a man by the name of John Roscoe came in, saying that he was bringing Finn the answer to one of the panels of the Development Board to Finn's proposal. He described himself as a Geographer and talked for quite a while. He had a civilian job in the Navy and kept talking about people who did well and had P7's & P8's in the various Departments. His wife worked for State Department geographer Dr. Samuel Boggs. He gave us a lot of dope on some of the changes in the Government. He said, that Byrd was out of the Navy and in the hospital for an operation. He gave us some interesting dope on Task Force 68. He told all about the rulings in and out. He came back later. We were trying to dress and pack and visit. Boyd came in for a chat. He said, he knew all about the trouble on expeditions and what he didn't know about this one, wouldn't hurt him.

At six o'clock, we went to the "Burton Island". Much to my surprise, I saw Jennie and Harry head for the "Edisto". In Ketchum's suite, we met Comdr. MacDonald, Skipper of the "Burton Island", and Comdr. Folger, Skipper of the "Edisto". They said the Darlingtons were being entertained in the Wardroom by Chief Engineer Daly. After dinner, the photographer came in and took our picture. The Icebreaker and their suite, was super duper. We all went to a movie on board , where the Darlingtons were present. Then we came back to the Skipper's cabin, had coffee, and our group came over on the beach to our shack, where we killed three bottles of champagne. We had a most enjoyable evening with them. They left 3:30 our time.

Friday, February 20, 1948

A steady stream of equipment moved from the Base to the ship. The ship was a beehive of action. By 3:30 in the afternoon, the greater mass of our equipment was aboard, and was being stowed away hurriedly. Our seven puppies, all of which had been born in the Antarctic, were taken aboard toward the last and then not without some difficulty. The Island had been their home. They knew of nothing else and the frightened pups had to be dragged forcibly along the bay ice to the ship's side where they were lifted over the side and placed aft on the ship's fantail. There, they were attached to their crates by six foot chains so that they would have freedom to move about. The oldest of the puppies was the handsome white-haired nine month old Kasco, the largest of all our dogs. The other six pups, all from the same litter, were seven months old. We took only these seven pups back to the States. Some of our older trustworthy companions were given to members of the two Navy Icebreakers as pets from the Antarctic, but we did not have enough to supply the enthusiastic demand. The rest of our dogs we left with the British, who were anxious to breed our species of husky with theirs.

It was decided that we would leave tonight at six o'clock. Ketchum wanted to get out of these waters before the Biscoe came in, because he was afraid they would get stuck here and ask for his help. We packed very hurriedly. Several people, including Roscoe, came in. Nichols came in mad that Pete had an office to himself aboard Ship and decided he did not want to use the desk in Ike's room, but wanted an office below. Finn got Pete in to discuss it and try to settle it, but everyone was on edge. Ken was over getting his teeth fixed on the Burton Island. Ketchum made everything available to us aboard both Ships. Around 3:30 we moved out to the Ship. Our stateroom was a mess with boxes everywhere. Finn went over to get his teeth examined, while I tried to straighten some things out. I was dead tired from nervous excitement.

Nichols went off with Appel in the helicopter to do geology nearby. John came in to say good-bye. Roscoe came in for a while. Ken came back, soon after Finn came back and we walked ashore together for the last time. Ken said, much water had passed under the bridge, since he first greeted us last March. Finn went alone up the snow covered rocky outcrop to the Flag Pole they had raised on the United States Antarctic Service Expedition back in 1941 and took down our flag for the last time. I helped him fold it.

The flag was a particularly large sized one which Fiske had put up in place of the usual one when he found out the Icebreakers were coming into Base. We took one last look around camp. Finn went through all of the buildings to see that the doors had been securely shut and that nothing of importance had been left behind. But there coming out of the Science Building was Andy Thompson, gathering-up his records and miscellaneous gear on his way. Butler came over from the British Camp to bid us good-bye. He had received word that the *"Biscoe"* was due there in a day or two and that she hoped to be able to get through the broken ice path. All of them would await her arrival and hope for the best. As Thompson, Finn, Ken, and I walked back to the ship for the last time, Butler again retraced how much water had passed under the bridge since first he had greeted us that day in March, nearly a year before. Our two groups had cooperated well together despite many predictions to the contrary. It was very sad to say goodby. Butler's keen understanding, integrity, and cooperative spirit had made our stay a most memorable one. We thought we would certainly meet again at some future date.

The "U.S.S. Edisto" departed a few hours before our sailing time in order to break up the ice along our route of travel. Shortly before we left, the helicopter landed Dr. Nichols on the flight deck of the "U.S.S. Burton Island". He and Dr. Afpel, Head of the Geology Department of Syracuse University, had been geologizing in nearby areas up until the very last minute. Nichols fortunately had stowed his hundreds of pounds of rocks on board before going out on his last field trip.

By the time we arrived at the ship, the icebreaker *"Burton Island"* had already maneuvered into position directly in front of the *"Port of Beaumont"*. A line from the *"Burton Island"* kept us following close in her path. Our propeller was made of bronze and had it come in contact with the heavy ice, there was the possibility of it becoming bent or even broken. Under the circumstances, it was not necessary for us to start up our engines until we were in the open sea.

> *Everyone was manning the rails of both ships and the helicopter was flying around taking pictures. We had already cast off our lines, when Finn and I climbed aboard. Ken climbed up the ladder to say good-bye to me. He reiterated his interest in coming to the Unites States at a later date.*
>
> *At six o'clock sharp, the breaker started. Most of the Britishers were standing on the ice nearby and their shouts of "Bon Voyage" as we waved good-bye faded in the distance. It was a thrilling sight to watch the Britishers and the camp slowly drift into the background, as the Icebreaker slowly pulled us out of the ice. Little by little, we left Stonington Island behind.*

Unfortunately, as circumstances worked out for him, this was the last time we would ever see Ken Butler. Slowly we made our way past the very familiar landmarks surrounding our Base. There on our port bow was Roman Figure Four Mountain; to the starboard, Neny Island; and in the distance I could distinguish the outlines of our abandoned camp buildings disappearing over the horizon. The tall radio antenna masts on the glacier were the last objects to be seen as we turned our eyes northward. My Diary records my feelings at the time.

> *I was not sorry to see it for the last time, even though, I was sure, I would never again see that beautiful scenery. I hope I shall remember the good times there, long after the unpleasant memories have been forgotten.*

There was a good feeling on board as everyone was glad to be on his way. Mac had gone over to the Icebreaker, at the last minute to get his teeth fixed. He wasn't on board when we pulled out, nor was Nichols, who was with Apel. Ketchum had asked us over to dinner, if we got out of the ice by six o'clock.

Clear water was encountered at the end of Red Rock Ridge and some straggling penguins who had not yet made their way northward with the season could be seen through the field glasses. As we neared the west coast of Adelaide Island, the ice fields blocked our way once more. These fields consisted of one and two year old pack ice, with huge tabular and glacier icebergs intermingled. They presented a formidable sight. In the past, Finn had seen such icebergs tip over without warning, thereby creating a floodwave easily capable of capsizing a ship the size of ours.

Once out of the ice, we sighed with relief at our good fortune. We had no way of knowing then, that seven days later the ice fields we had so cautiously plowed through would move out to sea and make the entire area easily navigable. Such things are hard to foretell, particularly when coping with Antarctic conditions.

We kept with the icebreaker, until we were about forty miles off the coast. It was about nine o'clock, when we stopped to anchor. Jennie was much in evidence. She had suddenly gotten much better and was around everywhere. It was obvious that she was pregnant. The icebreaker, Burton Island, tied alongside of us for the night. The Edisto was further ahead. Finn went over to the Burton Island to have a cavity filled. Buck Boyd brought me copies of the pictures taken the other night. Roscoe came over and chatted for several hours. Finn chatted for a few minutes with Ketchum after the dentist, came back, and we went to bed around midnight. We understood that Hassage had told one of the Chiefs, that it was well known the two women hadn't spoken to each other for six months. Sig went around straightening it out and told them Finn's side of the story.

Saturday, February 21, 1948

We slept fairly late this morning. I had just gotten dressed when MacDonald, the Burton Island's Skipper, came over and asked us aboard for a cup of coffee. We went over and chatted for quite awhile. He showed us things from Shackleton's and Scott's camp, which they had visited. He invited us to lunch, which we enjoyed. That morning Ketchum had sent the Edisto up to see how the British Ship was making out. While we were having lunch, Ketchum received a message from the British Captain saying he should be through the pack sometime that afternoon. Right after lunch, we got ready to take pictures of the 4 tons of dynamite, which they were setting off on one of the nearby islands for Andy's seismograph record (left with the British) at the Base and for the Geologist's rock business. We watched the fireworks, the blast, then the smoke, then the sound. The smoke mushroomed up exactly like the atomic bomb. The explosion was a large one, so the camera fiends were strategically located on the upper decks. I laughed, and thought how funny it would be, if the Chileans and Argentines could see it. Jorge, incidentally, has given the impression, that he practically ran everything on the whole expedition much to everyone's disgust. Robertson and I went down to the Ship's Service. I found nothing I wanted and someone was in the dentist office, so we came up on deck. There we met Bob Nichols, who introduced me to Dr. Afpel.

The geologists then took a boat out to inspect the results of the blast and collect some specimens of the loose rock.

Several of the men came up and wanted to take my picture. Personnel of both ships were fascinated by the two women on the expedition. I helped Finn clean up our stateroom and we got a lot done. The British ship was sighted and we watched their approach. The "John Biscoe" circled both our ships and then began signaling the Breaker. The Breaker announced "Get ready to receive ship on Port side". The British ship maneuvered and instead of coming up on the Breaker's port side, the "Biscoe" came up on our Starboard side and tied up alongside of us. The Navy men came over on our ship to handle the lines. One of the British Mates yelled "Throw the Beggars a Line". This made the Navy and our men very angry and they said as much. We reasoned, however, that it was probably a slang term. Ketchum signaled that he would like to have the British Captain to dinner.

Vivian Fuchs and Dr. Slesser came aboard our Ship immediately and brought us some mail. We also got the spare parts. We chatted about the usual things for some time. They were pleased, there had been such close cooperation between the two expeditions. They seemed to be completely blasé about the ice conditions. We promised to see them after dinner and the movie. After dinner, a Frenchman came on board from their ship and talked to Finn about Paul Emile Victor's expedition to Adelie Land next year. We went over to the movie. The Darlingtons were there. Ketchum came down at the last minute. The movie was, The Life of Ernest Ball". After the movie, he left, immediately, and we left and went over to the British Ship. Fuchs was having a conference with Nichols and Afpel, so we came back here.

The London Times Correspondent came in for a chat. He had already heard something about Jennie, I presume. Then Slesser and Fuchs came over and chatted until 10:30 or so and left to sail early tomorrow morning. We went to bed tired.

Don was still ranting about his medical office, which, he said, he was entitled to, according to international law. Finn threw the whole thing into Ike's hand.

Sunday, February 22, 1948

Nichols and Afpel started off early in the helicopter for Adelaide Island. The British ship sent a message to the Burton Island and she left immediately, to assist her. We were anchored alone. We got just about everything squared away. Several Navy men were on board working on the radio and the gyro. In the afternoon, Malcolm Davis and a Navy Officer came on board to say that Captain Folger had invited us and anyone else who cared to come over for the movie tonight. We chatted for quite a while and then they left. We decided not to go to the movie, but stay here for dinner instead, as all of the Darlington crowd was going over. We worked around here.

Nichols came back and said he had dinner with Folger. Later, Folger came over here to find out about the sailing tomorrow. Folger said, he had received a message from Ketchum to proceed with us at eight o'clock tomorrow morning, but it said nothing about towing and he couldn't because his gear was broken. He explained that, when he took a look at the "Biscoe" yesterday, he tried to help her through the pack and gave her his course, but she wouldn't follow him. He said, he was mad and came right back. Then he said, he was supposed to go in with her, if she needed help and he had waited around, but Ketchum went instead. He said, the only message which Ketchum received from the "Biscoe" was "Request that I be informed, if an Icebreaker intends to come to Stonington Island again this year". (They needed help, but didn't want to ask for it). Folger was disgusted and said he knew that had been arranged by Ketchum last night.

Folger asked me why we all hadn't come over to take a shower on his ship. I told him, there were a lot of strange characters floating around and Finn was anxious not to force them on anybody. He said, he understood. Harry knocked to say his boat was awaiting. Harry kowtowed to him all over the place. Folger was very nice to us. Harry opened doors for him and thanked him for everything. The everything, we found out later, was that he had taken some of the Darlington's luggage aboard for transporting back to the U.S. Harry works every angle.

Monday, February 23, 1948

We got underway with the "Edisto" about eight o'clock this morning. The Burton Island was in sight and soon caught up with us. The "Biscoe" followed her out and then changed course to head up the coast alongside of Adelaide Island. Don McLean steered us off course into some very heavy pack ice and the Edisto had to come breaking through and lead us out. We followed her for quite a while and then McLean went off course again. The Burton Island came in and threw us a line. Nichols secured the leader but, it snapped like a rubber band. This disgusted those aboard the Burton Island. Finn and Hassage, who had observed our poor seamanship, were so embarrassed, they had to leave the bridge. Finally, the line was sent over again and when we were in tow, McLean walked away from the wheel. Ketchum sent Ike a message saying either put a helmsman on that wheel and steer straight, or the consequences will be yours. Before this happened, Finn had sent a nice message to Ketchum thanking him and all the others for everything they had done. He got an answer back, "Glad to have been of some help to you, our motto is service with a smile ". Around dinner time, after we were just about through the pack, Ketchum gave orders to cast off. All hands went up on deck and cast the lines off. The "Burton Island" left us with an exchange of farewell blasts and final "Good Bye, Good Luck, and God Help You."

We continued through scattered pack ice fields to the open sea. The weather was good and with the long rollers from the northwest barely noticeable, we began making excellent headway.

With mixed feelings we watched the rugged outline of that vast frozen Continent, where we had just completed our year's work, disappear on the horizon. The spirit was high on board, and all hands looked forward to a rapid change from the polar life we had led to the more friendly conditions of civilized shores. The Antarctic weather, whose temperamental variableness we had contended with through thick and thin, seemed to pay us a final honor in the form of one of those rare but exquisite Antarctic sunsets. As we sailed northward, the sun dipped lower to the southwest; the ten thousand foot high mountains of Adelaide Island to the east of us were silhouetted against a dark Antarctic sky. As I turned my back upon it, I was certain this would be my last view of the Antarctic Continent.

The men gradually sorted their personal belongings. Their footwear soon changed noticeably from ski boots to lighter deck shoes. Ship's showers were most popular and in general the trend was toward forgetting the life of a polar camp in favor of the pattern followed in civilized society – but this did not last long.

Later in the evening, Kelsey received a message from the "Burton Island" asking, if we were all right in these waters. He replied, "Yes." Ike was acting hopeless. He hasn't a clue as to what it was all about. The Navy people were obviously pretty disgusted with him and he knew it. He was irritated with their remarks. The Breakers soon out distanced us.

After dinner, when it became dark, Ike and Harry were on watch on the bridge and Hassage in the Engine Room. Hassage called up to the Bridge and asked Ike if there was a lookout in the bow. The answer came back "None of your God Damn Business". Ike was obviously in one of his obstinate moods that he had exhibited several times at Base. Hassage turned over his watch to Robertson and went up to the Bridge. He reported to Captain Ike, that the engines were running at ten knots, that he had called the Bridge to ask about a bow lookout, which is correct according to International Law and we were traveling through icebergs and he informed Ike the answer he had gotten back from the Bridge. Ike said, yes, that was correct. Hassage said, he would like to be relieved of his duties as Chief Engineer and he would not stand a watch under such conditions. Ike relieved him and put Woody on. Shortly after this happened, we entered an icefield and began bumping hard pieces of ice everywhere and were forced to decrease our speed.

Hassage was furious. Ike threatened to call back the Icebreaker and take him off and have him examined. Finn went up to the bridge and stood there quietly. Ike tried to make him commit himself on Hassage and Finn told Ike it was his responsibility and not Finn's. The searchlight went bad and Ike was forced to stop the ship and drift around until daylight came. Hassage was in the right, but refused to take watch. Ike said, for the second time that Finn could pay his passage back from Valparaiso and he could get another Captain.

Tuesday, February 24, 1948

It started to get rough in the afternoon. I couldn't do much work then and took it easy from then on. By evening the ship was rolling pretty much. Got a message from the Icebreaker wondering if we were all right in these waters. Kelsey replied, that we were. Saw the last sight of icebergs today. Hassage was still standing deck watch, unhappy as he could be.

All hatches and companion ways were battered down and we prepared as much as was possible to meet the oncoming storm. The scientists (turned sailors) soon began to feel the effect of the rolling ship. One after another failed to show up at mealtime and finally only a bare minimum of men, enough to man the deck and engineering watches, were able to stand up against the ceaseless rolling and pitching. With the men available, however, all stations were manned in a seaman-like way.

Wednesday, February 25, 1948

The battle began today and lasted until Sunday morning, February 29, 1948. The seas got progressively worse each day. The overcast skies limited our visibility to almost zero. We rolled, and pitched constantly and winds blew with violent force. There was no heat on the ship.

When the ship's engines were first started the boiler providing her with heat worked well, but a few days later it developed some trouble and with the rush to get away and with the knowledge that we would be in warmer weather before too long, it had not been fixed.

The waves were as high as the Bridge. The highest waves were even higher than the top of the flying bridge and were estimated to be 35 to 40 feet in height. Many a good wash hit the deckhouse from abeam. At times we managed only to hold our own, making very little headway. The year which the ship had spent in the Antarctic began to show its effects. The snows had frozen-in between our deck seams and expanded them.

The ship took green seas over the deck and leaked to beat the band. Each time the ship shook throughout, then slowly rose about the water to ride over each successive wave. The whole stateroom was soaking wet. The bed was wet, the floor was wet, everything rolled around. Water two and three inches deep sloshed back and forth on the decks.

So with all the general dampness, we had no way of drying out or keeping warm, except by excessive amounts of clothing. It was pretty miserable. I doubt if any one of the men were able to get more than a cat nap in the five days that the ship tossed violently about.

Sig had great difficulty keeping the galley range going. After the second day out he had to give up serving hot meals altogether and just stayed in his bunk. The men ate as best they could, mostly biscuits, cheese, meat-cut sandwiches and pineapple juice. (To this day I can barely drink pineapple juice.)

> *Practically everyone was sea sick. Some couldn't even get up – like, Dodson, Owen, and Robertson. The men just made it, to stand their watches and then back to the bunk. Although I do not get seasick, I stayed in the bunk practically 24 hours a day. There was no place to go anyway. It was thoroughly miserable. When McLean was on watch, he never even pretended to stay on course, but remained 60 and 70 degrees off all the time. Finn decided we could make no headway at this rate and would never get to Valparaiso with the amount of fuel oil we had. Some days, we just held our own and hardly made any progress at all. The wind was blowing. Our greatest roll was 52 degrees to either side and we had much topside weight. Everyone was on edge and thoroughly unhappy. Lassiter slipped on the wet deck once and fell down and slid all the way across the room. He picked himself up, mad as a fire cracker, and about to say something, when he slipped again and repeated the same performance in the opposite direction. Kelsey standing nearby nonchalantly munching crackers, watched him wide-eyed. People watching say, it was just like a tennis match. Lassiter and Peterson made an attempt to fry some eggs and take them to those sick, but most of the fellows lost them anyway. The garbage pail spilled all over the mess hall floor. The corridors were wet and greasy. Water was every place. One of the puppies got hold of the American Flag and chewed it to shreds.*
>
> *Finn finally decided to head into the Straits of Magellan and to Punta Arenas to pick up a pilot and retrace our downward steps back through the inside passage to Valparaiso.*

We had not intended to go through the Straits of Magellan into Punta Arenas, Chile, on our return voyage, but rather to sail directly for Valparaiso, almost two thousand miles further to the north. However, after battling such seas without rest for five days and no sign of let-up, there was little we could do but make for the Straits to get a little respite from the impossible weather.

Sunday, February 29, 1948

Finally, this morning we arrived at Cape Pillar where we entered the Strait. This was indeed fortunate and spoke well for Smitty's navigation. He had done another outstanding job, particularly when considering that McLean steers 60 degrees off course.

After many days of stormy seas, with but few opportunities to obtain celestial sights, Smitty kept accurate checks on courses and distances during the voyage, and through his accurate dead reckoning, directed us safely to the entrance.

We steamed for several hours before the rolling ceased and we had peace at last. Finn and I immediately began to clean up our stateroom. He got the water off the floor and we tried to dry things out as best we could. The sick people began getting up and moseying around. Sig started to prepare the first meal in five days. Around six o'clock, we tried to anchor for the night. The ship rolled again and all Sig's food fell on the deck, making the galley just as messy as it had been, before he started to clean it. As Ike was not sure of the way, he decided to anchor for the night and continue at day break. The spot where he picked to anchor, however, was too deep and they could not find bottom, so the engines were started once more and we steamed around the Straits all night. We rolled constantly. Around ten o'clock, Sig had the stew ready. It was bitter cold on the ship and that stew certainly tasted good. Robertson came in our Stateroom and had dinner with us. Finn and I together wrote an article for NANA on the last few days. Earlier in the day, a Norwegian tanker passed by us in the Strait. We went to bed tired but glad we were out of the storm.

Monday, March 1, 1948

When daylight came, the ship started on its way again. We passed much beautiful scenery. Bob Nichols spent most of the afternoon in here chatting with us. We believe that the Darlingtons intend leaving in Punta Arenas and the general feeling is good riddance. Sig had a good dinner tonight of fricassee chicken. It was delicious and everyone ate heartily. We arrived at Punta Arenas around nine o'clock, much too late to go ashore. We anchored between two Chilean destroyers and Finn wondered if Kaare Olsen was on one of them. Everyone had channel fever and civilian clothes were being brought out of suitcases. Everyone washed up and a general gay feeling prevailed throughout the ship.

As we rode safely at anchor that evening, the events of the entire expedition, both pleasant and unpleasant, passed slowly in review. Isolation was behind us; all hands had been returned safely to civilization; there was no doubt that the expedition's plans had been fulfilled; the future evaluation of our accomplishments was for others to decide. The huge task of working up its results had just begun. Subsequent events proved our year's work in the Antarctic contributed a great deal of worthwhile results to the exploration and world scientific knowledge of that region, thanks to the men whose initiative, ingenuity, and unfailing determination made this possible.

Tuesday, March 2, 1948

Before Finn left the ship this morning , a small boat came alongside and delivered him a message. It was from Comdr. Olsen inviting us to dinner tonight.

This was the first of many social invitations over the next few days. Our return to civilisation was to be one long round of cocktail parties and dinners. Many of them with friends we had made on the way down. We had our first lunch ashore at the Cosmos Hotel.

It was wonderful to eat lettuce again and we enjoyed a steak which was so tender it almost fell apart under a fork. (The year before there had been a warning from our State Department not to touch lettuce or any fruit that couldn't be peeled. In the middle of my third salad, I remembered this. Fortunately, I had no bad consequences),

Over the next few days I did a lot of shopping. It was pure ecstasy! Only a woman who has been deprived of shopping for a year could ever understand how I felt. I felt like a giggling schoolgirl again. I had a dress made out of some wonderful new silk material that I bought. I wouldn't say that I was the only one who enjoyed this new found liberty. Finn had a suit made and bought a new jacket. When we got back to the ship we found that the Darlingtons had gone ashore today as had Don and Andy. It looked to me by our bathroom, that Jenny was gone for good. I couldn't say that I was sorry.

Thursday, March 4, 1948

After a couple of days of most enjoyable social engagements Finn and I were rather tired.

> *While we were in bed we heard Harry and Jennie come aboard, take the rest of their bags, and Chinook and say a few good-byes and leave. Next morning we found out that Harry had accused Robertson of trying to kill him, with that one bad Beechcraft engine. Robertson argued with him and finally, Harry apologized, but Robertson was so affected by the accusation, that he cried all night long, being a little tight anyway. Sig asked Ike why he didn't put Hassage back as Chief Engineer and that started off a war. Ike said, cause Hassage was a quitter. Hassage heard this and let Ike have it, who also called him a mutineer, and told him to get off the Ship. Hassage lost all control and ranted and raved, saying he was packing and would leave as soon as he could get a boat, that no one would call him a quitter, that someone would pay for his transportation back to the States and that as long as he could borrow a cent of money, he would take Ike to court to see who was right. Finn tried to calm him down, but he shook his fist in Finn's face. Lassiter, Smitty, and Nichols all tried to talk to him, but this only infuriated him more. He screamed and yelled for a couple of hours and then there was silence of a sort so everyone went to sleep. The following day Hassage was calm and eventually went back to his job as Chief Engineer without further difficulty between the two.*

Friday, March 5, 1948

> *The last people came aboard this morning Don, Andy, and Mac. Don and Andy hadn't been aboard, since they left the first day and had left others to stand their watch for them. Finn was ashore to get his suit, my suit, and the pilot and Harry came down to see the above off, when Finn was waiting to go back to the Ship. Finn felt extremely relieved to be rid of Harry and Jennie. Before he went ashore this*

morning, he had a long talk with Hassage and told him he would be put in the same class with the Darlingtons, if he left here. This made him mad, but seemed to calm him down considerably. He decided to go back to the engine room and work with Lassiter. This was agreeable with Ike, so to all outward appearances last night's rumpus was straightened out.

The Chilean Frigate from the Antarctic anchored in the harbor this morning. Her Skipper and three other men from the Ship came aboard with Finn. One very nice man, who was an architect from Santiago, wanted to see us when we reached there. They viewed the Ship and Finn showed them his new maps. I gave them expedition paper as a souvenir. The newspaper man came aboard and took many pictures of us all for the papers. When they left, we made preparations to sail. Finn had said good-bye to everyone in town for us. It was a rare perfectly beautiful day. The sun was brilliant. We sat on deck for quite a while, chatting with Lassiter. Finn bought me a pretty little working watch in Punta Arenas. We viewed unclimbed Mt. Sarmiento. Kelsey said Fiske had sold some clothes in Punta Arenas to an oil man and received a check for $300. Finn and I wrote a story for NANA. Kelsey received some very good messages for us tonight.

Saturday, March 6, 1948

Finn and I worked most of the day, as we steamed quietly through the Island channels. Bill and Finn got the expedition's pictures straightened out. Everyone seems to be in good humor on board, except Lassiter, who has some more ideas about leaving in Valparaiso or Panama. The morning was sunny, but the afternoon cloudy and misty. We were making very good time and expect to be in Valparaiso next Friday.

Sunday, March 7, 1948

Another nice quiet peaceful day through the channels. The pilot is most interesting. He has seen a lot of shipping and had many experiences in his time. Lassiter was up in the air, because Finn doesn't want him to leave in Panama, as he wants to do. In the early afternoon, we anchored at Port Eden, where the Indians are and the Chilean Air Forces have a station. Sure enough the Indian canoes started paddling toward our ship, even though it was raining hard. Finn told them, he did not want any trading of Government property with the Indians. Jorge was just about to throw over some brand new Government underwear, when Lassiter stopped him and told him to get Finn's permission, which, of course, he did not give. The Chilean Air Force Officer with the beard came on board and said four of his men had dysentery and asked for some medicine. Finn told McLean to give him what he wanted. He told us that the weather outside was bad, but that it should be clearing shortly. We decided to anchor until morning. Fiske, Jorge, Peterson, Thompson, McClary. and Nichols went ashore for a trip. Latady and Finn took pictures of the maps for the American Geographical Society article all afternoon. After dinner, Lassiter had a chat with me about his leaving in Panama. I said, I thought Finn needed him and wanted him to continue with the expedition until it was over, which was when it entered the U.S. Although Lassiter had written up a bad message to the Army for Finn's O.K. saying his work on the expedition was over and he was now only doing routine ship work, for which he was not sent by the Army to do, and requesting he be recalled from the expedition, the reason I gave him, seemed to satisfy him and he decided to continue as before. He feels Finn has been too nice to the people, who opposed him once and are now jumping on the band wagon, at the last minute.

I have now six letters finished and ready to mail in Valparaiso. Kelsey came in and as usual we had a long chat after his schedule.

Monday, March 8, 1948

We steamed all day again today through the channels. The morning was cloudy and misty off and on, but the afternoon brought the sun and all the picture takers. We were all on deck, as we passed through the English Narrows. The lake, which followed, was lovely with its scenery.

Lassiter said, it equals the beauty of any lake he has ever seen, including Lake Tahoe and Lake Louise. The weather report from the outside was good, so we headed for the open. Finn and I spent all day correcting and retyping his American Geographical Society article. We reached the open sea around dinner time and started to roll slightly, because of the long swells. We entered the sea in about 46 degrees. The Roaring Forties were not as roaring, as the sixties had been by a long cry. I tried to work, but, actually, got very little done in the evening. Capt. Flenberg came in for a chat. He certainly is an interesting story teller and has had many hair raising experiences.

Tuesday, March 9, 1948

We had a slight roll all today, but it calmed down considerably by evening. More and more information is coming in on Larry Fiske's deal in Punta Arenas. He also sold McLean's camera, apparently. He did get a $300 check for the stuff, according to Kelsey. Robertson heard "Butch", the head driller offer to settle with Fiske for everything, so they left for the Scandinavian Bar where Sig saw Butch make out a check and give it to Larry. Kelsey and Robertson say, that he would leave the ship in a jacket and return in only a windproof. This happened twice. Jorge tells Finn, that he saw Larry pack up a bag full of stuff on board ship including a new pair of ski boots and give the bag to Butch, who carried it ashore. The really funny thing about this whole thing is, that after Fiske sold the equipment. which Finn had gotten for the expedition, Fiske offered to lend Finn some money, if he needed it. We told Nichols, who bluntly asked Fiske how he came by all this sudden wealth. Fiske replied, that he had cashed several checks in Punta Arenas, but didn't explain where he had gotten them. We worked all day long on the A.G.S. article. Nichols is reviewing and correcting it.

Wednesday, March 10, 1948

The weather was absolutely beautiful all day today. It is getting very hot, however. Last night, we slept with only a sheet over us. Nichols, Finn and I worked solidly all day long on the A.G.S. article. It is a terrible job and I am afraid we are rushing it too much. In the afternoon, Finn and I joined Thompson, Jorge, Robertson and Lassiter on the forward deck and took a sun bath. It was certainly nice to feel the warm and hot rays of the sun again. We didn't roll at all – the sea was as smooth as silk. Andy came in and told me about the very brief report he was writing and made promises for a longer one, a month to six weeks after we arrived. He also wants to go to Cordoba, Argentine to have his dip circle calibrated the time we are in Chile. He said, it was to his advantage to turn in a good report to Finn as he wanted to continue in this work. I just about finished going over the A.G.S. report by the time to go to bed. What a job!

Friday, March 12, 1948

Arrived Valparaiso around 7 p.m. Left Valparaiso Thursday, March 18, 1948.

Thus ended my Diary exactly one year after I started it. As we entered the harbor of Valparaiso after having been in Antarctica for one year, flags were flying and whistles were blowing. Some on board thought it was in our honor. But a little reflection made us realize, that was not a possibility. Later we learned that the commotion was in honor of Chilean President Alfonso Gonzalles Vidella's first visit to the city from his home in Santiago after having made a dash to the northern tip of Palmer Peninsula to spend one day dedicating a new Chilean Base at Hope Bay. Our fifteen minutes of fame was only in our minds.

With the departure of the Darlingtons, we had become an infinitely more cohesive group with considerably less contention and stress. After a very pleasant few days, we sailed northward to Panama and up the east coast of the United States to New York City to a very exciting home coming. While still at anchor, Sir Hubert came aboard with the customs agents. He was very anxious to view the maps Finn had made over the extension to the areas he had once covered by plane. We welcomed him with open arms.

As we passed the Statue of Liberty, no native or immigrant had ever gazed upon it with a heart more full of gratitude and relief than did I.

HOME AT LAST! FREEDOM AT LAST! NEVER, NEVER AGAIN!!!

Tugs with their horns and fire hoses squirting water into the air conducted us to the Navy pier where our families, friends and officials greeted us. It was a thrilling and heady time. There are no words to describe the sheer joy I felt in being back home and among family and friends.

The following evening the American Geographical Society had arranged a large reception and program for us at the Engineers Society Hall. Our friend Larry Gould (Dr.Laurence McKinley Gould), President of Carleton College in Northfield, Minnesota, better known as Mr. Antarctica, was Master of Ceremonies. Many prominent Antarctic celebrities, including Sir Hubert Wilkins and Lincoln Ellsworth (the only time I ever met him, as he died not long after), and members of the Explorers Club were present.

We were gratified that the expedition was considered an unqualified success in terms of its scientific and geographical results. Without funds of his own and against great odds, Finn's sheer determination had launched his expedition. With Congressional approval for the loan of a Navy ship, he solicited funds and equipment from scientific organizations and private individuals. The Air Force lent him planes for exploration and aerial photography, as well as cold weather clothing for testing in severe climatic conditions. The Office of Naval Research gave him a small contract to carry out research in many scientific disciplines. Our 183 foot wooden ship the "Port of Beaumont" was manned and operated by expedition personnel and sailed to Marguerite Bay, off the Antarctic Peninsula where it was frozen in for the duration. Our party of 23 spent the long, dark, cold winternight ashore preparing to tackle geographical problems on the sun's return. The aviation personnel, including Finn as navigator, supported by British and American ground teams, made numerous flights and mapped known and previously unknown land to the south and southwest of the treacherous Weddell Sea. Here the last unknown coastline in the world was delineated; it stretches from the Peninsula to the southernmost point in the Weddell Sea to Coats Land, a distance of about 450 miles. Scientists at the Base and out in the field with dog teams conducted investigations in 11 branches of science. Thanks to the superb competence of our two Air Force pilots, James Lassiter and Charles Adams, mountain ranges with huge glaciers were discovered in the newly explored "Edith Ronne Land" an area more than twice the size of Texas, all of which Finn claimed in the name of the United States.

The 100 new features discovered include Isaiah Bowman Peninsula, Gould Bay, Mount Merle Tuve, LeMay Mountain Range, Sweeney and Lowell Thomas Mountains and many others recognizing members of the expedition. The correlation and location of all of the newly discovered features Finn located on sketch maps sent to the American Geographical Society from Valparaiso, Chile. Complete maps were made by the society even before the expedition ship reached New York. This also proved to be a "first" in the history of exploration. A full description of the geographical and scientific accomplishments of the expedition were published in the June 1948 issue of the Geographical Review of the American Geographical Society of New York. Fifteen scientific accounts were published by the Office of Naval Research as well as other publications by the Air Force, the Army, Scientific Monthly, Explorers Journal, etc. and the popular account in "Antarctic Conquest," Finn's own story, by G.P.Putnam's, New York. This was the book which I had spent many hours helping to draft while in our little shack down South.

The expedition cost a total of less than $50,000, and was financed on a shoe-string, but the accomplishments of its 23 members, as indicated in the foreword of "Antarctic Conquest" by Dr. Isaiah Bowman, were much greater than many much larger and costlier expeditions of the time. Finn's work was widely recognized in the scientific and geographical polar field. He was also the first American postmaster ever to formally set up a post office in the Antarctic and was thus given official backing to an otherwise privately financed and operated polar expedition.

All this was achieved despite the active opposition of a few members of the expedition. It has never ceased to amaze me how some people can so quickly lose any veneer of social grace or any pretence of intelligence. Ultimately, however, it seems to me that their deliberate attempts to sabotage the work which we set out to achieve merely became a footnote to the success of the rest of the team.

Cdr. Gerald Ketchus USN Commander of Task Force #39 consisting of the Navy Icebreakers Burton Island and Edisto visit the Ronnes

Jackie and Finn going aboard the Burton Island Icebreaker for dinner

Port of Beaumont arrives in New York

The NY boy scouts welcome home fellow boy scouter Art Own, center

Greeting well-wishers on arrival in New York

The Ronne expedition's arrival in New York

The entire expedition group, minus the Darlingtons and Jorge DiGeorgio, pose on the deck of the ship upon return to New York. Standing: Ike Schlossback, Dr. Don McLean, Capt. James Lassiter, Chuck Hassage, Larry Fiske, Commander Finn Ronne, Jackie Ronne, Ernest "Woodie" Wood, Bill Latady, Jimmy Robertson, Bob Nichols, Harcly "Pete" Peterson, Sig Gutenko. Kneeling: Chuck Adams, Bob Dodson, Walter "Smitty" Smith, Nelson "Mac" McClary, Art Owen, and Andy Thompson.

XVIII

Antarctica Made My Life

For the next several years we wrote reports, articles, a book, *Antarctic Conquest*, toured the USA and Scandinavia lecturing until our daughter Karen was born in March 1951. I settled down and was happy to be just a housewife and mother. Our primary interest in Antarctica never left us, however. Members of our expedition, as well as those who had been south with Finn previously were in and out of our home, our correspondence, and lives routinely. Most of these visits were pleasant but we had several strange phone calls from Harry Darlington over the years. He rang from time to time, usually at 2 a.m., and always dead drunk, to tell Finn "I just met someone who is a bigger son of a bitch than you are" and hung up. There is no doubt that he and his cohorts spread their malicious gossip to anyone who was prepared to listen. Putting up with something like this was more than compensated for by the very wonderful people that I got to meet. Some of the very illustrious personalities in the field were still alive, and I felt very privileged to be a part of it all and to be accepted by pioneering colleagues in the polar field, as well as by the popular press. Although the expedition, without a doubt, had been the most stressful year of my life, it continued to shape and influence greatly the many different people I met and the things I did for the rest of my life.

Finn consistently focused his public relations efforts on promoting the expedition's important scientific research findings and geographical conquests. The news media saw the story appealing to the popular culture as a story about the first women in the Antarctic. As a result, I became fairly well known and was often invited to give lectures, all over the United States and overseas. I still am invited to give them all over the world. But I felt uncomfortable in the spotlight, as I also was conscious about taking some of the spotlight away from Finn's accomplishments. It was a heady experience being the focus of so many magazine and newspaper articles, recognizing my unique role in Antarctic history. I was a normal gal from Baltimore and suddenly I was newsworthy, meeting famous people, and appearing on TV shows. One of the more unusual personalities that I met was ventriloquist Edgar Bergen, with dummy Charlie MacCarthy. I also met his little daughter, Candace, who grew up to become a major TV and movie actress. One of my greatest pleasures has been the time spent as a very active member of the Society of Woman Geographers, an international group of outstanding women of achievement in their various fields, who have published and/or otherwise contributed to the benefit of man/woman kind. My three years as their president in the late seventies and early eighties was a great honor, and the time I spend with them has always been sheer delight.

Finn continued to present plans to several government agencies for additional U.S. presence in Antarctica and they were well received. Ruth and Harold Dudley made many valuable suggestions to further such a program. It was not unusual for them to be at our home discussing ideas three times a week. They introduced us to Senator Francis Case, who became very interested and most helpful along with other Government officials including Congressman Thor Tollefson and many others.

Eventually, a group of scientists including Dr. Lloyd Berkner and Larry Gould drew up plans for U.S. participation in a huge program during International Geophysical Year 1956-8. There were many ramifications before final plans for this worldwide scientific event took shape and were approved. Although not well at the time, Admiral Byrd was asked to be the technical head of the U.S. Antarctic Program. Finn was asked to be the Scientific and Military Leader of one of the bases. Ellsworth Station, was eventually established near Gould Bay, deep in the Weddell Sea, a feature Finn had discovered and named on our expedition in 1948. From here he continued the work of exploration started then and was also able to assist the departure of Vivian Fuchs on his great Trans-Antarctic Expedition. I received his radio reports sent into the Navy Department by radio and rewrote them for articles in the New York Times and North American Newspaper Alliance.

Despite the fact that I had said I would never go back to Antarctica, like so many of the men before me, when the opportunity arose, I was eager to return. In 1959, when the Argentine Government asked me to be their guest on their first commercial tourist cruise to Antarctica, I started packing my bags before hanging up the telephone. It was just a short two-week trip. Finn, who was a guest on board their Icebreaker, the General San Martine, was able to hitch a ride on a small Chilean ship and joined me half way. Having breakfast served to you in bed in your stateroom, was a new wrinkle in polar exploration and not all that hard to take. A good dress, nylon stockings and high-heeled shoes were suddenly not so out of place in Antarctica after all.

We visited several Argentine and Chilean Bases on the northern part of the Antarctic Peninsula and cruised through the magnificent Lemaire and Neumayer Channels. I was particularly pleased to see Deception Island, from where our friend, Sir Hubert Wilkins, had made the first Antarctic flight and also delighted to re-acquaint myself with my friends, the penguins.

The development of Polar cruises also led us to visit the North when we had the chance to charter a yacht with some friends and visit Spitsbergen. It was fascinating to me how like the Antarctic the Arctic was in some ways and yet so very, very different in others. During this same time period, I helped Finn write and edit his books, *Antarctic Command, Ronne Antarctic Research Expedition*, and *Antarctica, My Destiny*.

Then in 1971, in recognition of our family's long involvement in Antarctic exploration, my husband and I were asked by the U.S. Department of Defense to go directly to the South Pole in December in honor of Amundsen's 60th Anniversary of its attainment. This was my husband's ninth (and last) journey south covering a 38-year span, including four overwinterings of 15 or more months' duration. At that time, to our knowledge, Finn Ronne had sledged more miles behind a dogteam than any other man. He was well aware of the grueling effort required in advancing Antarctic frontiers. Although at the time, much initial exploration of the Continent had been accomplished by the trusty huskies, today dogs are no longer allowed on the Continent for ecological reasons. Our trip to the Pole was taken by more modern means. "Roald Amundsen should see us now," I said to my husband as we settled into the bucket seats of the Hercules C-130 turbo jet flying us to the Pole. Once, the Norwegian explorer had driven his dog teams across the Ross Ice Shelf, over perilous crevasses, up steep glaciers to the 10,000-foot high polar plateau. It took Amundsen's party two months of difficult sledging to reach the South Pole on December 14, 1911. Now, sixty years later, we retraced the route in three hours – about an hour and a half of flight time for each month of their tortuous struggle.

Although the round trip from McMurdo Sound on Antarctica's icy coast to the geographical South Pole can be achieved by air in one good flying day, women who had made the trip were scarcer than penguin chicks at a zoo. Many women have crossed the Antarctic Circle via tourist ships in recent years, but you could count in an ice tray those who have contributed to on-the-spot history of the Continent. The pristine icy scenery we were surveying from the relative warmth and safety of the huge ski-equipped Navy plane's cockpit was not new to me. Although it was my third venture to the Antarctic Continent, it was my first to 90 degrees South, where all the meridians meet.

Below us, the polar bound tracks of Amundsen, Scott, and Shackleton had long since been obliterated by the shifting winds. Not only were we on our way to pay homage to the remarkable feats of willpower, stamina, and courage of these early pioneers, but we intended to observe the great progress that had taken place since.

The majestic and terrifying beauty of the Beardmore Glacier defies description. Bordered on either side by high mountains, this wide flowing frozen river moves its ice masses from the high polar plateau precipitously down to the Ross Ice Shelf. As we flew southward, numerous dense crevassed areas disrupting its surface could be seen from the safety of our vantage position in the cockpit of the plane. With brilliant sky overhead and only a few scattered clouds on the distant horizon, the sharp ridges and black rock outcrops stood in distinct contrast to the dramatic ice panorama of our flight track below.

Continuously, we climbed up the steep glacier, so formidable to the early explorers, until we reached the edge of the 10,000-foot high polar plateau. An eternally white virgin surface stretched as far as the eye could see. For the next 200 miles we scanned the endlessly white horizon for the Pole Station. Finally, we spotted movement on the distant snowy surface where men were preparing for our arrival. Soon we were on the ground at 90 DEGREES SOUTH!

It was bitterly cold! We noticed it at once, particularly on our faces. The chill factor was 80 degrees below 0, Fahrenheit, although the temperature was a mere minus 20. We marveled at those who had made it the hard way. Never could we know the feeling of those intrepid men who had endured so much hardship and incredible sacrifice. For us it had been spectacular and embarrassingly easy.

Newcomers are ushered directly to the Pole, a few yards from the makeshift runway. We had just become the first husband and wife team to set foot there. I was the seventh woman to stand at the pole. The first six were woman journalists who Admiral George Dufek had jump together, simultaneously from the airplane during his command in the late 1950's, ten years after I had spent a year in Antarctica.

The "Ceremonial Pole" itself was about ten feet high and decorated like a barber pole. It was surrounded by the fluttering flags of the sixteen signatory nations to the 1959 Antarctic Treaty. The treaty "froze" national claims and opened the Continent to science and peaceful purposes only. As we staved off frostbite, the photographers recorded my husband's presentation of two historic photographs to Deep Freeze's commanding officer, Admiral Leo McCuddin. One was of Amundsen at the Pole in December 1911, and the other of Scott at the pole one month later.

Hurriedly, we ducked into the entrance of our Amundsen-Scott base and carefully descended the chiseled icy steps to buildings and their connecting tunnels buried some twenty feet beneath the surface. I thought the lighted Christmas tree in the entrance space at the bottom of the steps looked particularly sad and lonely in its isolation. I was glad I was not going to be here this Christmas.

As we toured the station, the various scientific research programs came alive. geological, biological and upper atmospheric information was being systematically inventoried at all of our Antarctic bases, along with similar occurrences in other areas of the world. Some immediate applications of the results already obtained provide us with more accurate predictions in long-range radio transmission and weather forecasting, not to mention some legal and political problems connected with the already known mineralization of the continent. In a somewhat lighter vein, a fascinating three year study of the sleep and dream patterns of personnel was being conducted to help understand human adaptation to isolation.

Our stay at the Pole station was concluded with a leisurely meal of steak, cafeteria style, after which we made a short-wave radio broadcast to Lowell Thomas, a friend of many years. The three and a half hour flight back to McMurdo (our main U.S. staging area) was uneventful, but for me the day will remain forever the most meaningful of my life.

The next morning we flew to Cape Royds. We intended to spend only an hour or so at the hut used in 1907-09, by British leader Sir Ernest Shackleton when his party attempted to sledge to the Pole by manhauling their heavy loads. They came within 97 miles of their hard fought goal before adverse conditions forced them to turn back. It would have been impossible for them to have reached the Pole and return alive.

After viewing the austere conditions of a polar camp from yesteryear and photographing many nesting penguins in a nearby rookery, we climbed into the two UH-1N helicopters and strapped down for takeoff. Suddenly, our previous 20 mile visibility changed so rapidly that after five miles of flight we ran into whiteout conditions. There was no visible horizon and no depth perception. Sea ice, glaciers and sky all appeared as one and made us feel as though we were maneuvering in a bottle of milk. As both helicopters swung around, they informed Ground Control at McMurdo that we were returning to Cape Royds. I was a lone woman with seventeen men at Shackleton Base and we were marooned! I began to have uncomfortable recollections of my year's stay in the Antarctic and second thoughts about why I was here today.

We were hungry, tired and generally uncomfortable. Soon the efficient crew brought out their only survival gear and lit a small gasoline stove to prepare a meal. It took a while to melt the several million year old hard blue ice chipped from a nearby glacier. Into the uncontaminated water went a combination of chicken, spaghetti, beef, and everything else readily available to make the most delicious 18 cups of 'hooch' any of us had ever tasted. The Antarctic diet had certainly progressed in the last few years. Then we made another try.

The pilots followed along the coast, hoping we could stay close enough to the glacier fronts and rocky outcrops abutting the sea to find our way back to McMurdo. But again, the curtain of white dropped. In a flash reaction we made a sharp bank towards the last visible crevasses at the edge of the ice barrier.

As we jolted around 180 degrees, I thought we were going to crash into the glacier front, but the skillful pilot righted the craft and we returned again to Cape Royds.

By now we had seen more of the volcanic ash, penguins and Shackleton's hut than we cared about. It was easy to conclude we really didn't want to become heroes after all. Walking 40 miles back to McMurdo was out of the question. In our path lay mountainous terrain dotted with crevasse filled glaciers pouring down the valleys from Mt. Erebus. Nor could we reach the base over the sea ice pierced with wide open water leads quite impossible to cross. Our return depended solely upon the two helicopters and our next try would have to be successful as there was insufficient gas left for a third abortive attempt.

Left momentarily to our individual reveries, I had no difficulty imagining the men of the top Command back at McMurdo figuratively tearing their hair. Innocently enough, I had become a good example of why, in those times, the U.S. Navy had to swallow hard each time it permitted a woman to enter its once exclusively male domain. Long ago, I had broken this tradition, but, now my safety was clearly the Navy's responsibility. Mentally, I cringed at the sticky situation, and could only surmise the assessment that must be taking place.

As time wore on, the dingy hut took on new dimensions. In spite of a New Zealand Government notice cautioning all visitors from removing any item whatsoever from the historic shrine, we began to eye the corroded cans of Bird's Egg Powder, Cabbage, Ox Tongue, weathered boxes of hard tack biscuits, and bottles of brandy with more than casual indifference. Only a musty bottle on the medical shelf labeled Padagoric the remedy for diarrhea and dysentery provided the necessary restraint.

Dirty torn socks, worn mukluks, inadequate shoes, old blankets, well used pieces of canvass and unappealing seal skins, covered with layers of volcanic dust had been fascinating testimony to the hardships of long past era when we first arrived. Now, the longer we remained, the cleaner the surroundings appeared. Subconsciously, each of us picked out a corner or niche on a hard bench, which might possibly afford some relative comfort during the forthcoming night. Every 30 minutes or so we had to move around to keep our circulation going. There was a stove. Had there been fuel, a note indicating the old relic did not function property dissuaded us from the probable fire hazard.

Clearly, an overnight experience under these conditions would separate "the men from the boys."

Fortunately, no one was put to the ultimate test. During one of our forays out for exercise, we noticed a small break in the dense cloud cover. Slowly, the patch began to grow. We were enthralled. When the sun finally broke through, eighteen elated visitors bounded up the volcanic slag hill to the waiting helicopters without a backward glance. Someone up there had delayed our moment of truth. Forty-five minutes later we were thawing out in McMurdo's familiar surroundings. The episode made a believer out of me. Never again did I go further than the mess hall without taking my own survival gear. Today the rules demand it of everyone.

My husband died in 1980, and although I continue to give spot lectures, as before, there was every reason to believe my active Antarctic "career" was over. However, some twenty-three years after having accompanying him to the Pole, I received a surprise invitation to be the guest lecturer in February 1995 on Abercrombie and Kent's tourist cruise ship *"Explorer"*. Their unpublicized objective was to get me back to our Base on Stonington Island, where we had spent a year on the Ronne Antarctic Research Expedition forty-seven years before. This had recently become the first American Historic Site in Antarctica and an internationally recognized Antarctic Heritage site. Ice conditions being what they are in that area, I gave them a thirty-percent chance of penetrating the pack ice. We were unbelievably lucky, and made it, within that year's two and a half-week ice free span.

I had never expected to gaze upon Stonington Island's magnificent scenery again. I was delighted to have my daughter with me, however, as we crossed the Antarctic Circle, I was painfully aware this was the first time I was there without my husband and it was hard not to shed a tear. In spite of a very strong wind, the ship made its way cautiously through the pack ice and eventually anchored in front of Stonington Island. With great consideration from the staff, Karen and I were taken ashore first in one of the zodiacs, and oh, so slowly we plowed our way through knee deep snow, me falling now and then, to the old buildings. When constructed in 1940, they were built to last fifty years and they had done so relatively well. The Machine Shop was no longer there and the canvas covering was missing from the Bunkhouse, Science Building and our small 12 foot square shack. Only the four walls were standing; everything inside the buildings had been stripped, cleaned out – liberated, gone!

By standing on a couple of good sized rocks, I was able to peer into one of the two windows of my old 12x12 boarded up hut. There was nothing there. The bunk, the small heating stove, the book shelves, the desk, the table, were all gone. Just a totally empty room – except for my memories. The plywood tunnel that had given us access to the Main Bunkhouse had long since blown away.

Upon entering the main door of the Bunkhouse, a well-boarded vestibule allowed visitors to view the huge empty room beyond. Previous personnel from the now vacant British Base nearby had built an artificial floor over the ice, which covered the original floor, in order to store their dead seals in the building. Once the hub of all our camp activities, the large building was stripped of everything: two tiers of bunks lining either wall, the long mess table with all of its chairs, and all galley equipment including a 1400 lb. stove. The only thing visible was that considerable build-up of hard, dirty ice covering the galley area, which had accumulated as the result of a long since broken skylight windowpane allowing the snows access.

The Science Building also was devoid of everything except for a good sized table containing a small museum of artifacts, some broken, found around camp by a recent three man team sent by the National Science Foundation to shore-up, repair and preserve the camp as the first American Historic Site in Antarctica. Metal plaques had been placed on all the buildings attesting to the action, including one marking the "Ronne Hut". Suddenly, my old little shack where I had hibernated for a year, while I unwittingly made history, had become an internationally recognized historic building worthy of being preserved, partly because I had lived there. My daughter, Karen Ronne Tupek, by now a government historic preservation architect, had made and brought along three large panels depicting the story of the Ronne Expedition from press clippings, photographs, text captions, and a reprint from my diary entry of March 12, 1947, when I became the first American woman to set foot on the continent. One panel depicted her father's career; another was about me and my life during my unplanned venture; and the third told about the story of the successful expedition as a whole. They were encased in sheets of heavy plexiglass sealed with waterproof tape at the edges and screwed into the wooden walls near the museum, with the hope they might survive future thefts and/or moisture for a few years.

Together, Karen and I walked the 200 yards over the rocky hill to see the British Base, a new one since I was there, but no longer occupied, then we went up to our old flag pole on the Island's highest point. The sloping glacier foot on which we had often skied and which was our only access to the larger glacier leading up to the high plateau dividing the peninsula, was no longer there. In the intervening years it had gradually receded making Stonington a true island without access to the mainland as in the past.

Words can hardly describe how I felt as I stood once again in this place and re-lived all of the memories that lay hidden within its walls. All of the joys and sorrows, the happy times and the petty rows that had been something of a trauma for me then, flooded through my mind. It was an unforgettable lesson in raw basic human nature without any of the veneer of civilization. It is not something that I would want to repeat. It was only by re-visiting these memories in this place that I was able once and for all to face them down and finally feel able to share them with the world. Free at last!

With very mixed feelings, I said goodbye to our Base the second time and headed back to our ship, again very certain that I would never again view this magnificent scenery which had had such a large influence over my life. This young girl from a conservative family had certainly seen some unexpected things.

Almost despite myself, I had become a true Antarctican. When a person has once overwintered in the Antarctic, a great desire to return again will invariably occur. I have known many men who, prior to their return to the United States had made up their minds to the contrary, but after a few months in civilization, each in turn would take measures to ascertain how soon the next expedition would depart. Now I found that I was no different. The wild rugged grandeur of nature at its most primitive, and man's untiring battle to survive and cope with the worst that it has to offer, are the strong ties of the Continent which continue to draw Antarcticans back, even on a tourist ship. In retrospect, the sparse comforts of camp life seem to outweigh the obvious disadvantages such as the dangers and hardships of cold, blizzards, crevasse filled terrain, and other familiar hazards. Those days of piercing winds, blinding snowstorms, freezing temperatures, tired muscles, and irritability, are soon forgotten. Only the pleasant experiences remain.

So it has been with expeditions in the past and so it was with our expedition. The road had been long and at times quite bumpy. The innumerable problems and seemingly insurmountable obstacles were hurdles with the passage of time and now one could take the opportunity to think how actually enjoyable the time had been spent. It's not the cold or the inconvenience of camp life; it's dealing with your fellow human beings in isolation that is the most difficult. This really is one of the most beautiful places in the world. At the time, I was sure

I would never ever return here under any circumstances but, when the opportunity occurred, under different circumstances, I was only too happy to return to that magical place. Having been a member of the expedition made my life, I wouldn't give up that year's experience for anything in the world. It was the trip of a lifetime.

Times have changed radically; large, exploratory private expeditions are a thing of the past, government expeditions have taken over with sufficient funds to pay participants and thus establish financial control over incentives and insubordination. Advancement in aviation has provided greater movement for shorter periods of time and the introduction of tourist cruises has provided quick trips for thousands who, otherwise, would never have had an opportunity to view the magnificent of continents. During the year I spent there in 1947-48, there were less than 100 people on the entire continent the size of the United States and Mexico combined. While during the year of 1996, there were 4,500 tourists there alone, not counting those operating the many bases where scientific investigations were being conducted year round by many countries. Nearly 10,000 people were there in 1998.

In 1997 and 1998, I celebrated my fiftieth anniversary in Antarctica, on the two tourist ships I have lectured on in recent years, the *"Explorer"* in 1997, and also the *"Marco Polo"* in 1998. Along with their parents, my two grandchildren went with me in early 1998 as the fourth generation in Antarctica. I have often tried to stay in the background so as not to overshadow my remarkable husband but when those around me toasted me as "Antarctica's First Lady" in many ways I wondered if, at my age, I shouldn't simply accept the applause and smile sweetly – so I did.

Daughter Karen was born in 1951

Jackie points to map where Finn named newly discovered land "Edith Ronne Land", later named "Ronne Ice Shelf," after her

Jackie and Finn toured around the US and Europe, lecturing about their experiences

Jackie in an ice cave in 1971

Finn and Jackie at South Pole in December 1971 with Commanding Officer Admiral Leo McCuddin

Jackie returned to Stonington Island Base in 1995

Jackie shows daughter Karen around the base. Here, they pose in front of the Ronne Hut.

Jackie lectured on board tourist cruises to the Antarctic

Emperor penguin with a chick resting on its feet to keep warm.

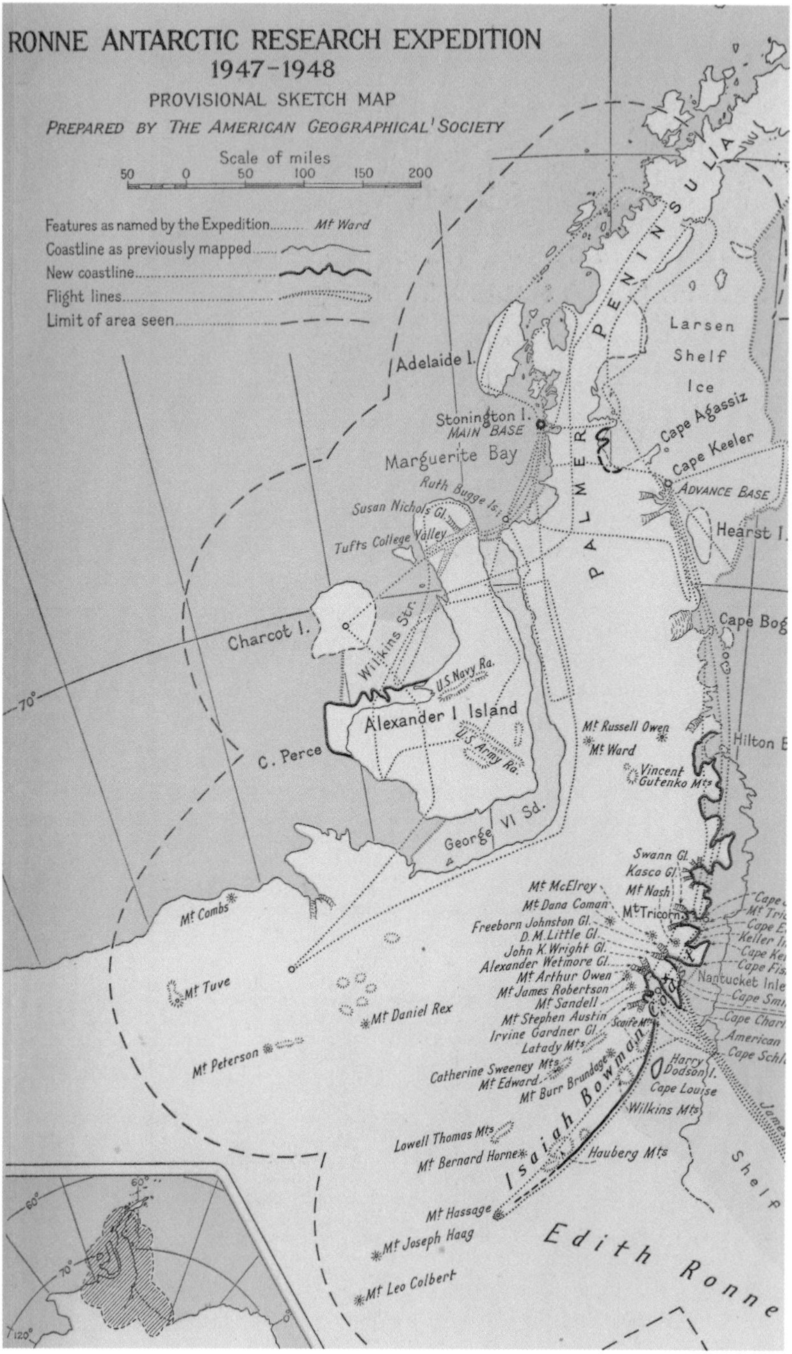
RONNE ANTARCTIC RESEARCH EXPEDITION
1947–1948
PROVISIONAL SKETCH MAP
PREPARED BY THE AMERICAN GEOGRAPHICAL SOCIETY
Scale of miles
50 0 50 100 150 200
Features as named by the Expedition......... Mt Ward
Coastline as previously mapped.......
New coastline.......................................
Flight lines...
Limit of area seen.................................
PALMER PENINSULA
Larsen Shelf Ice
Adelaide I.
Stonington I.
MAIN BASE
Marguerite Bay
Cape Agassiz
Cape Keeler
ADVANCE BASE
Hearst I.
Ruth Bugge Is.
Susan Nichols Gl.
Tufts College Valley
Charcot I.
Wilkins Str.
U.S. Navy Ra.
Cape Bog
70°
Alexander I Island
U.S. Army Ra.
C. Perce
George VI Sd.
Mt Russell Owen
Mt Ward
Vincent Gutenko Mts
Hilton B
Swann Gl.
Kasco Gl.
Mt McElroy
Mt Nash
Mt Dana Coman
Mt Tricorn
Freeborn Johnston Gl.
D.M. Little Gl.
John K. Wright Gl.
Alexander Wetmore Gl.
Mt Arthur Owen
Mt James Robertson
Mt Sandell
Mt Stephen Austin
Scaife Mt
Irvine Gardner Gl.
Latady Mts
Catherine Sweeney Mts
Mt Edward
Mt Burr Brundage
Harry Dodson I.
Cape Louise
Wilkins Mts
Isaiah Bowman Coast
Lowell Thomas Mts
Mt Bernard Horne
Hauberg Mts
Mt Hassage
Mt Joseph Haag
Mt Leo Colbert
Edith Ronne
Shelf
Nantucket Inle
American
Mt Combs
Mt Tuve
Mt Daniel Rex
Mt Peterson
60°
70°
120°

Biography

Edith "Jackie" Maslin Ronne

Born Edith Ann Maslin on October 13, 1919, she was raised in a conservative, private Baltimore family. Her father, Charles Jackson Maslin, worked several jobs, his last being with the B&O Railroad. Her mother, Elizabeth Parlett Maslin, could have taught school but like a proper married woman of her day, she stayed home instead and reviewed Edith's homework every night making sure she never went to school without knowing her lessons letter perfect.

According to Edith, she spent three "marvelous" summers away from home at a Girl Scout summer camp, Camp May Flather, in Virginia. It was at camp where she acquired her nickname "Jackie". In the 1930's, Baltimore, Maryland did not believe in co-education in their public schools so she graduated from Eastern High School at sixteen without ever having a date, except when she arranged for a classmate's brother to take her to the senior prom.

Jackie's first two years in college were spent at the College of Wooster in Wooster, Ohio. Then she transferred to George Washington University in Washington, D.C. In order to be near the university, Jackie moved to live with her aunt and uncle in Chevy Chase, Maryland, who were financing her education. The first person she recognized on campus was a girl from Girl Scout Camp. To her friends, she introduced Edith as Jackie, and everyone felt the name better fit her personality than Edith. Since that time she has been called Jackie.

At George Washington University, Jackie joined Phi Mu Sorority, had a great social life, and in 1940 graduated with a major in History and a minor in English. When she graduated, it was not easy to find a job with a "mere" undergraduate degree. Therefore, Jackie began a typing and shorthand course while looking for work. The National Geographic Society offered her a job. After about nine months, she sought and found a government job at the Civil Service Commission paying twice the salary of the National Geographic Society. A few months later she moved on to the State Department where she would remain for over five years serving in several different positions from file clerk to International Information Specialist in the Near and Far Eastern Division of Cultural Affairs.

In 1942, she met the polar explorer Lieutenant Finn Ronne (who would later advance to the rank of Captain) on a blind date and over the ensuing months, Jackie enjoyed his maturity (Finn was 20 years her senior), nationality, "charming" Norwegian accent, and stories of exploration. Finn proposed to Jackie before Christmas of 1943 and they were married on March 18, 1944.

Finn Ronne was a great organizer, planner, and leader; and in 1947 he commanded the last privately funded expedition to Antarctica despite roadblocks and obstacles erected by Admiral Byrd and associates and the British who currently occupied the area of Antarctica where the Ronne Expedition was destined. (Once the Ronne Expedition reached the frozen continent, the Americans and British worked closely together.) Nevertheless, regardless of a small budget and crew, the Ronne Expedition departed from Beaumont, Texas on January 25, 1947 where Finn selected Beaumont Eagle Scout Arthur Owen to join the expedition. Jackie edited all of Finn's correspondences and reports and was to be in charge of the domestic side of the expedition. However, instead of remaining stateside, she resigned her position with the State Department to accompany her husband on his fifteen month Ronne Antarctic Research Expedition.

As Expedition Recorder-Historian, Jackie Ronne wrote the news releases for the North American Newspaper Alliance; kept a daily history of the expedition's accomplishments, which formed the basis for her husband's book Antarctic Conquest published by Putnam in 1949. She also made routine daily seismographic and tidal observations when the geophysicist was in the field during summer trail program.

Jackie Ronne became the first American woman to set foot on the Antarctic Continent. (Before her, only the wife of a Norwegian whaling captain had done so very briefly.) Mrs. Ronne, along with the wife of one of the expedition's pilots, became the first two members of an over-wintering expedition and to spend a year in the Antarctic. No woman had ever lived in the Antarctic before this, nor did any do so for the following twenty-five years, until women scientists occasionally accompanied their scientific husbands in recent years. The 400,000 square mile area newly discovered by the Ronne Antarctic Research Expedition was named EDITH RONNE LAND by the U.S. Board on Geographic Names, making it one of the very few land areas honoring a woman of non-royal birth. After 20 years on the maps, the feature was renamed RONNE ICE SHELF, an area which is second only to the great Ross Ice Shelf.

Jackie Ronne has lectured extensively throughout the U.S. and in numerous foreign countries. In addition to collaborating with her husband in various scientific and popular accounts, she has written numerous articles including those for the annual editions of the Britannica, Americana, and Funk and Wagnalls encyclopedias, as well as many articles for the NORTH AMERICAN NEWSPAPER ALLIANCE.

Upon the invitation and sponsorship of the Argentine Government in 1959, she participated in the first commercial tourist cruise to Antarctica. In 1962, she made a trip to the Arctic Islands of Spitsbergen, visiting Norwegian and Russian coal mining stations, on a Norwegian sealing vessel which penetrated the pack ice to within 600 miles of the North Pole.

In 1971, upon the invitation of the Secretary of Defense, she accompanied her husband as a guest of the U.S. Navy to McMurdo Sound, Antarctica, and made a flight to the South Pole Station, as the first husband and wife team and 7th woman to do so, in observance of the 60th Anniversary of Amundsen's attainment of the Pole on December 14, 1911, (on which Finn Ronne's father, Martin Ronne, was a member).

In addition, Jackie held various offices in the Society of Woman Geographers; The Columbian Women of George Washington University; the United Nations Association and the National Society of Arts and Letters. She assisted in civic organizational work in various capacities and is listed in Who's Who of American Women. Jackie received a special Congressional Medal for American Antarctic Exploration, was elected President of the Society of Woman Geographers from April 1978-1981. She was the recipient of a special Achievement Award Columbian College of George Washington University and dedicated a Polar Section to National Naval Museum. She was a special Guest Lecturer aboard Abercrombie and Kent's Antarctic Cruise Ship "Explorer" in February and March 1994 and aboard the Orient Lines ship the "Marco Polo" in January and February 1996. Jackie also returned to her former Antarctica base at Stonington Island as a guest lecturer. In her lifetime, she has made 15 trips to Antarctica.

Jackie Ronne has one daughter, Karen Tupek, and two grandchildren. Both her daughter and granddaughter were also Girl Scouts. Her grandson is a Scout and engineering student (like his grandfather Finn Ronne who was a mechanical engineer with postgraduate studies in naval architecture) with aspirations to make the 2008 US Olympic rowing team.

Currently, Jackie Ronne resides in Bethesda, Maryland and is as active and quick-witted as ever. She returns to Beaumont, Texas on November 11, 2004 for the opening of the Ronne Expedition and Arthur Owen Museum Exhibit at the Clifton Steamboat Museum, the debut of her book "Antarctica's First Lady", a reunion of the surviving six crew members from the Ronne Antarctic Research Expedition, and the unveiling of her Adventures of the Elements character card, the Jackie Ronne card. These events to honor Jackie Ronne, the Arthur Owen family, and the expedition are being coordinated by Three Rivers Council #578, Boy Scouts of America, which is the same Boy Scout Council area that was involved in the 1947 expedition. Philanthropist, historian, and Clifton Steamboat Museum owner, David Hearn Jr., has made this historically significant event possible by funding the publication of her book and the extensive Ronne Exhibit at his museum including digitizing and preserving over 16,000 feet of film from the expedition.

Scouts and Scouters have an opportunity to earn a special medal commemorating the Ronne Expedition and Art Owen.

At a Port of Beaumont reception in August 2004, representatives from the Boy Scouts, City of Beaumont, and Clifton Steamboat Museum welcome Jackie Ronne back to Beaumont.

The Clifton Steamboat Museum in Beaumont, Texas, honors heroes, past, present, and future. Military and civilian heroes are represented in displays featuring Texas battles, the Republic of Texas and its statehood, the Civil War in Texas and Louisiana, the Steamboat Era, WWI, WWII, Korea and Vietnam. Upper galleries hold sculpture, artworks, a historical Boy Scout exhibit, and hand-crafted ship models.

In a photo taken prior to the expedition, Art Owen of Beaumont is pictured in his Eagle Scout uniform.

This Jackie Ronne Character Card for the *"Adventures of the Elements"* scientific trading card game was unveiled at the Ronne Expedition Reunion, held in Beaumont on November 11, 2004, honoring Jackie Ronne and the other expedition members. The educational and entertaining game uses "real" people, including Ronne Expedition members Jackie Ronne and Art Owen as role models for game players. Visit *www.adventuresoftheelements.com* for more information.